KAZAN

$$3$$

GAKU ★ MIYAO

KAZAN

Translators
Alex Mizuno
Dominic Mah

Editors
Dominic Mah
Renee Adams

Production Artists
Atsuko Hattori
Kelly Lin
Nicole Shi

US Cover Design
Yuki Chung

Lettering Fonts
Comicraft
www.comicbookfonts.com

President
Robin Kuo

Publisher
ComicsOne Corporation
47257 Fremont Blvd
Fremont, CA 94538
www.ComicsOne.com

First Edition: May 2001
ISBN 1-58899-067-2

CONTENTS

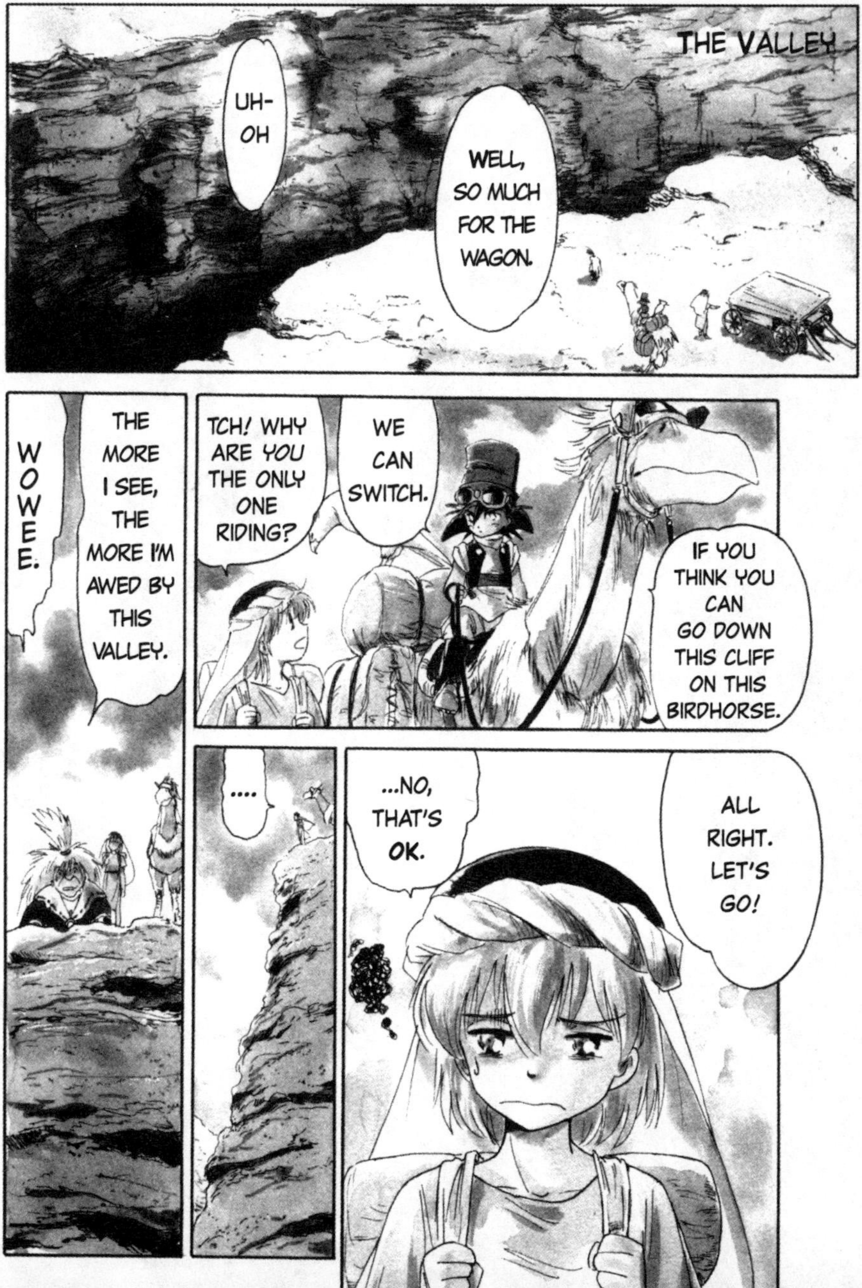
THE VALLEY
UH-OH
WELL, SO MUCH FOR THE WAGON.
WOWEE.
THE MORE I SEE, THE MORE I'M AWED BY THIS VALLEY.
TCH! WHY ARE YOU THE ONLY ONE RIDING?
WE CAN SWITCH.
IF YOU THINK YOU CAN GO DOWN THIS CLIFF ON THIS BIRDHORSE.
....
...NO, THAT'S OK.
ALL RIGHT. LET'S GO!

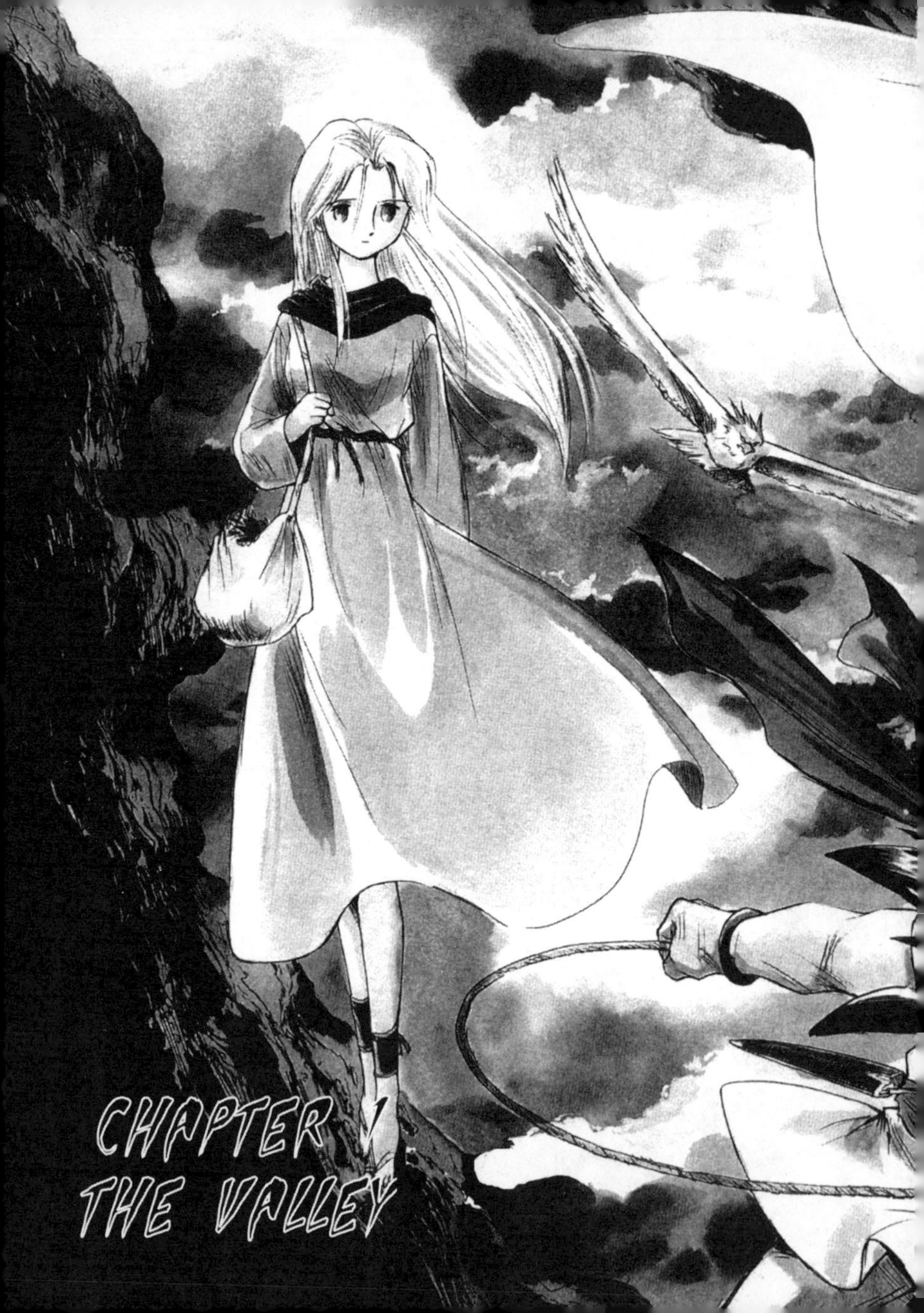
CHAPTER 1
THE VALLEY

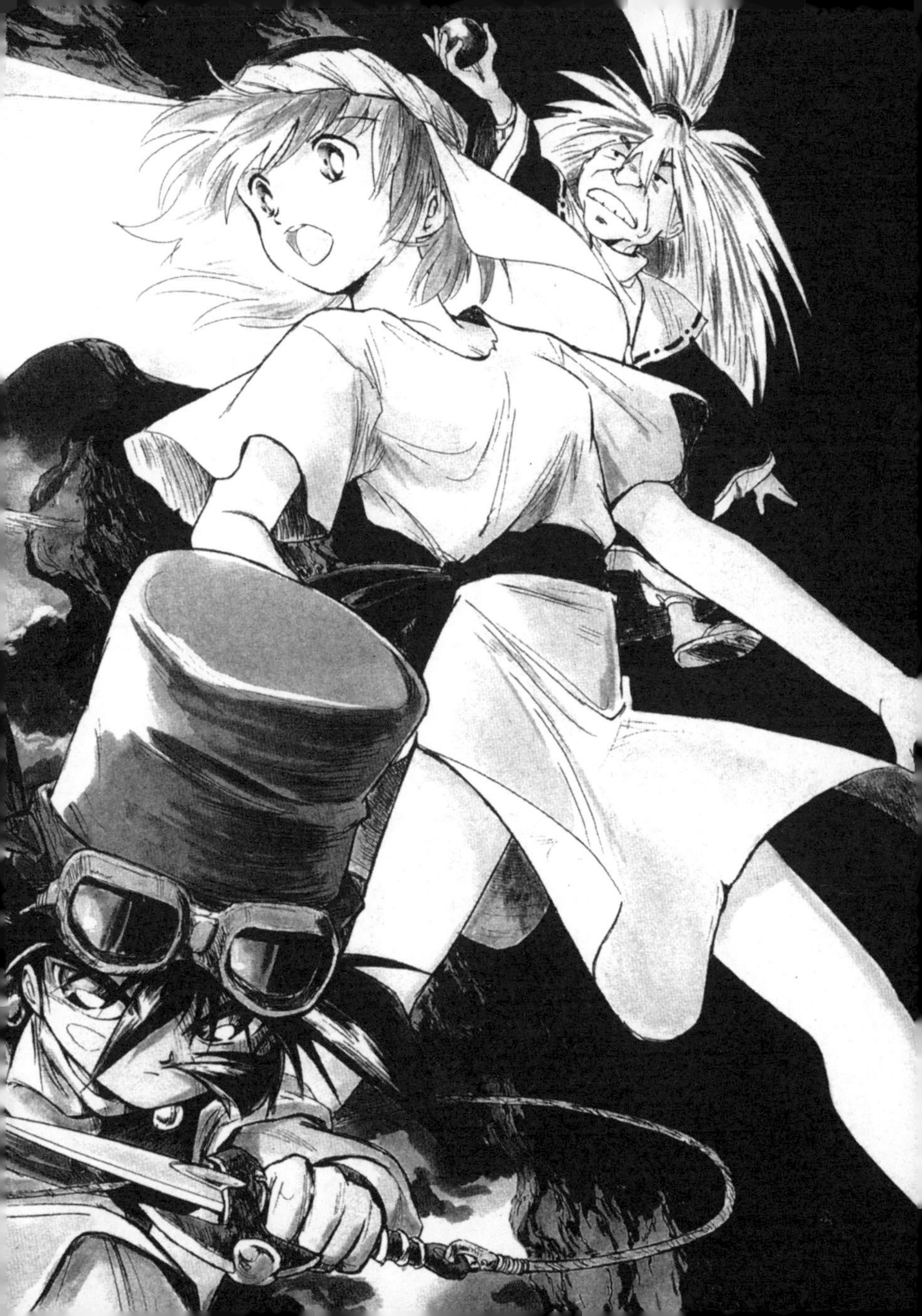

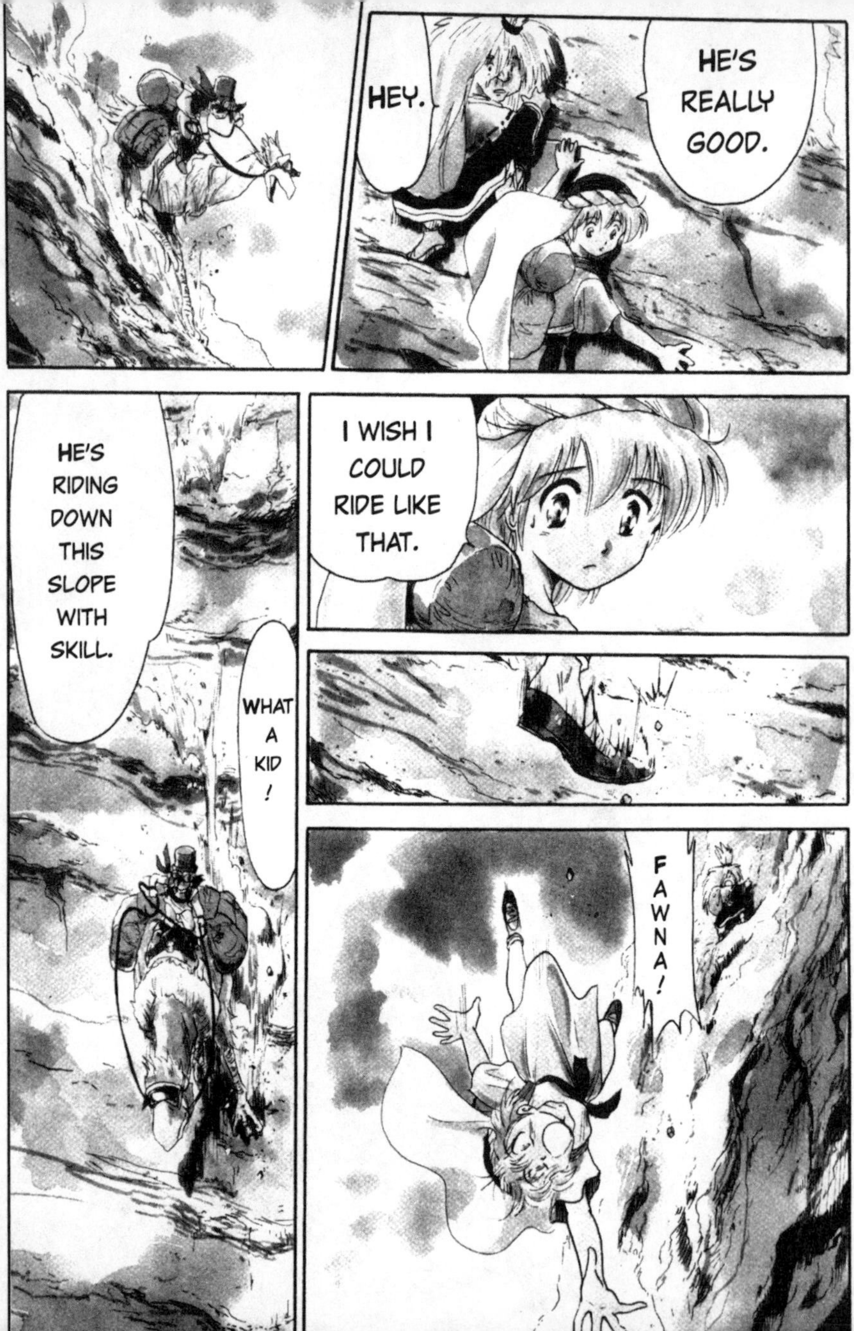
HEY.
HE'S REALLY GOOD.
HE'S RIDING DOWN THIS SLOPE WITH SKILL.
WHAT A KID!
I WISH I COULD RIDE LIKE THAT.
FAWNA!

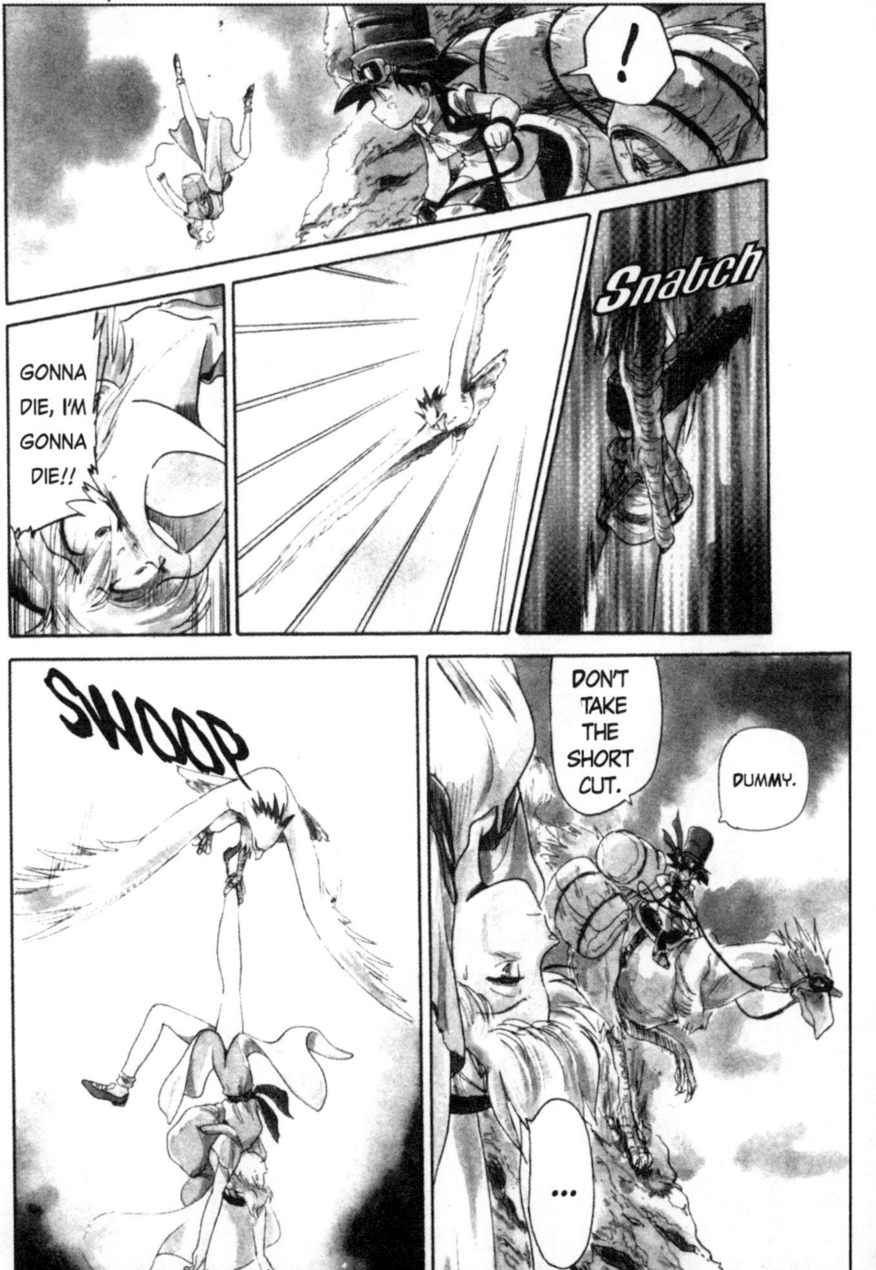
!
Snatch
GONNA DIE, I'M GONNA DIE!!
SWOOP
DON'T TAKE THE SHORT CUT.
DUMMY.
...

ZZZZZZZZZZZ

ZZZZZZZZZZZ

GOLDENE

MY ...

MY LORD! I HAVE BAD NEWS!

WHAT ?!

WHAT HAPPENED TO THE COMMUNICATION TOWERS?!

9

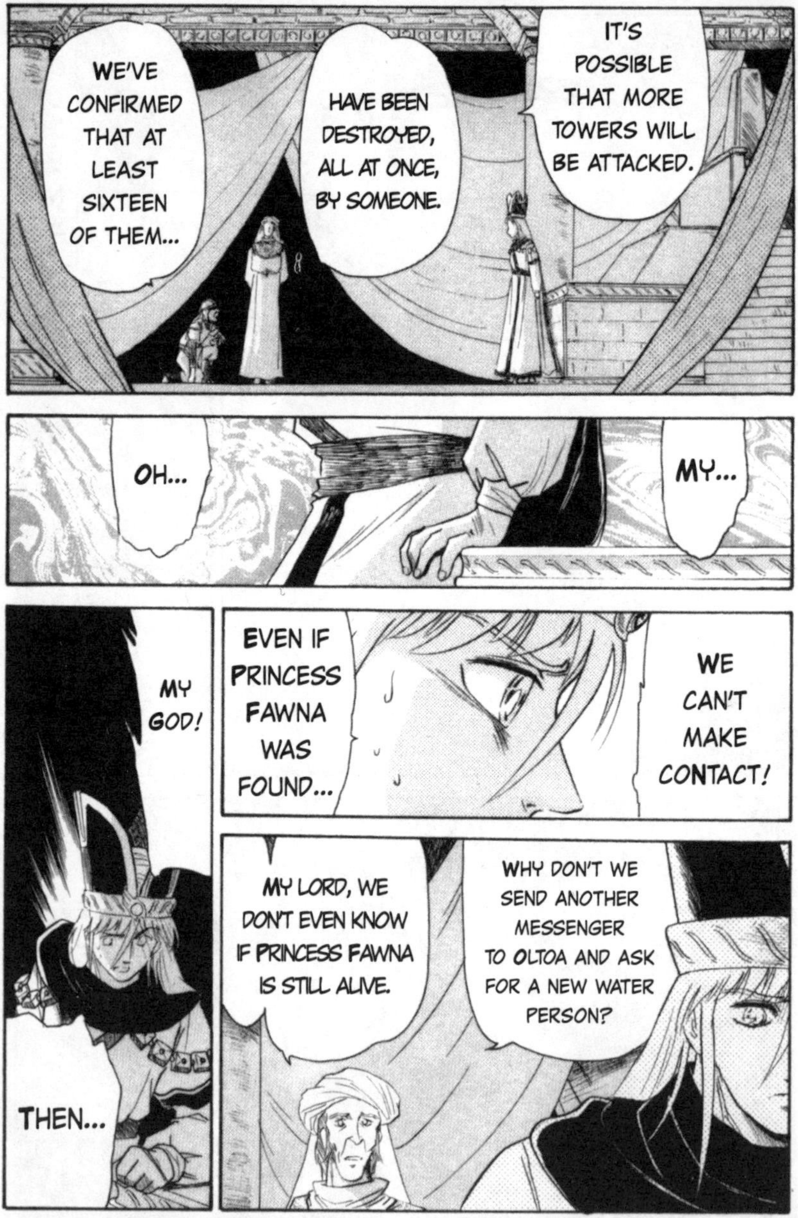
WE'VE CONFIRMED THAT AT LEAST SIXTEEN OF THEM...
HAVE BEEN DESTROYED, ALL AT ONCE, BY SOMEONE.
IT'S POSSIBLE THAT MORE TOWERS WILL BE ATTACKED.
OH...
MY...
MY GOD!
EVEN IF PRINCESS FAWNA WAS FOUND...
WE CAN'T MAKE CONTACT!
MY LORD, WE DON'T EVEN KNOW IF PRINCESS FAWNA IS STILL ALIVE.
WHY DON'T WE SEND ANOTHER MESSENGER TO OLTOA AND ASK FOR A NEW WATER PERSON?
THEN...

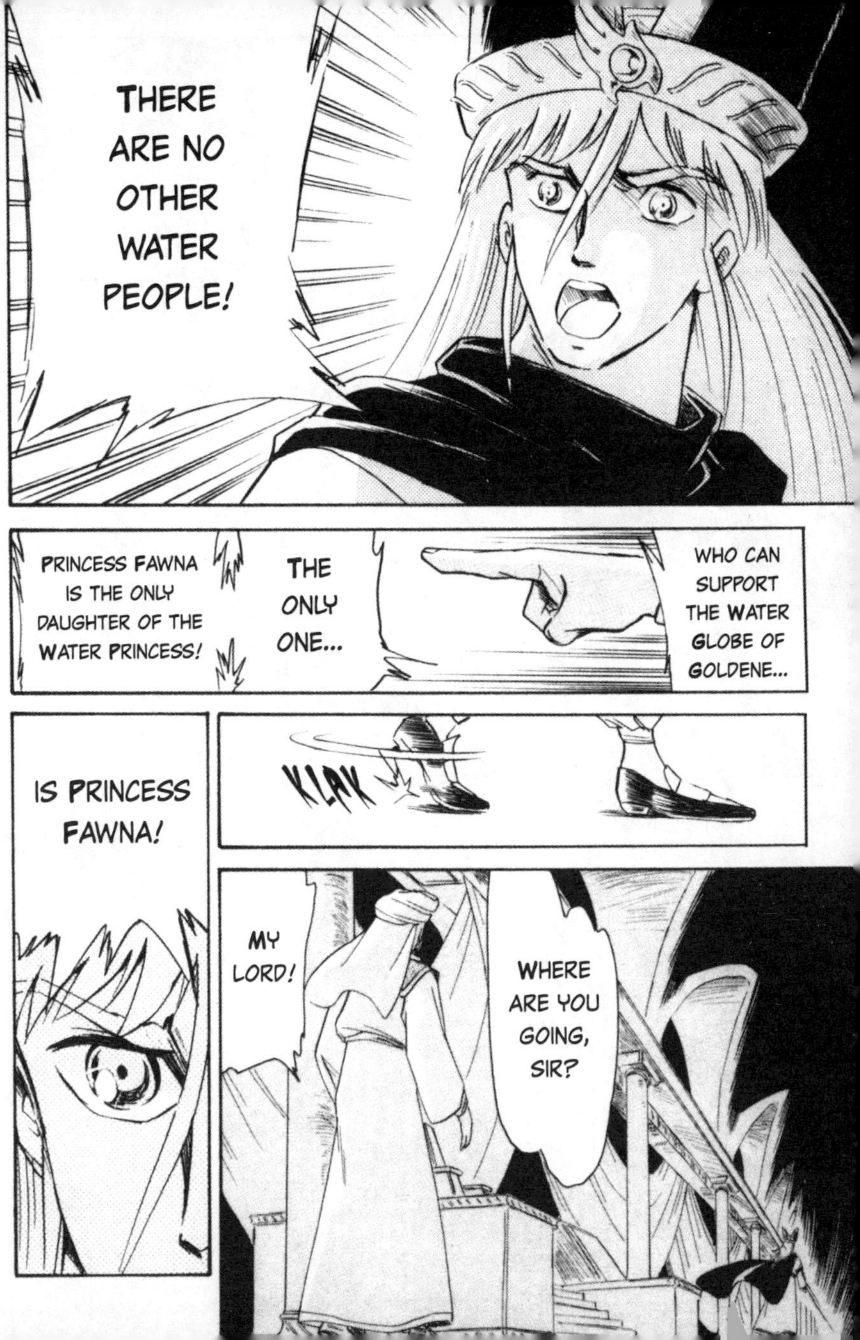
THERE ARE NO OTHER WATER PEOPLE!
WHO CAN SUPPORT THE WATER GLOBE OF GOLDENE...
THE ONLY ONE...
PRINCESS FAWNA IS THE ONLY DAUGHTER OF THE WATER PRINCESS!
KLAK
IS PRINCESS FAWNA!
WHERE ARE YOU GOING, SIR?
MY LORD!

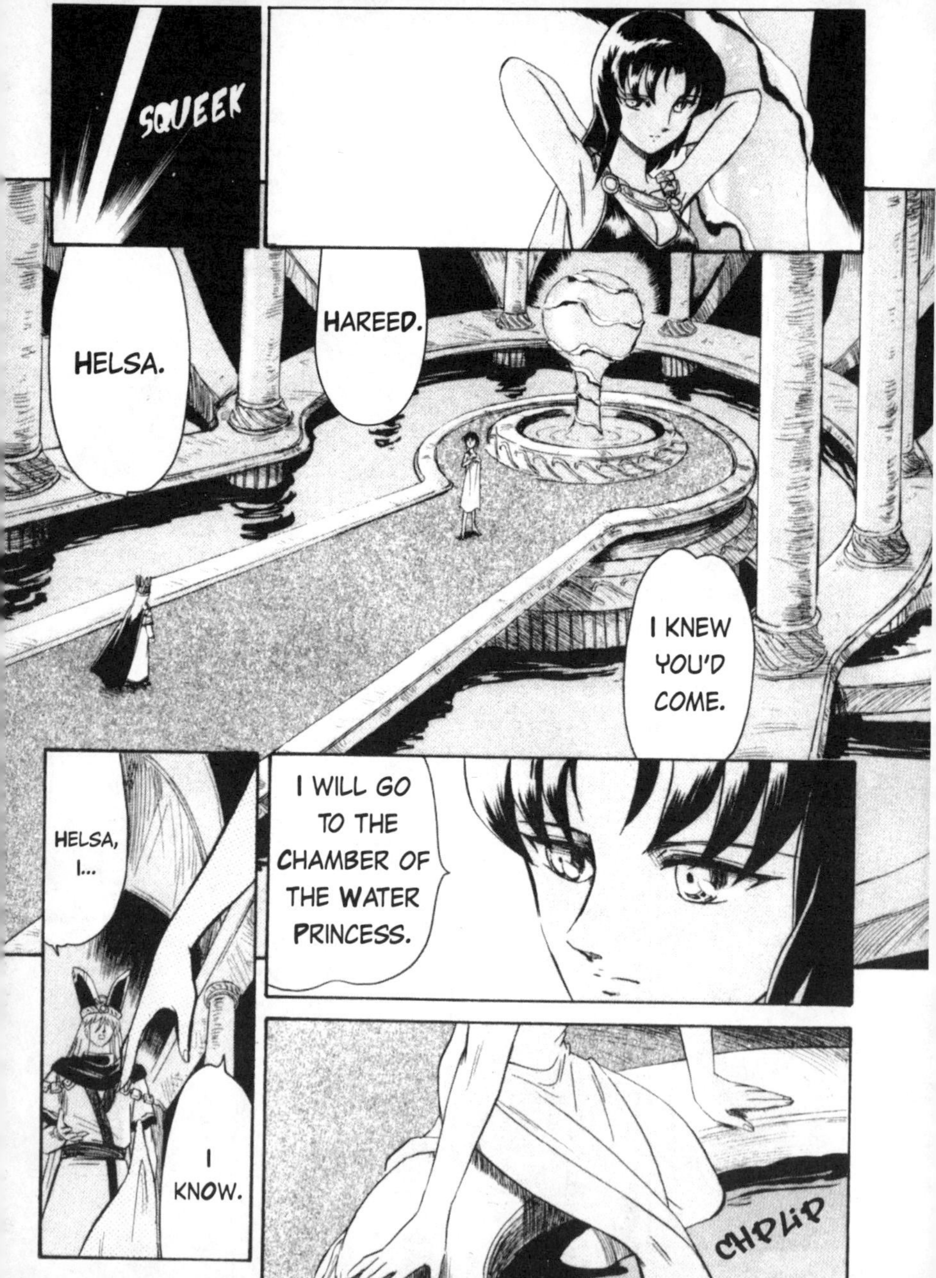
SQUEEK
HAREED.
HELSA.
I KNEW YOU'D COME.
I WILL GO TO THE CHAMBER OF THE WATER PRINCESS.
HELSA, I...
CHPLIP
I KNOW.

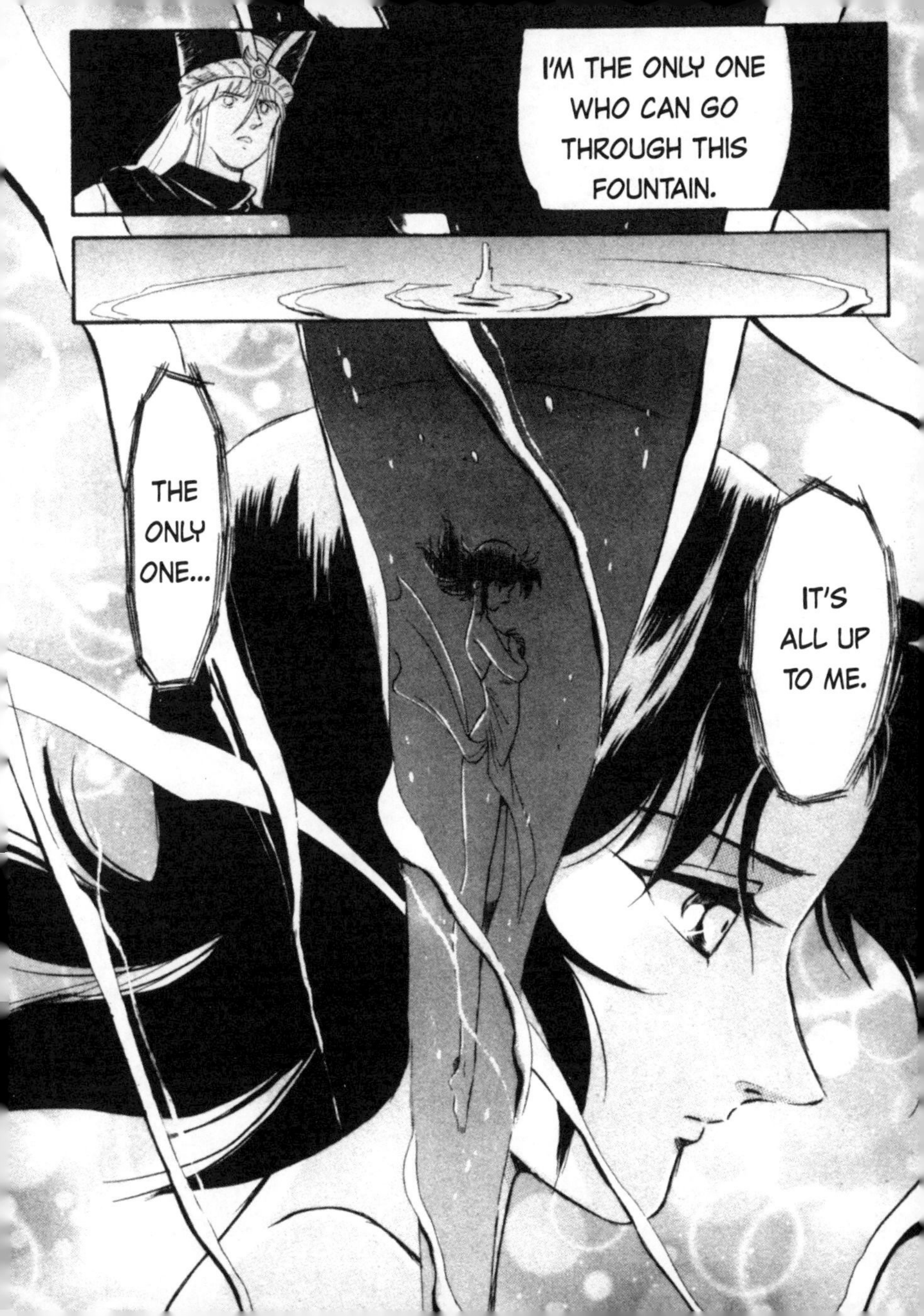
I'M THE ONLY ONE WHO CAN GO THROUGH THIS FOUNTAIN.
IT'S ALL UP TO ME.
THE ONLY ONE...

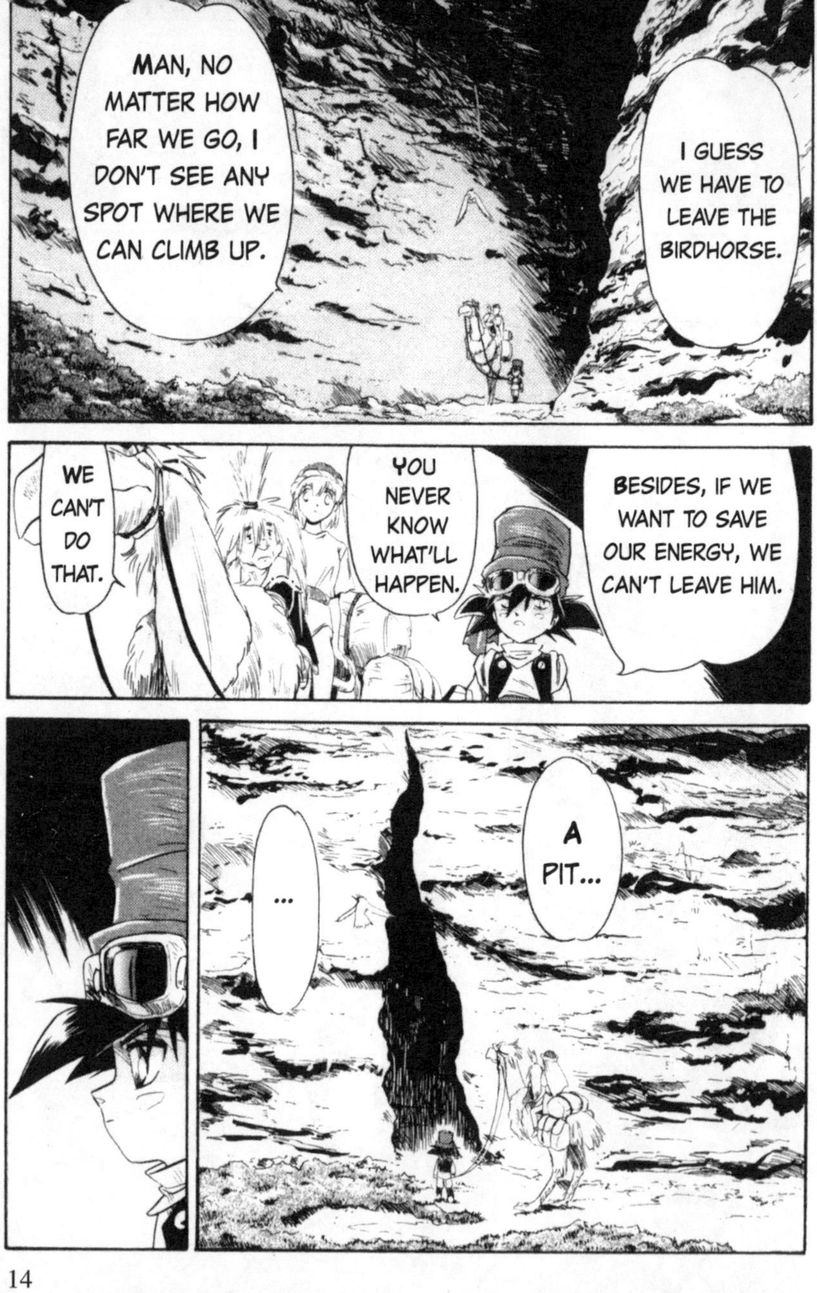
MAN, NO MATTER HOW FAR WE GO, I DON'T SEE ANY SPOT WHERE WE CAN CLIMB UP.
I GUESS WE HAVE TO LEAVE THE BIRDHORSE.
WE CAN'T DO THAT.
YOU NEVER KNOW WHAT'LL HAPPEN.
BESIDES, IF WE WANT TO SAVE OUR ENERGY, WE CAN'T LEAVE HIM.
A PIT...
...

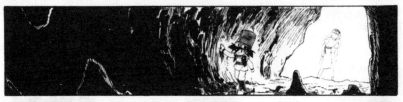

HA! KAZAN SUCKS HIS FINGER.

I'M CHECKING THE WIND, STUPID.

WIND?

YUP.

JUST A LITTLE, BUT IT'S BLOWING FROM THE OTHER END.

HMM. JUST THIS AREA IS COVERED WITH MOSS.

ARBEY, ARBEY.

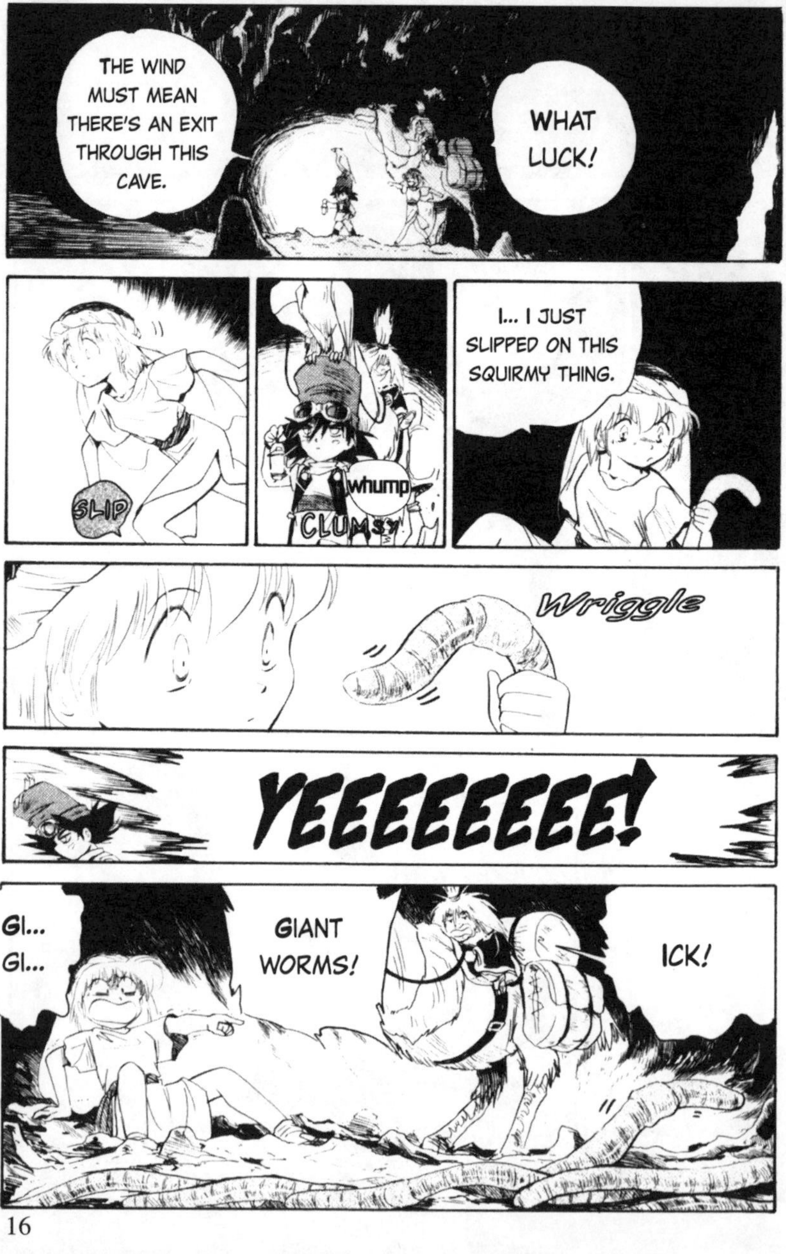
THE WIND MUST MEAN THERE'S AN EXIT THROUGH THIS CAVE.
WHAT LUCK!
SLIP
whump
CLUMSY
I... I JUST SLIPPED ON THIS SQUIRMY THING.
Wriggle
YEEEEEEEEE!
GI... GI...
GIANT WORMS!
ICK!

AHA, THEY'RE ON THEIR WAY TO EAT THAT MOSS.

SKRITCH SKRATCH

WHA-WHAT'S THAT SOUND?

IT'S COMING FROM THE OTHER SIDE.

SKRITCH SKRATCH

GET OUT OF THERE!

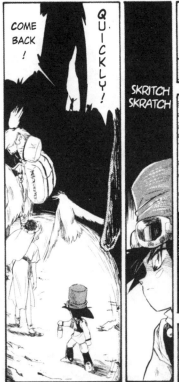
COME BACK !

QUICKLY!

SKRITCH SKRATCH

RUN !

WHAT ?

BACK TO THE ENTRANCE !

RAMBLE

I DON'T GET IT!

RAMBLE

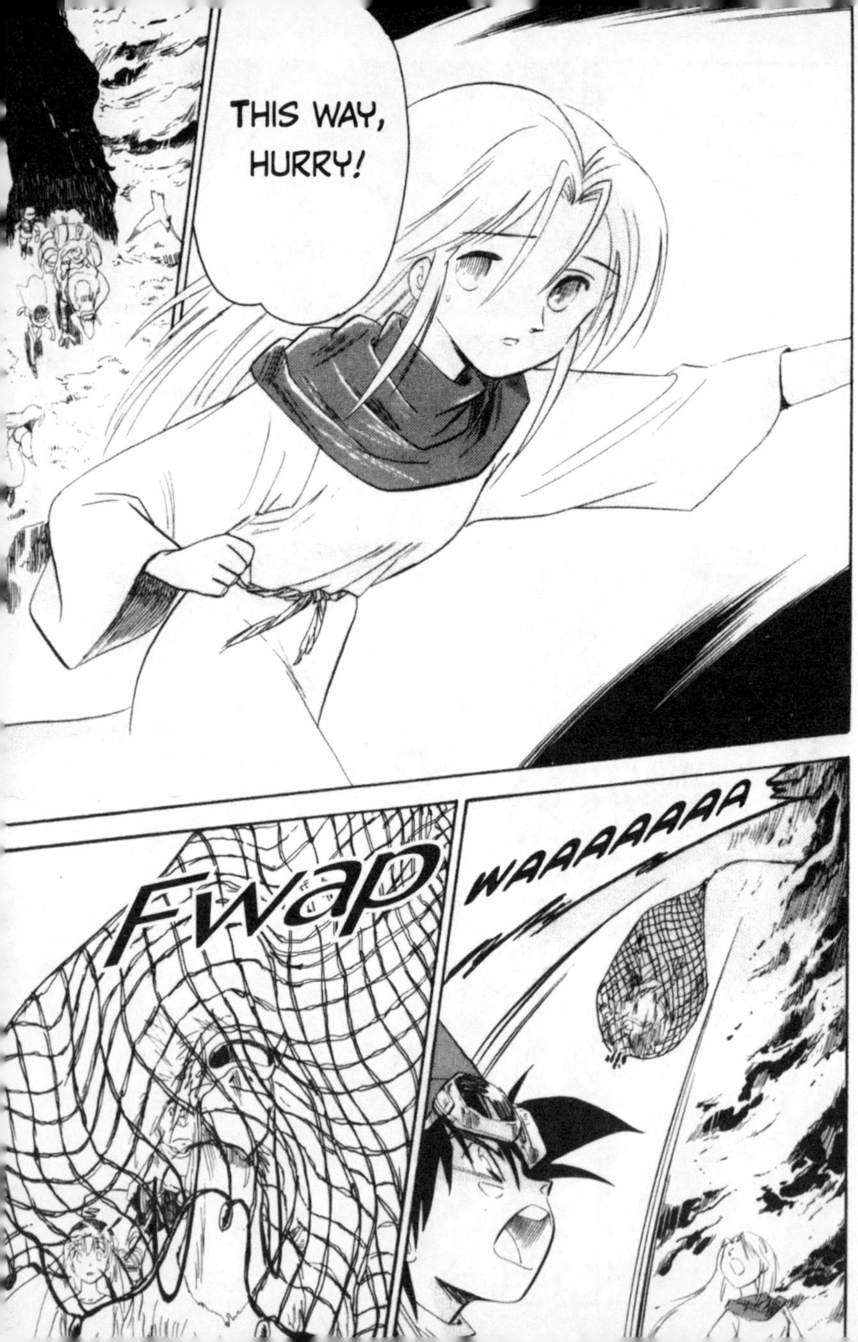
THIS WAY, HURRY!
Fwap
WAAAAAAAA

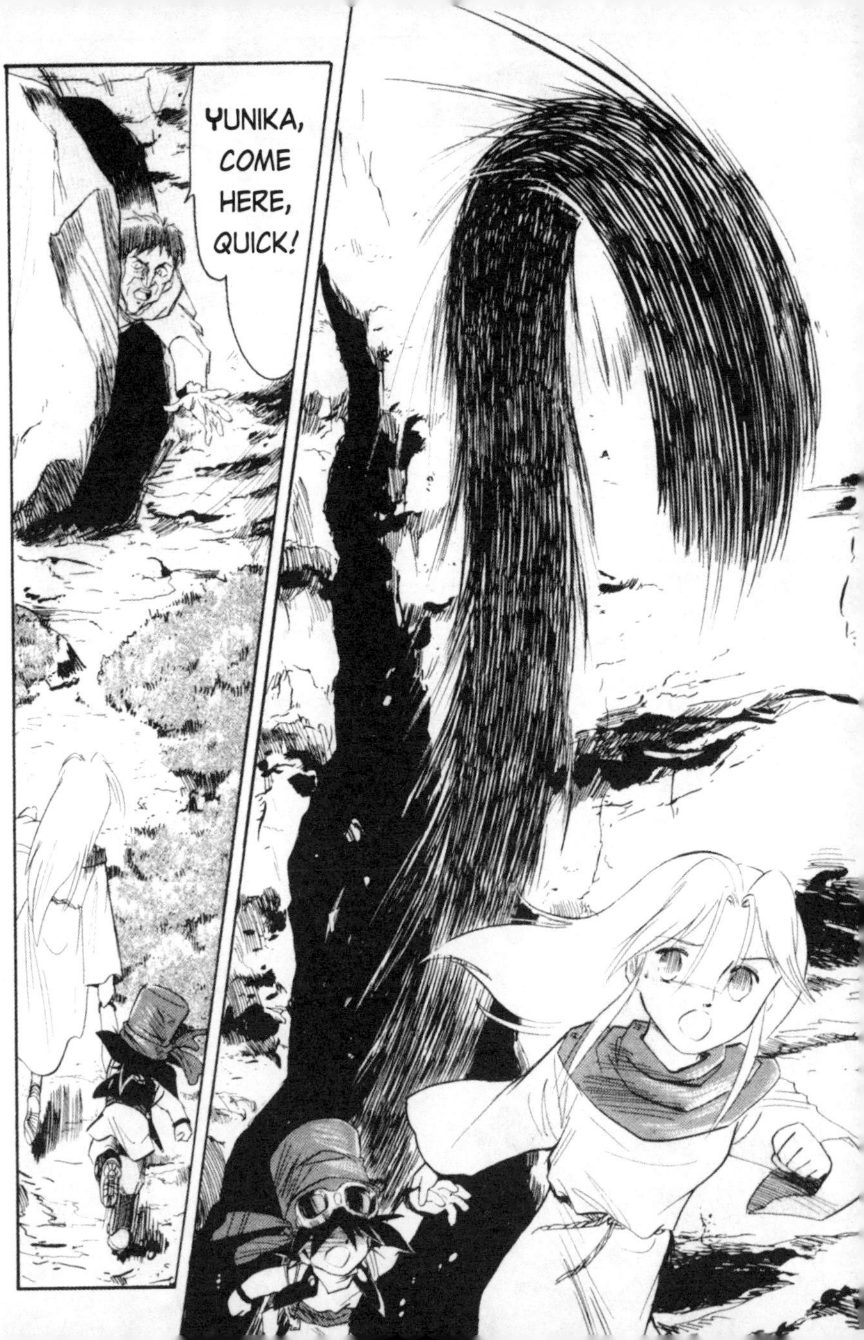
YUNIKA, COME HERE, QUICK!

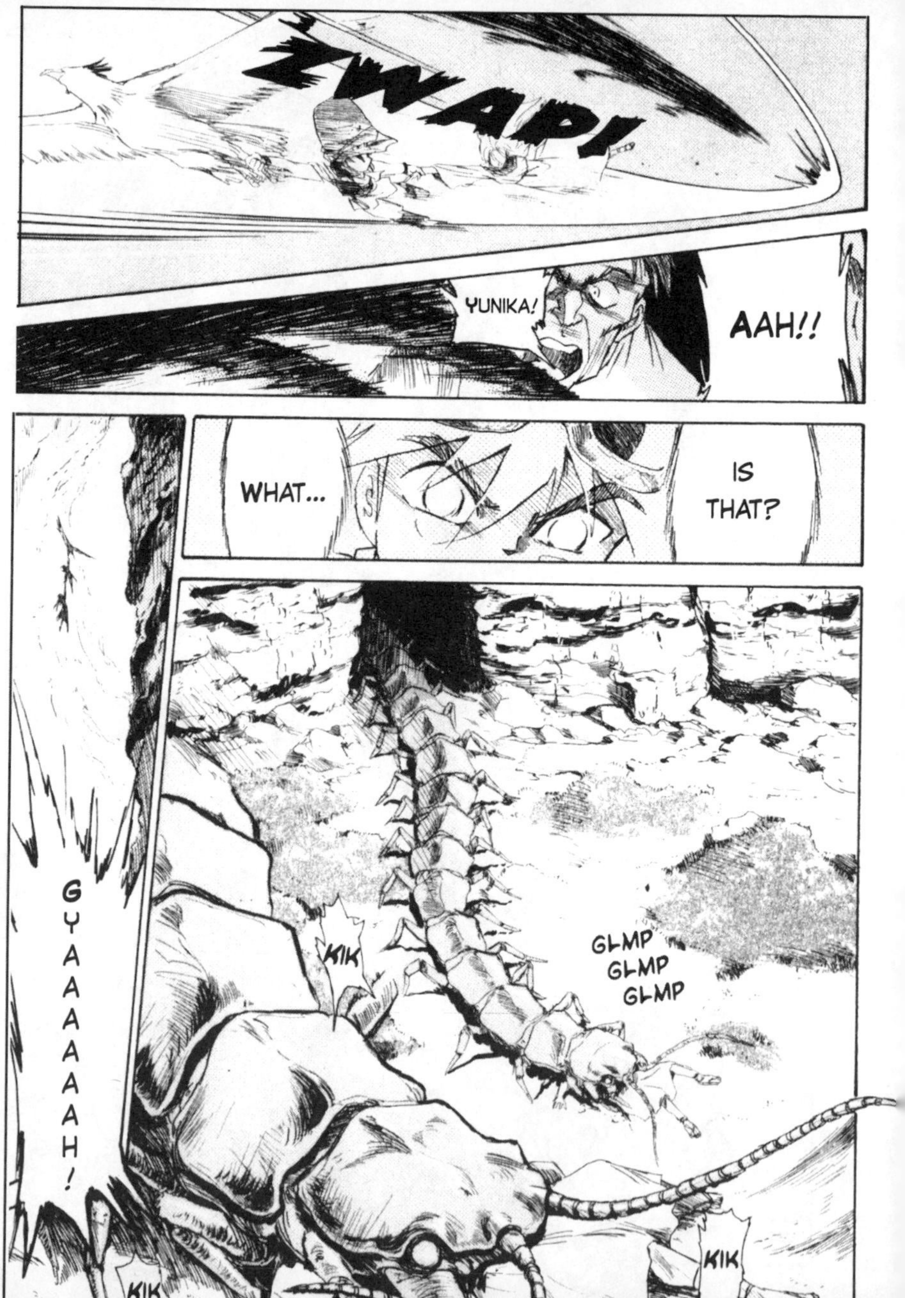
ZWAP!
AAH!!
YUNIKA!
IS THAT?
WHAT...
GLMP GLMP GLMP
KIK
KIK
KIK
GYAAAAAAAAH!

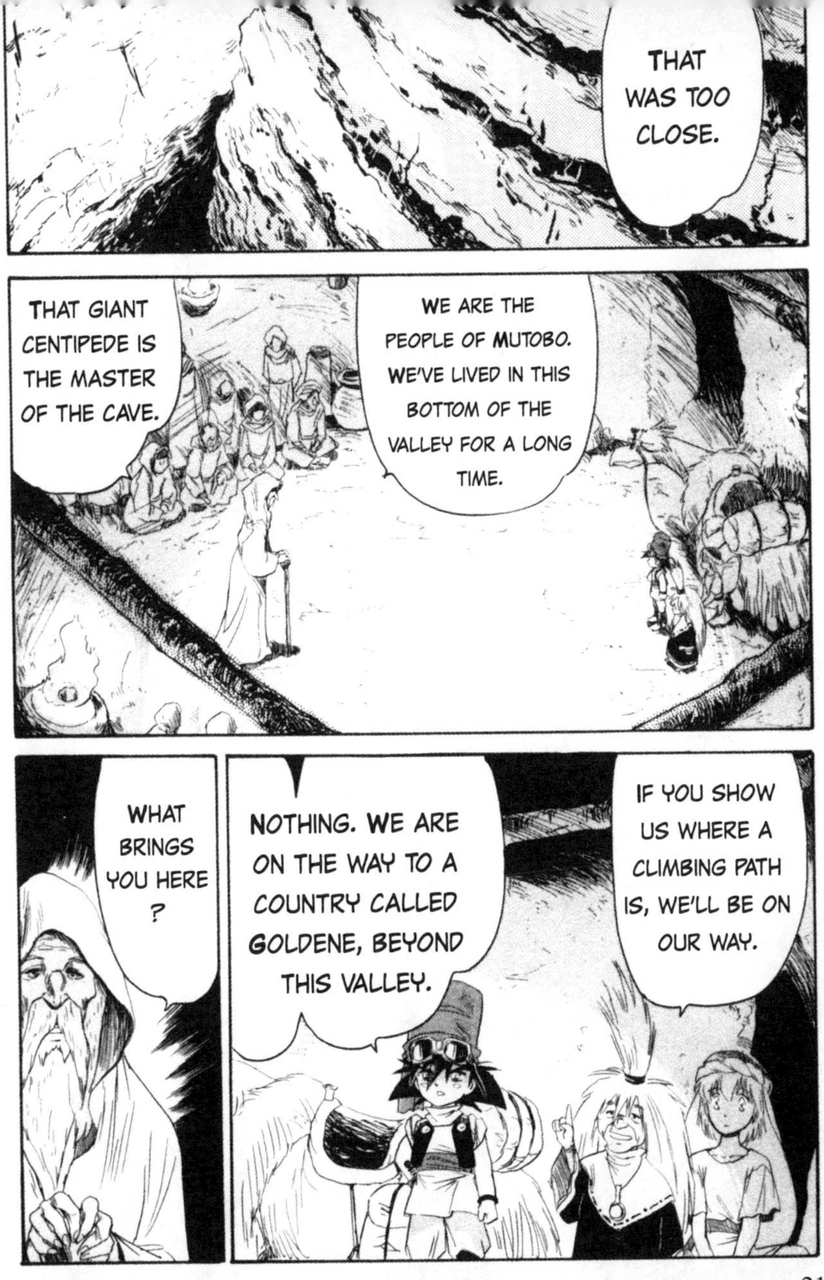
THAT WAS TOO CLOSE.
THAT GIANT CENTIPEDE IS THE MASTER OF THE CAVE.
WE ARE THE PEOPLE OF MUTOBO. WE'VE LIVED IN THIS BOTTOM OF THE VALLEY FOR A LONG TIME.
WHAT BRINGS YOU HERE ?
NOTHING. WE ARE ON THE WAY TO A COUNTRY CALLED GOLDENE, BEYOND THIS VALLEY.
IF YOU SHOW US WHERE A CLIMBING PATH IS, WE'LL BE ON OUR WAY.

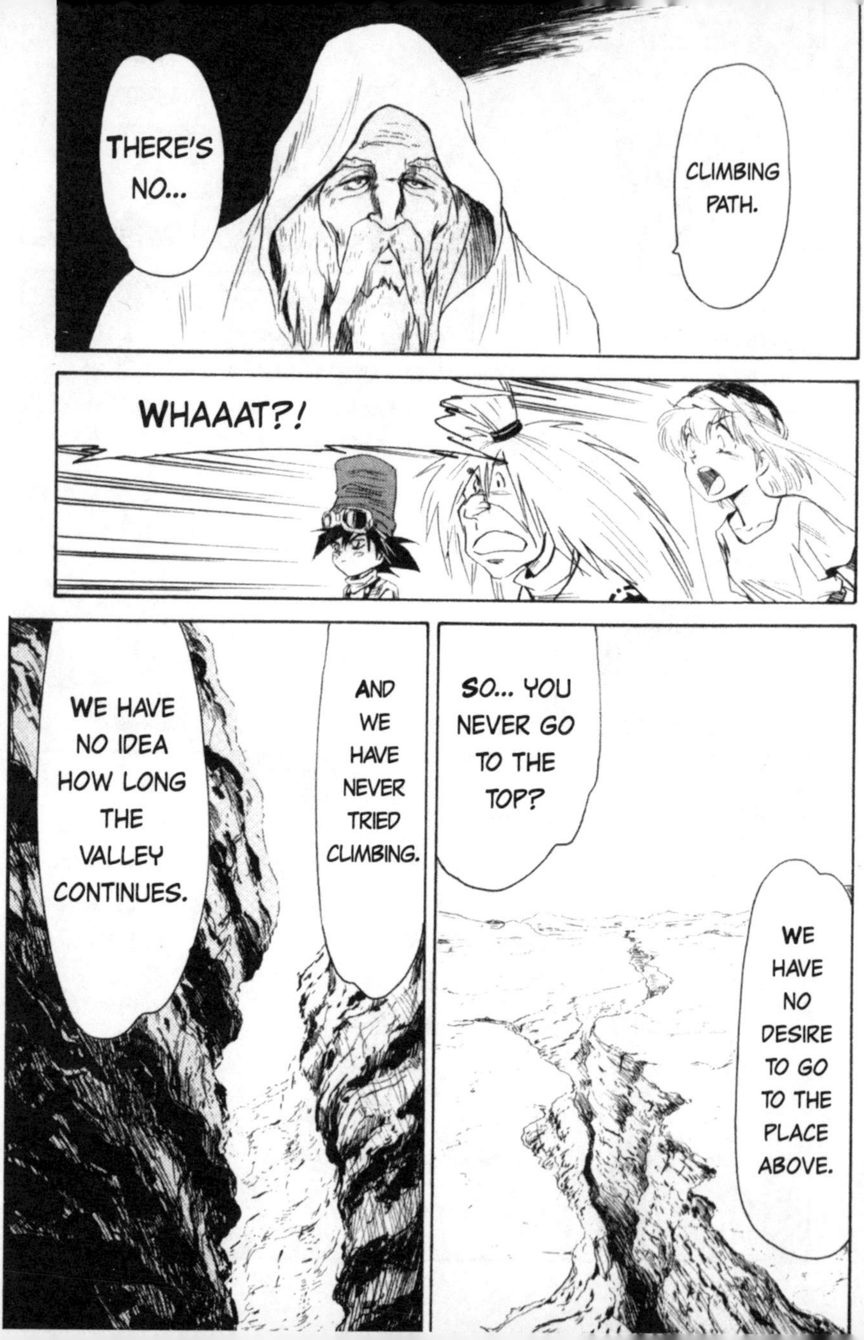
THERE'S NO...
CLIMBING PATH.
WHAAAT?!
SO... YOU NEVER GO TO THE TOP?
AND WE HAVE NEVER TRIED CLIMBING.
WE HAVE NO IDEA HOW LONG THE VALLEY CONTINUES.
WE HAVE NO DESIRE TO GO TO THE PLACE ABOVE.

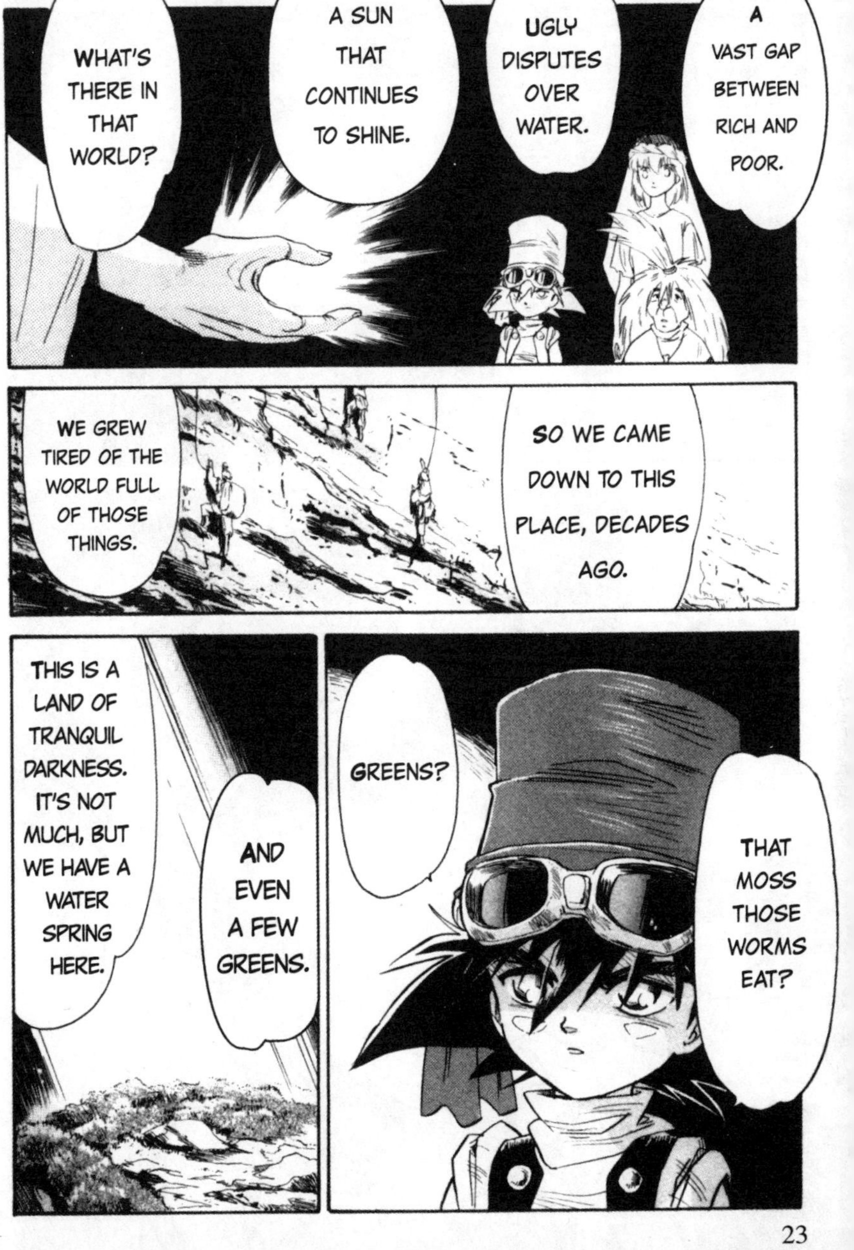
WHAT'S THERE IN THAT WORLD?
A SUN THAT CONTINUES TO SHINE.
UGLY DISPUTES OVER WATER.
A VAST GAP BETWEEN RICH AND POOR.
WE GREW TIRED OF THE WORLD FULL OF THOSE THINGS.
SO WE CAME DOWN TO THIS PLACE, DECADES AGO.
THIS IS A LAND OF TRANQUIL DARKNESS. IT'S NOT MUCH, BUT WE HAVE A WATER SPRING HERE.
AND EVEN A FEW GREENS.
GREENS?
THAT MOSS THOSE WORMS EAT?

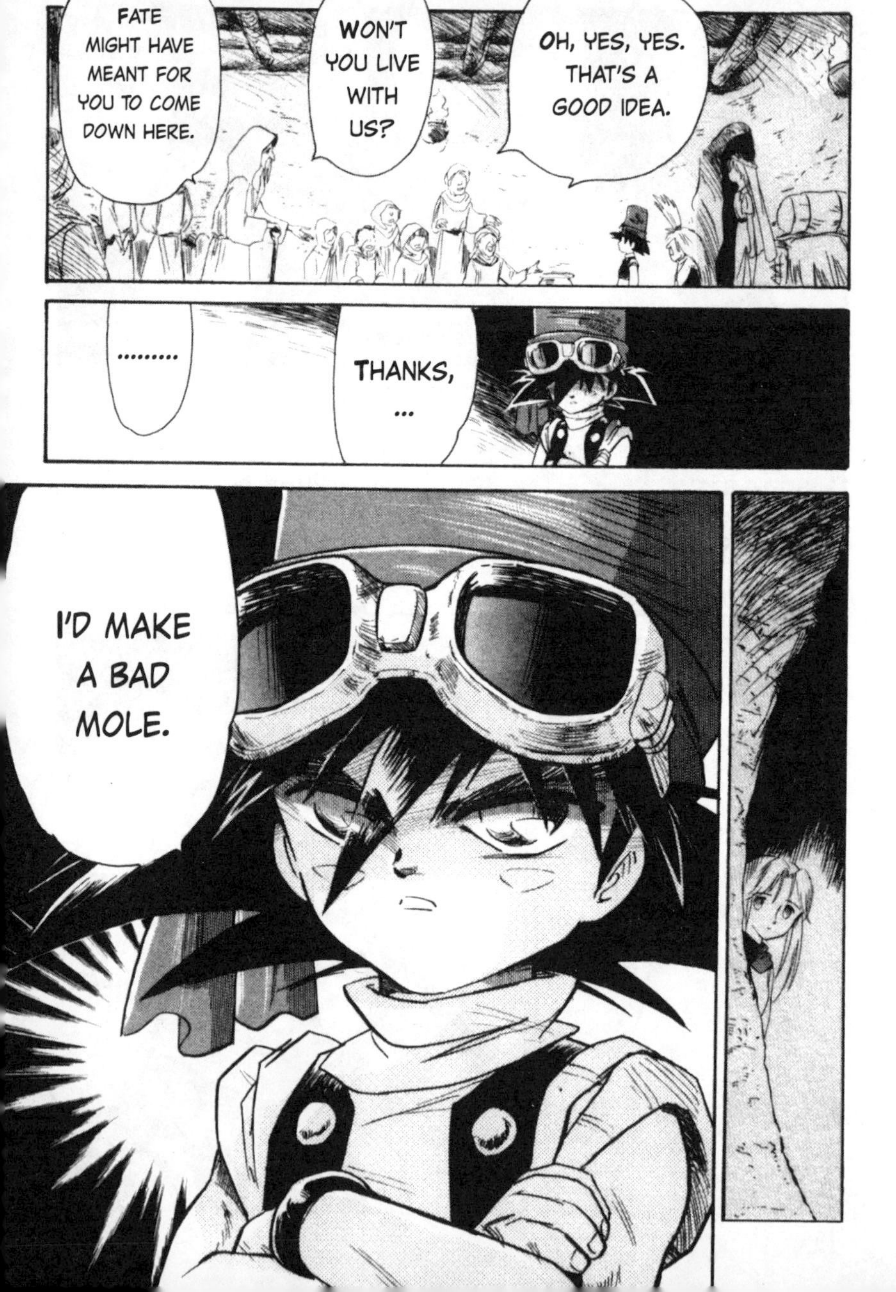
FATE MIGHT HAVE MEANT FOR YOU TO COME DOWN HERE.
WON'T YOU LIVE WITH US?
OH, YES, YES. THAT'S A GOOD IDEA.
....
THANKS, ...
I'D MAKE A BAD MOLE.

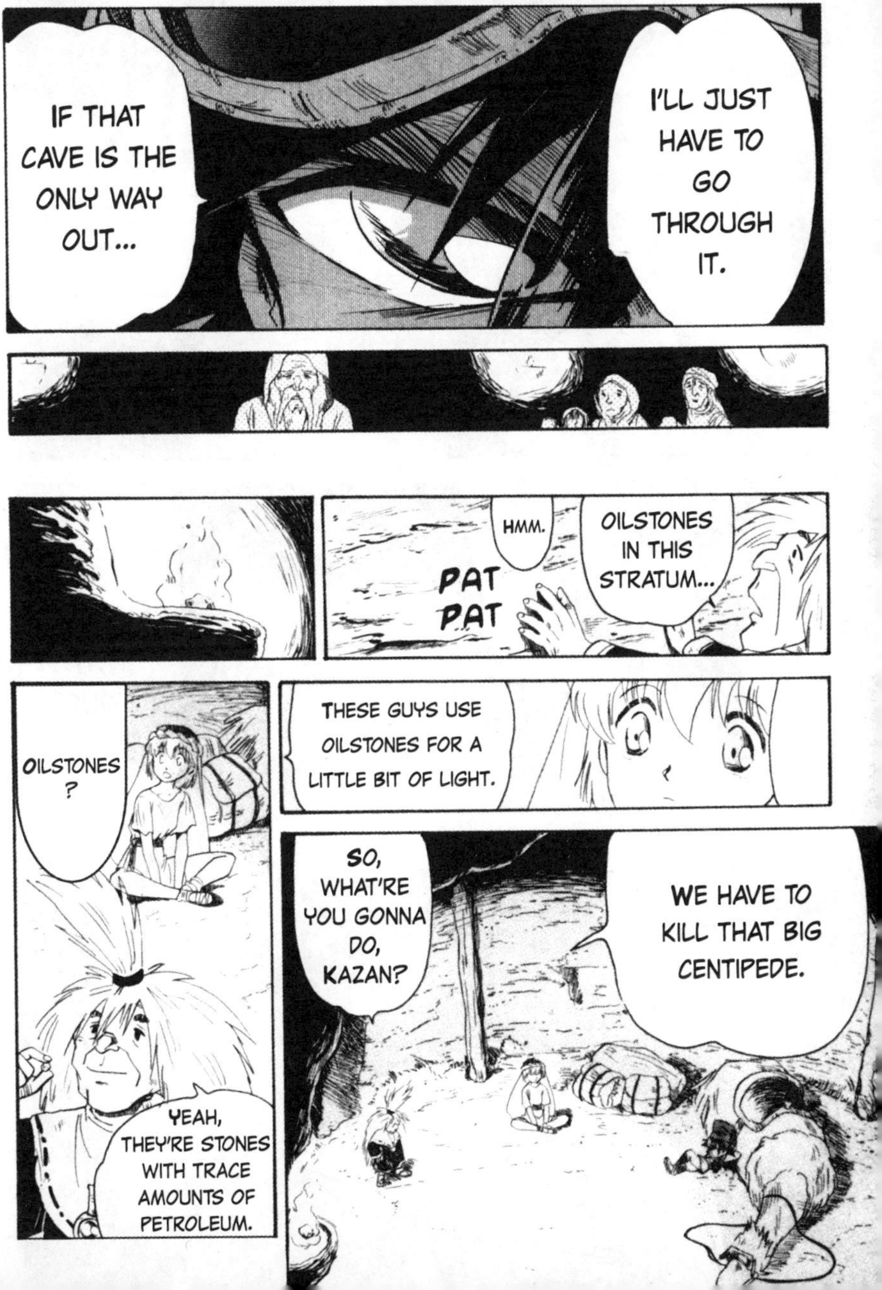
I'LL JUST HAVE TO GO THROUGH IT.
IF THAT CAVE IS THE ONLY WAY OUT...
OILSTONES IN THIS STRATUM...
PAT PAT
HMM.
THESE GUYS USE OILSTONES FOR A LITTLE BIT OF LIGHT.
OILSTONES ?
YEAH, THEY'RE STONES WITH TRACE AMOUNTS OF PETROLEUM.
WE HAVE TO KILL THAT BIG CENTIPEDE.
SO, WHAT'RE YOU GONNA DO, KAZAN?

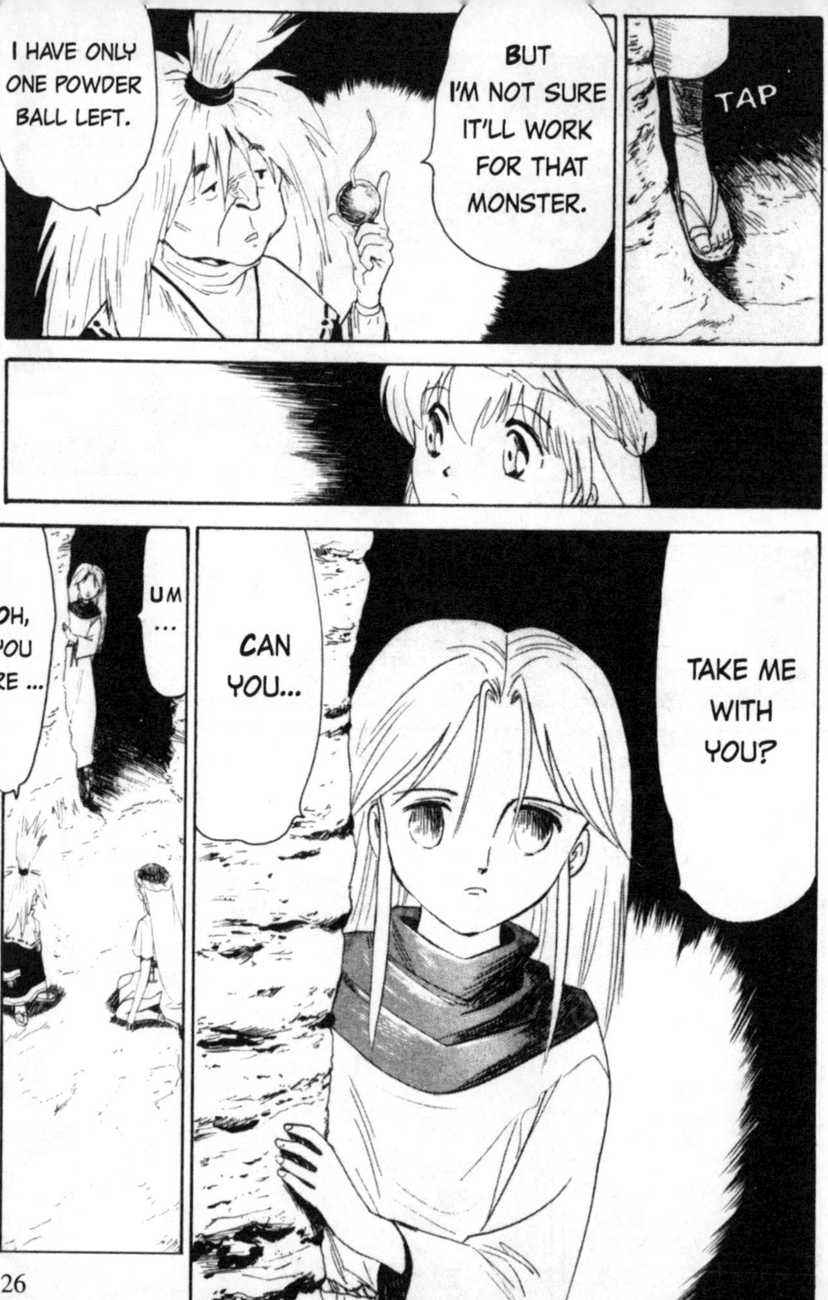
I HAVE ONLY ONE POWDER BALL LEFT.
BUT I'M NOT SURE IT'LL WORK FOR THAT MONSTER.
TAP
OH, YOU ARE ...
UM ...
CAN YOU...
TAKE ME WITH YOU?

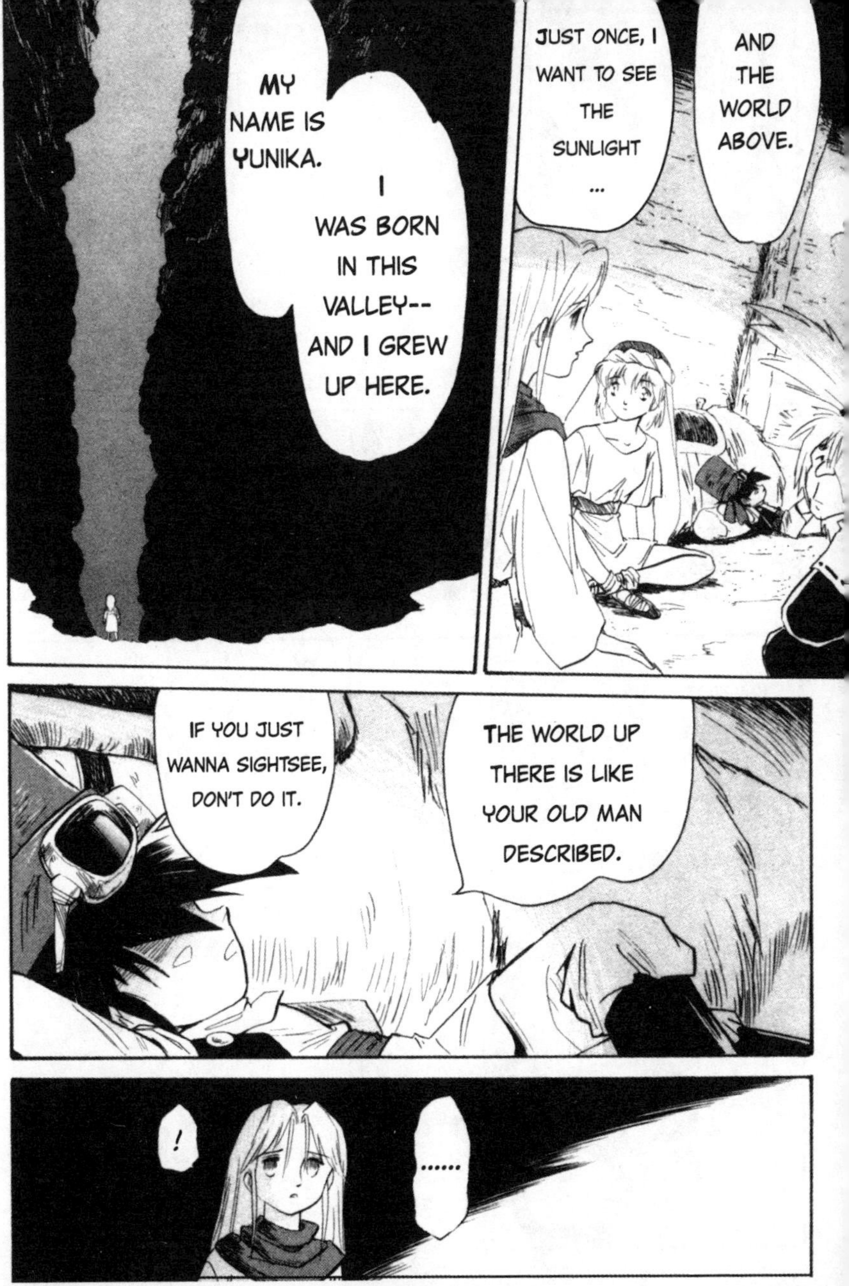
MY NAME IS YUNIKA.
I WAS BORN IN THIS VALLEY-- AND I GREW UP HERE.
JUST ONCE, I WANT TO SEE THE SUNLIGHT ...
AND THE WORLD ABOVE.
IF YOU JUST WANNA SIGHTSEE, DON'T DO IT.
THE WORLD UP THERE IS LIKE YOUR OLD MAN DESCRIBED.
!
......

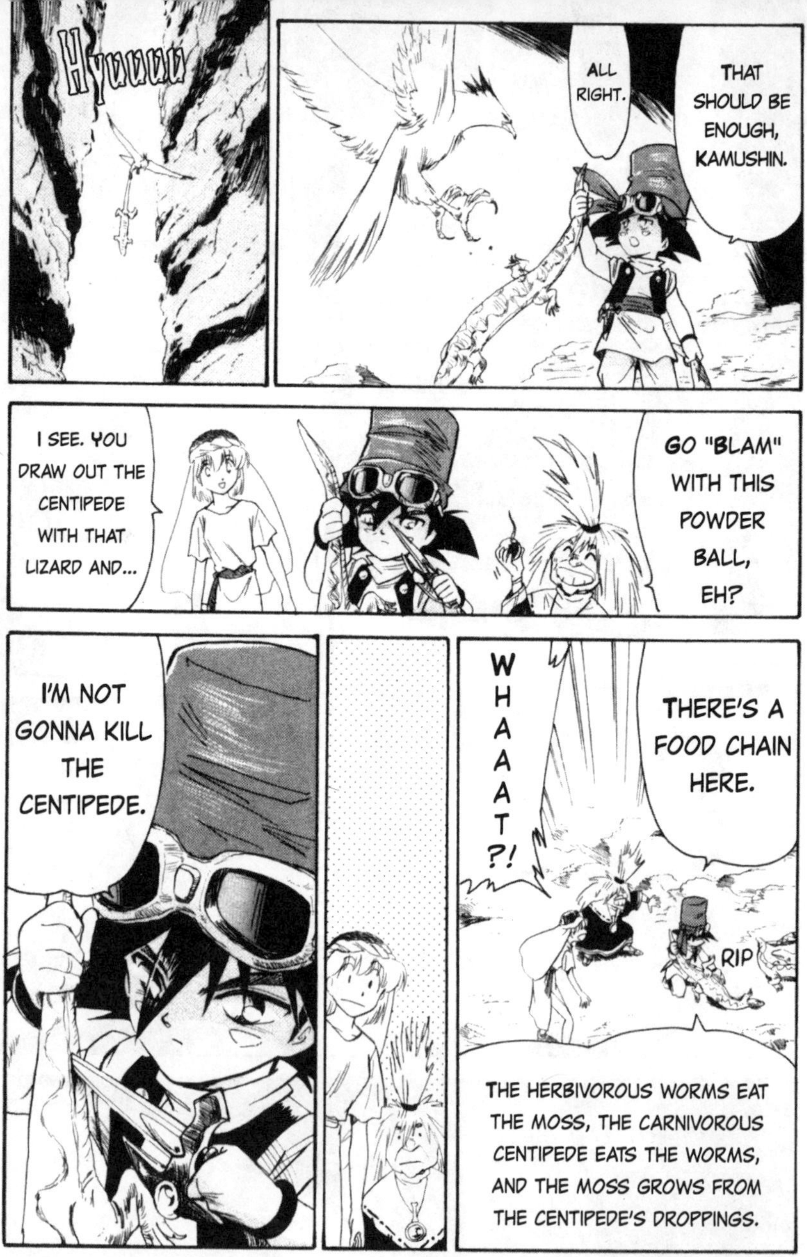
Hyuuuu
ALL RIGHT.
THAT SHOULD BE ENOUGH, KAMUSHIN.
I SEE. YOU DRAW OUT THE CENTIPEDE WITH THAT LIZARD AND...
GO "BLAM" WITH THIS POWDER BALL, EH?
I'M NOT GONNA KILL THE CENTIPEDE.
WHAAAAT?!
THERE'S A FOOD CHAIN HERE.
RIP
THE HERBIVOROUS WORMS EAT THE MOSS, THE CARNIVOROUS CENTIPEDE EATS THE WORMS, AND THE MOSS GROWS FROM THE CENTIPEDE'S DROPPINGS.

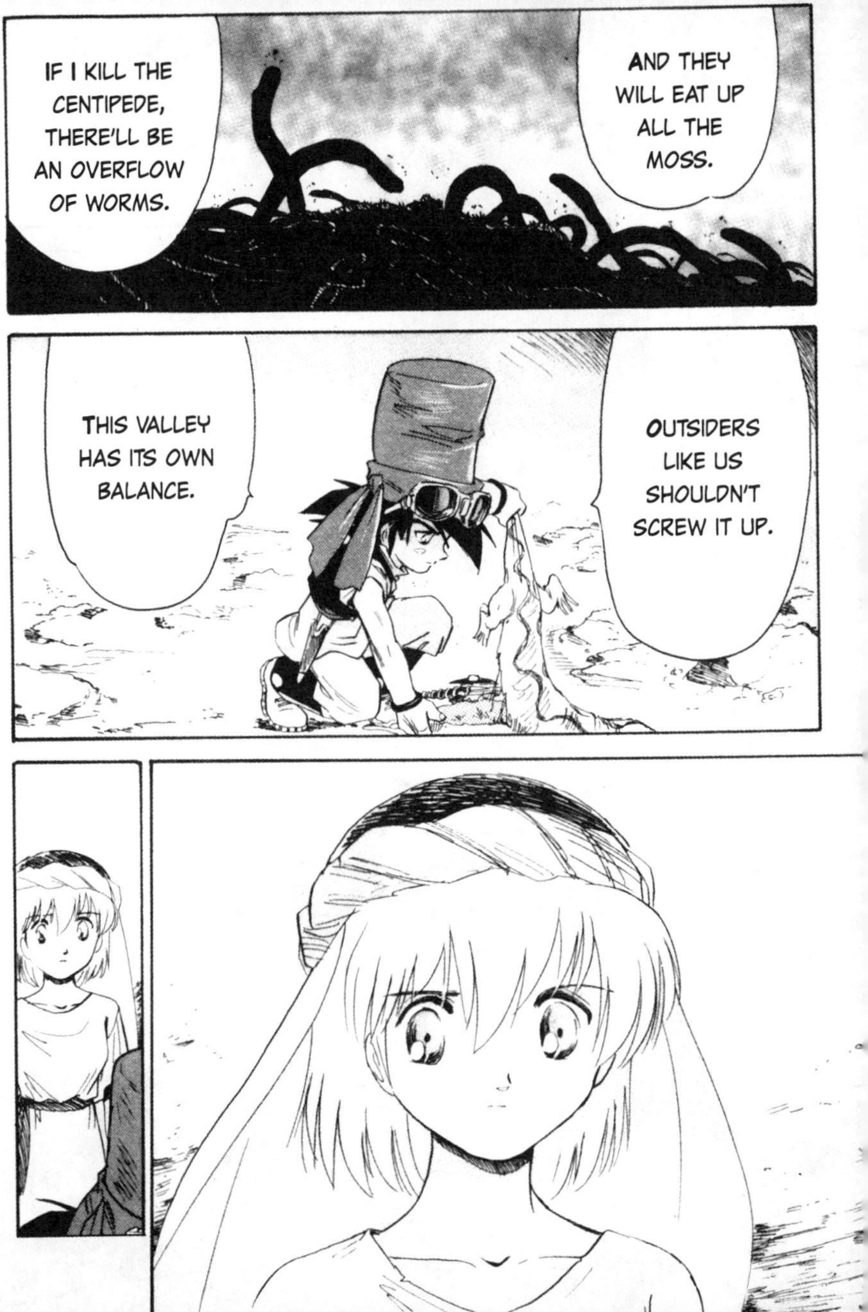
IF I KILL THE CENTIPEDE, THERE'LL BE AN OVERFLOW OF WORMS.
AND THEY WILL EAT UP ALL THE MOSS.
THIS VALLEY HAS ITS OWN BALANCE.
OUTSIDERS LIKE US SHOULDN'T SCREW IT UP.

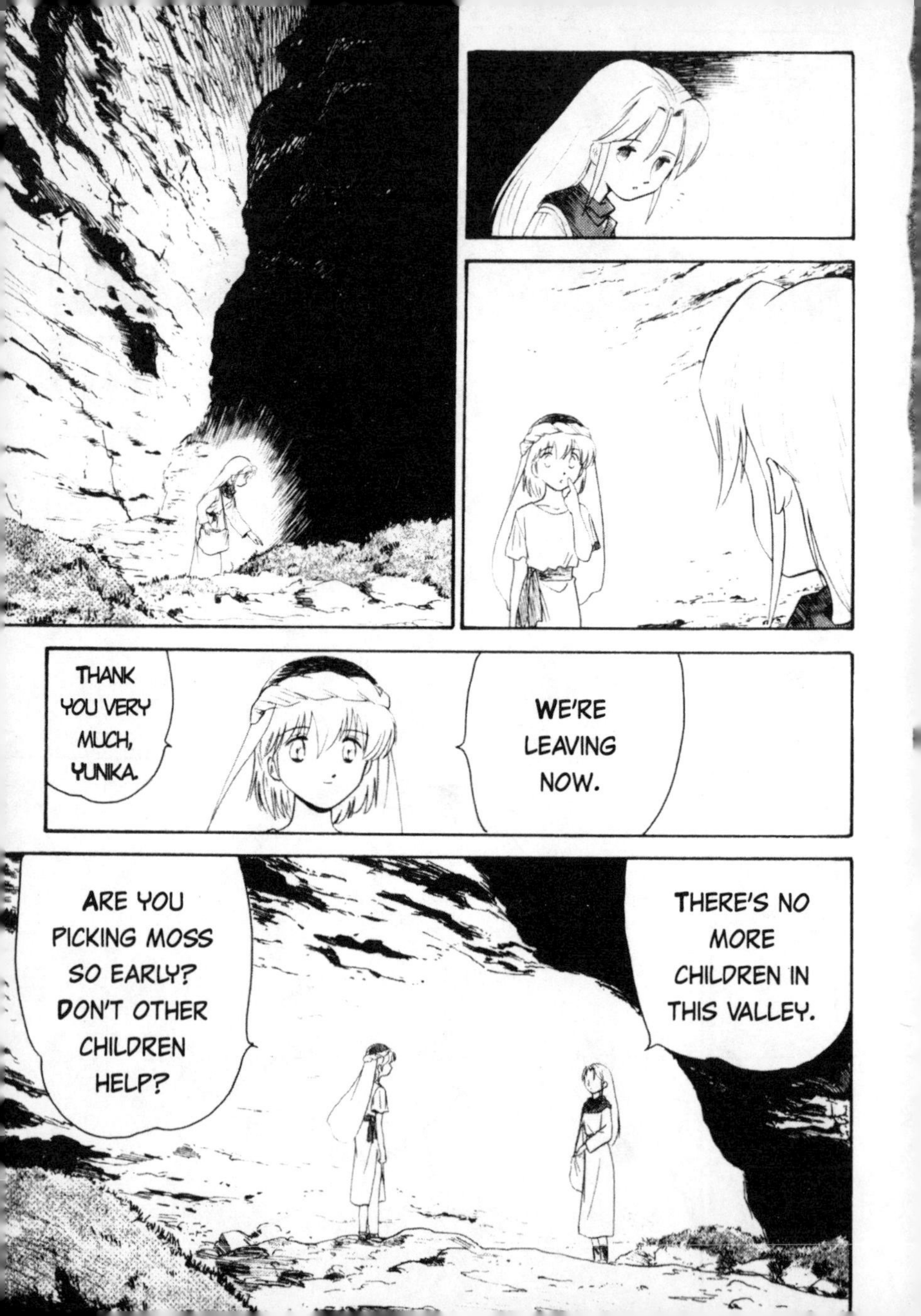
THANK YOU VERY MUCH, YUNIKA.
WE'RE LEAVING NOW.
ARE YOU PICKING MOSS SO EARLY? DON'T OTHER CHILDREN HELP?
THERE'S NO MORE CHILDREN IN THIS VALLEY.

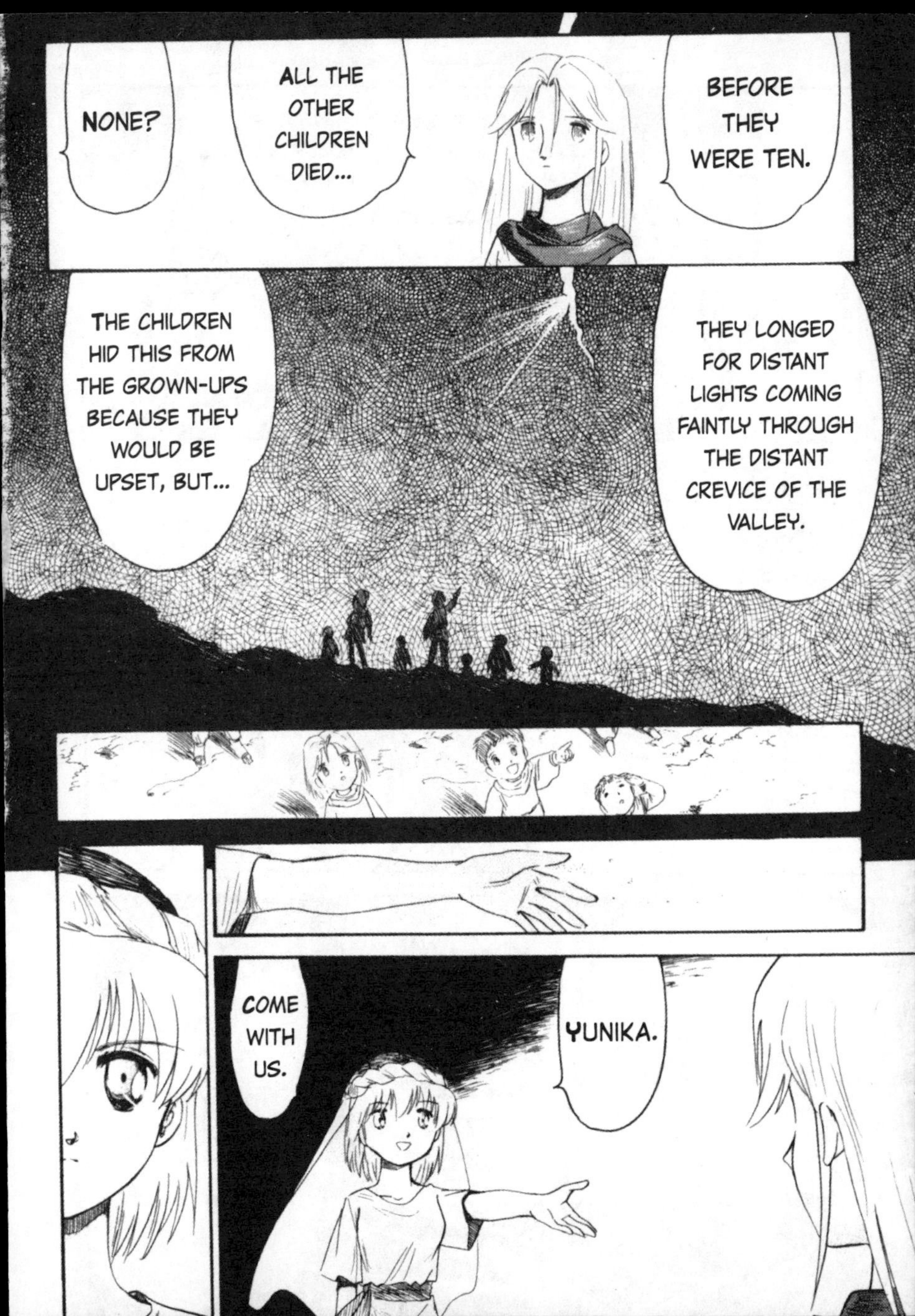
BEFORE THEY WERE TEN.
ALL THE OTHER CHILDREN DIED...
NONE?
THEY LONGED FOR DISTANT LIGHTS COMING FAINTLY THROUGH THE DISTANT CREVICE OF THE VALLEY.
THE CHILDREN HID THIS FROM THE GROWN-UPS BECAUSE THEY WOULD BE UPSET, BUT...
YUNIKA.
COME WITH US.

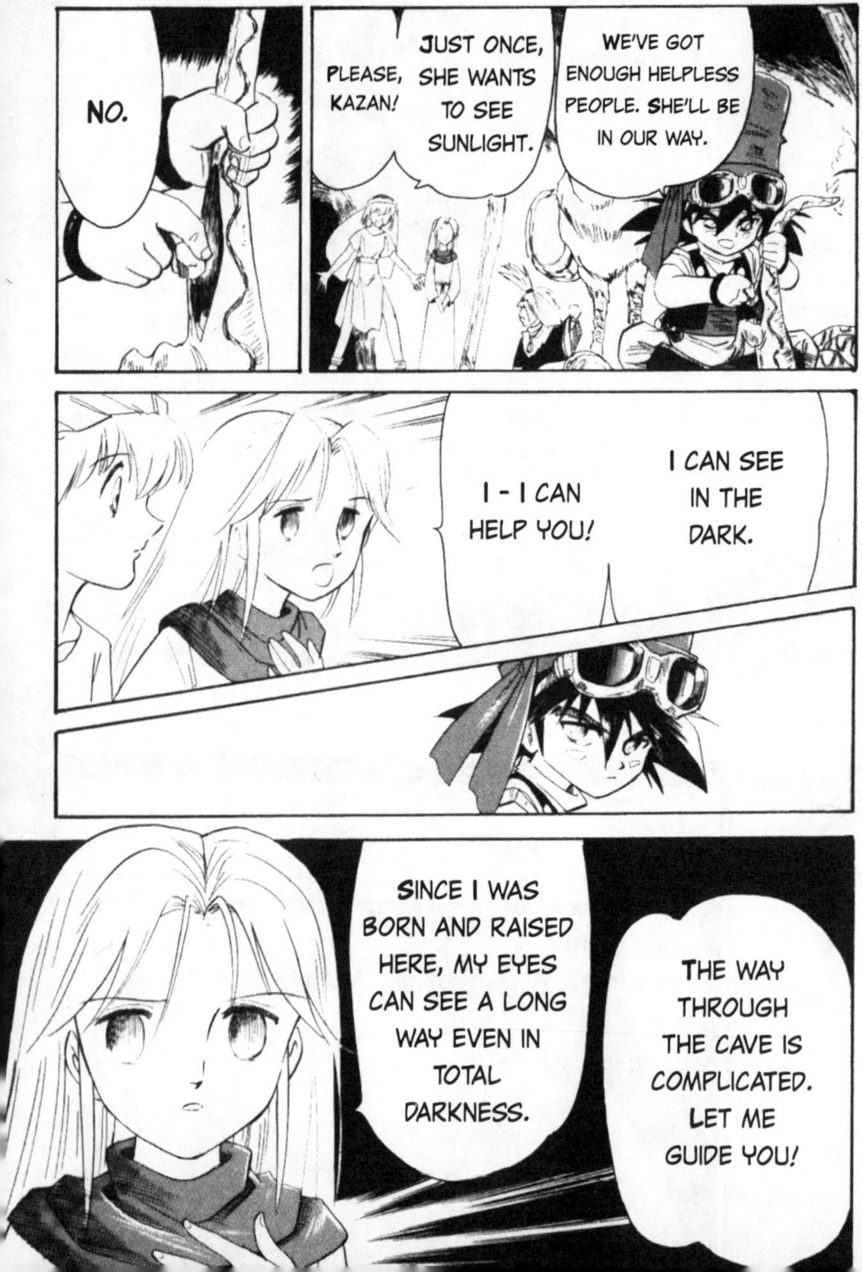
NO.
PLEASE, KAZAN!
JUST ONCE, SHE WANTS TO SEE SUNLIGHT.
WE'VE GOT ENOUGH HELPLESS PEOPLE. SHE'LL BE IN OUR WAY.
I - I CAN HELP YOU!
I CAN SEE IN THE DARK.
SINCE I WAS BORN AND RAISED HERE, MY EYES CAN SEE A LONG WAY EVEN IN TOTAL DARKNESS.
THE WAY THROUGH THE CAVE IS COMPLICATED. LET ME GUIDE YOU!

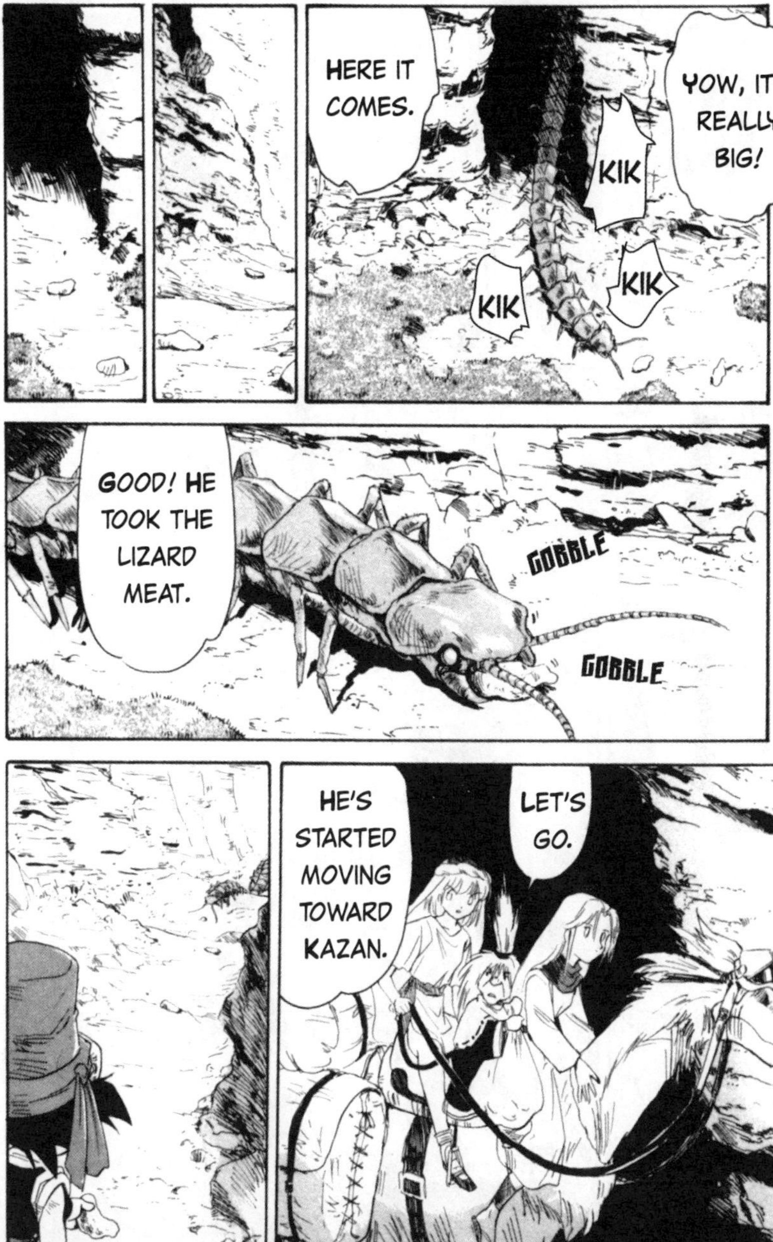
HERE IT COMES.
YOW, IT'S REALLY BIG!
KIK
KIK
KIK
GOOD! HE TOOK THE LIZARD MEAT.
GOBBLE
GOBBLE
LET'S GO.
HE'S STARTED MOVING TOWARD KAZAN.

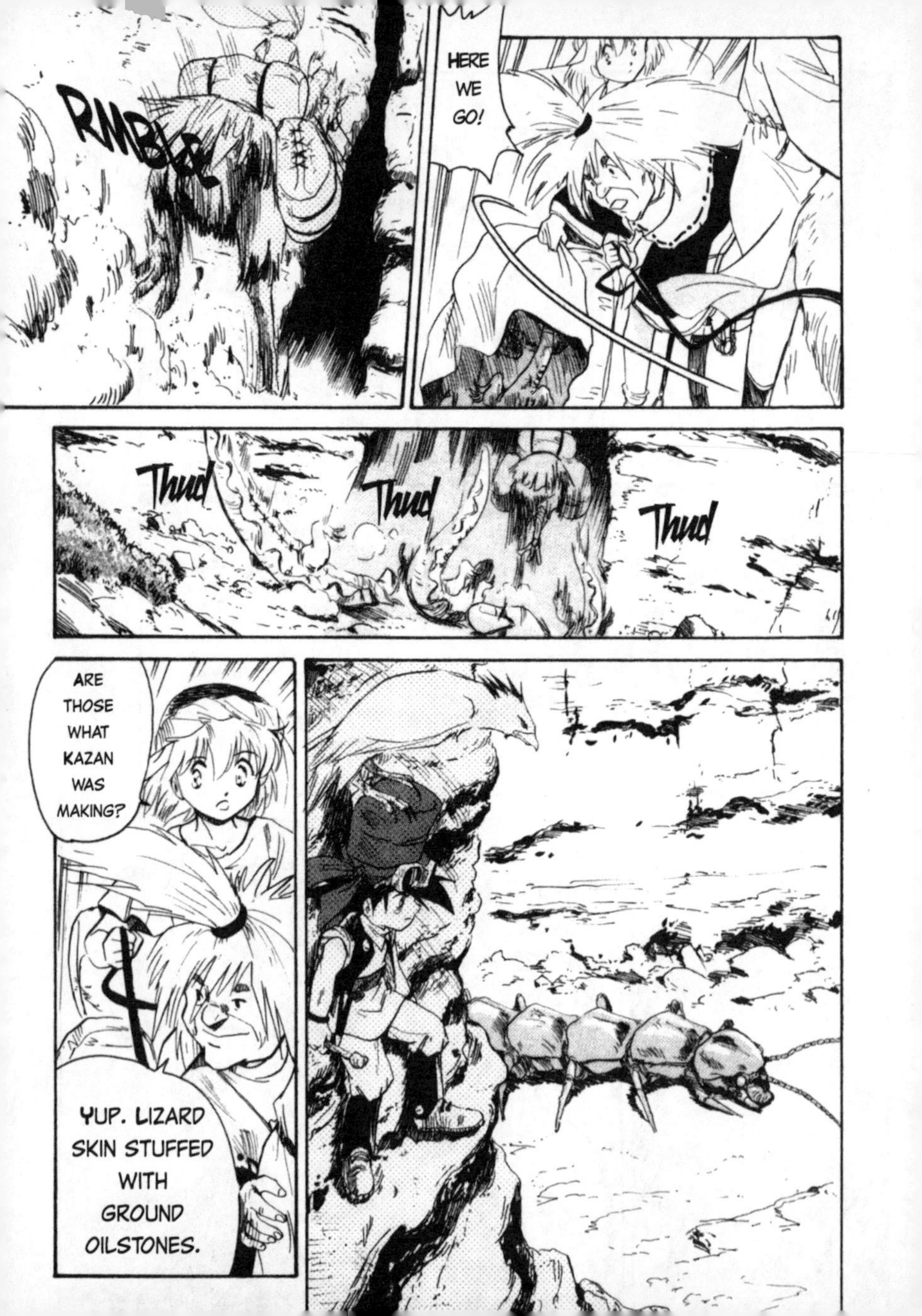
RMBLE
HERE WE GO!
Thud
Thud
Thud
ARE THOSE WHAT KAZAN WAS MAKING?
YUP. LIZARD SKIN STUFFED WITH GROUND OILSTONES.

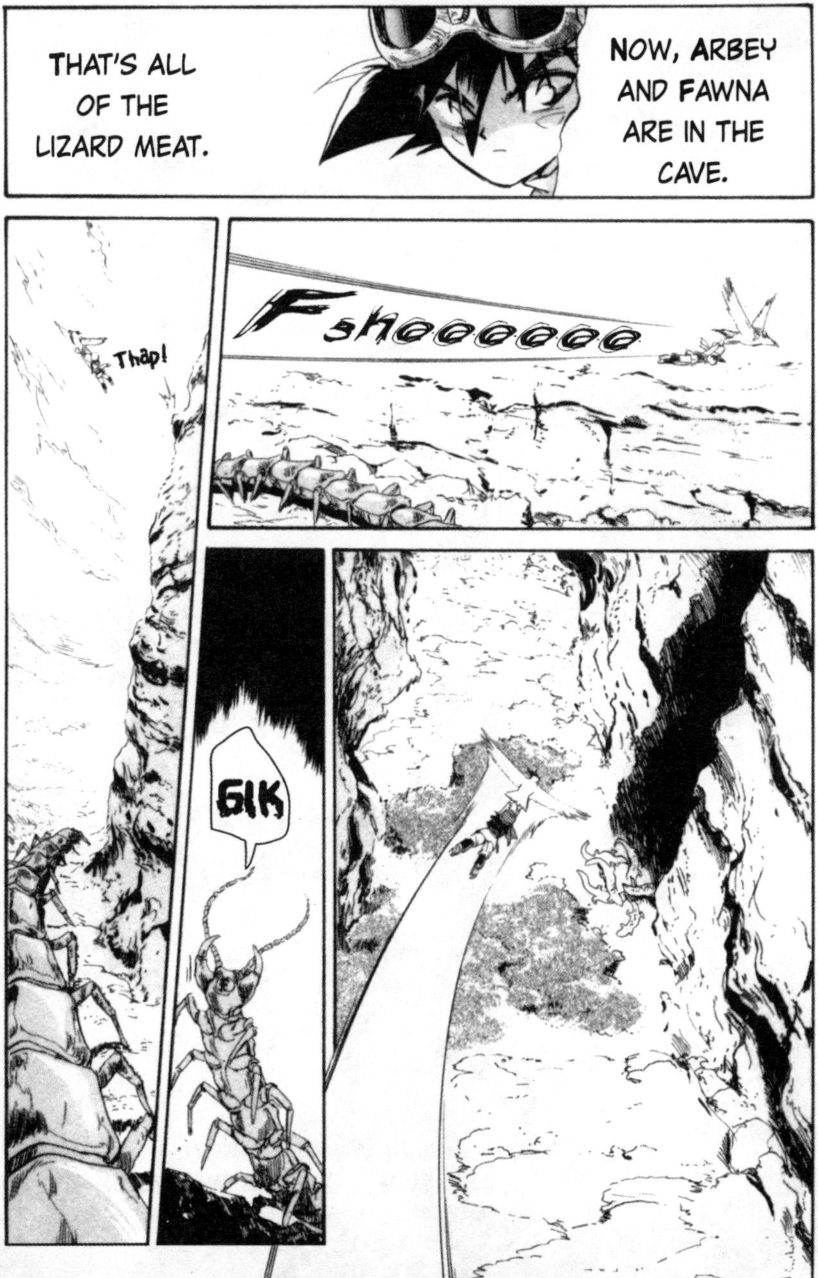

THAT'S ALL OF THE LIZARD MEAT.
NOW, ARBEY AND FAWNA ARE IN THE CAVE.
Thap!
Fshoooooooo
GIK

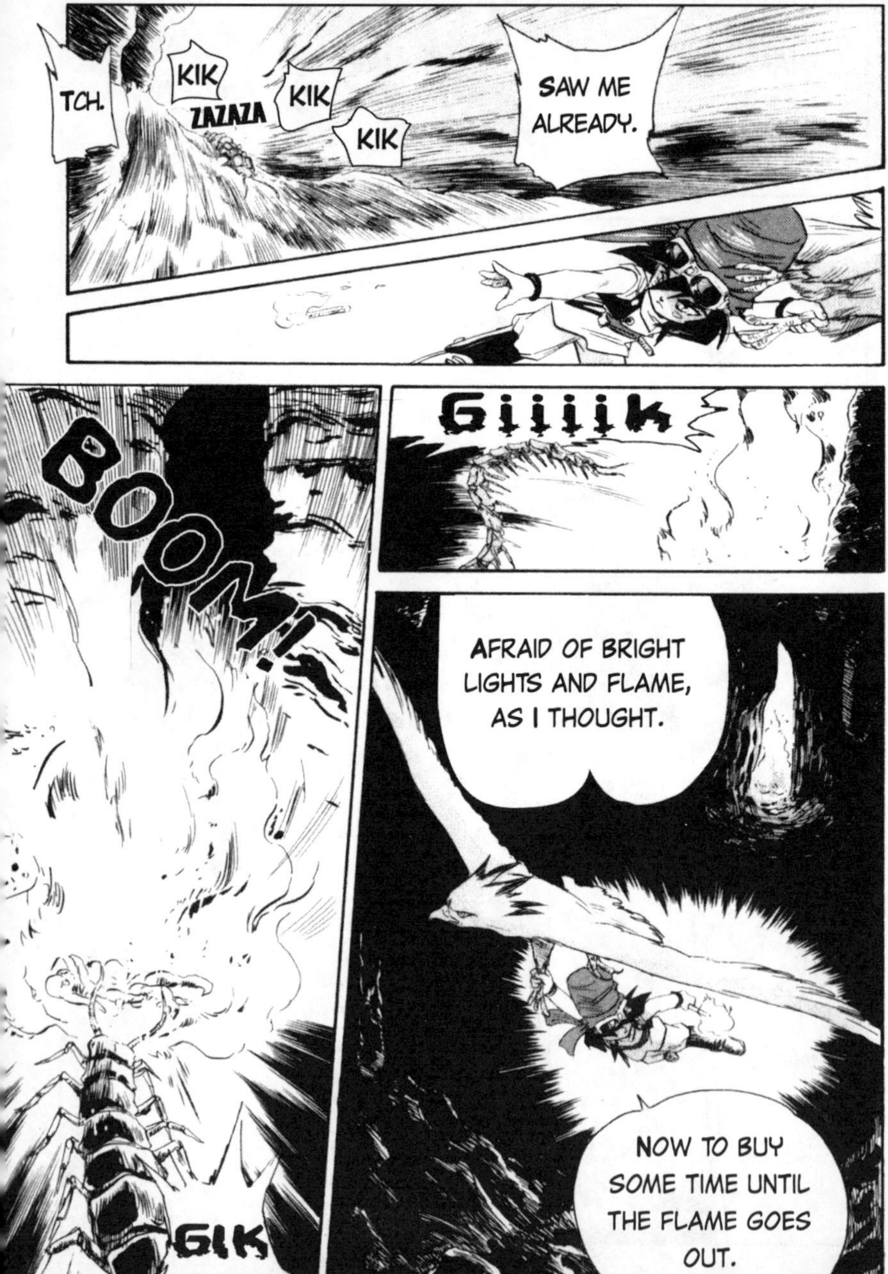
TCH.
KIK
ZAZAZA
KIK
KIK
SAW ME ALREADY.
BOOM!
GIK
Giiiik
AFRAID OF BRIGHT LIGHTS AND FLAME, AS I THOUGHT.
NOW TO BUY SOME TIME UNTIL THE FLAME GOES OUT.

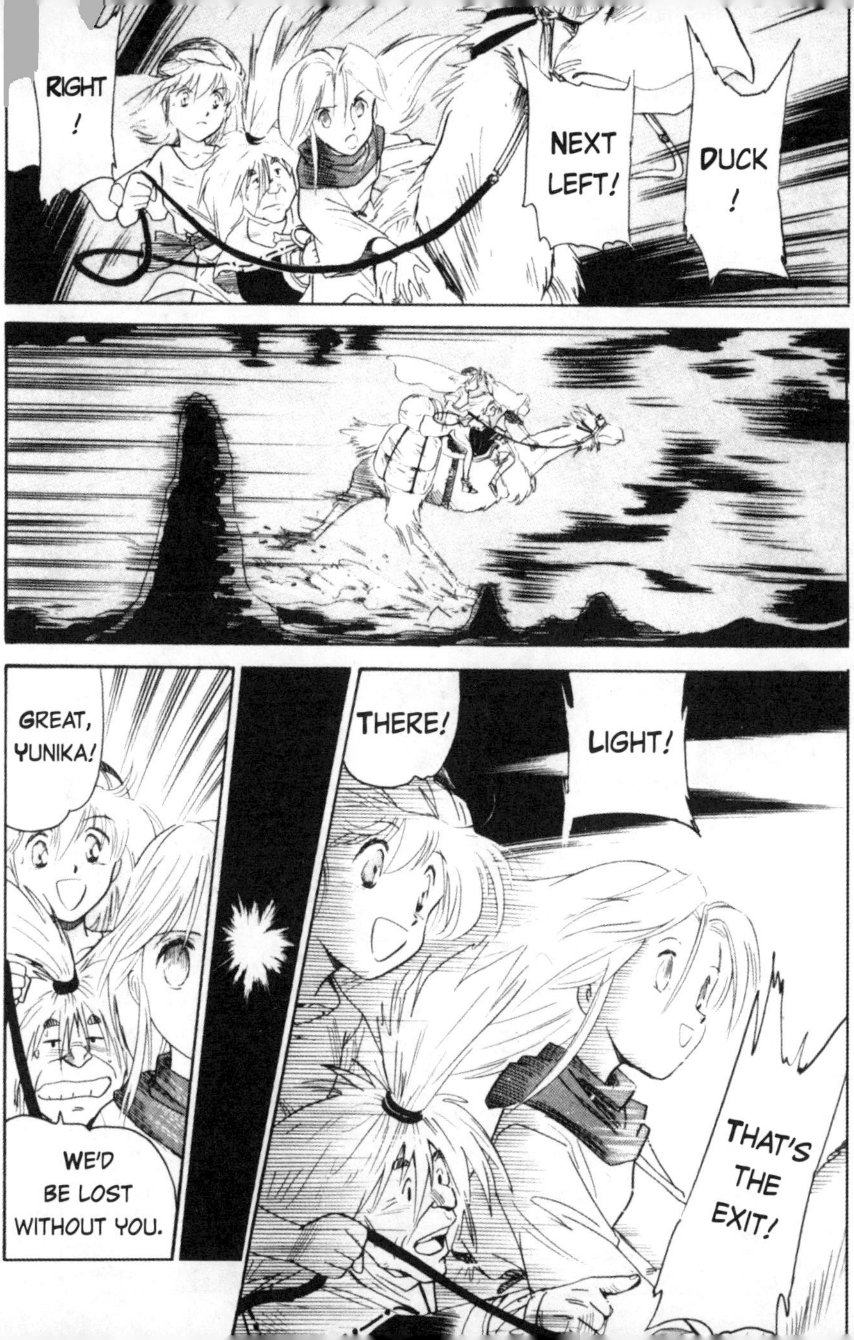
DUCK!
NEXT LEFT!
RIGHT!
LIGHT!
THERE!
THAT'S THE EXIT!
GREAT, YUNIKA!
WE'D BE LOST WITHOUT YOU.

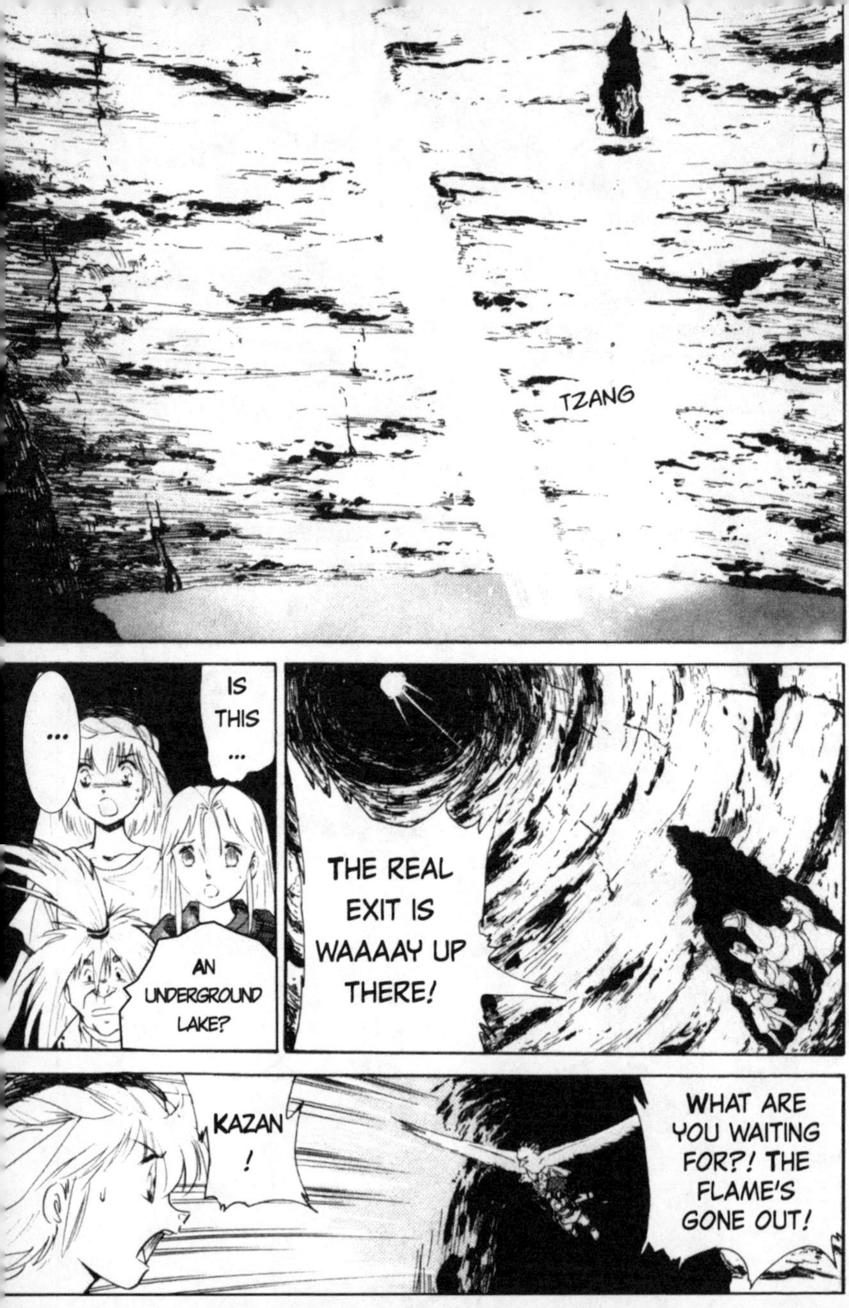
TZANG
IS THIS ...
...
AN UNDERGROUND LAKE?
THE REAL EXIT IS WAAAAY UP THERE!
KAZAN!
WHAT ARE YOU WAITING FOR?! THE FLAME'S GONE OUT!

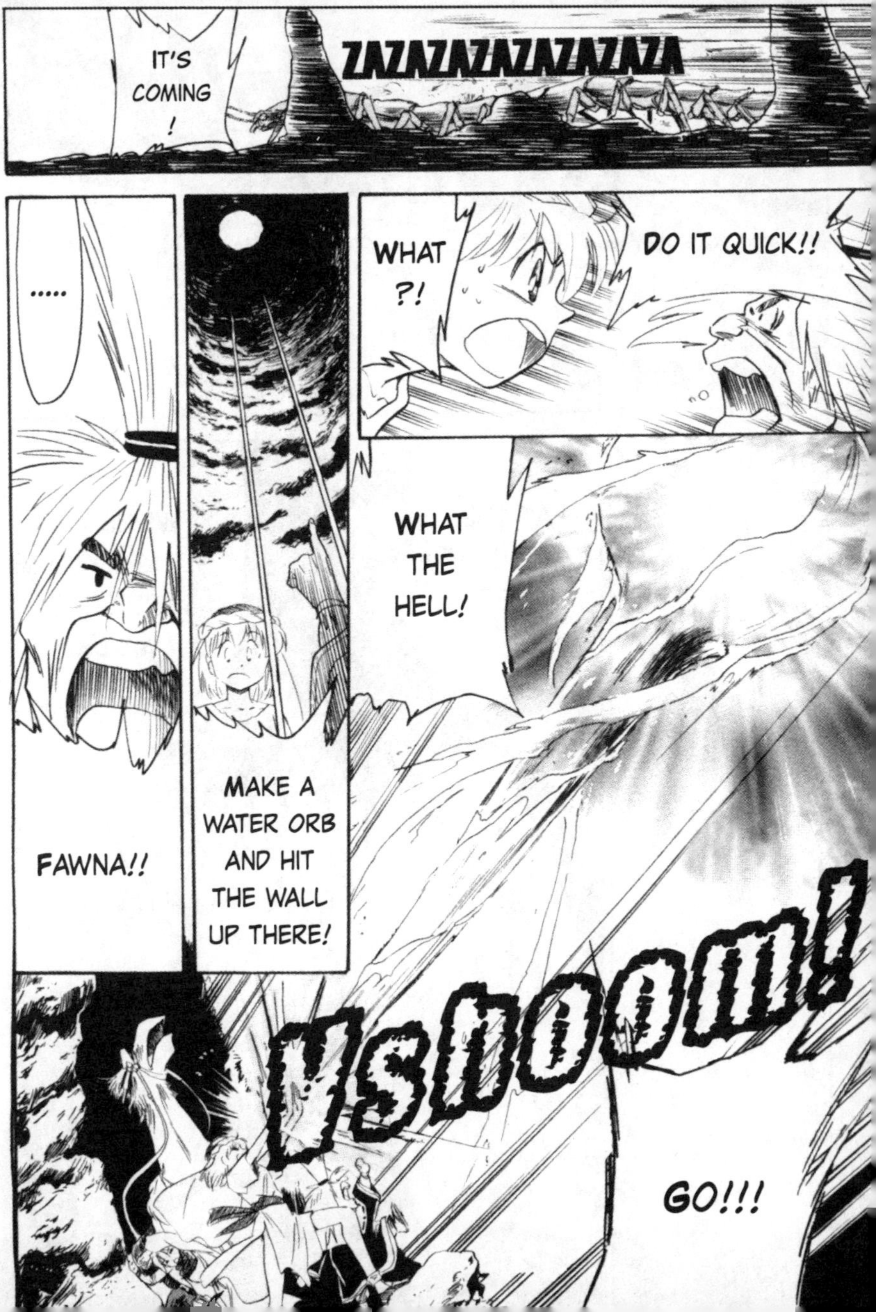
IT'S COMING!
ZAZAZAZAZAZAZAZA
.....
FAWNA!!
MAKE A WATER ORB AND HIT THE WALL UP THERE!
WHAT?!
DO IT QUICK!!
WHAT THE HELL!
VSHOOOM!
GO!!!

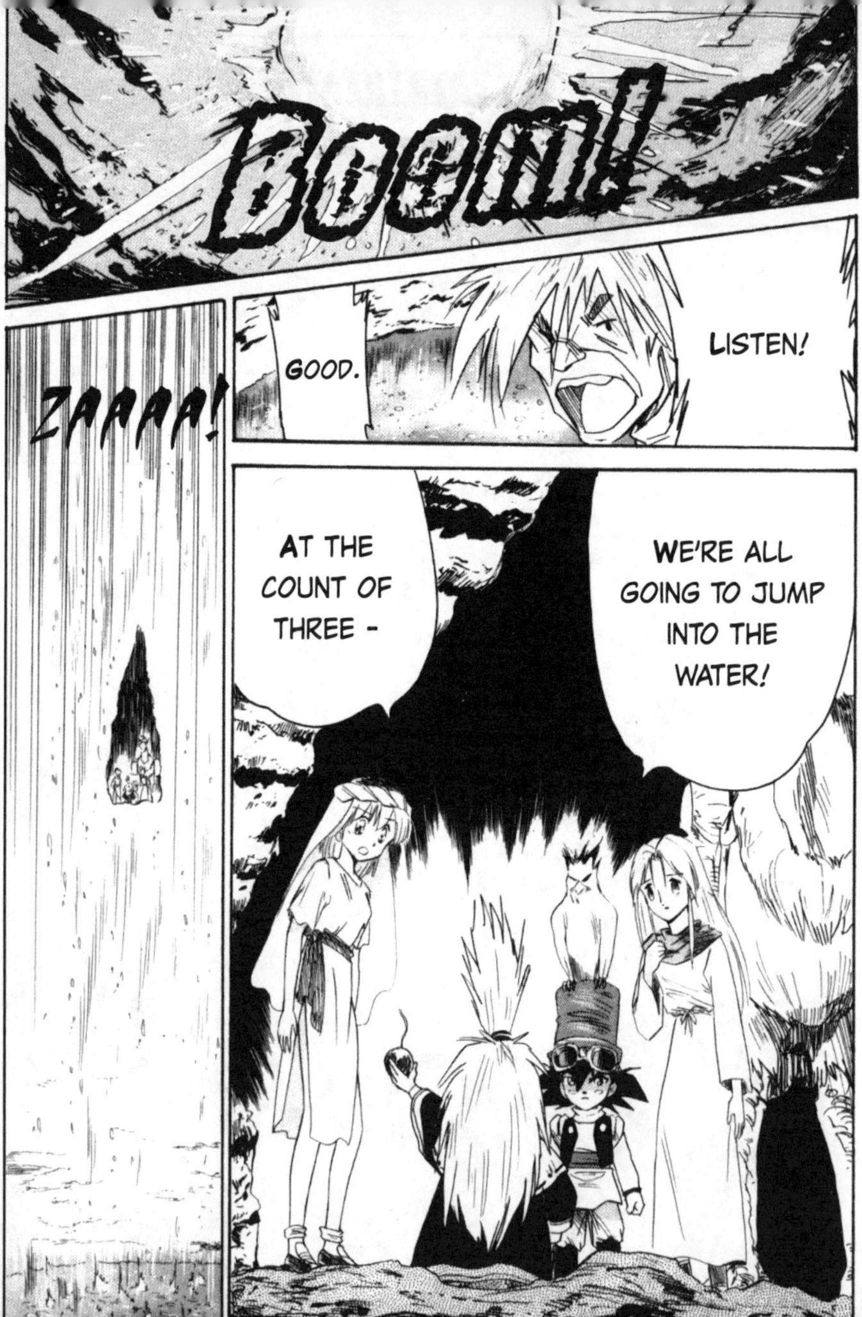
BOOOM!
LISTEN!
GOOD.
ZAAAA!
WE'RE ALL GOING TO JUMP INTO THE WATER!
AT THE COUNT OF THREE -

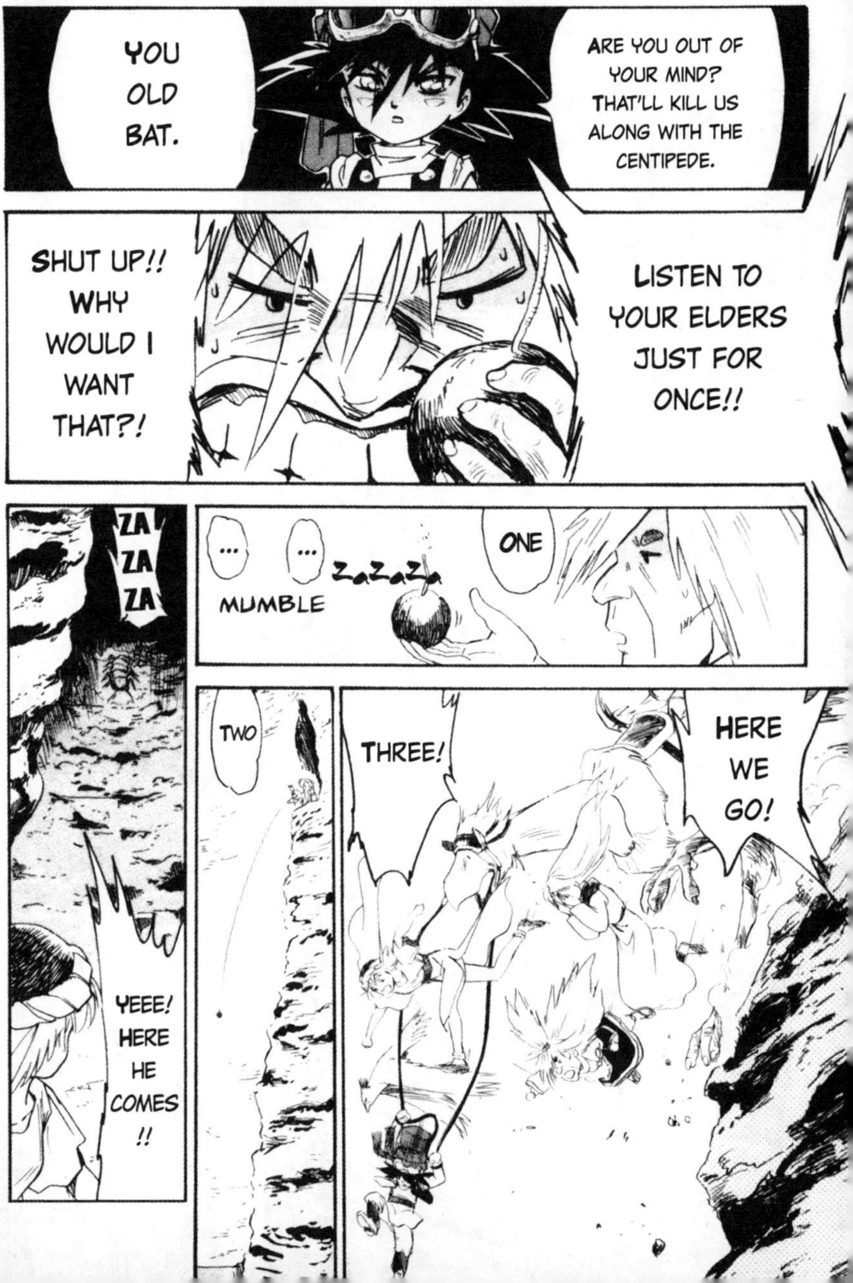
YOU OLD BAT.
ARE YOU OUT OF YOUR MIND? THAT'LL KILL US ALONG WITH THE CENTIPEDE.
SHUT UP!! WHY WOULD I WANT THAT?!
LISTEN TO YOUR ELDERS JUST FOR ONCE!!
ZA ZA ZA
...
...
ZaZaZa
MUMBLE
ONE
TWO
THREE!
HERE WE GO!
YEEE! HERE HE COMES !!

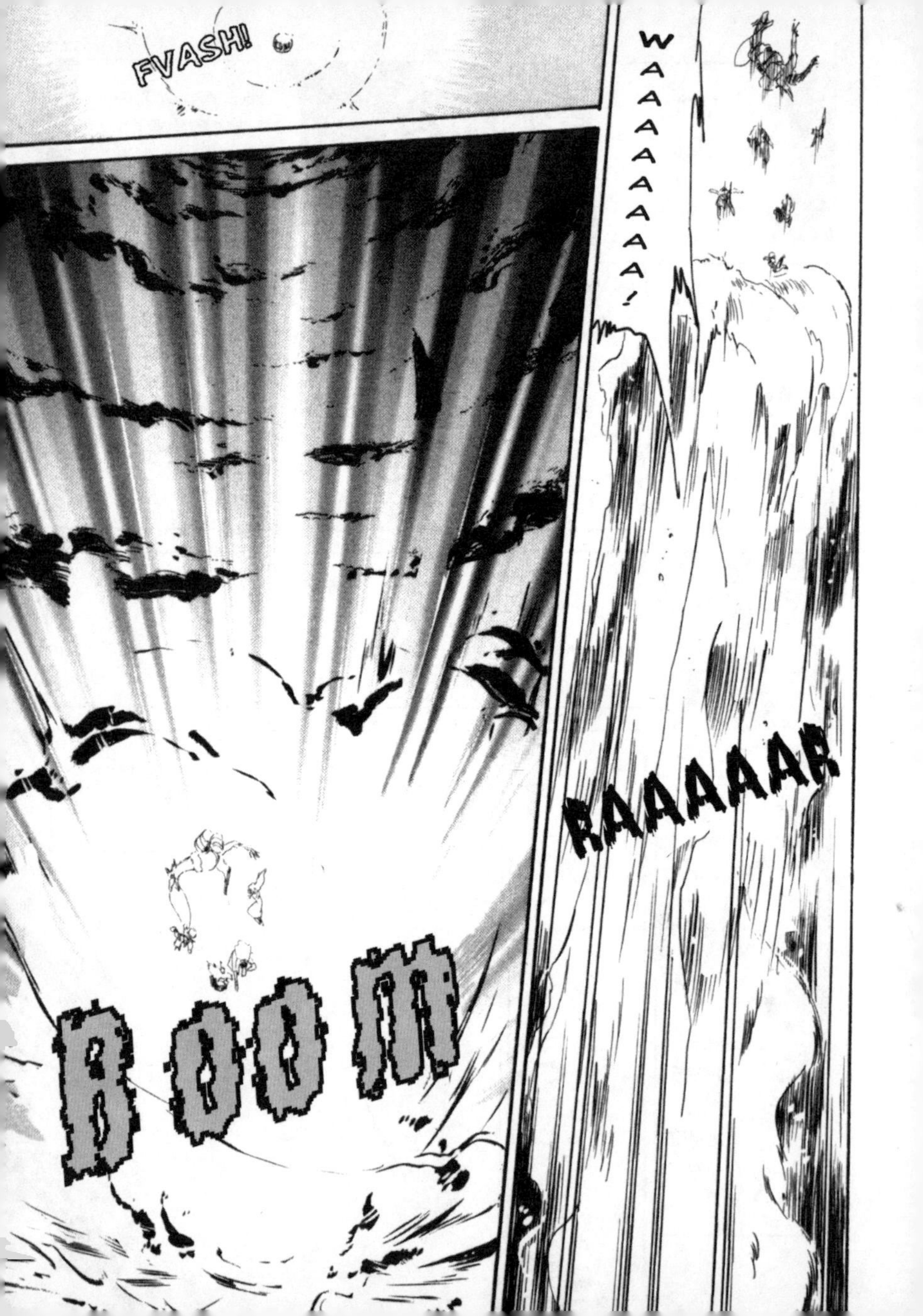
FVASH!
WAAAAAAAAAAA!
RAAAAAAR
BOOM

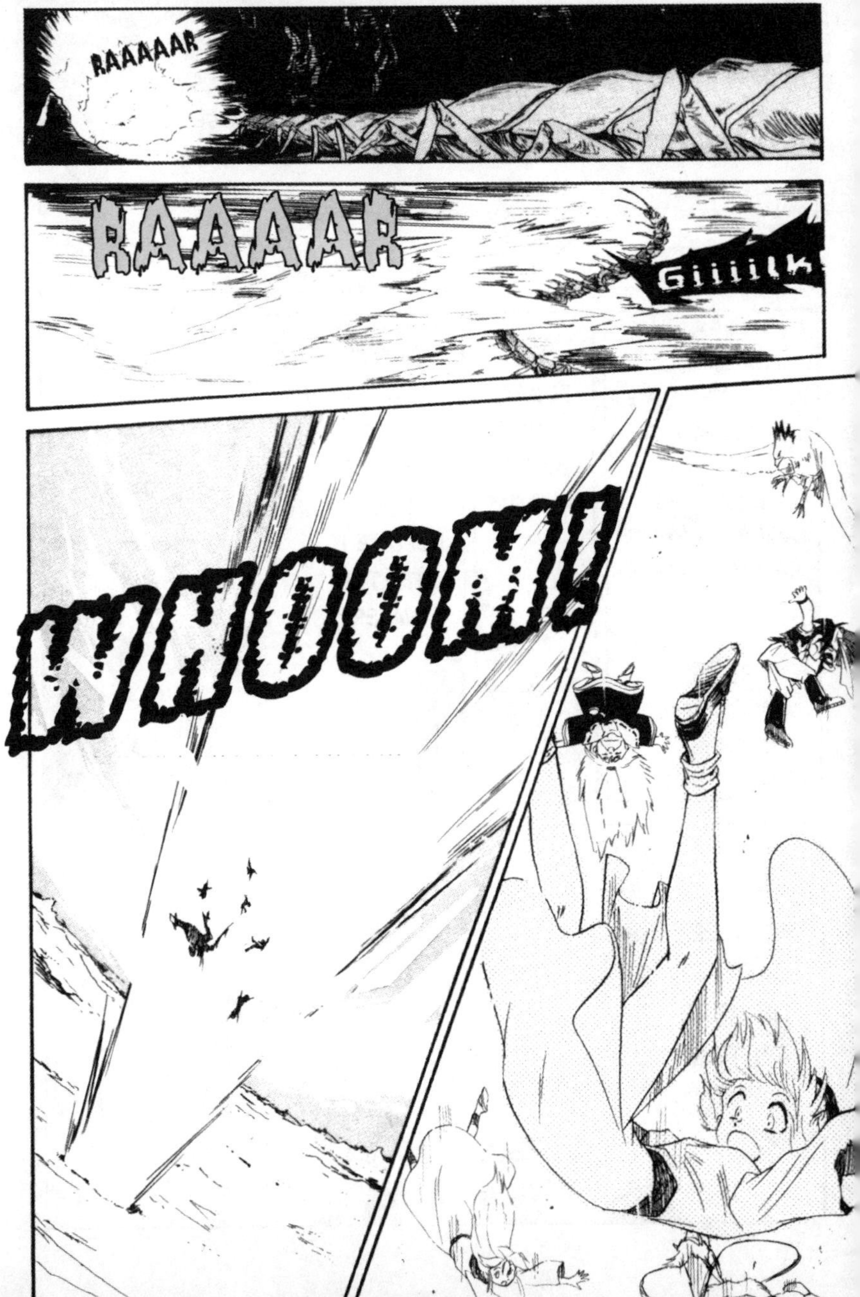
RAAAAAR
RAAAAR
Giiiilk
WHOOM!

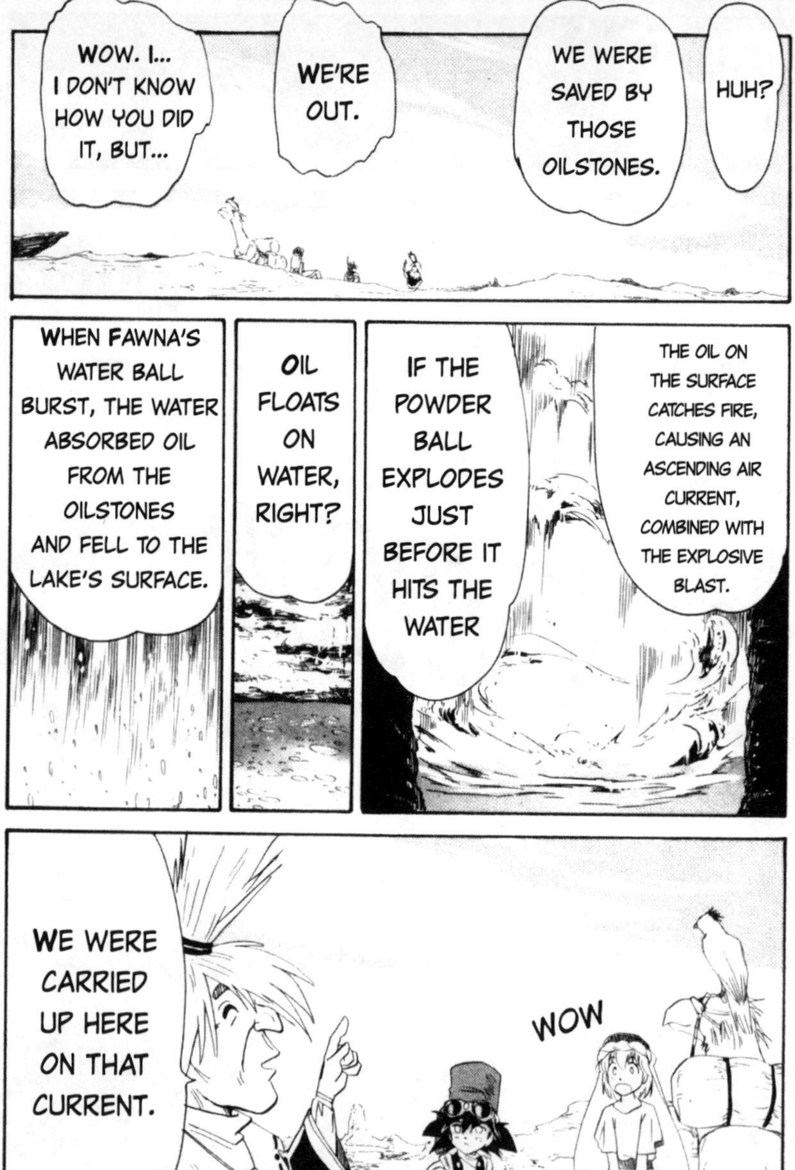
WOW. I... I DON'T KNOW HOW YOU DID IT, BUT...
WE'RE OUT.
WE WERE SAVED BY THOSE OILSTONES.
HUH?
WHEN FAWNA'S WATER BALL BURST, THE WATER ABSORBED OIL FROM THE OILSTONES AND FELL TO THE LAKE'S SURFACE.
OIL FLOATS ON WATER, RIGHT?
IF THE POWDER BALL EXPLODES JUST BEFORE IT HITS THE WATER
THE OIL ON THE SURFACE CATCHES FIRE, CAUSING AN ASCENDING AIR CURRENT, COMBINED WITH THE EXPLOSIVE BLAST.
WE WERE CARRIED UP HERE ON THAT CURRENT.
WOW

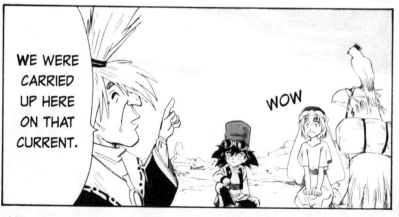

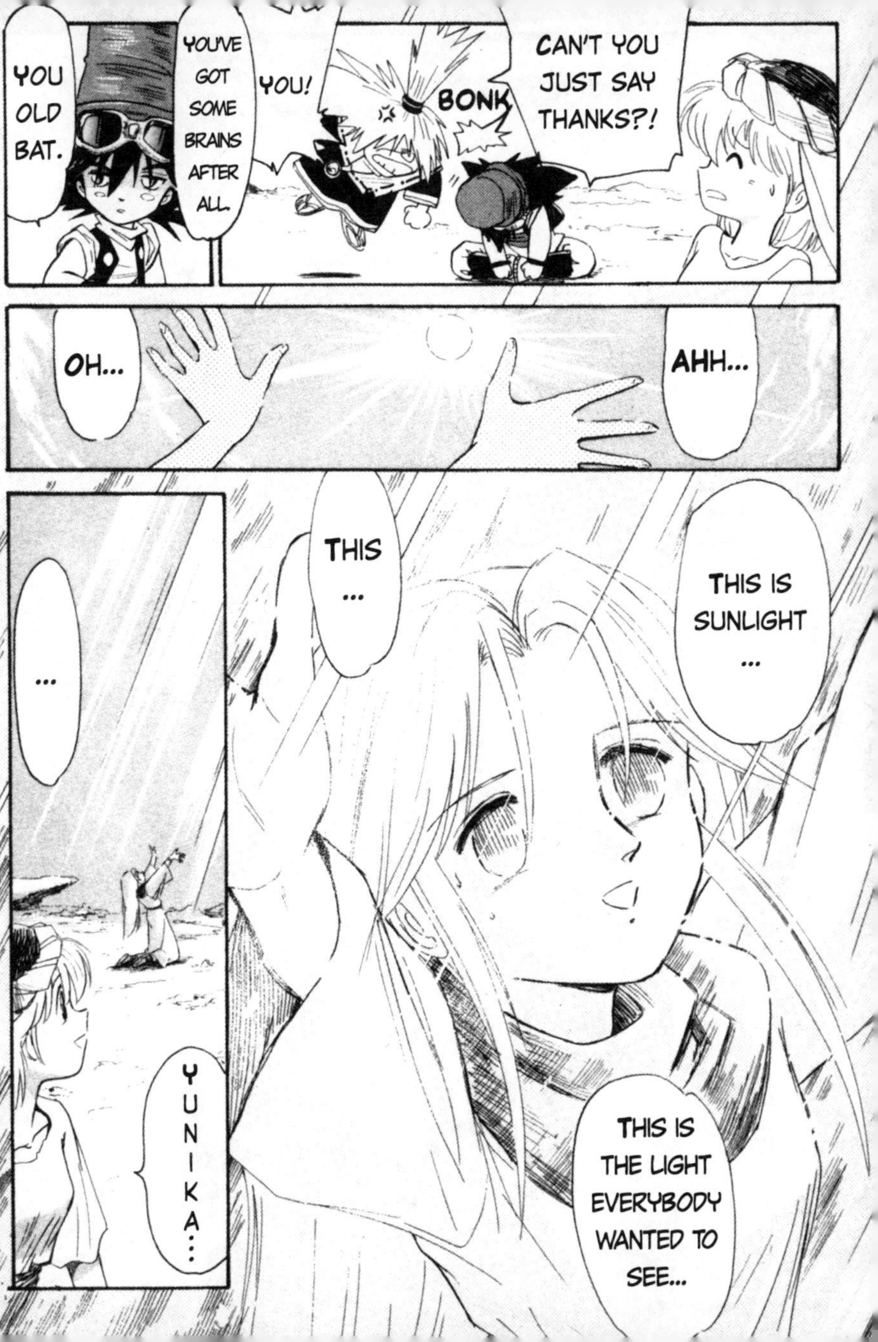
YOU OLD BAT.
YOU'VE GOT SOME BRAINS AFTER ALL.
YOU!
BONK
CAN'T YOU JUST SAY THANKS?!
OH...
AHH...
...
THIS ...
THIS IS SUNLIGHT ...
YUNIKA...
THIS IS THE LIGHT EVERYBODY WANTED TO SEE...

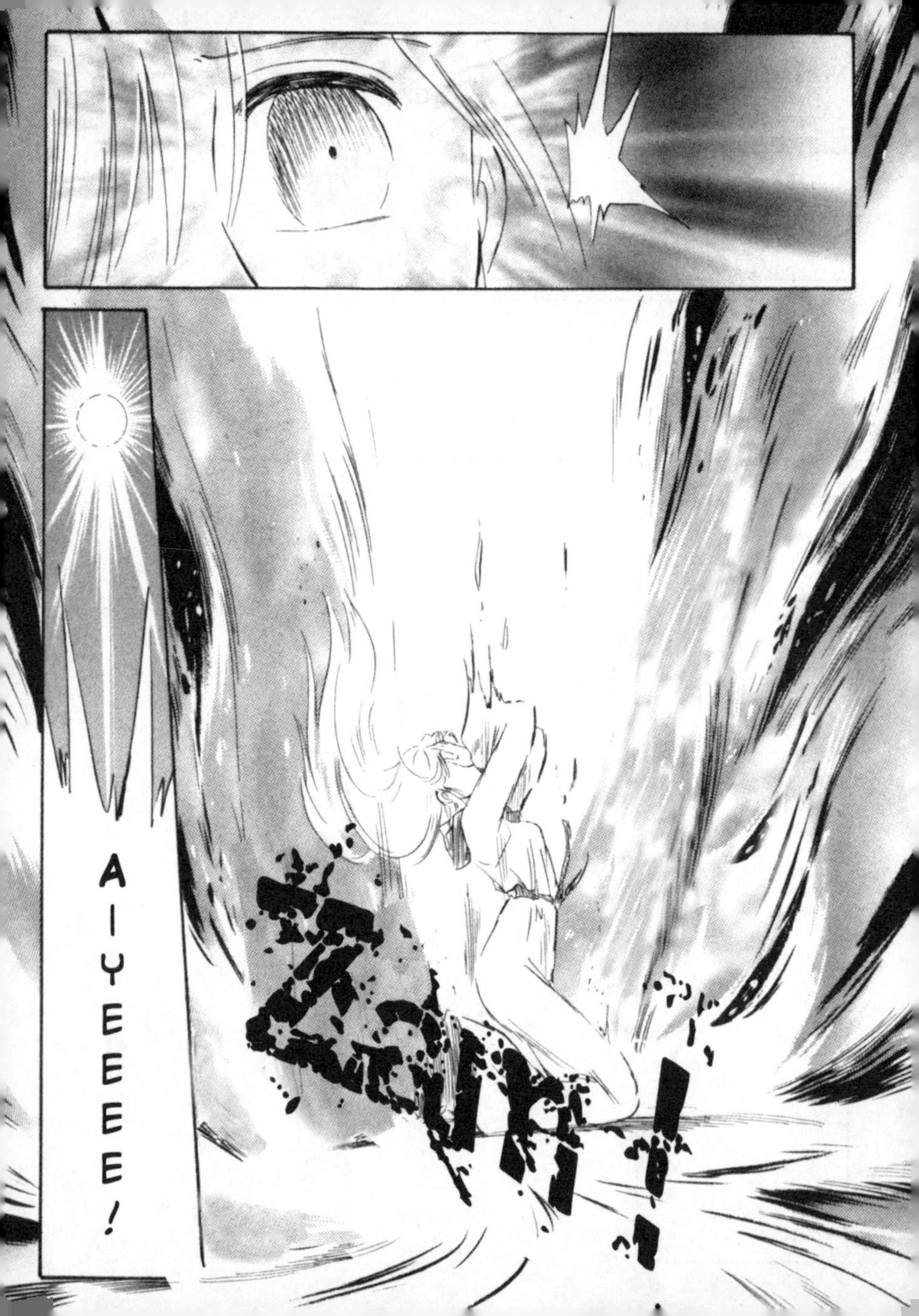
AIYEEEEE!

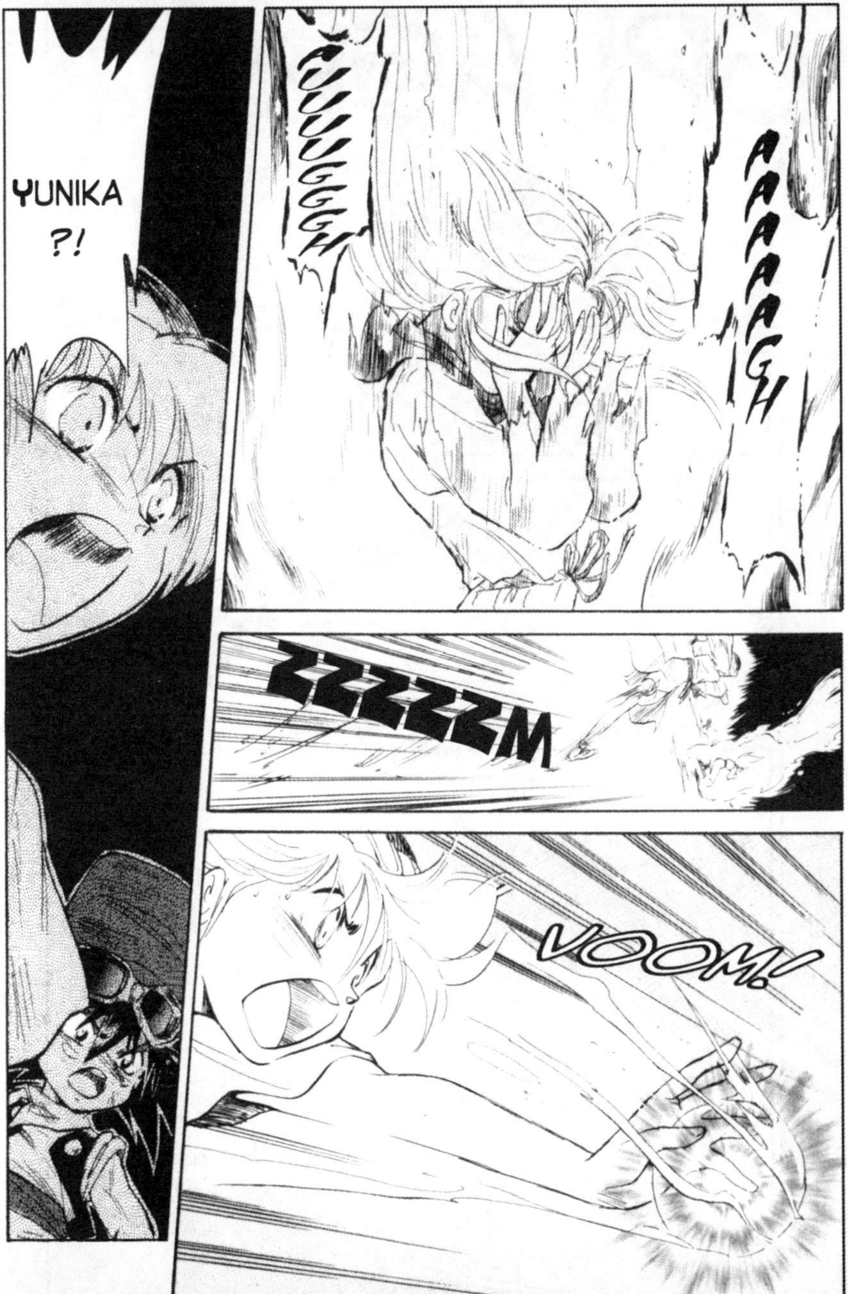
AAAAAAGH
RUUUUUGGGH
YUNIKA ?!
ZZZZZZM
VOOOM!

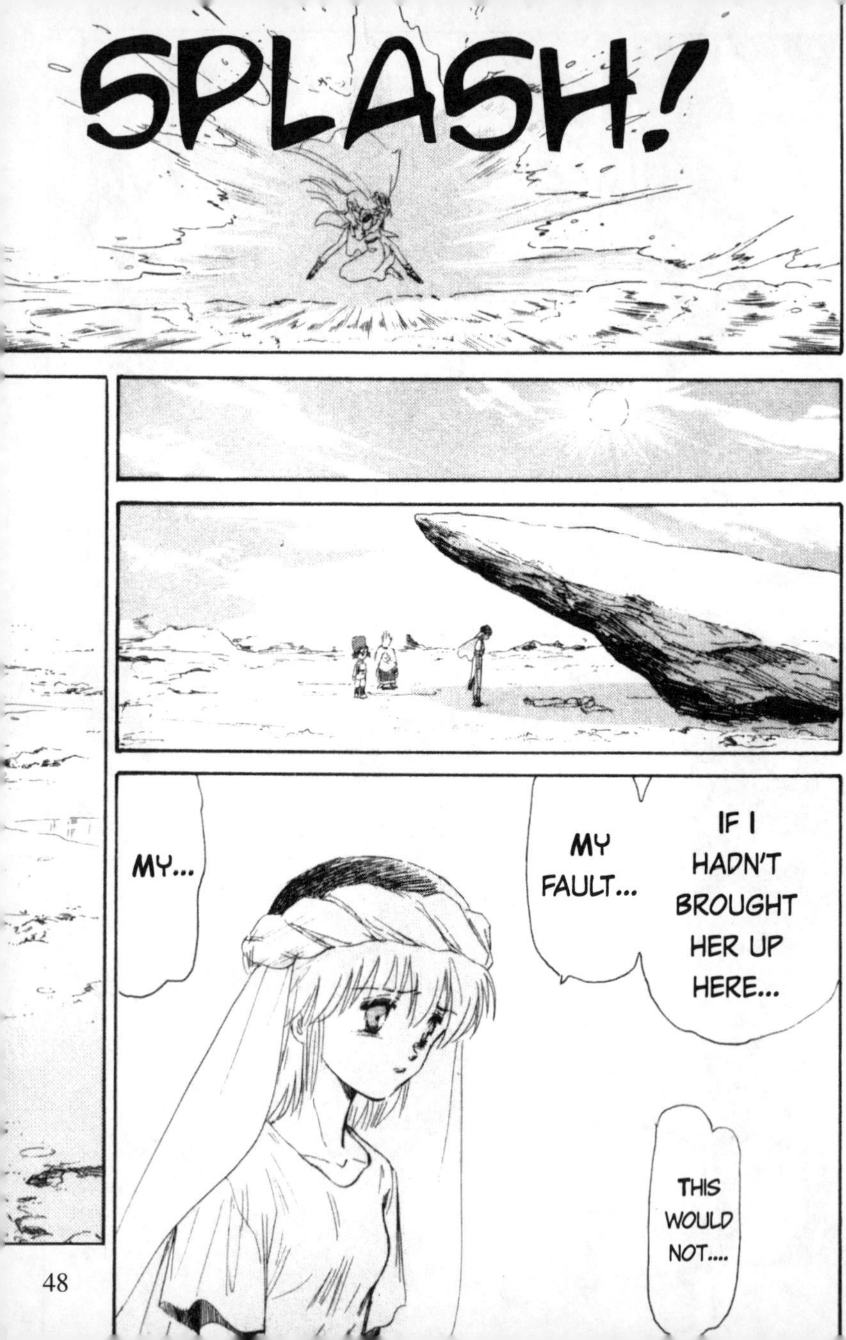
SPLASH!
MY...
IF I HADN'T BROUGHT HER UP HERE...
MY FAULT...
THIS WOULD NOT....

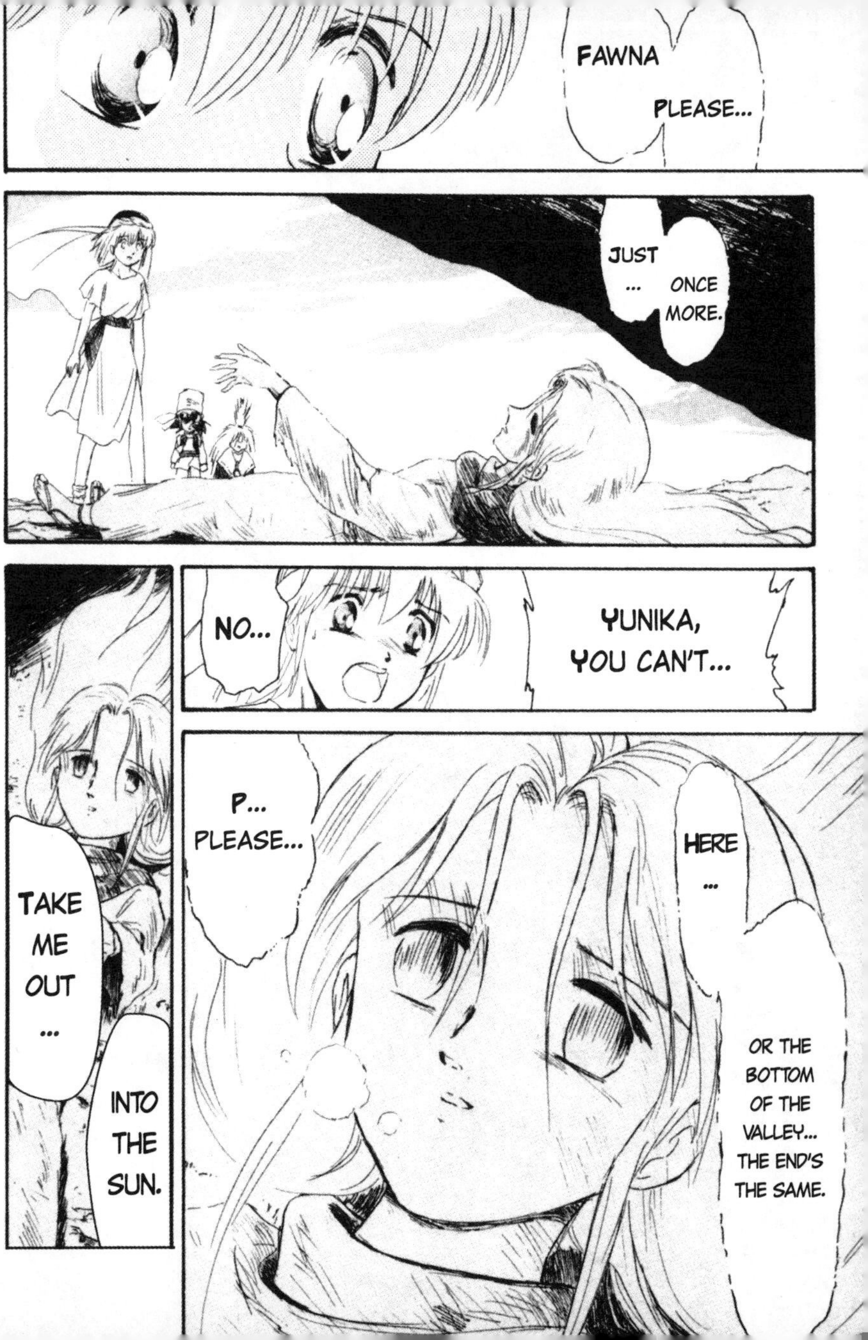
FAWNA
PLEASE...
JUST ... ONCE MORE.
TAKE ME OUT ...
INTO THE SUN.
NO...
YUNIKA, YOU CAN'T...
P... PLEASE...
HERE ...
OR THE BOTTOM OF THE VALLEY... THE END'S THE SAME.

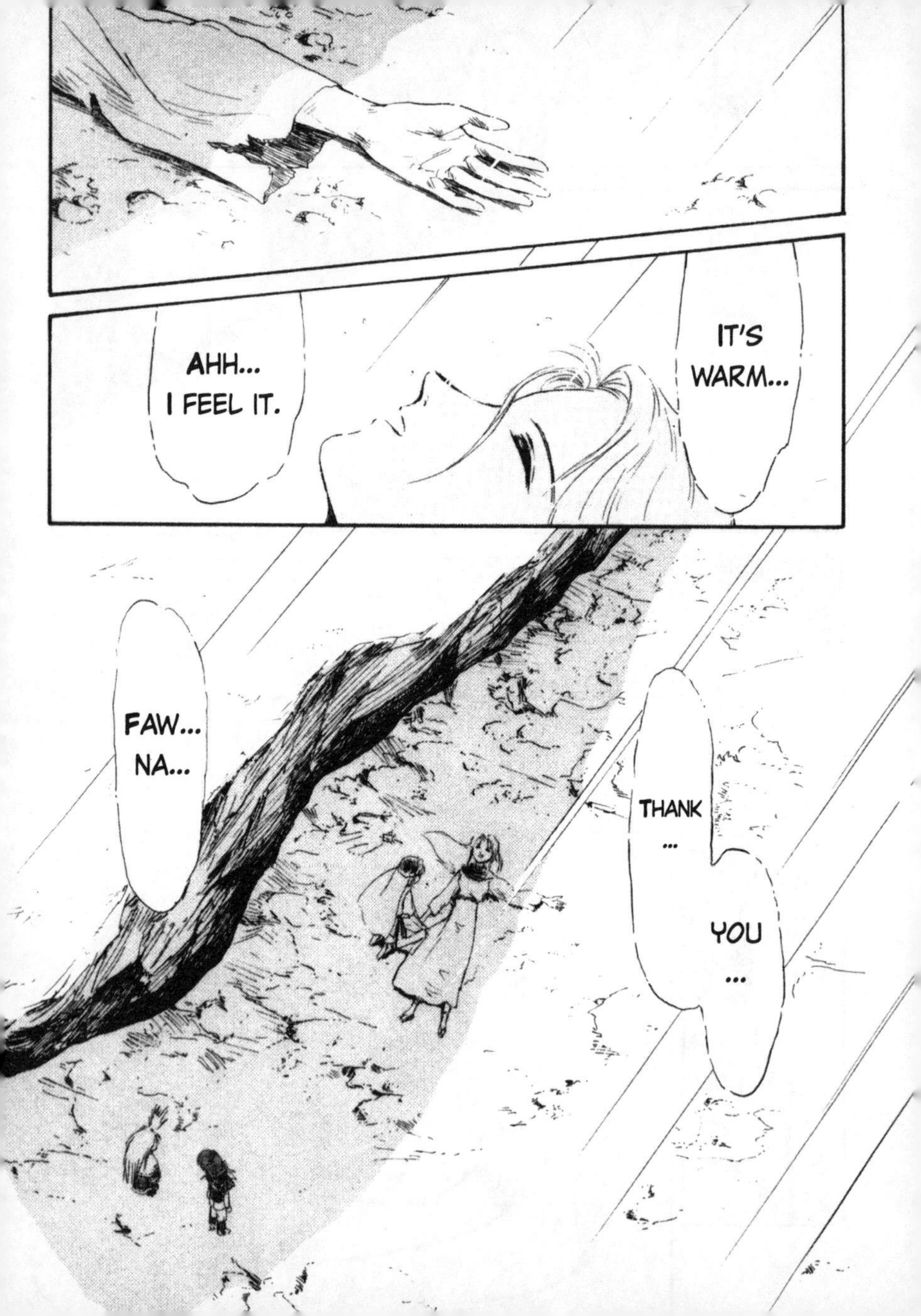
IT'S WARM...
AHH... I FEEL IT.
THANK... YOU...
FAW... NA...

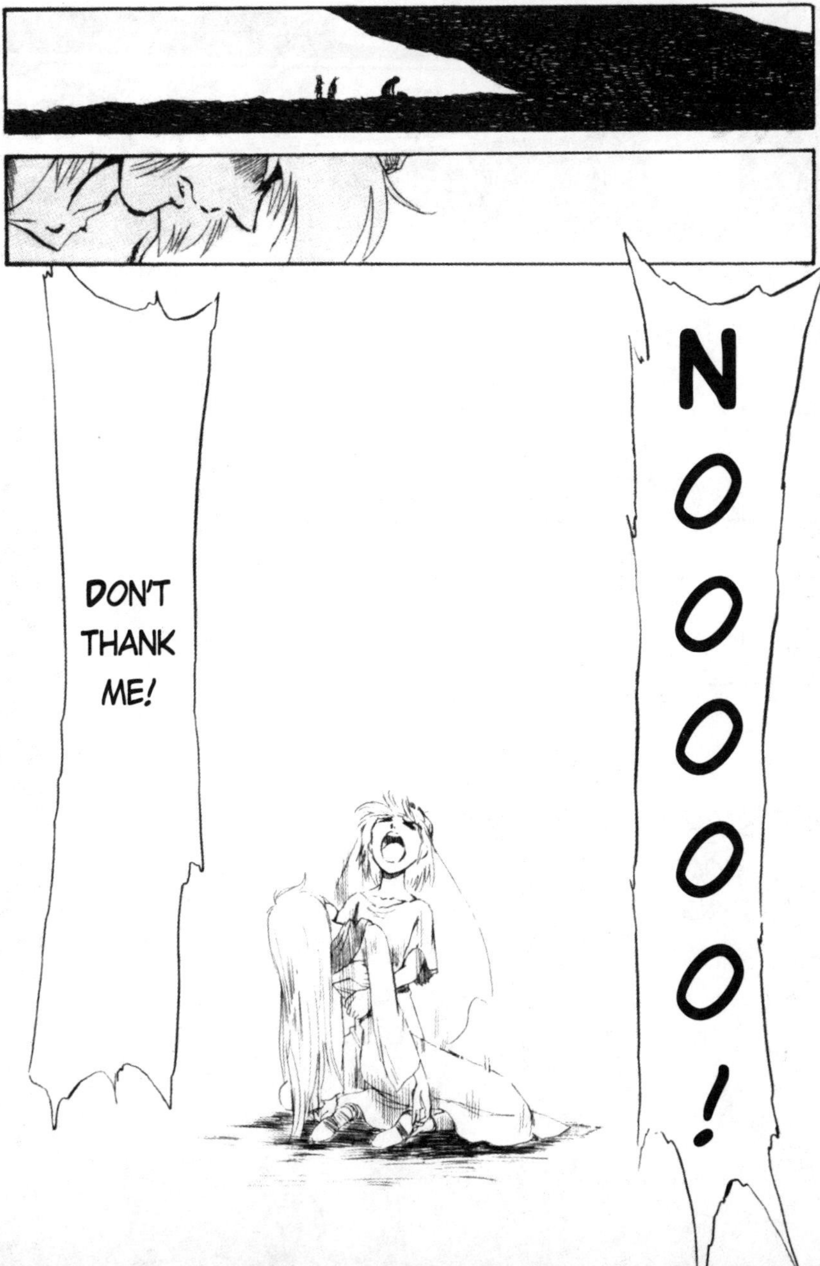
NOOOOOO!
DON'T THANK ME!

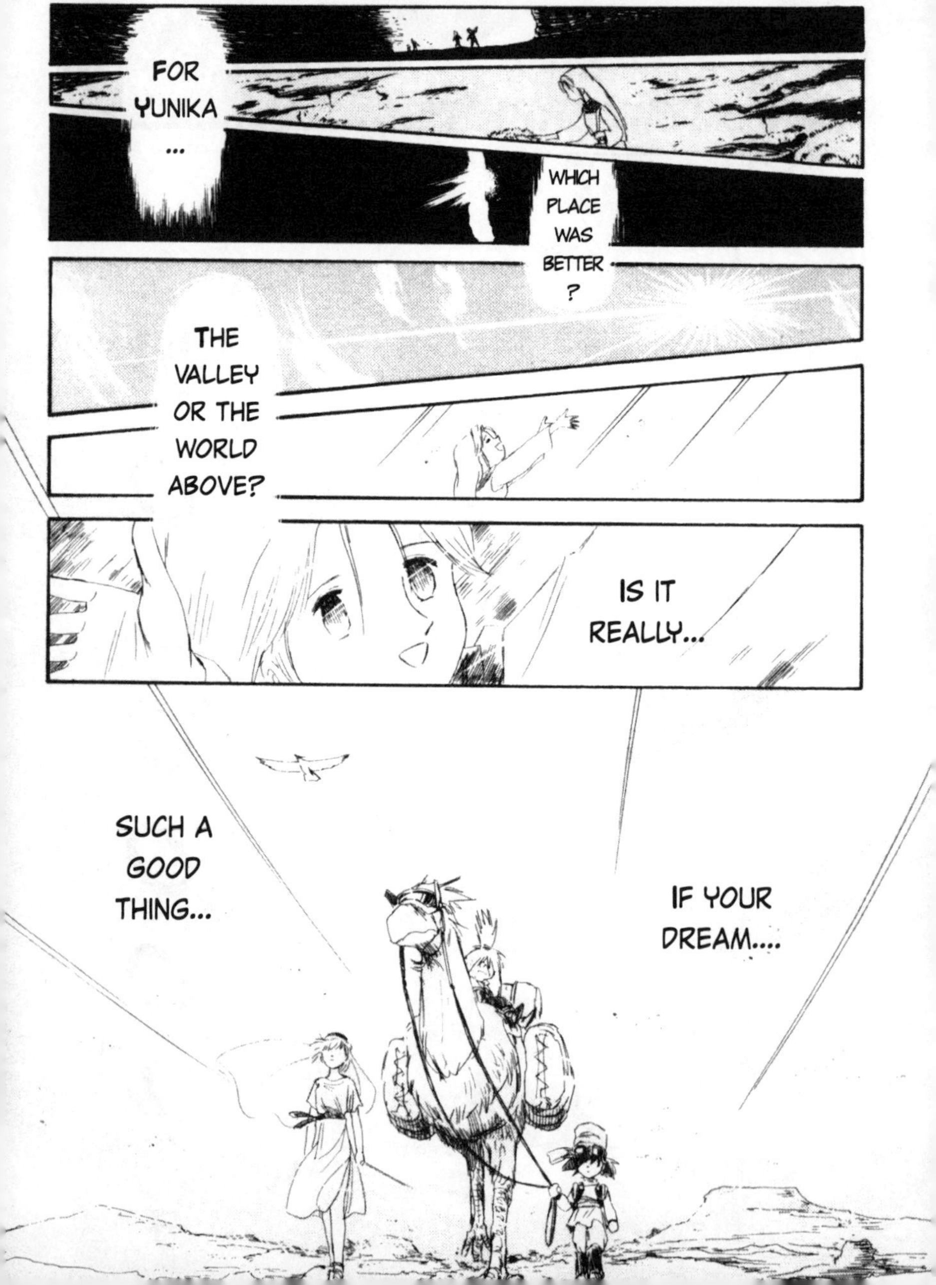
FOR YUNIKA ...
WHICH PLACE WAS BETTER ?
THE VALLEY OR THE WORLD ABOVE?
IS IT REALLY...
IF YOUR DREAM....
SUCH A GOOD THING...

...COMES
TRUE?

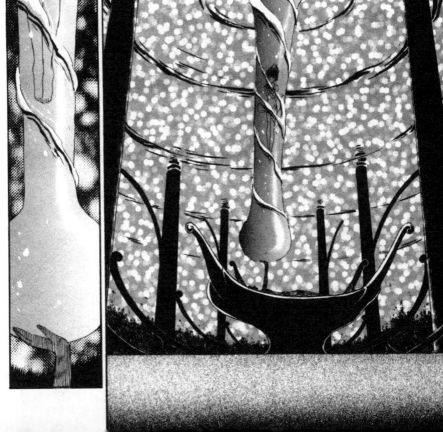

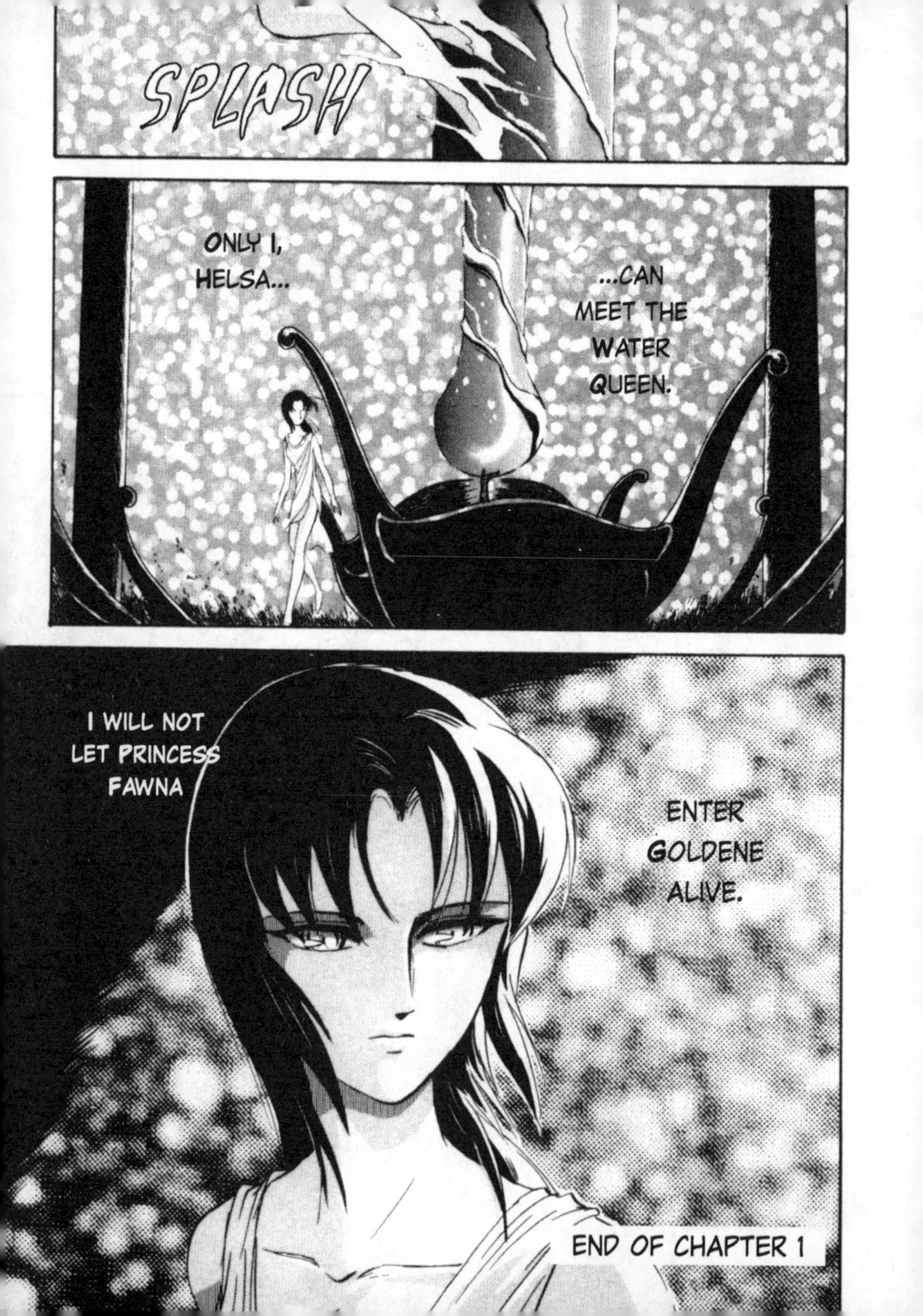
SPLASH
ONLY I, HELSA...
...CAN MEET THE WATER QUEEN.
I WILL NOT LET PRINCESS FAWNA
ENTER GOLDENE ALIVE.
END OF CHAPTER 1

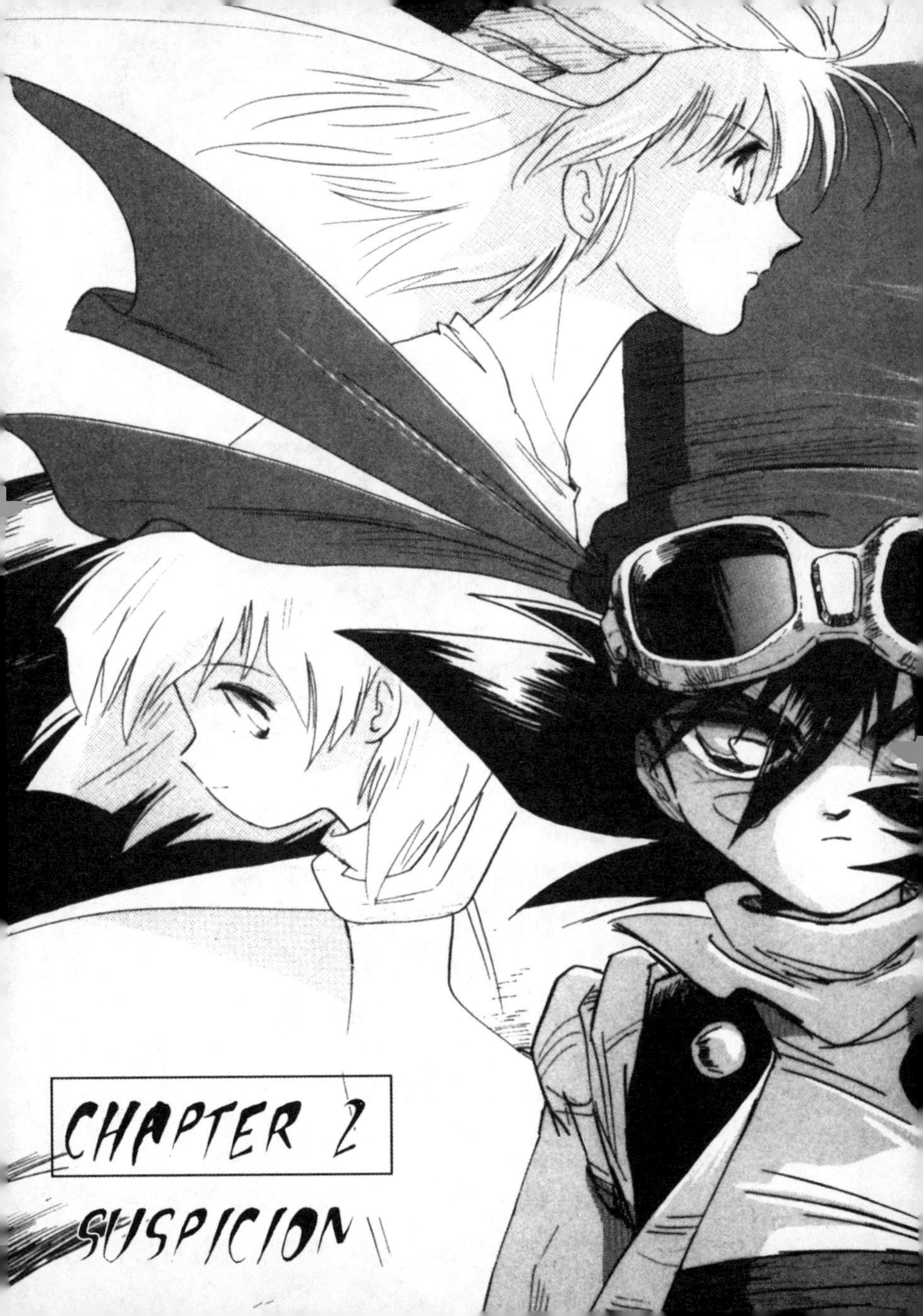
CHAPTER 2
SUSPICION

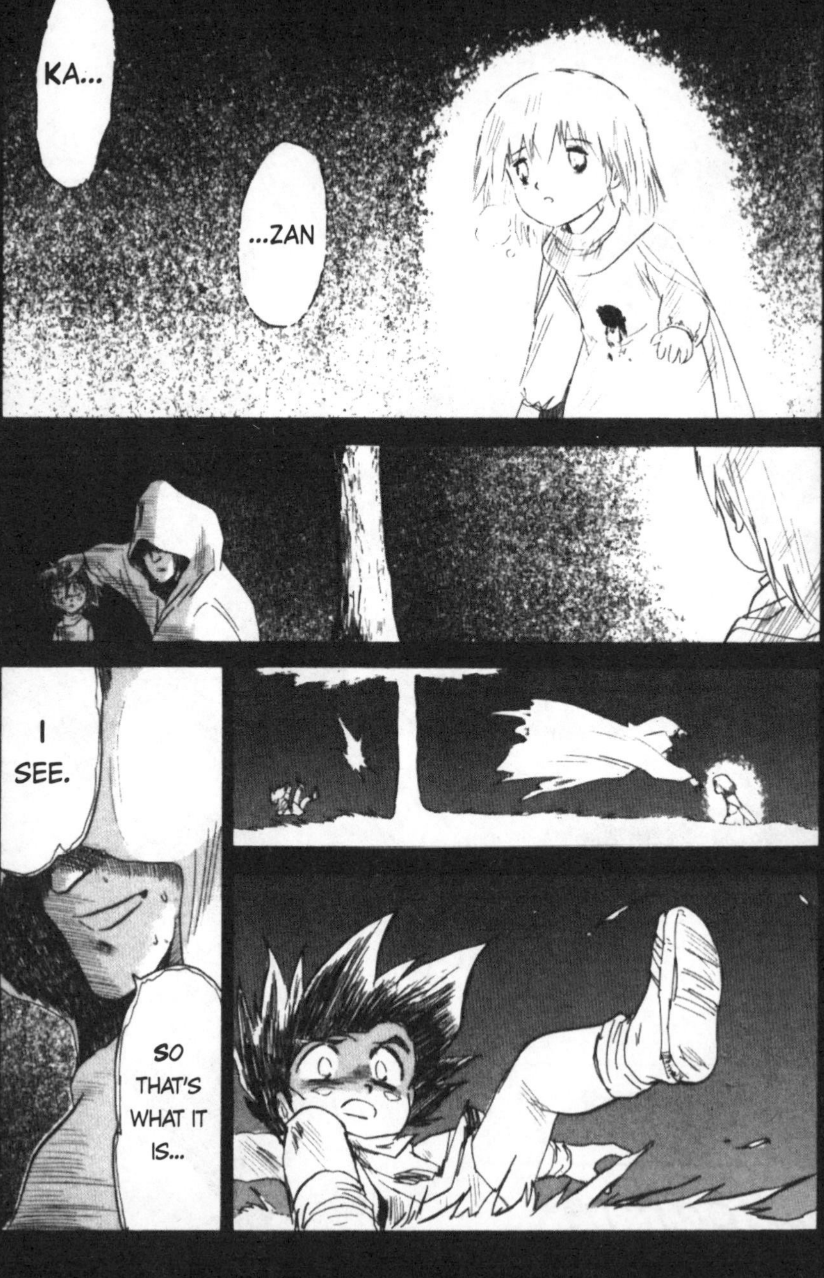
KA...
...ZAN
I SEE.
SO THAT'S WHAT IT IS...

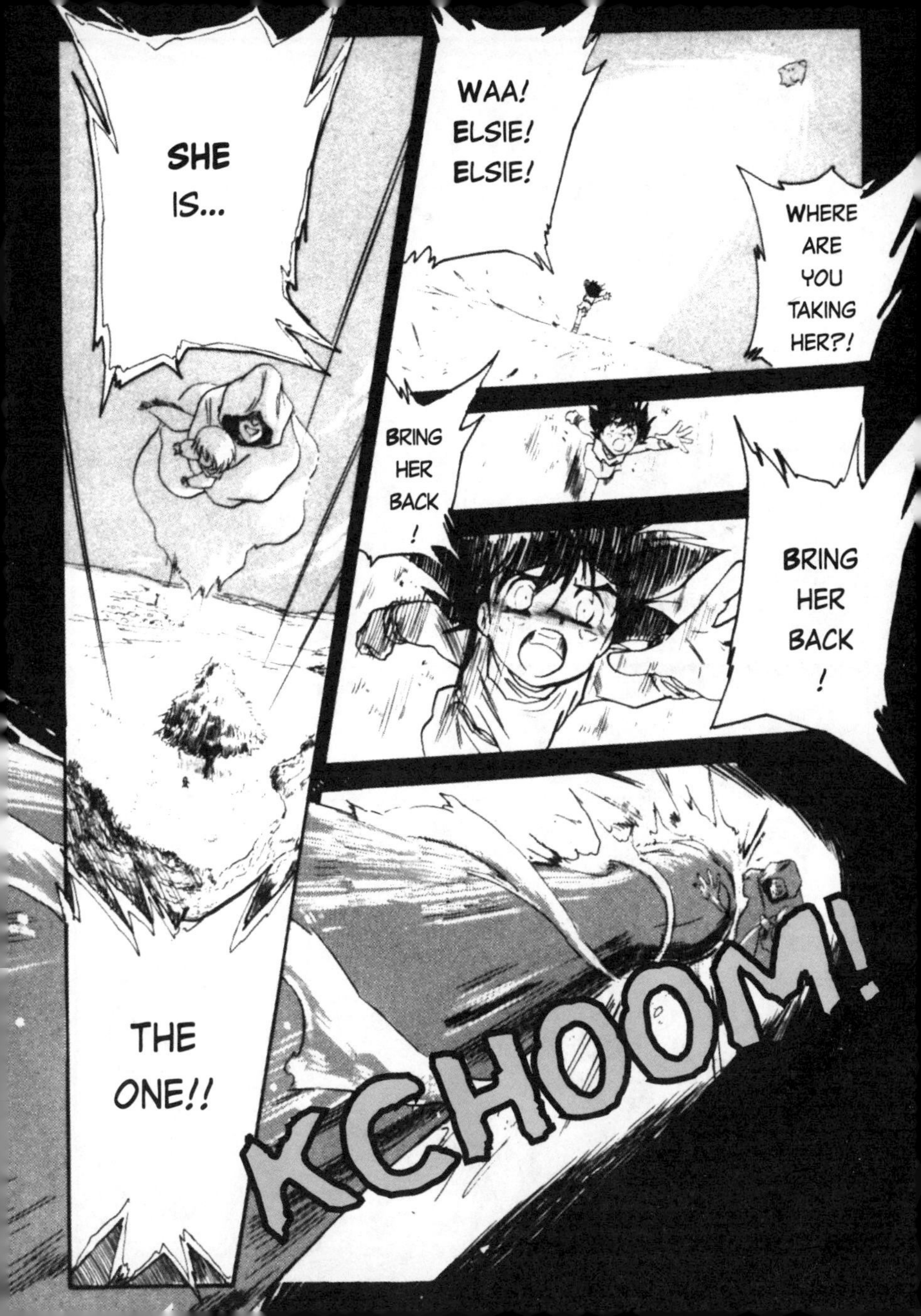

WAA! ELSIE! ELSIE!
WHERE ARE YOU TAKING HER?!
BRING HER BACK!
BRING HER BACK!
SHE IS...
XCHOOM!
THE ONE!!

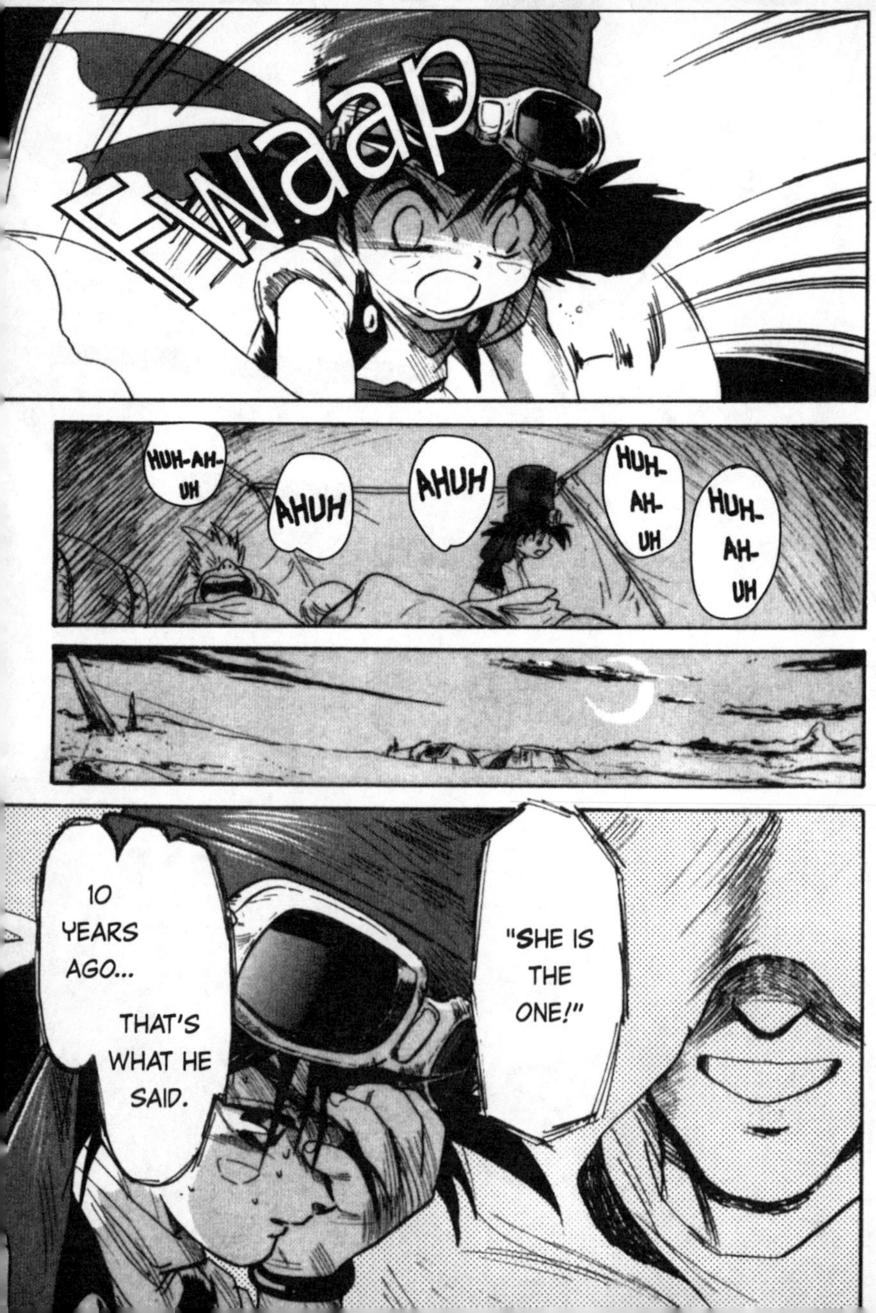
FWaaap
HUH-AH-UH
AHUH
AHUH
HUH-AH-UH
HUH-AH-UH
10 YEARS AGO...
THAT'S WHAT HE SAID.
"SHE IS THE ONE!"

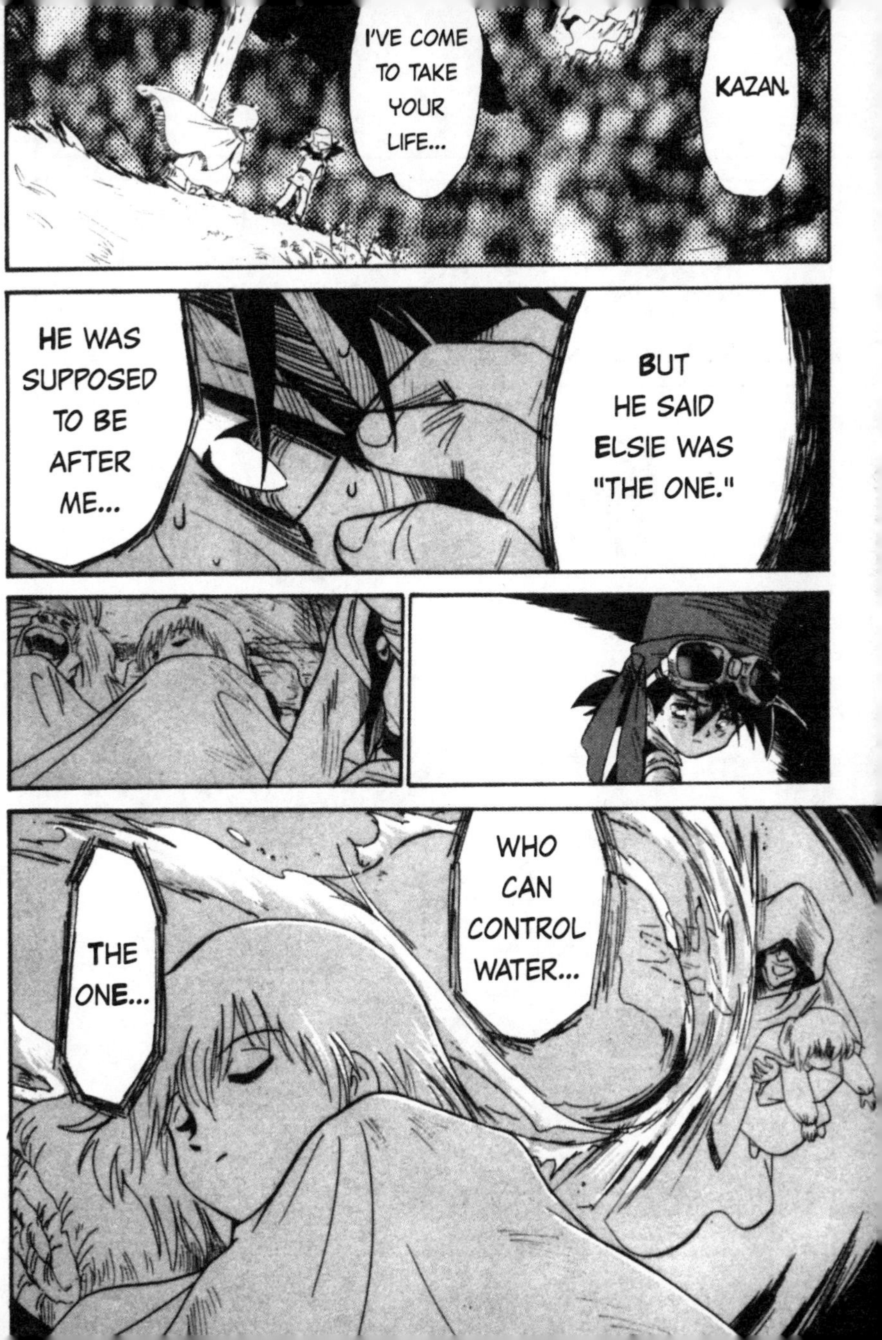
I'VE COME TO TAKE YOUR LIFE...
KAZAN.
HE WAS SUPPOSED TO BE AFTER ME...
BUT HE SAID ELSIE WAS "THE ONE."
THE ONE...
WHO CAN CONTROL WATER...

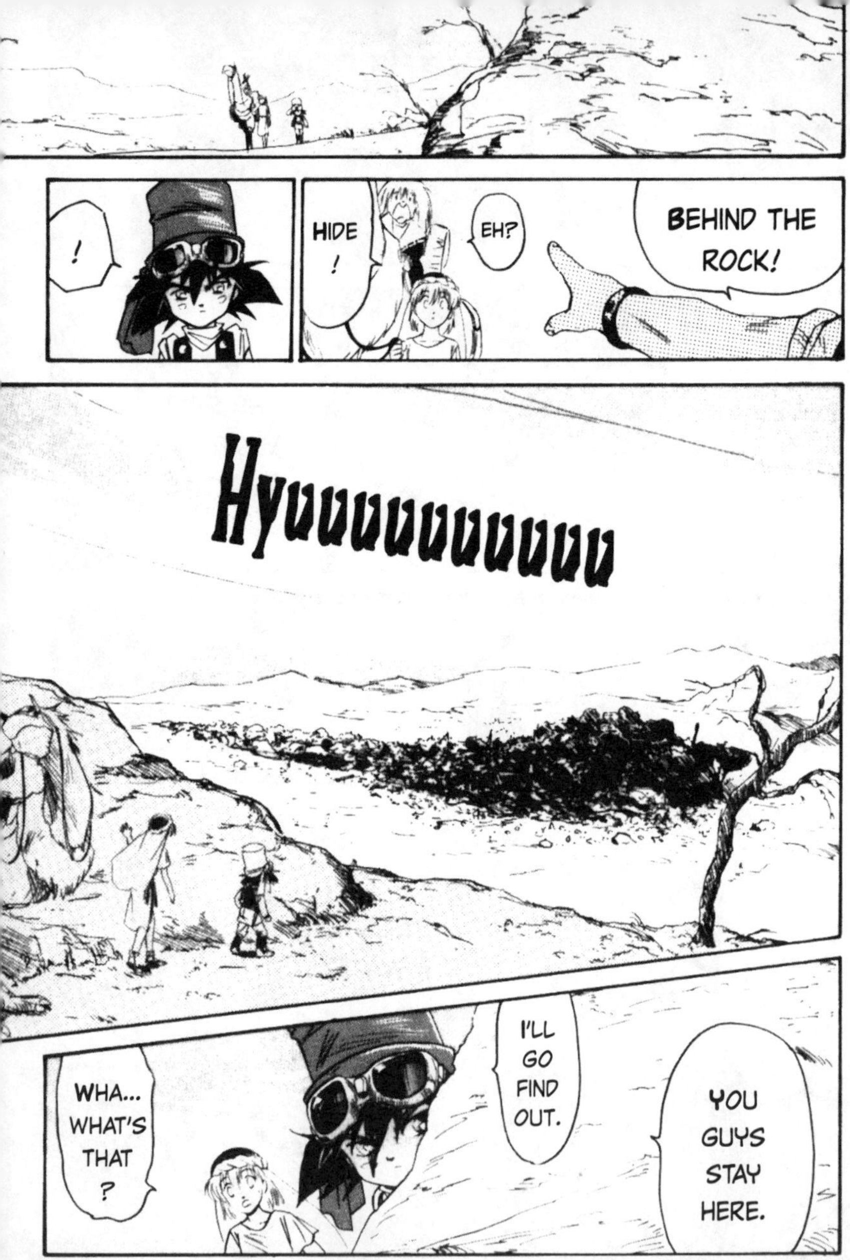
!
HIDE!
EH?
BEHIND THE ROCK!
Hyuuuuuuuuuu
WHA... WHAT'S THAT?
I'LL GO FIND OUT.
YOU GUYS STAY HERE.

Snag!

FWIP

Hyuuuu

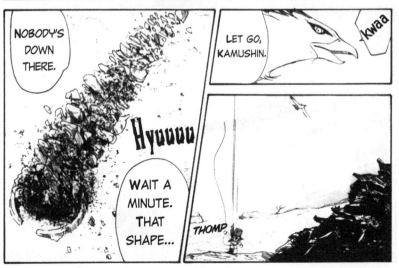

NOBODY'S DOWN THERE.

Hyuuuu

WAIT A MINUTE. THAT SHAPE...

LET GO, KAMUSHIN.

Kwaa

THOMP

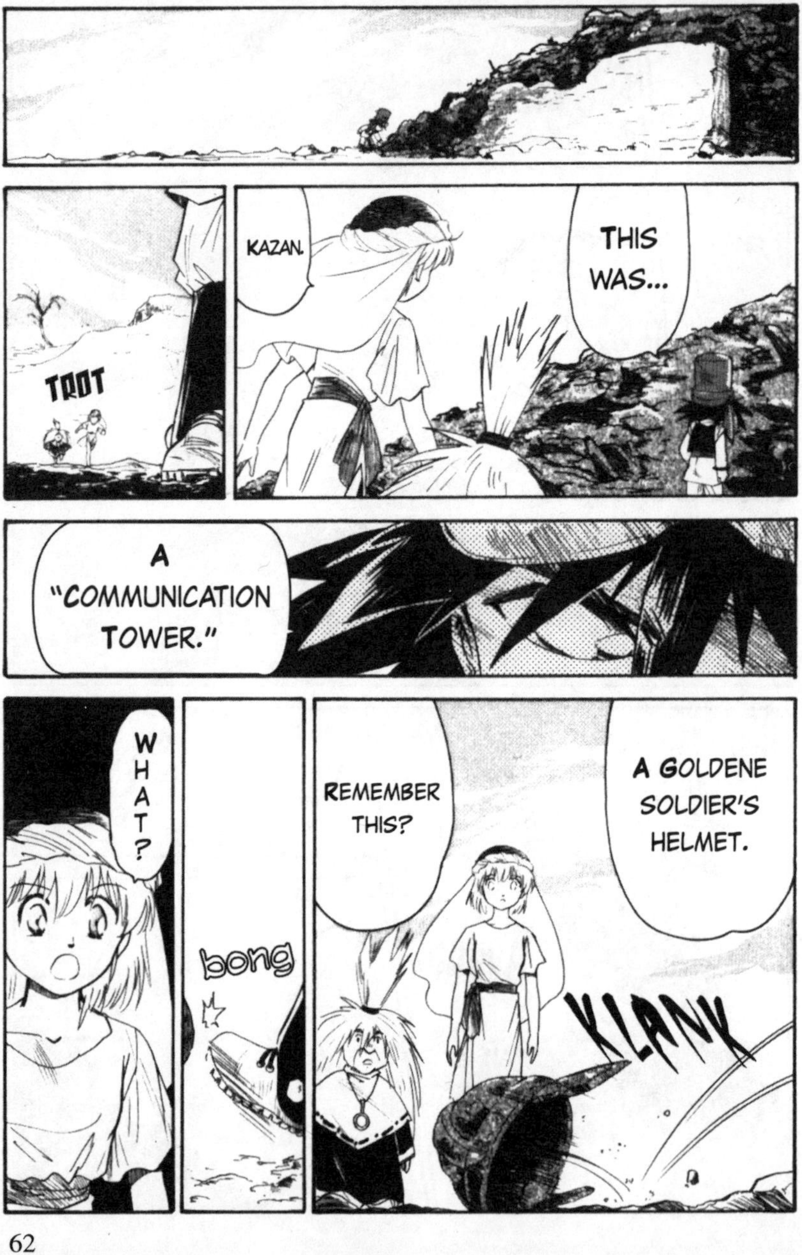

TROT
KAZAN.
THIS WAS...
A "COMMUNICATION TOWER."
WHAT?
bong
REMEMBER THIS?
A GOLDENE SOLDIER'S HELMET.
KLANK

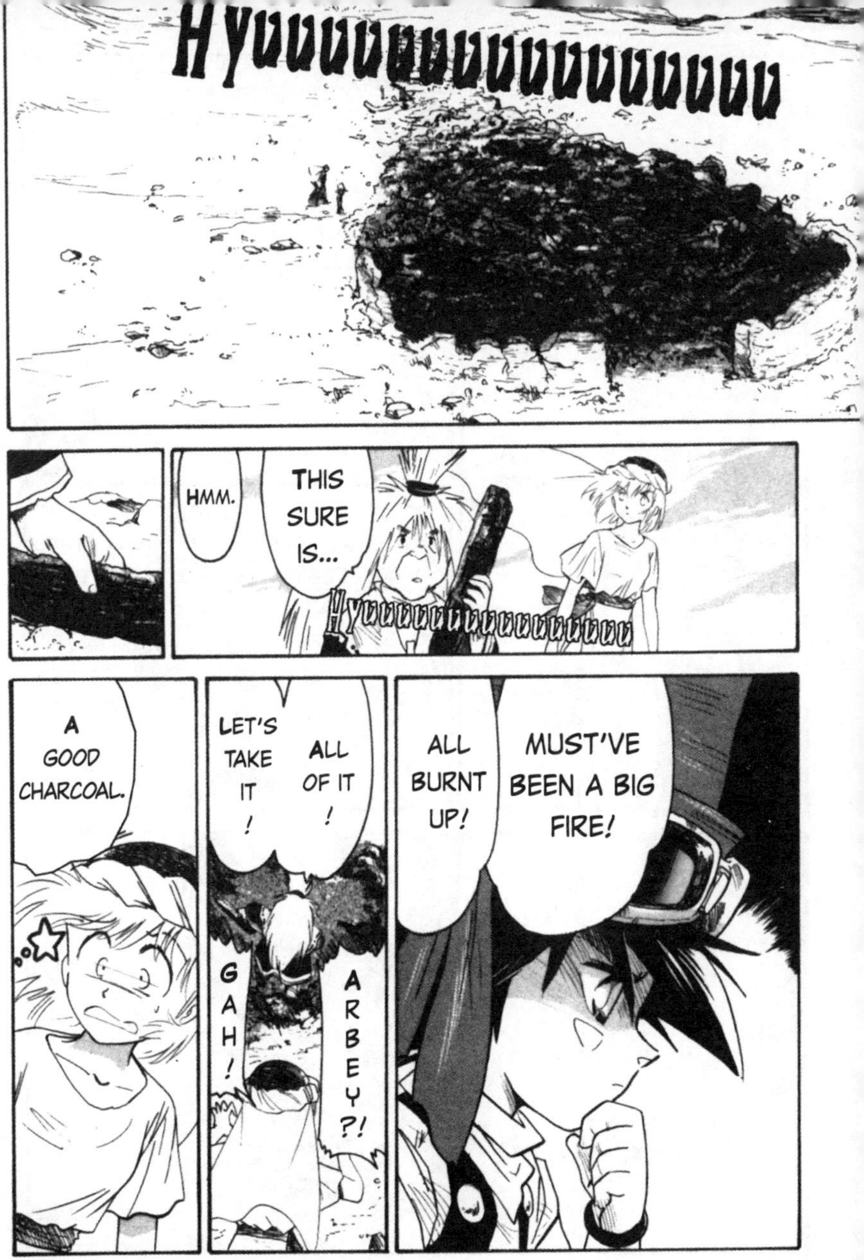
HYUUUUUUUUUUUUUUUU
THIS SURE IS...
HMM.
HYUUUUUUUUUUUUUUUUUU
MUST'VE BEEN A BIG FIRE!
ALL BURNT UP!
ALL OF IT!
LET'S TAKE IT!
ARBEY?!
GAH!
A GOOD CHARCOAL.

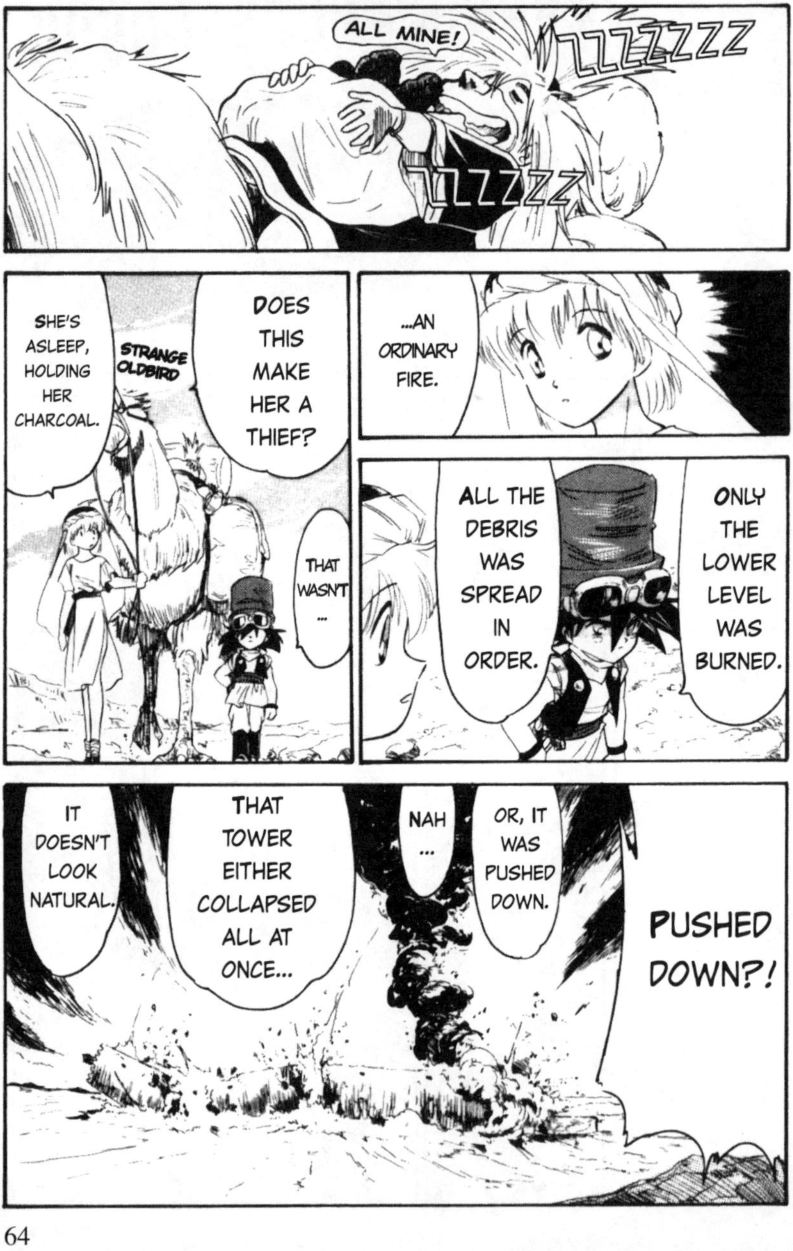

ALL MINE!
ZZZZZZZZ
ZZZZZZ
SHE'S ASLEEP, HOLDING HER CHARCOAL.
STRANGE OLDBIRD
DOES THIS MAKE HER A THIEF?
THAT WASN'T ...
...AN ORDINARY FIRE.
ALL THE DEBRIS WAS SPREAD IN ORDER.
ONLY THE LOWER LEVEL WAS BURNED.
IT DOESN'T LOOK NATURAL.
THAT TOWER EITHER COLLAPSED ALL AT ONCE...
NAH ...
OR, IT WAS PUSHED DOWN.
PUSHED DOWN?!

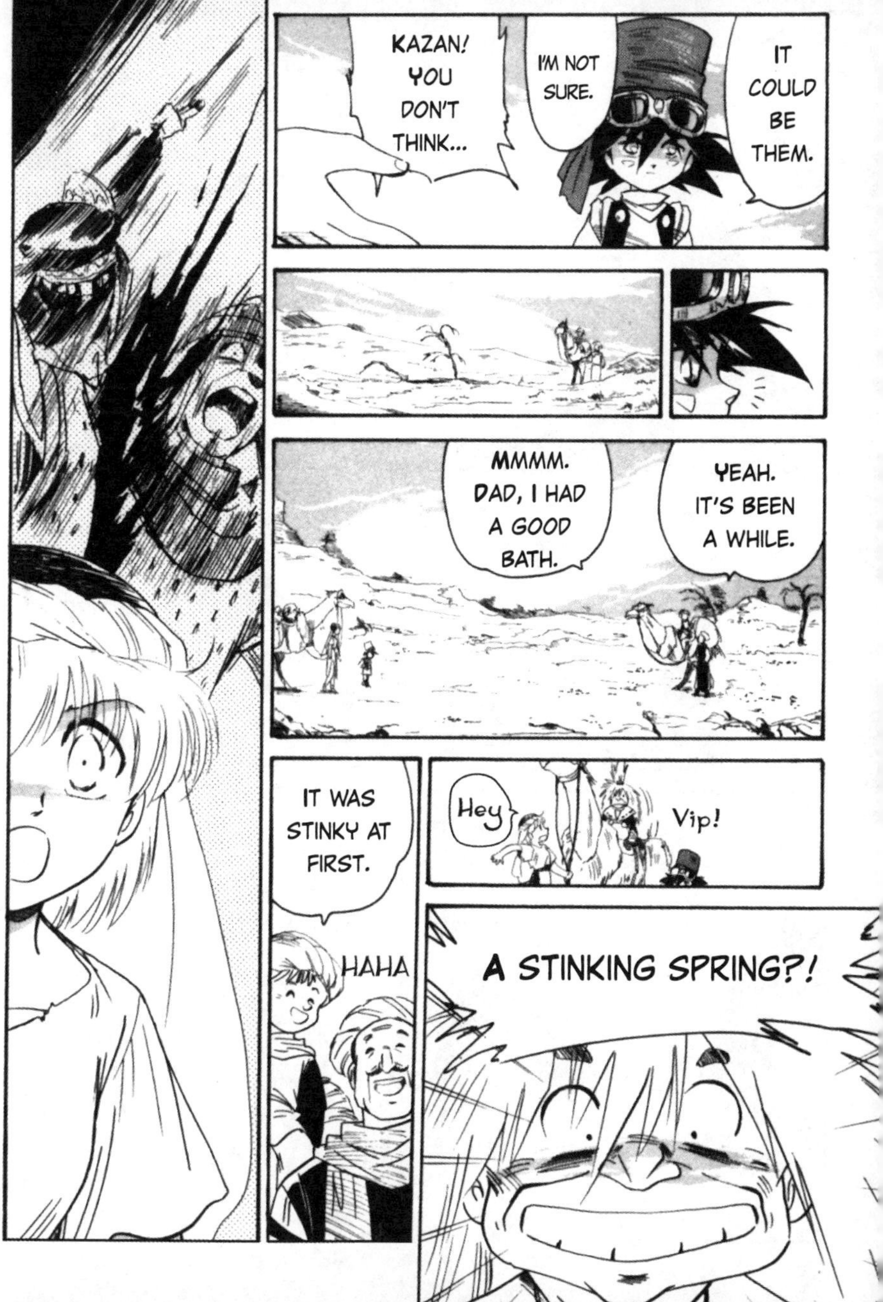
KAZAN! YOU DON'T THINK...
I'M NOT SURE.
IT COULD BE THEM.
MMMM. DAD, I HAD A GOOD BATH.
YEAH. IT'S BEEN A WHILE.
IT WAS STINKY AT FIRST.
HAHA
Hey
Vip!
A STINKING SPRING?!

A SPRING! A SPRING!

NOTHING BEATS A SPRING FOR OLD PEOPLE.

WHAT'S THAT WEIRD SMELL?

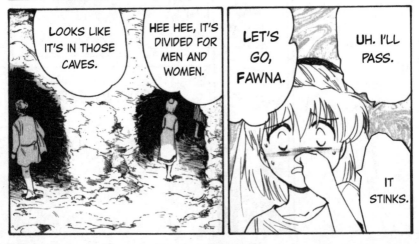

LOOKS LIKE IT'S IN THOSE CAVES.

HEE HEE, IT'S DIVIDED FOR MEN AND WOMEN.

LET'S GO, FAWNA.

UH. I'LL PASS.

IT STINKS.

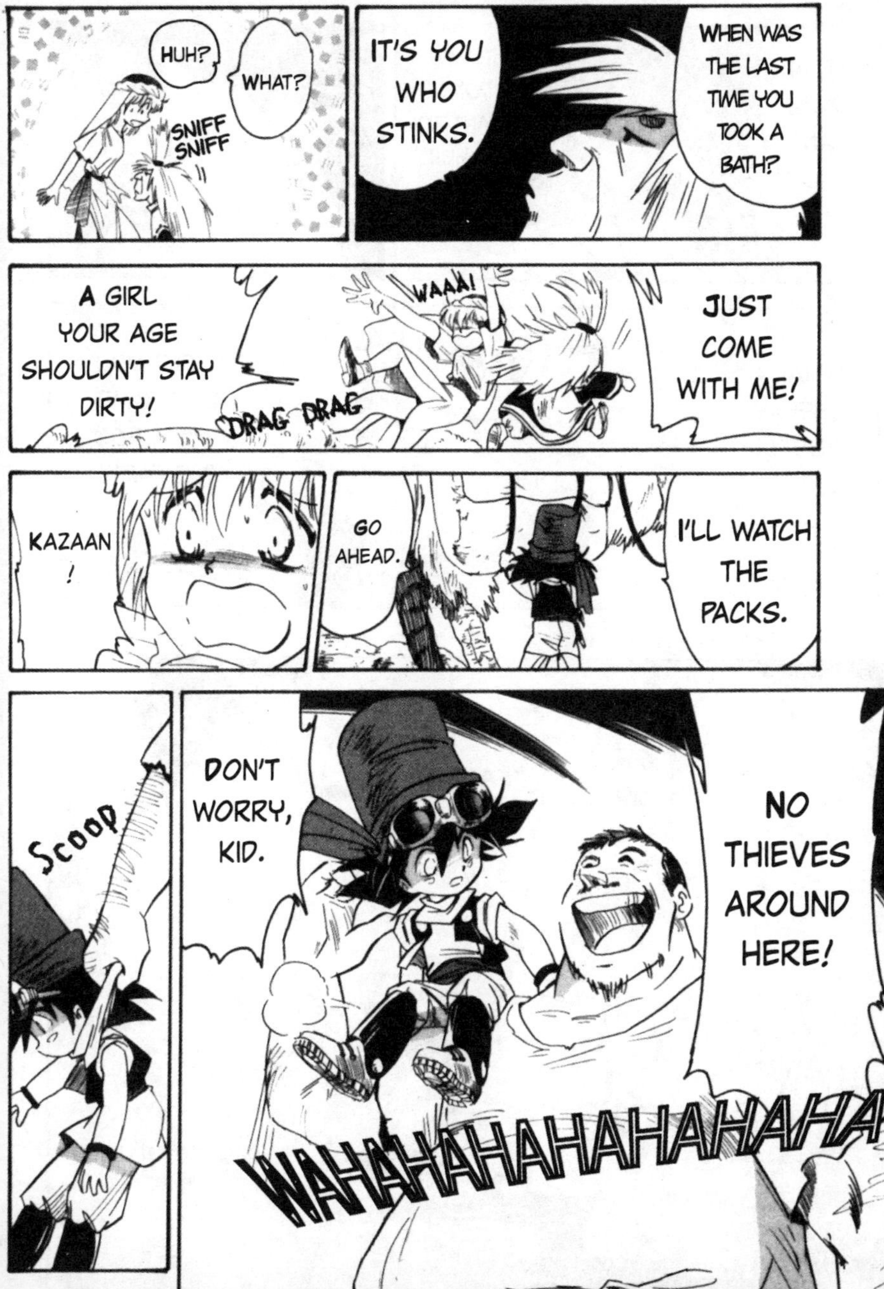
HUH?
WHAT?
SNIFF SNIFF
IT'S YOU WHO STINKS.
WHEN WAS THE LAST TIME YOU TOOK A BATH?
A GIRL YOUR AGE SHOULDN'T STAY DIRTY!
WAAA!
DRAG DRAG
JUST COME WITH ME!
KAZAAN!
GO AHEAD.
I'LL WATCH THE PACKS.
Scoop
DON'T WORRY, KID.
NO THIEVES AROUND HERE!
WAHAHAHAHAHAHAHAHA

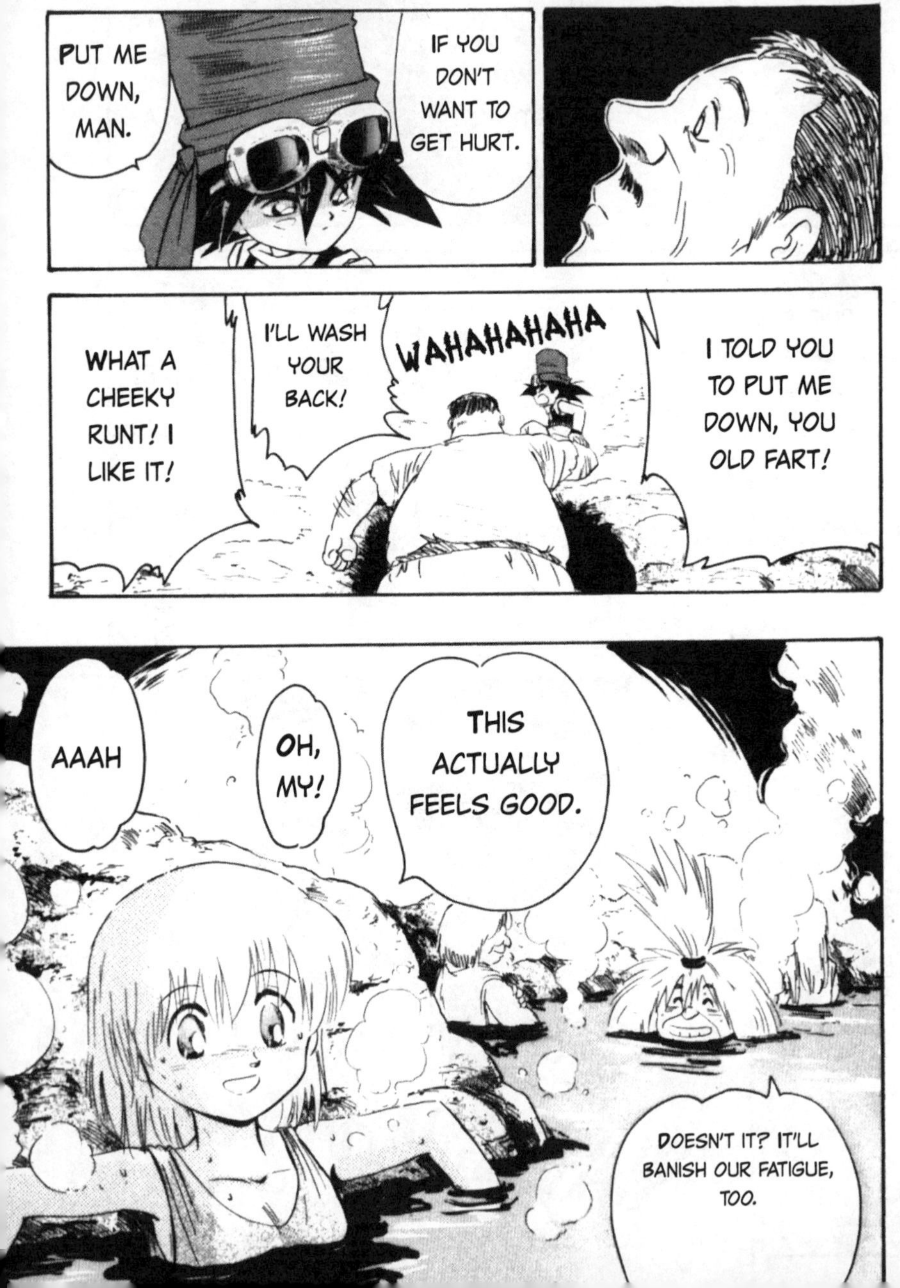
PUT ME DOWN, MAN.
IF YOU DON'T WANT TO GET HURT.
I TOLD YOU TO PUT ME DOWN, YOU OLD FART!
WAHAHAHAHA
I'LL WASH YOUR BACK!
WHAT A CHEEKY RUNT! I LIKE IT!
THIS ACTUALLY FEELS GOOD.
OH, MY!
AAAH
DOESN'T IT? IT'LL BANISH OUR FATIGUE, TOO.

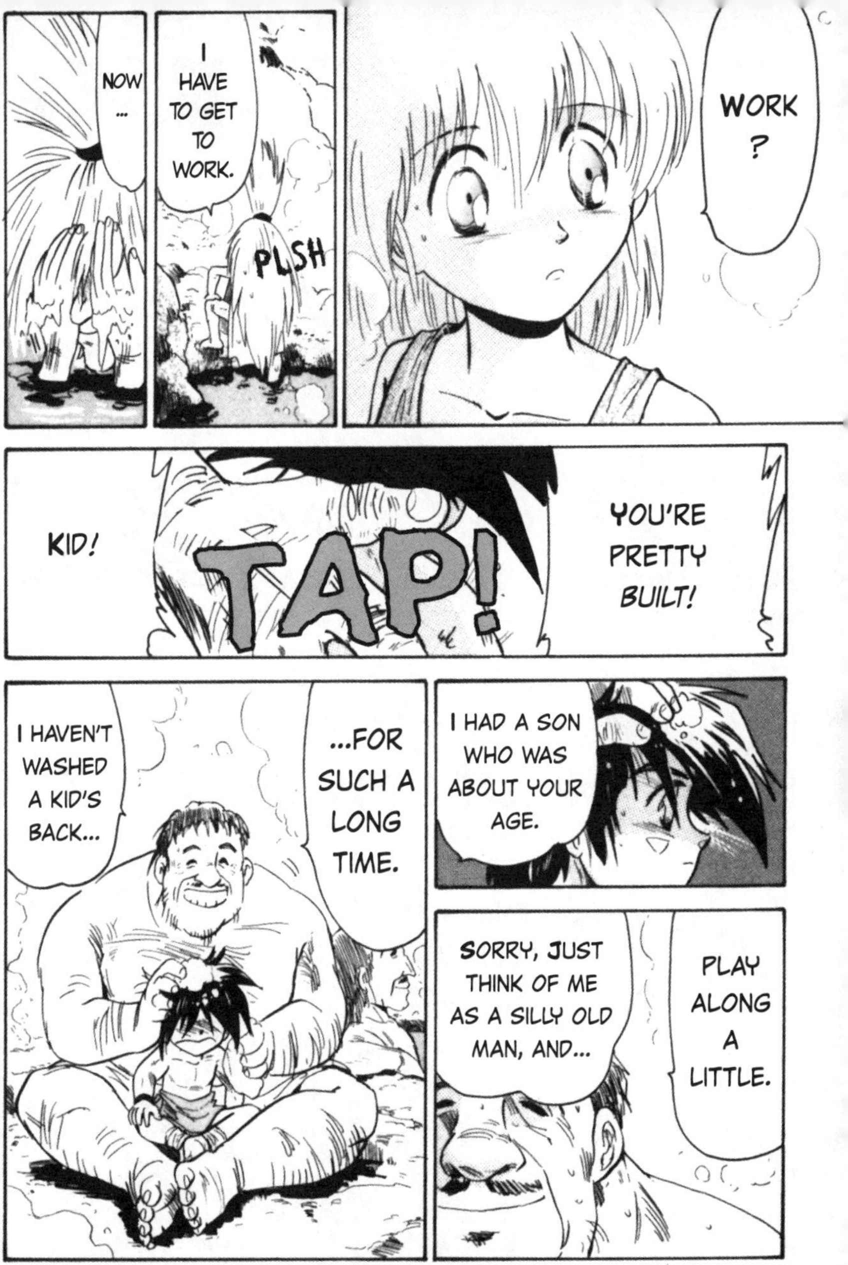
NOW ...
I HAVE TO GET TO WORK.
PLSH
WORK ?
KID!
TAP!
YOU'RE PRETTY BUILT!
I HAVEN'T WASHED A KID'S BACK...
...FOR SUCH A LONG TIME.
I HAD A SON WHO WAS ABOUT YOUR AGE.
SORRY, JUST THINK OF ME AS A SILLY OLD MAN, AND...
PLAY ALONG A LITTLE.

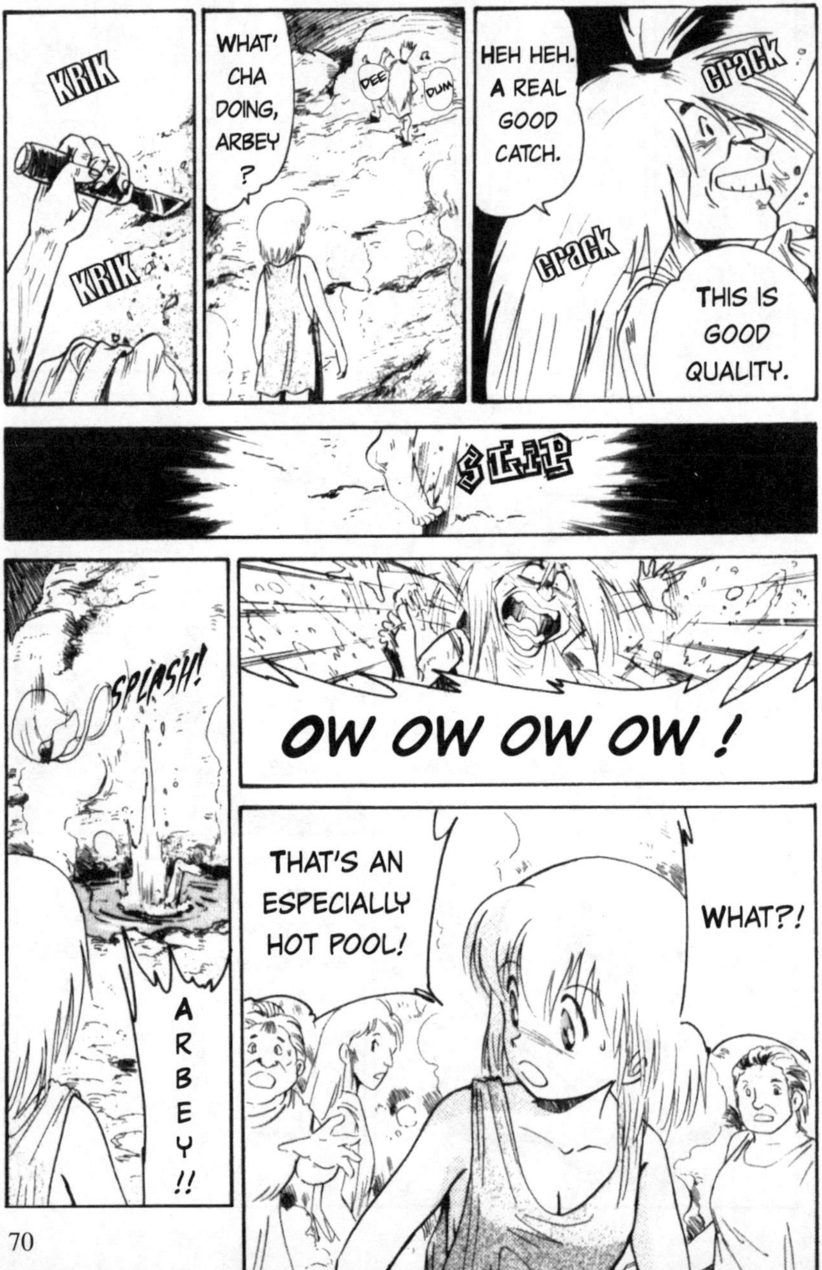
KRIK
KRIK
WHAT'CHA DOING, ARBEY?
DEE
DUM
HEH HEH. A REAL GOOD CATCH.
crack
crack
THIS IS GOOD QUALITY.
SLIP
OW OW OW OW!
SPLASH!
ARBEY!!
THAT'S AN ESPECIALLY HOT POOL!
WHAT?!

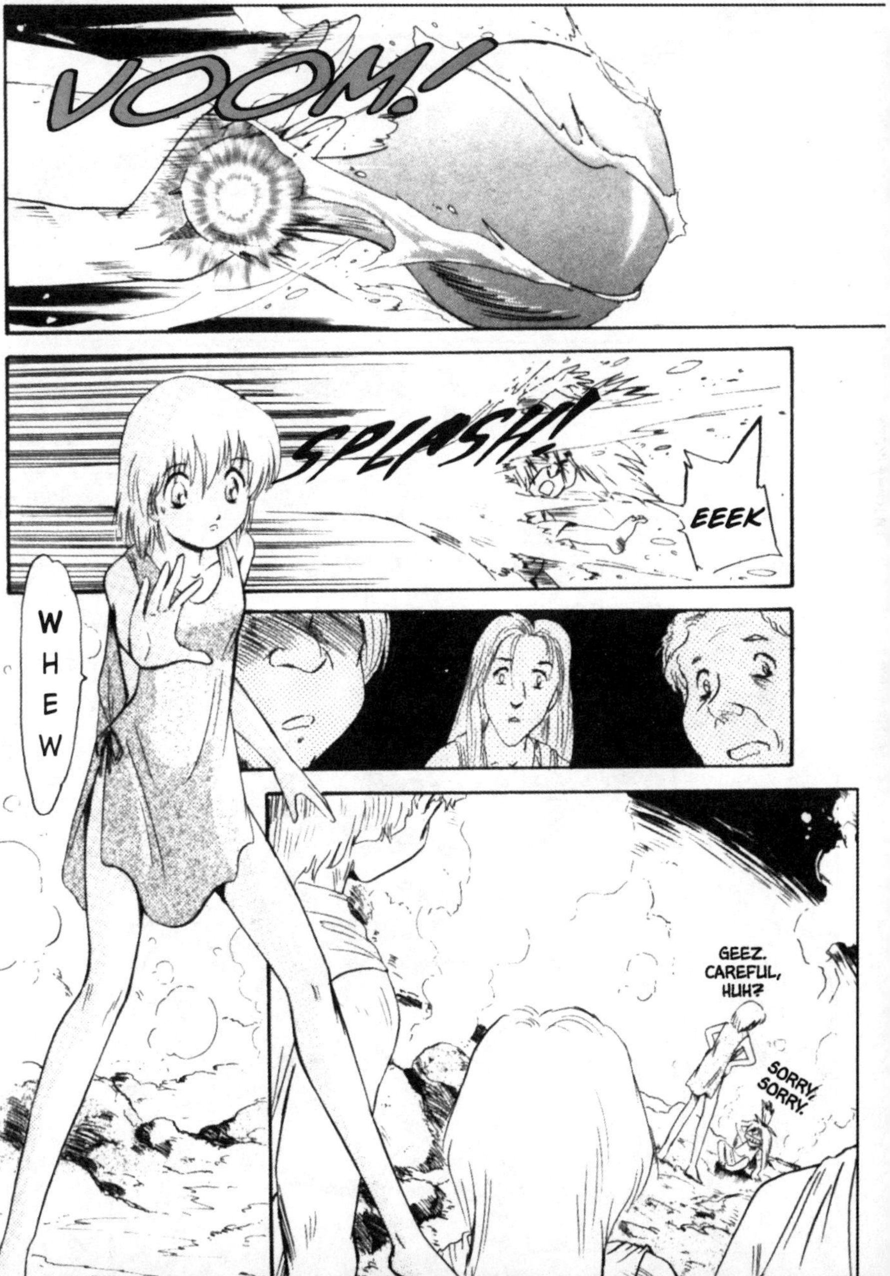
VOOM!
SPLASH!
EEEK
WHEW
GEEZ. CAREFUL, HUH?
SORRY, SORRY.

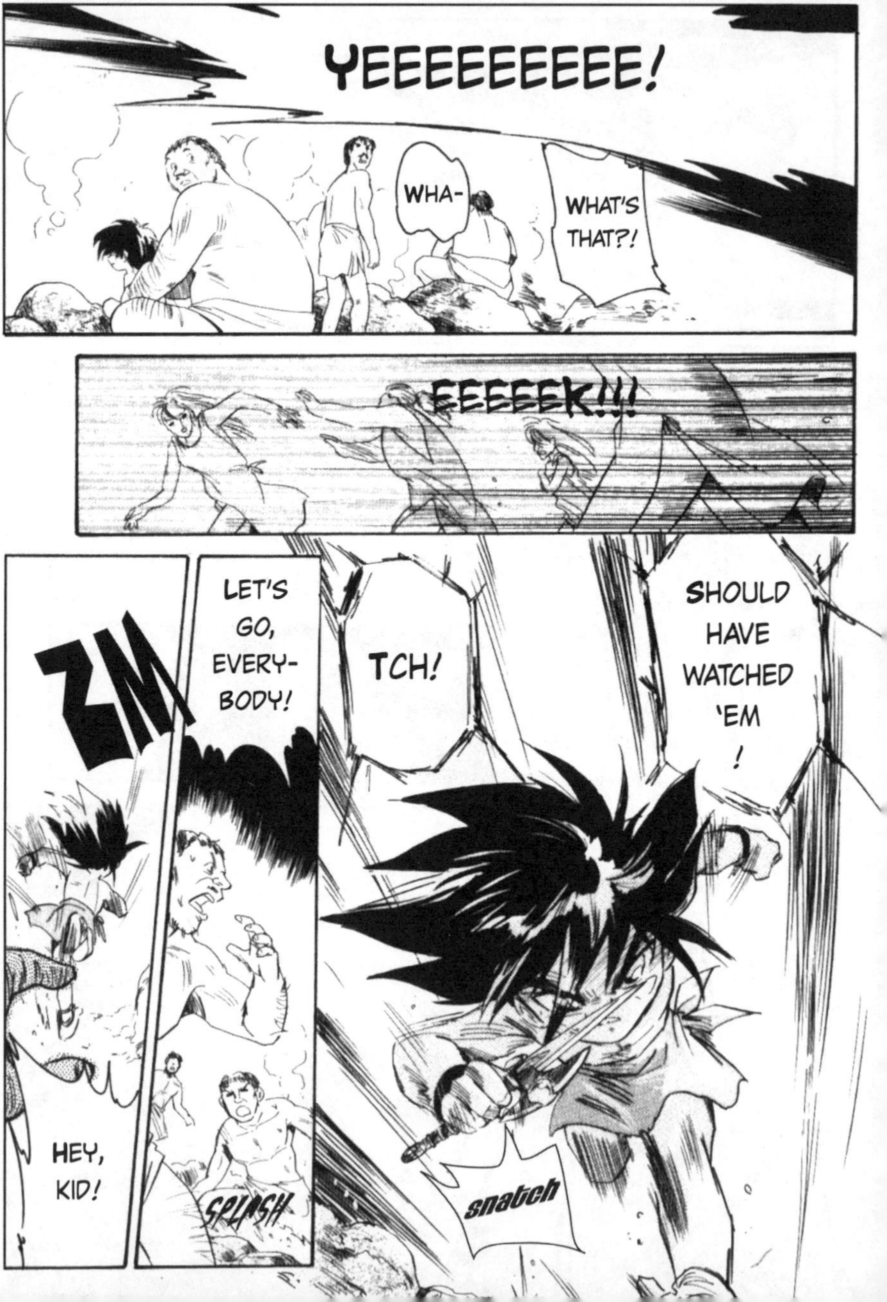
YEEEEEEEEEE!
WHA-
WHAT'S THAT?!
EEEEEK!!!
ZM
LET'S GO, EVERY-BODY!
HEY, KID!
SPLASH
TCH!
SHOULD HAVE WATCHED 'EM!
snatch

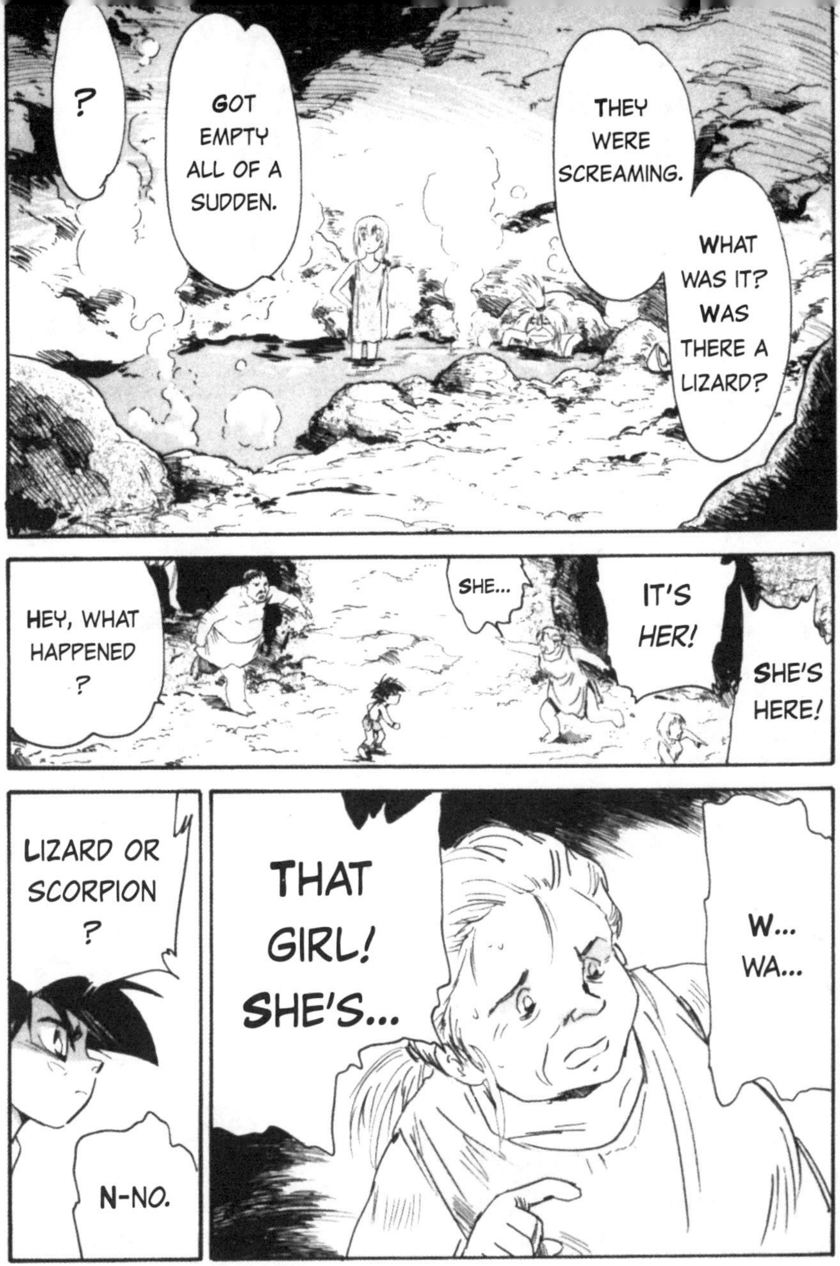
THEY WERE SCREAMING.
WHAT WAS IT? WAS THERE A LIZARD?
GOT EMPTY ALL OF A SUDDEN.
?
SHE'S HERE!
IT'S HER!
SHE...
HEY, WHAT HAPPENED?
W... WA...
THAT GIRL! SHE'S...
LIZARD OR SCORPION?
N-NO.

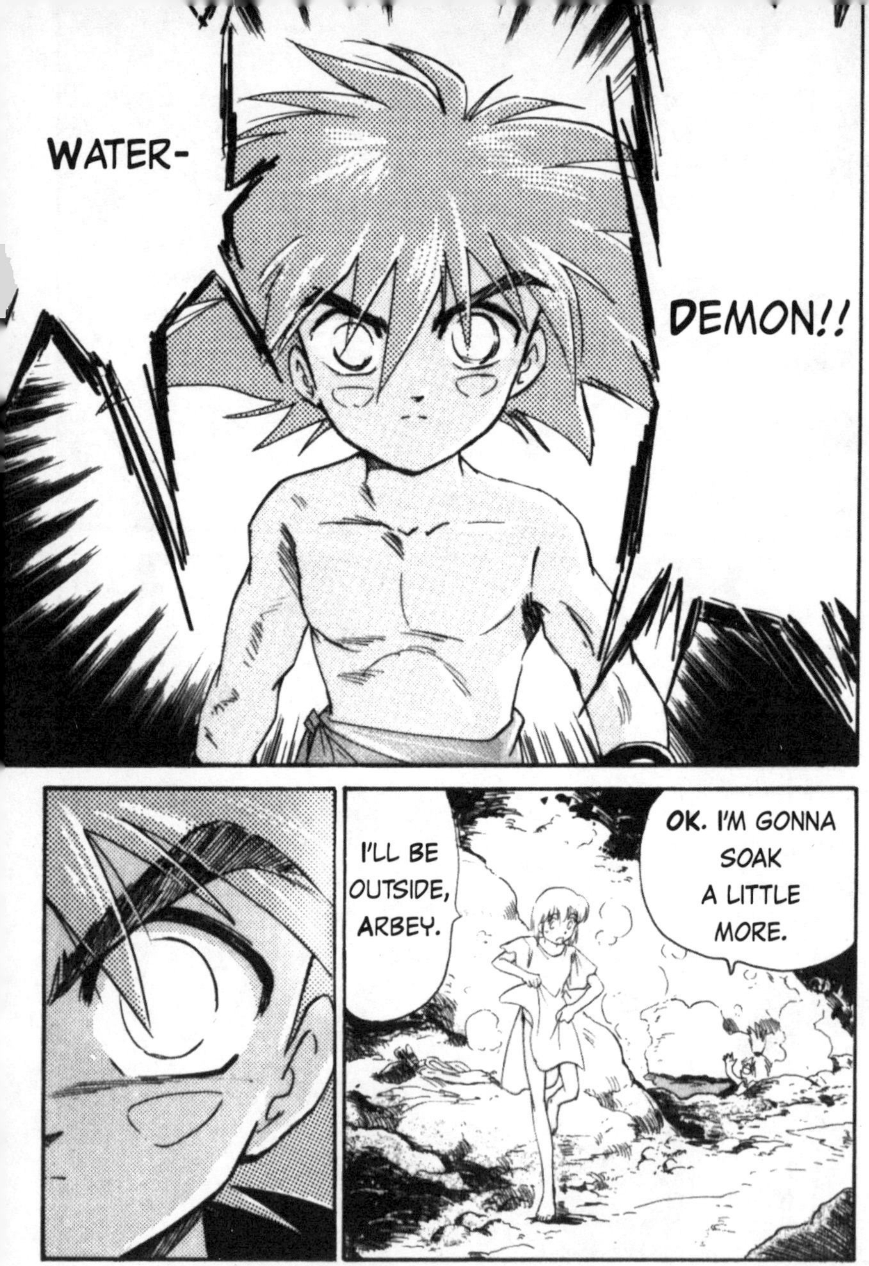
WATER-
DEMON!!
OK. I'M GONNA SOAK A LITTLE MORE.
I'LL BE OUTSIDE, ARBEY.

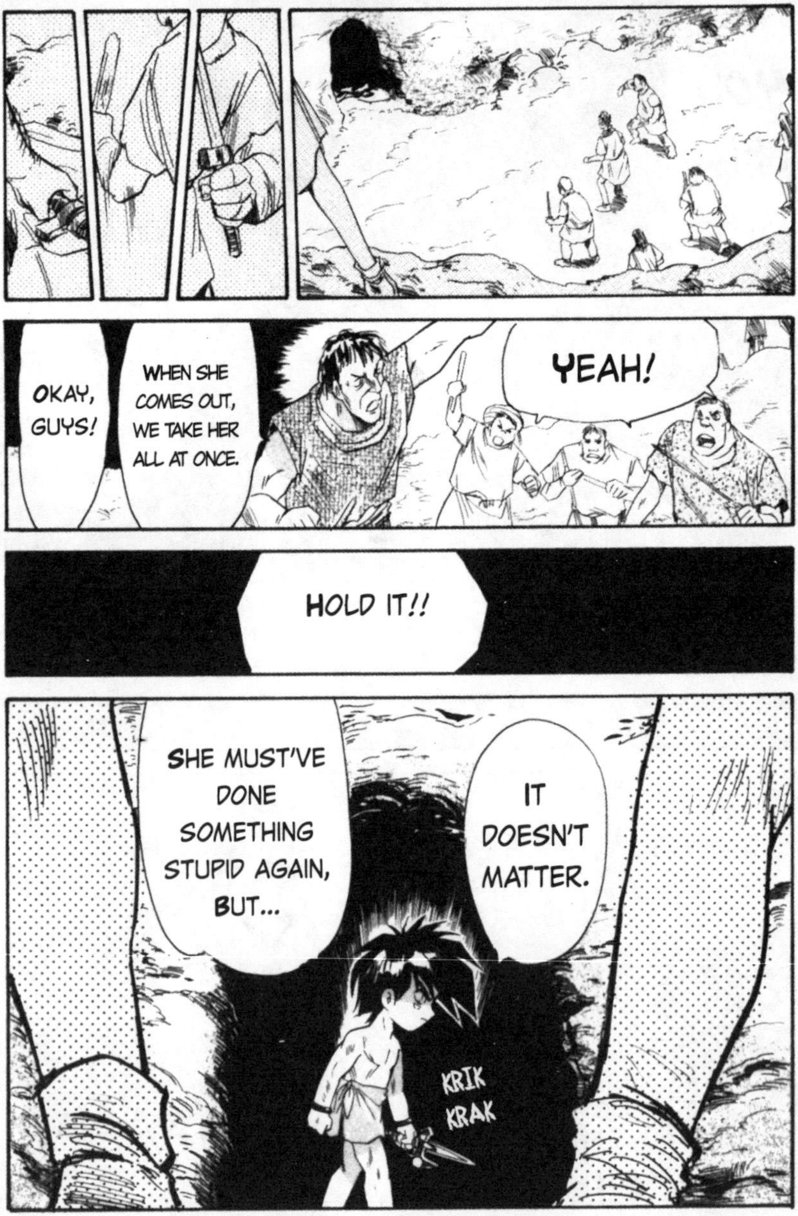
OKAY, GUYS!
WHEN SHE COMES OUT, WE TAKE HER ALL AT ONCE.
YEAH!
HOLD IT!!
SHE MUST'VE DONE SOMETHING STUPID AGAIN, BUT...
IT DOESN'T MATTER.
KRIK KRAK

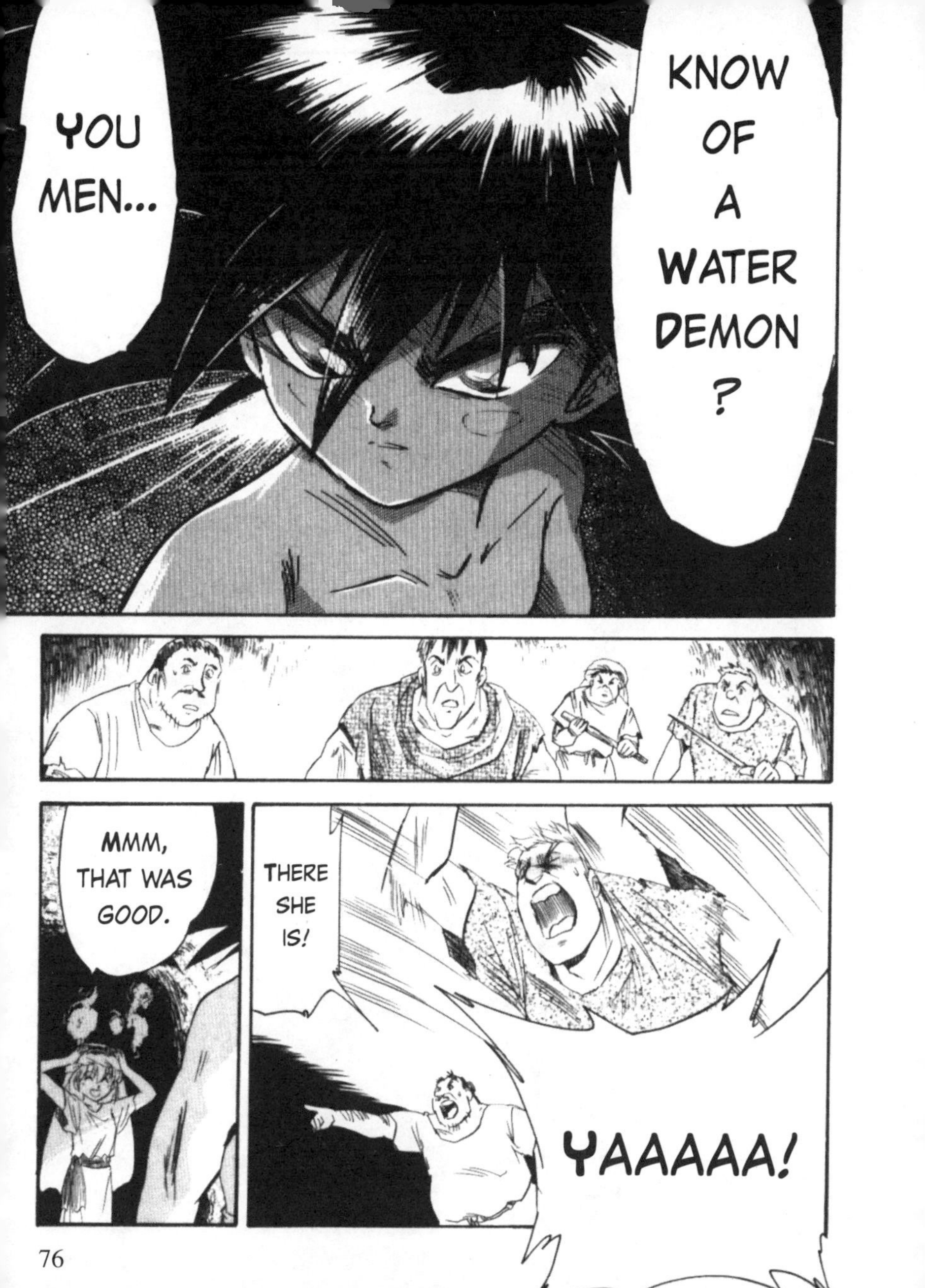
YOU MEN...
KNOW OF A WATER DEMON?
MMM, THAT WAS GOOD.
THERE SHE IS!
YAAAAA!

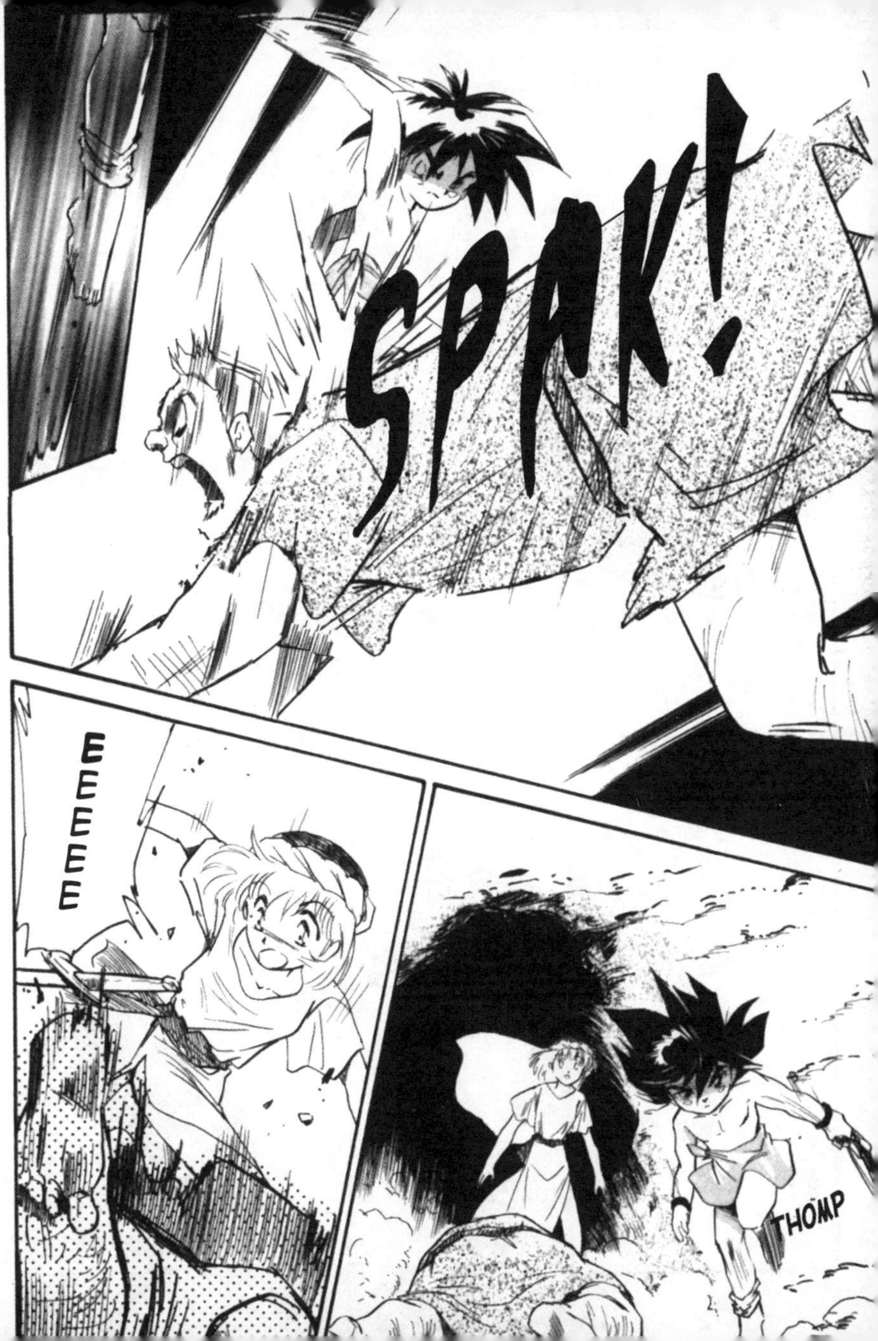
SPAK!
EEEEEE
THOMP

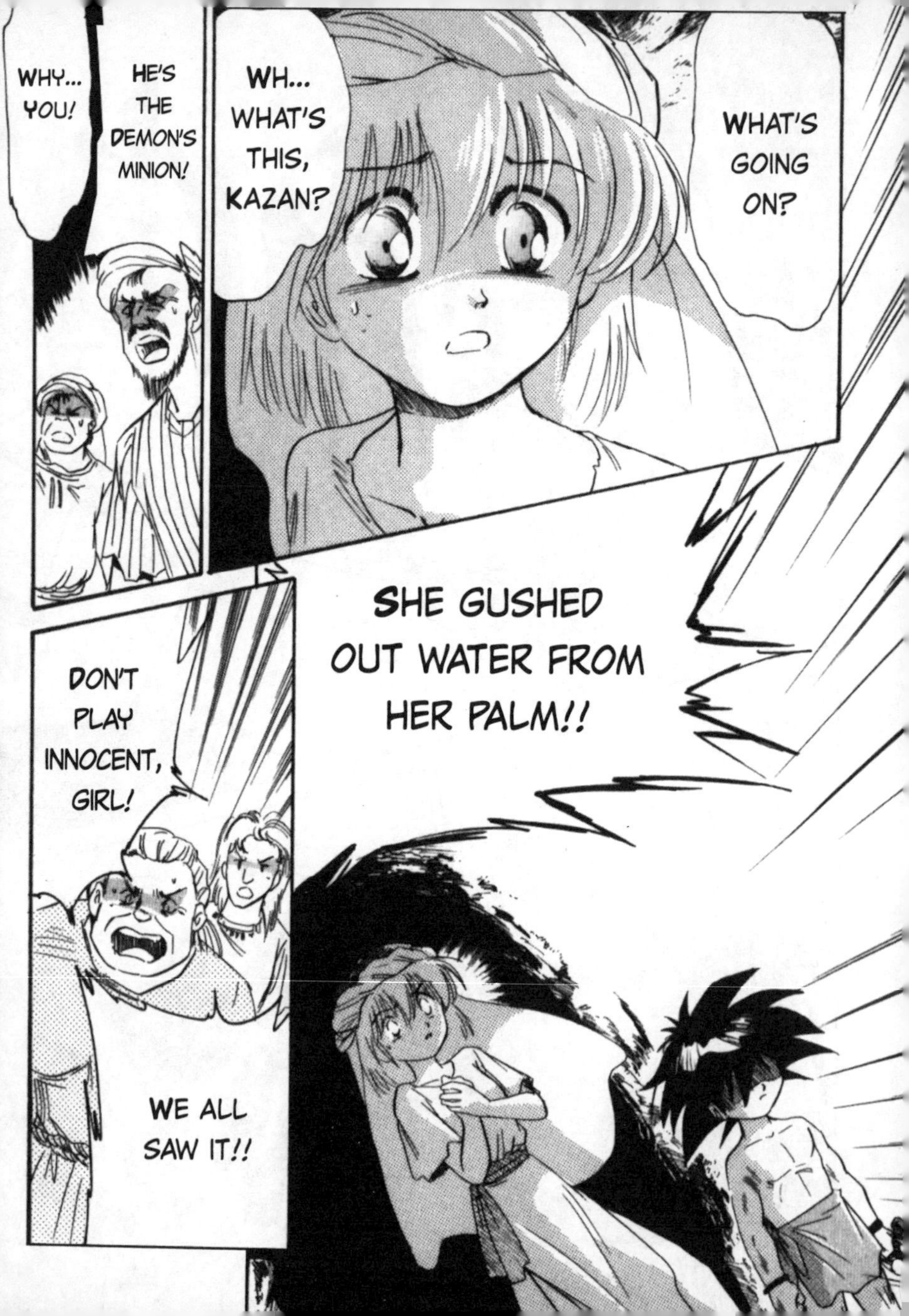
WHAT'S GOING ON?
WH... WHAT'S THIS, KAZAN?
HE'S THE DEMON'S MINION!
WHY... YOU!
SHE GUSHED OUT WATER FROM HER PALM!!
DON'T PLAY INNOCENT, GIRL!
WE ALL SAW IT!!

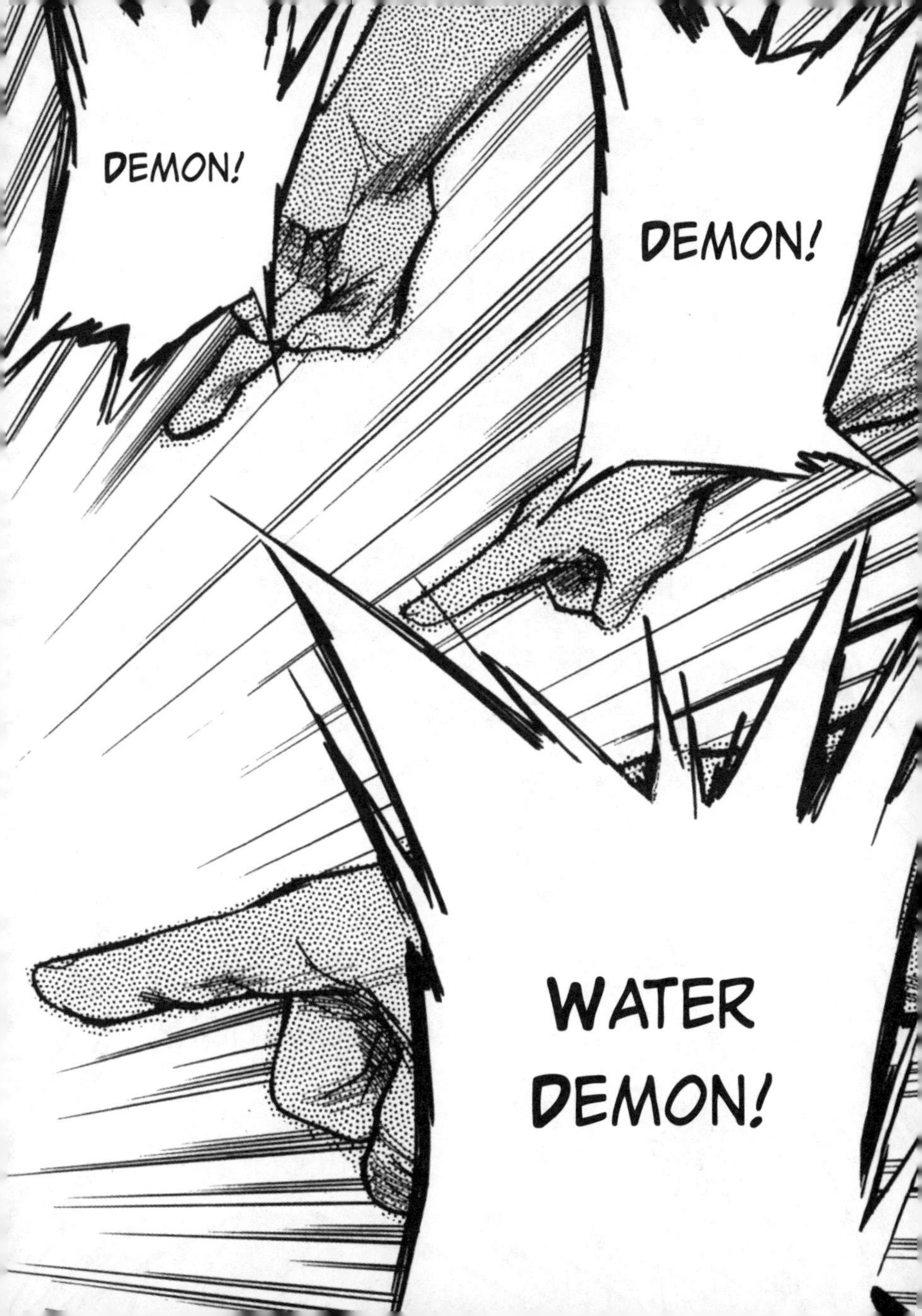
DEMON!
DEMON!
WATER
DEMON!

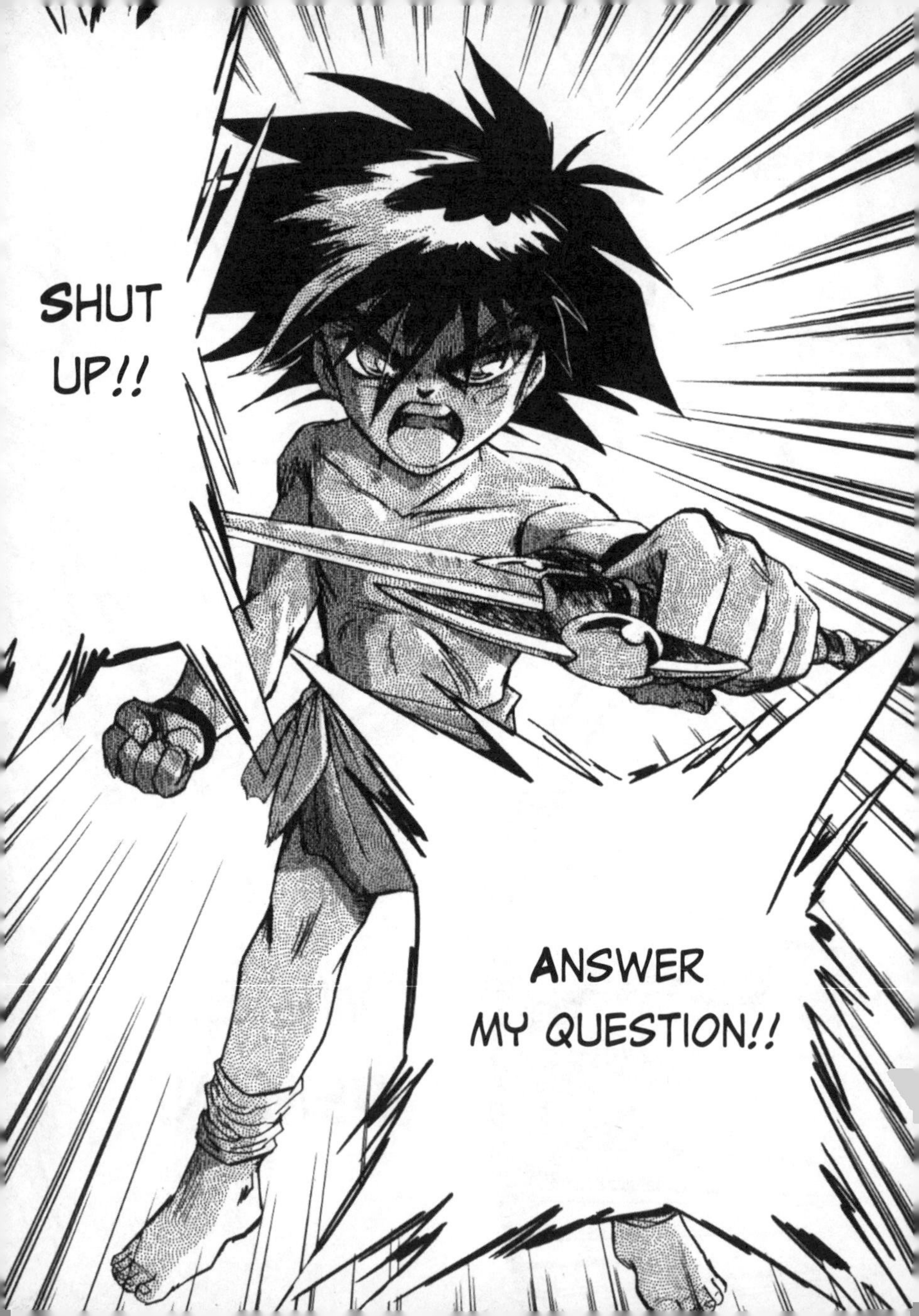
SHUT UP!!
ANSWER MY QUESTION!!

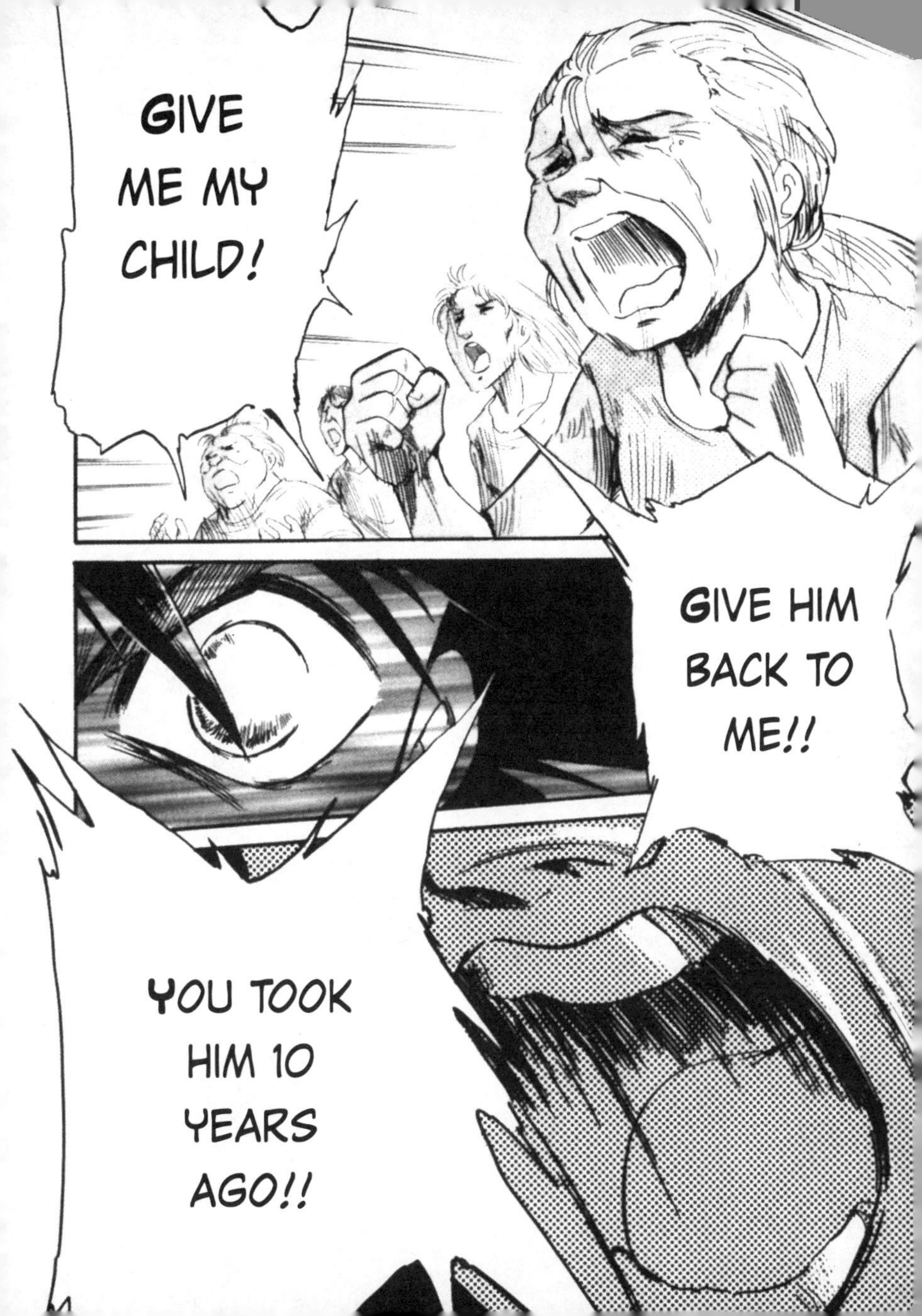
GIVE ME MY CHILD!
GIVE HIM BACK TO ME!!
YOU TOOK HIM 10 YEARS AGO!!

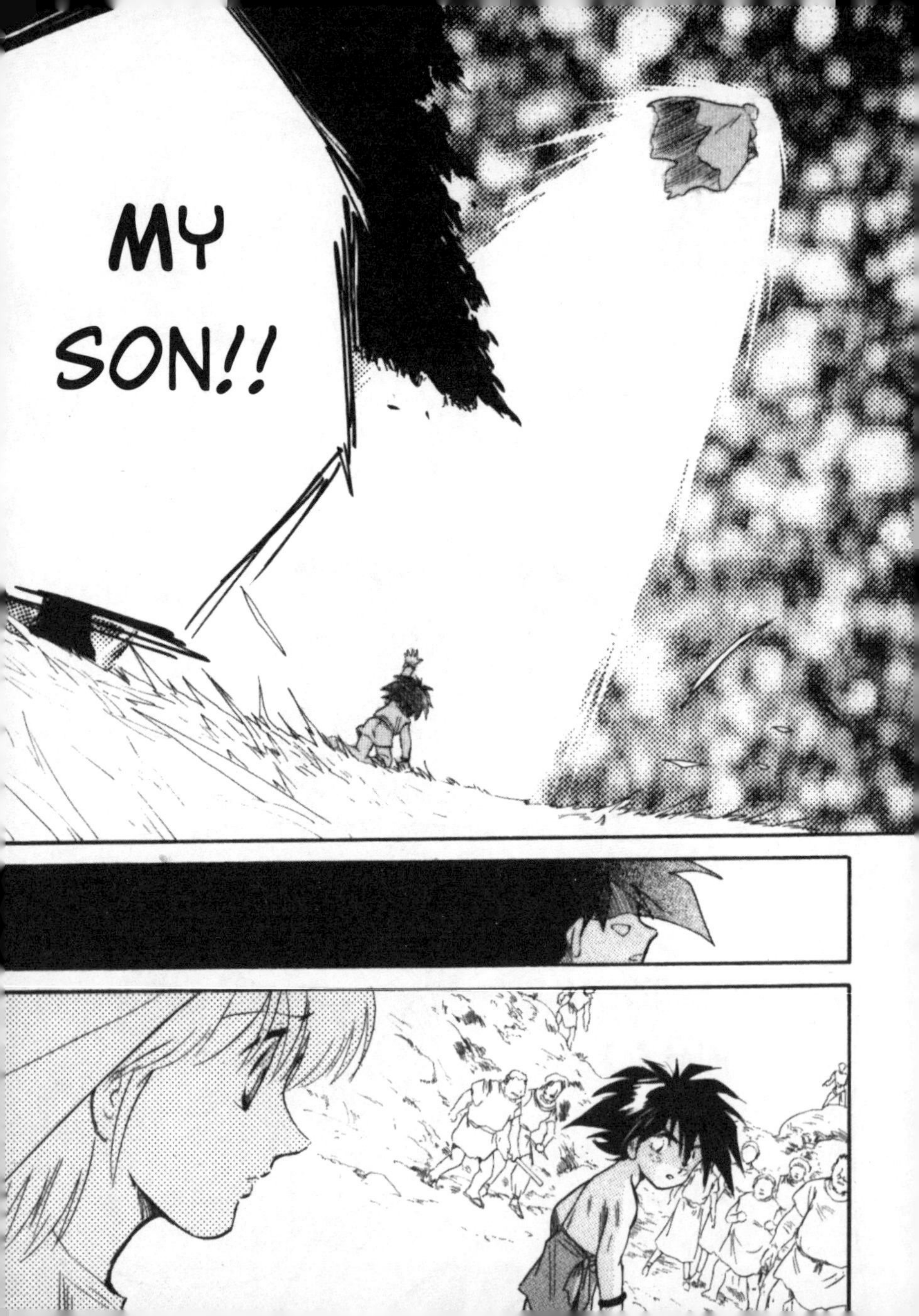
MY SON!!

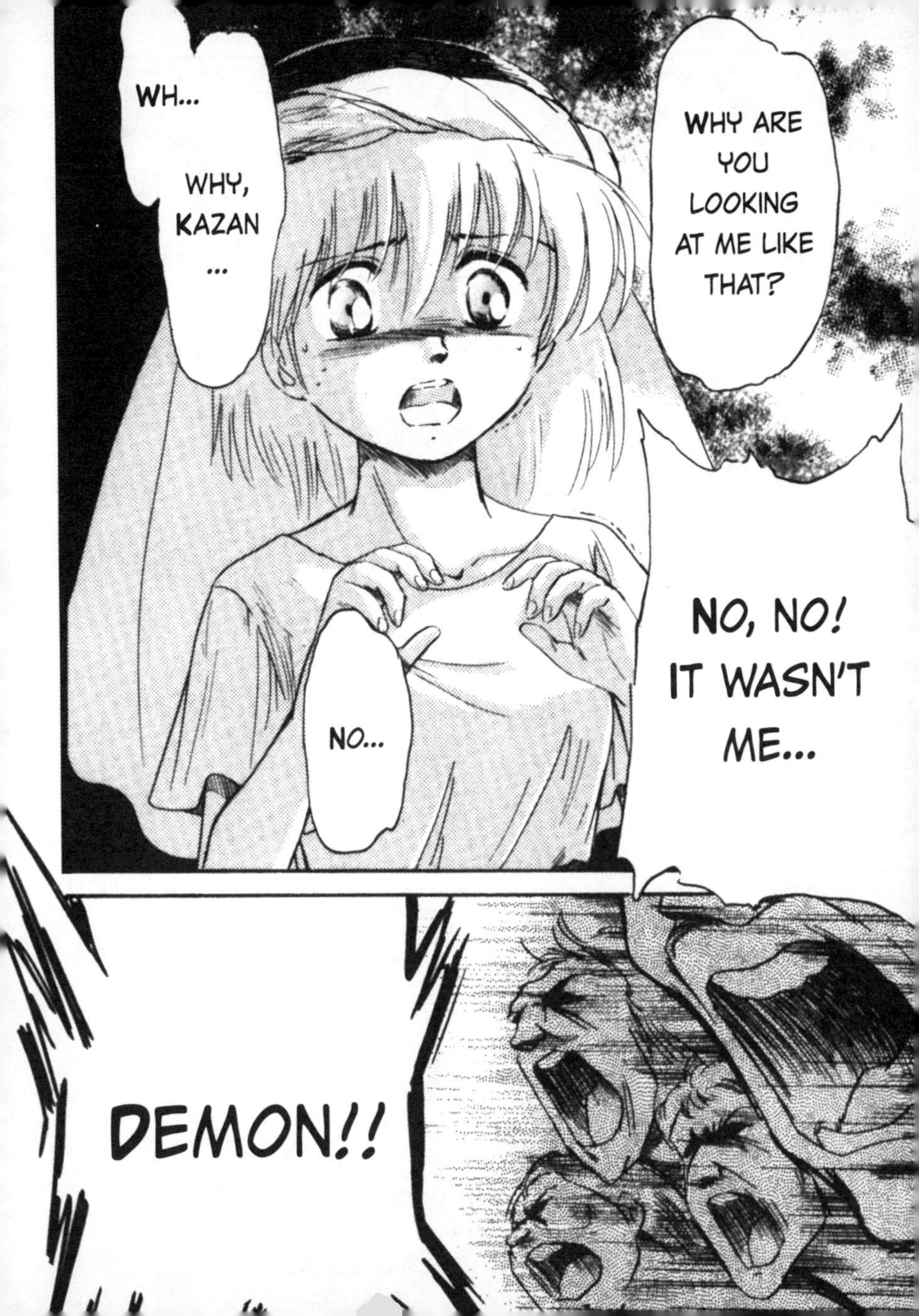
WHY ARE YOU LOOKING AT ME LIKE THAT?
WH...
WHY, KAZAN ...
NO, NO! IT WASN'T ME...
NO...
DEMON!!

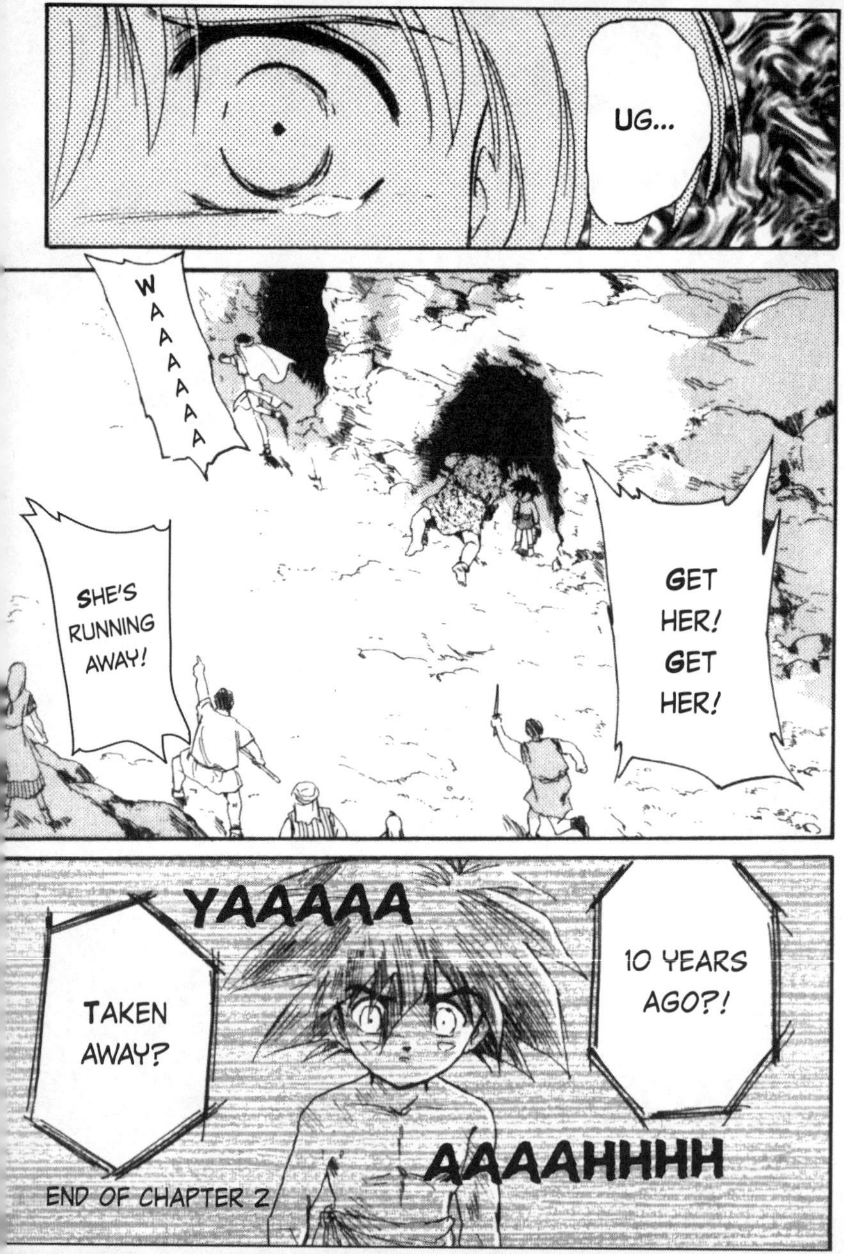
UG...
WAAAAAAAAA
GET HER! GET HER!
SHE'S RUNNING AWAY!
10 YEARS AGO?!
YAAAAA
TAKEN AWAY?
AAAAHHHH
END OF CHAPTER 2

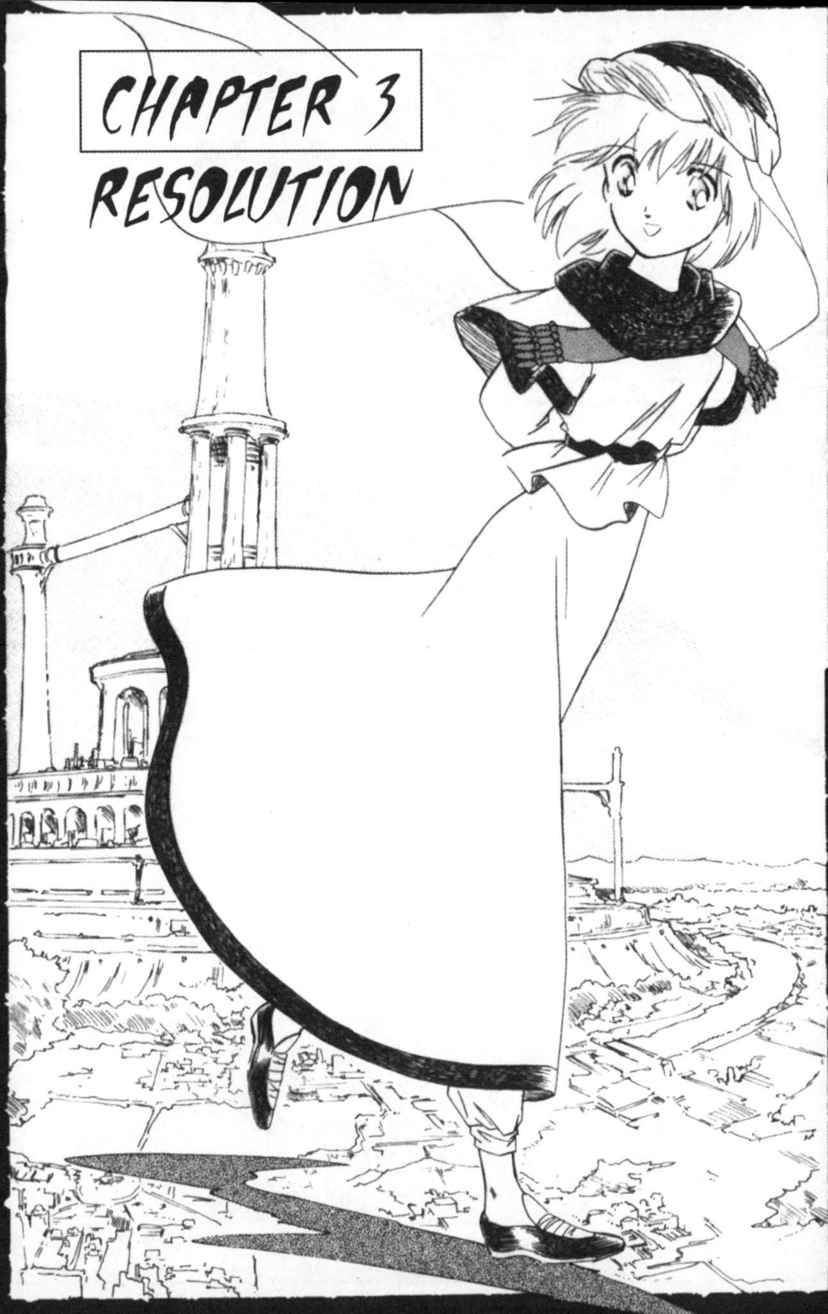
CHAPTER 3
RESOLUTION

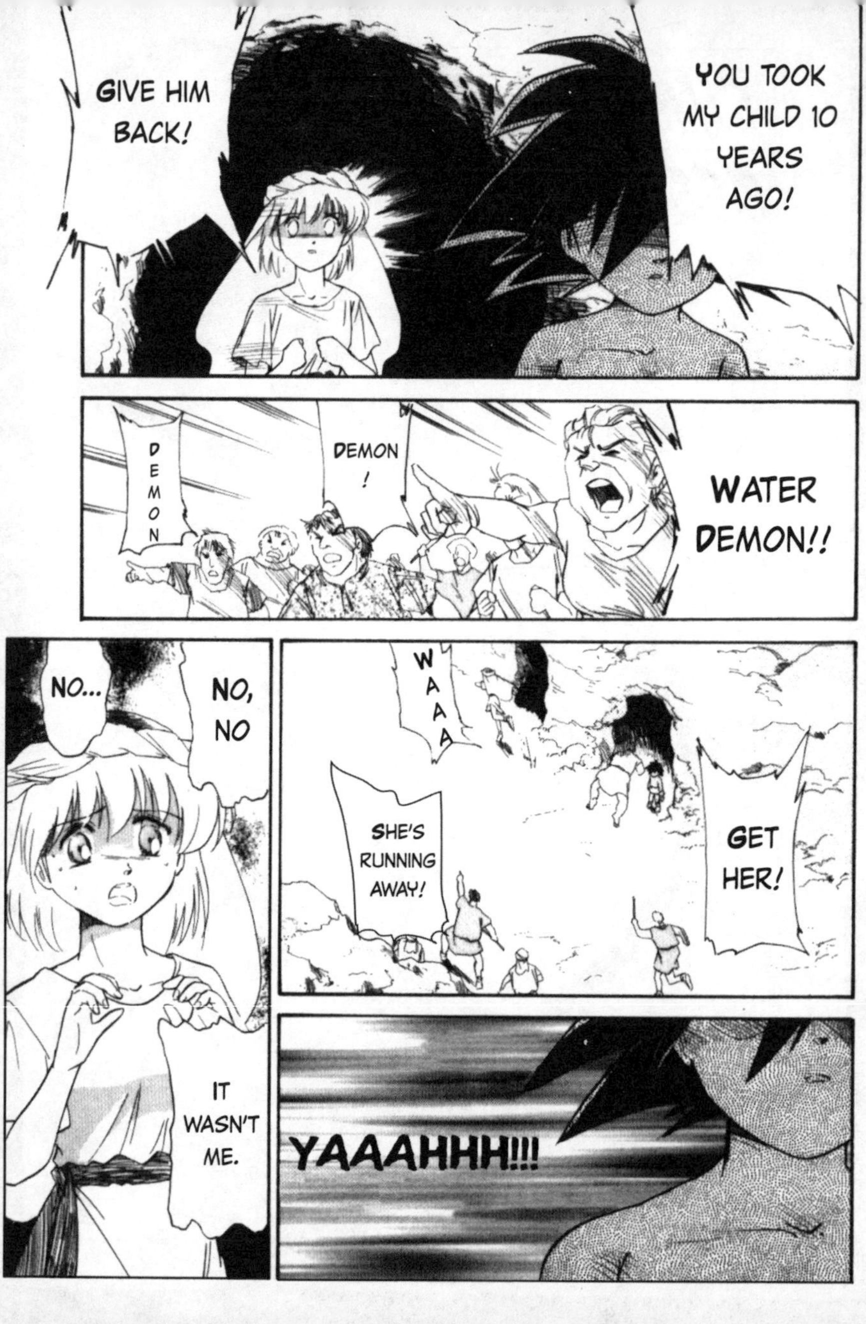
GIVE HIM BACK!
YOU TOOK MY CHILD 10 YEARS AGO!
DEMON
DEMON!
WATER DEMON!!
NO...
NO, NO
IT WASN'T ME.
WAAAA
SHE'S RUNNING AWAY!
GET HER!
YAAAHHH!!!

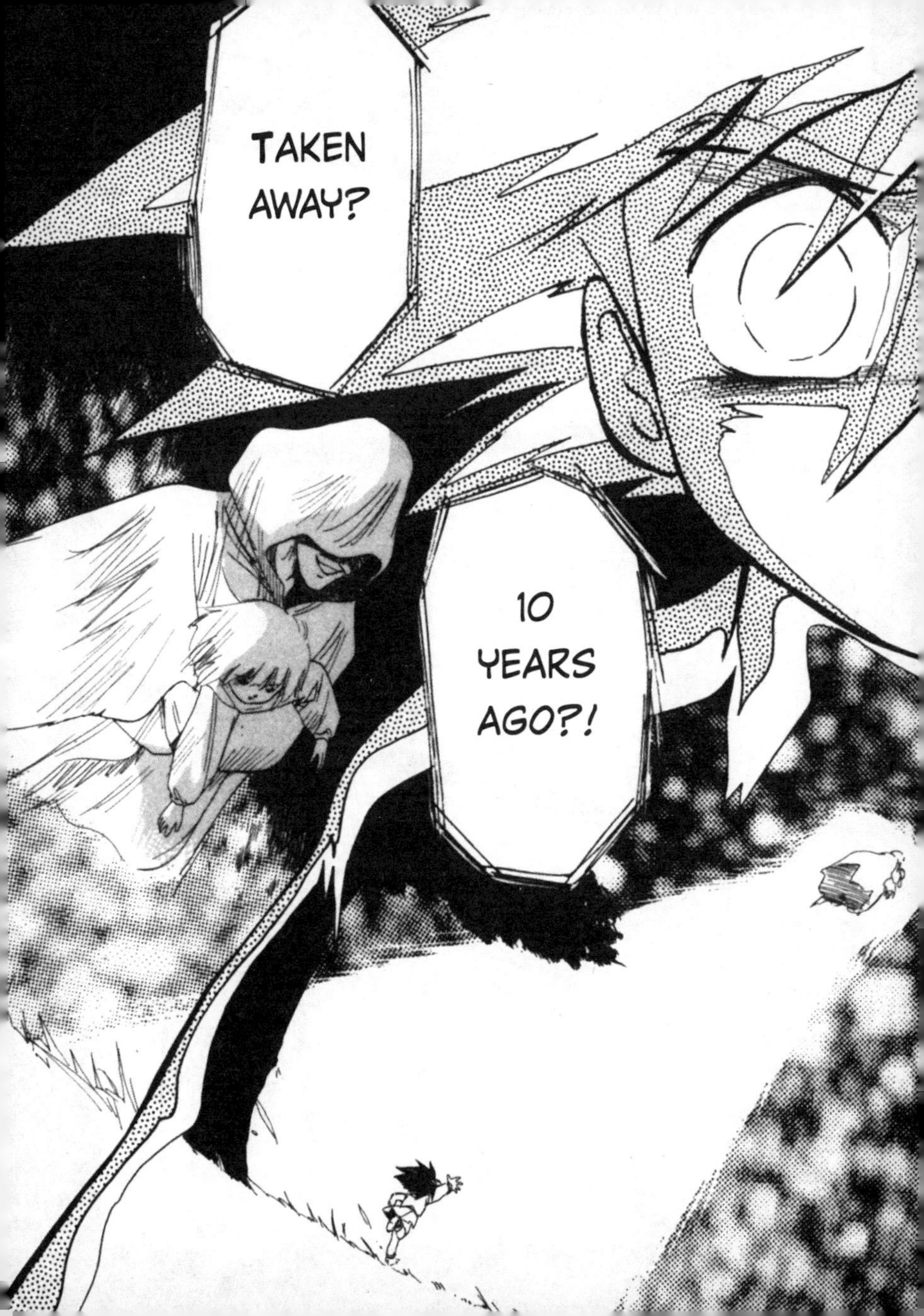
TAKEN AWAY?
10 YEARS AGO?!

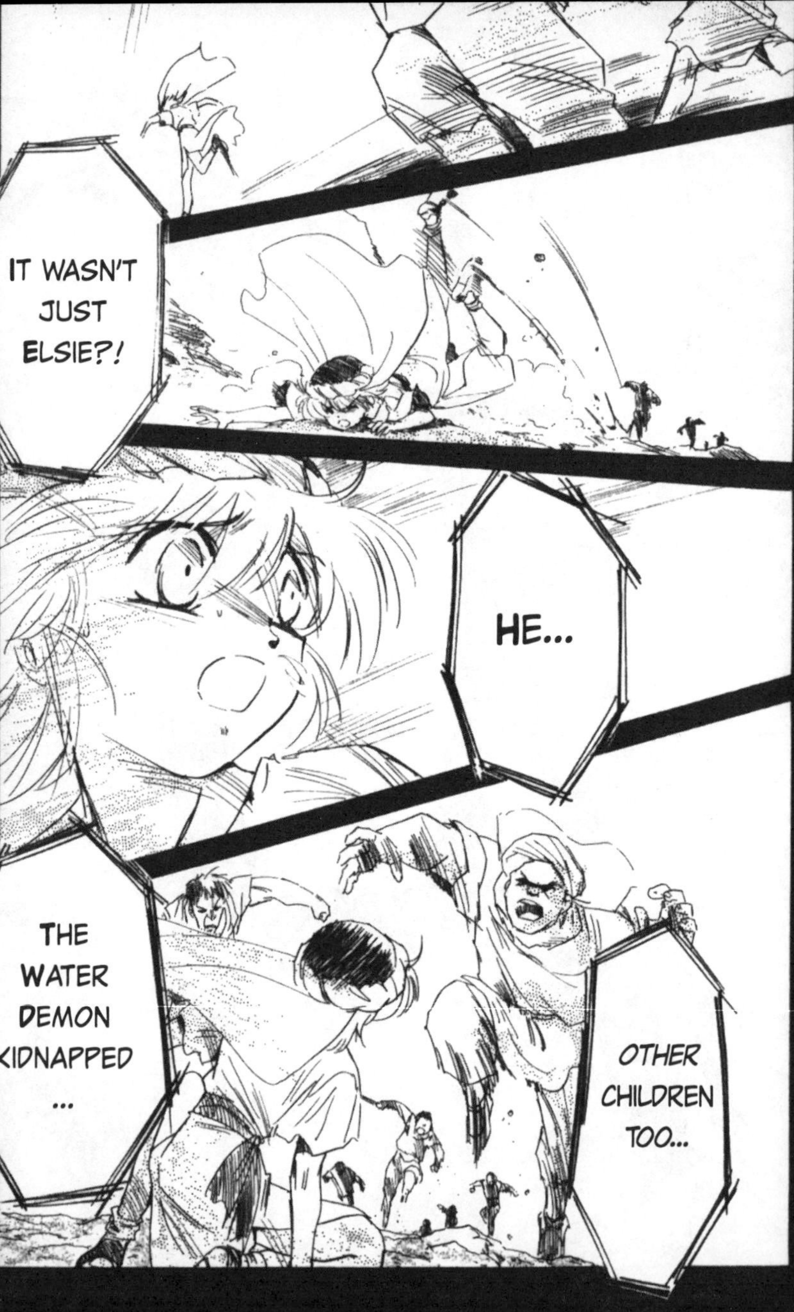
IT WASN'T JUST ELSIE?!
HE...
THE WATER DEMON KIDNAPPED ...
OTHER CHILDREN TOO...

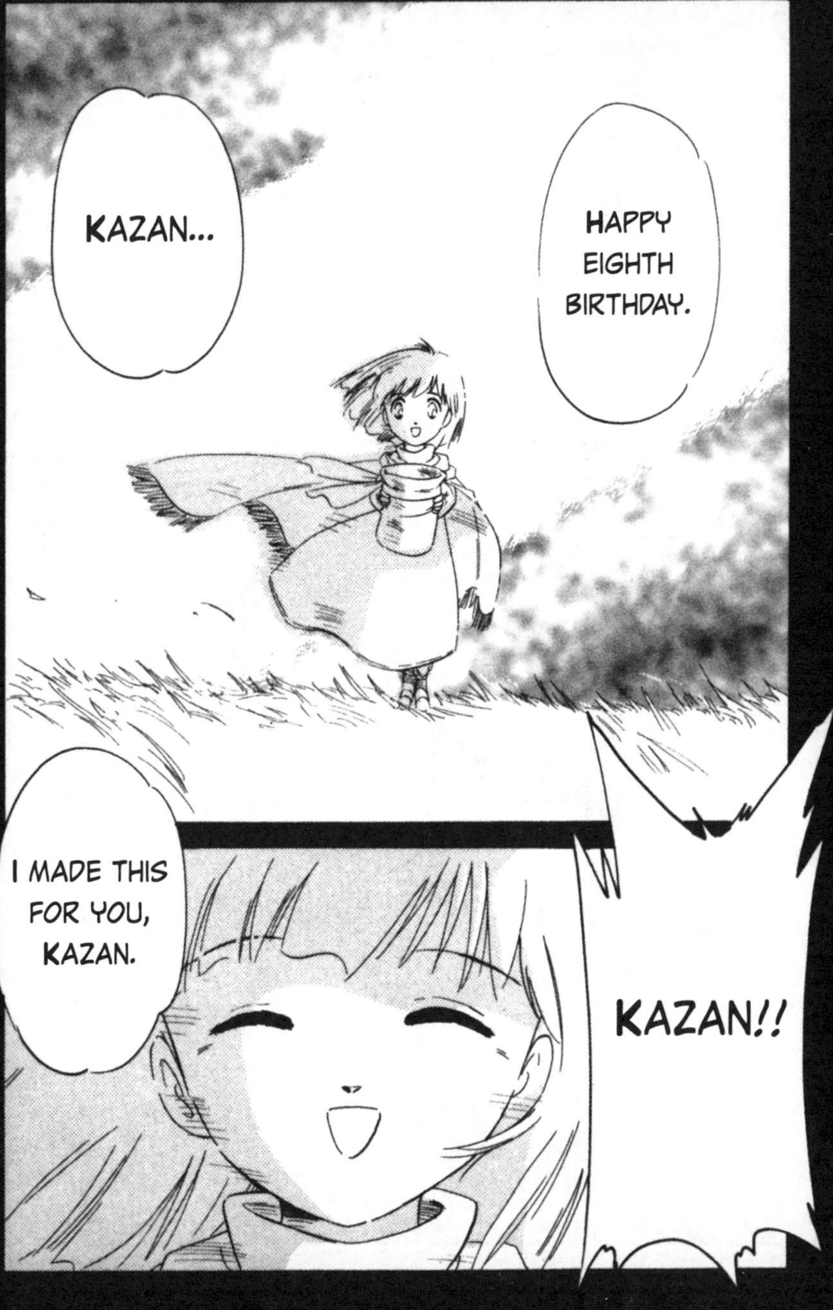
HAPPY EIGHTH BIRTHDAY.
KAZAN...
KAZAN!!
I MADE THIS FOR YOU, KAZAN.

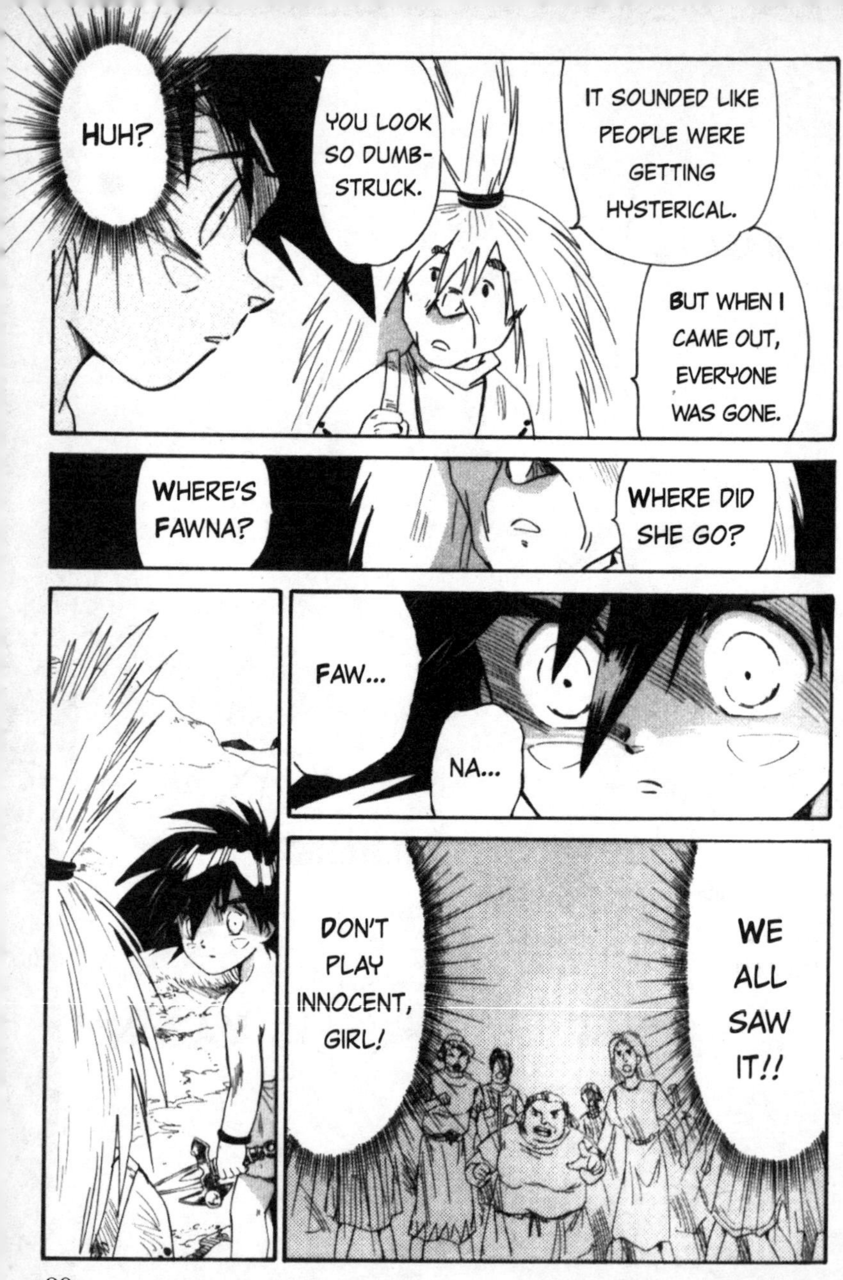
HUH?
YOU LOOK SO DUMB-STRUCK.
IT SOUNDED LIKE PEOPLE WERE GETTING HYSTERICAL.
BUT WHEN I CAME OUT, EVERYONE WAS GONE.
WHERE'S FAWNA?
WHERE DID SHE GO?
FAW...
NA...
DON'T PLAY INNOCENT, GIRL!
WE ALL SAW IT!!

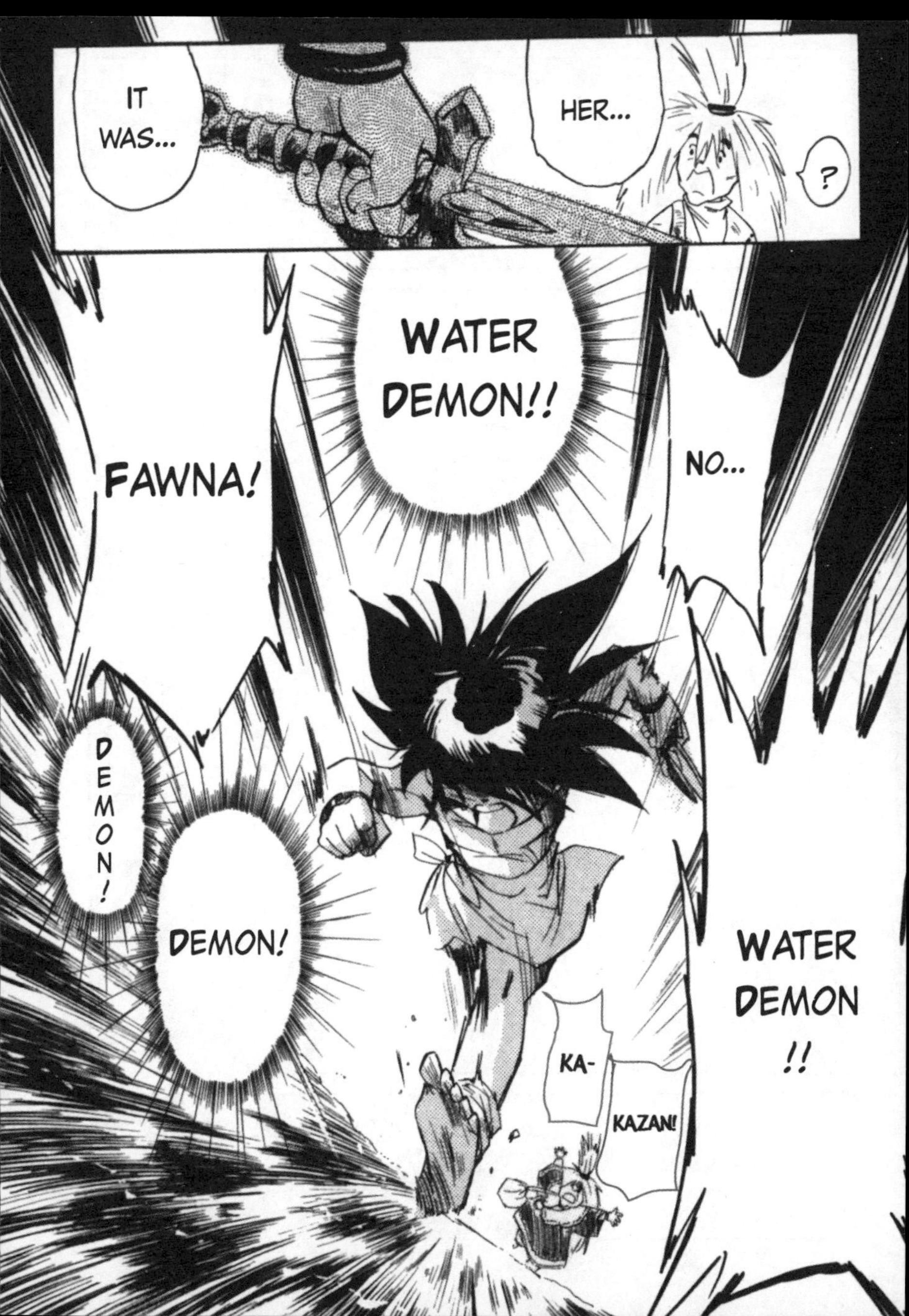
IT WAS...
HER...
?
WATER DEMON!!
FAWNA!
NO...
DEMON!
DEMON!
WATER DEMON !!
KA-
KAZAN!

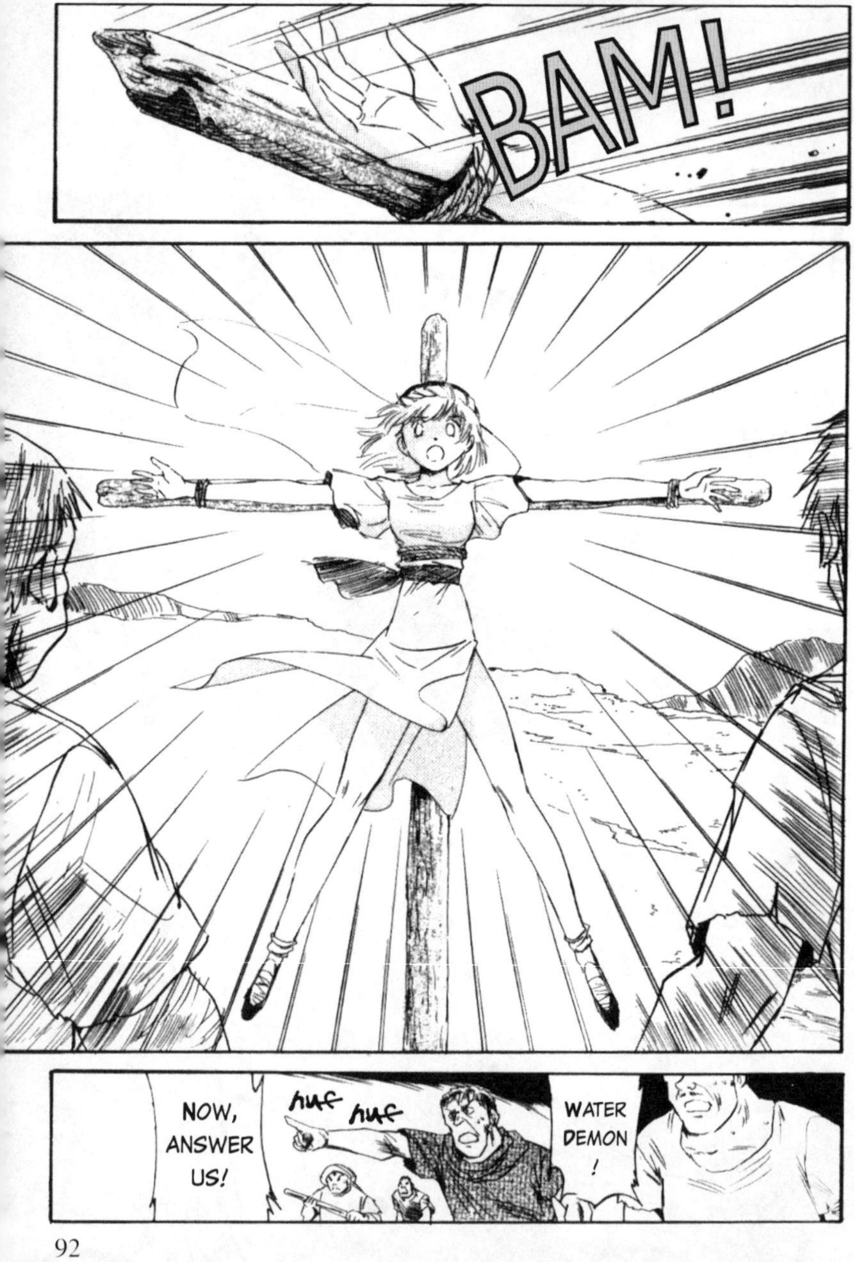
BAM!
WATER DEMON !
huf huf
NOW, ANSWER US!

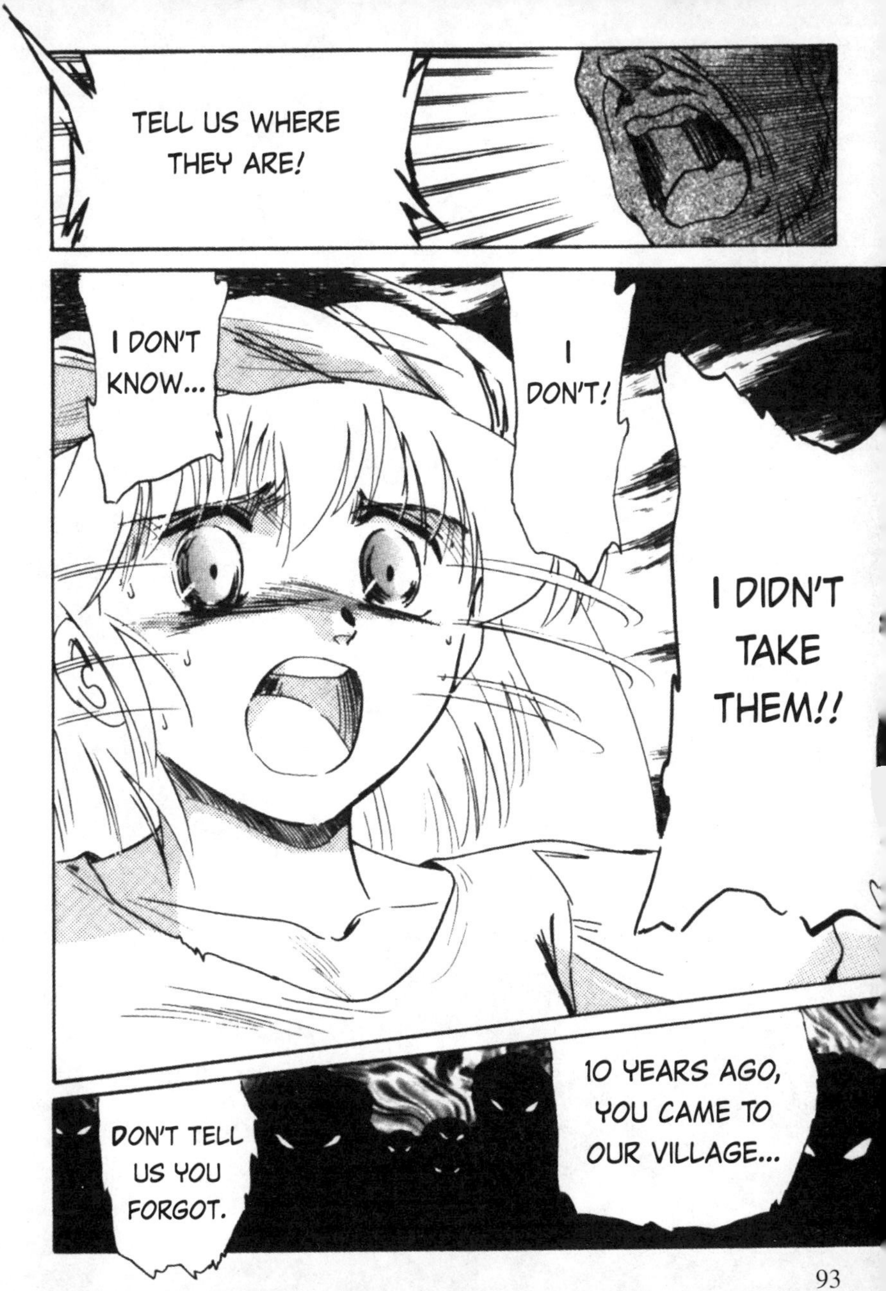
TELL US WHERE THEY ARE!
I DON'T KNOW...
I DON'T!
I DIDN'T TAKE THEM!!
10 YEARS AGO, YOU CAME TO OUR VILLAGE...
DON'T TELL US YOU FORGOT.

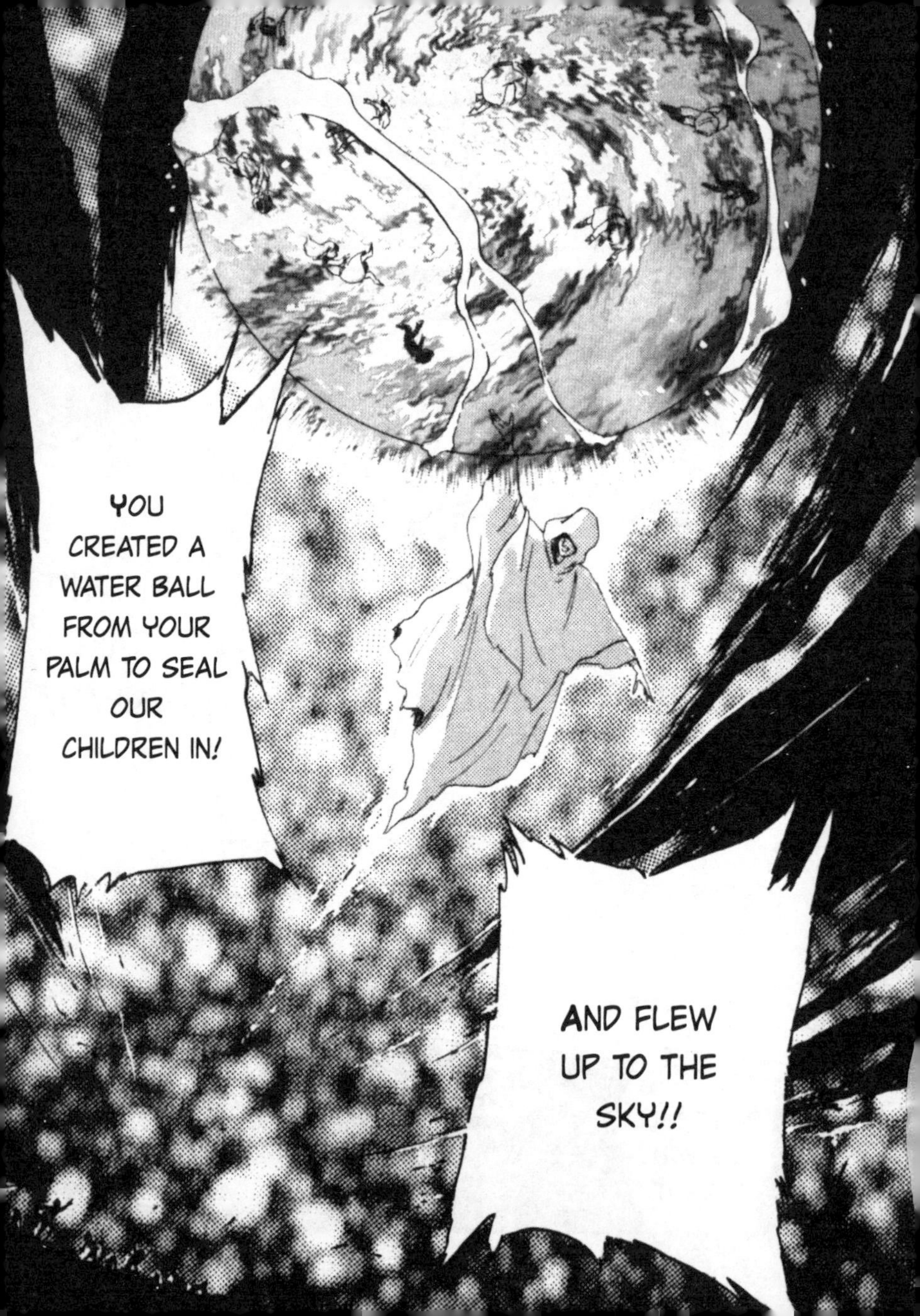
YOU CREATED A WATER BALL FROM YOUR PALM TO SEAL OUR CHILDREN IN!
AND FLEW UP TO THE SKY!!

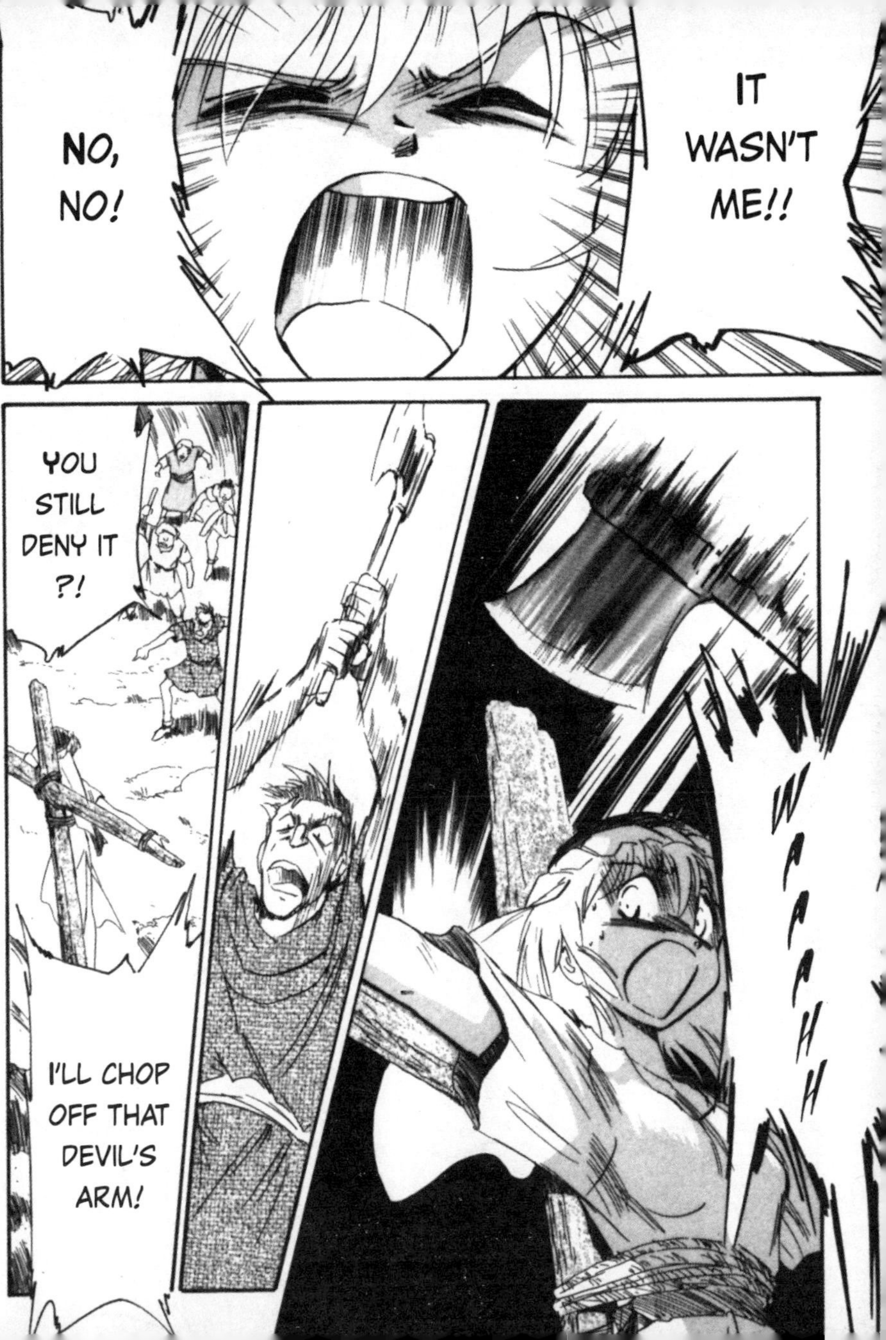
IT WASN'T ME!!
NO, NO!
WAPPAHH
YOU STILL DENY IT ?!
I'LL CHOP OFF THAT DEVIL'S ARM!

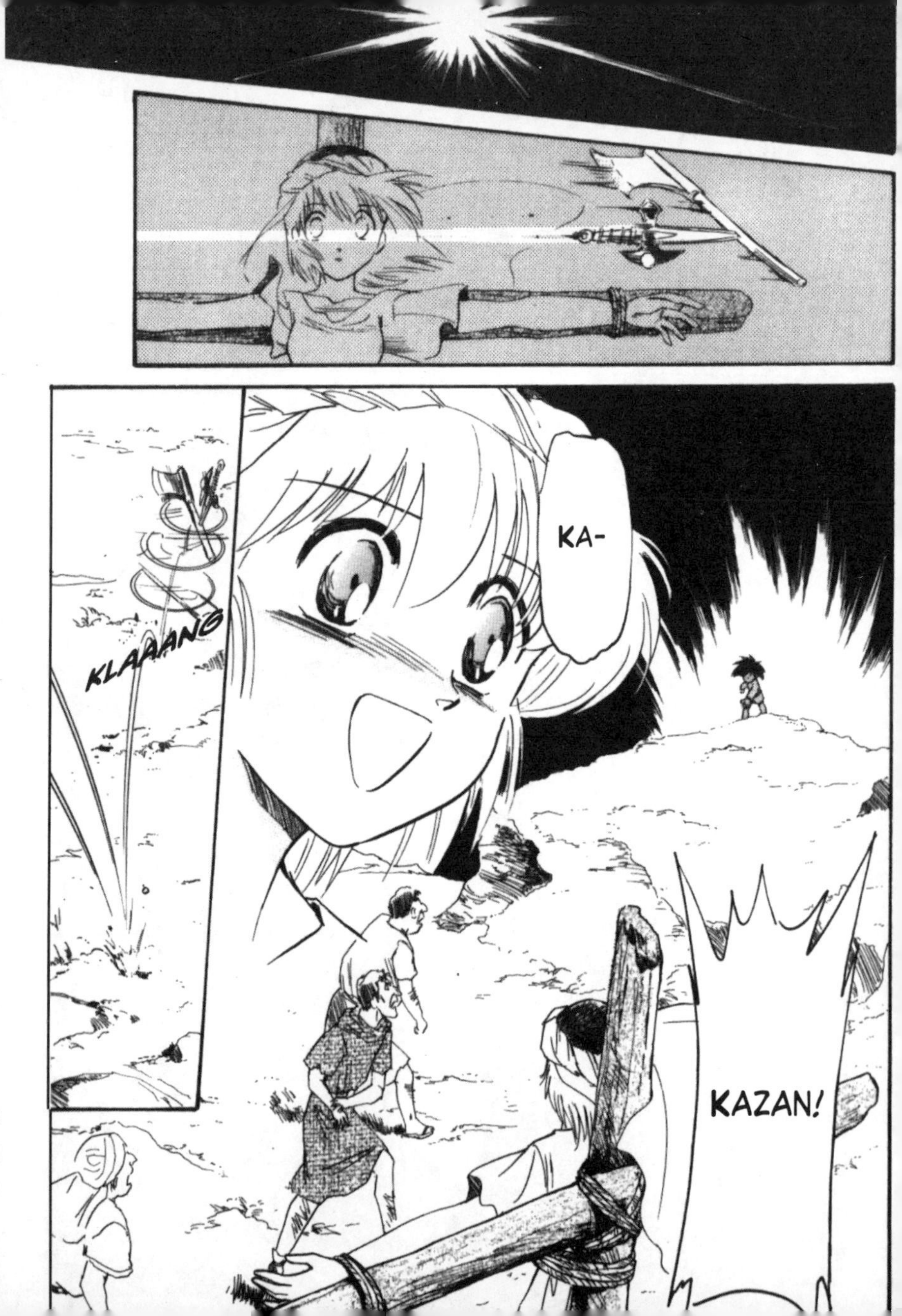
KLAAANG
KA-
KAZAN!

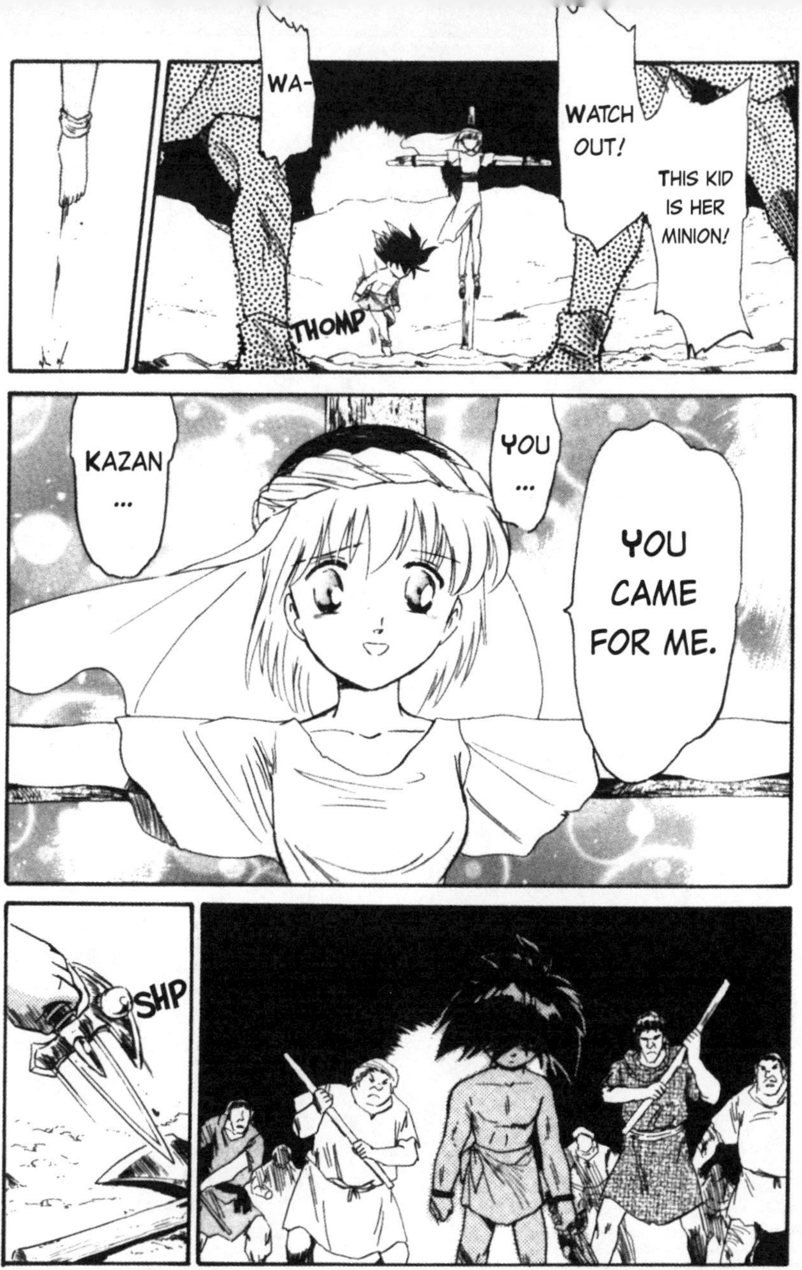
WA-
WATCH OUT!
THIS KID IS HER MINION!
THOMP
KAZAN ...
YOU ...
YOU CAME FOR ME.
SHP

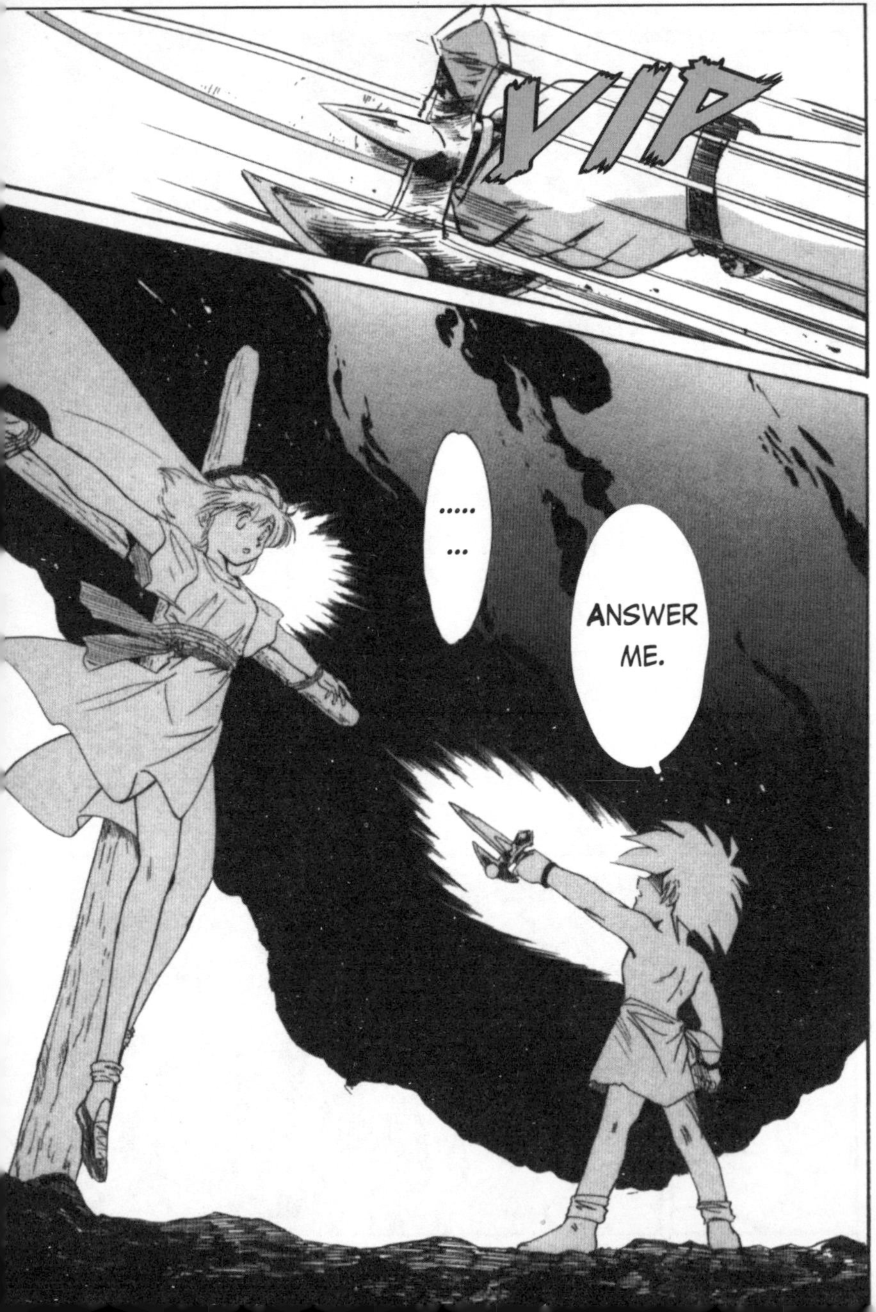
VIP
......
...
ANSWER ME.

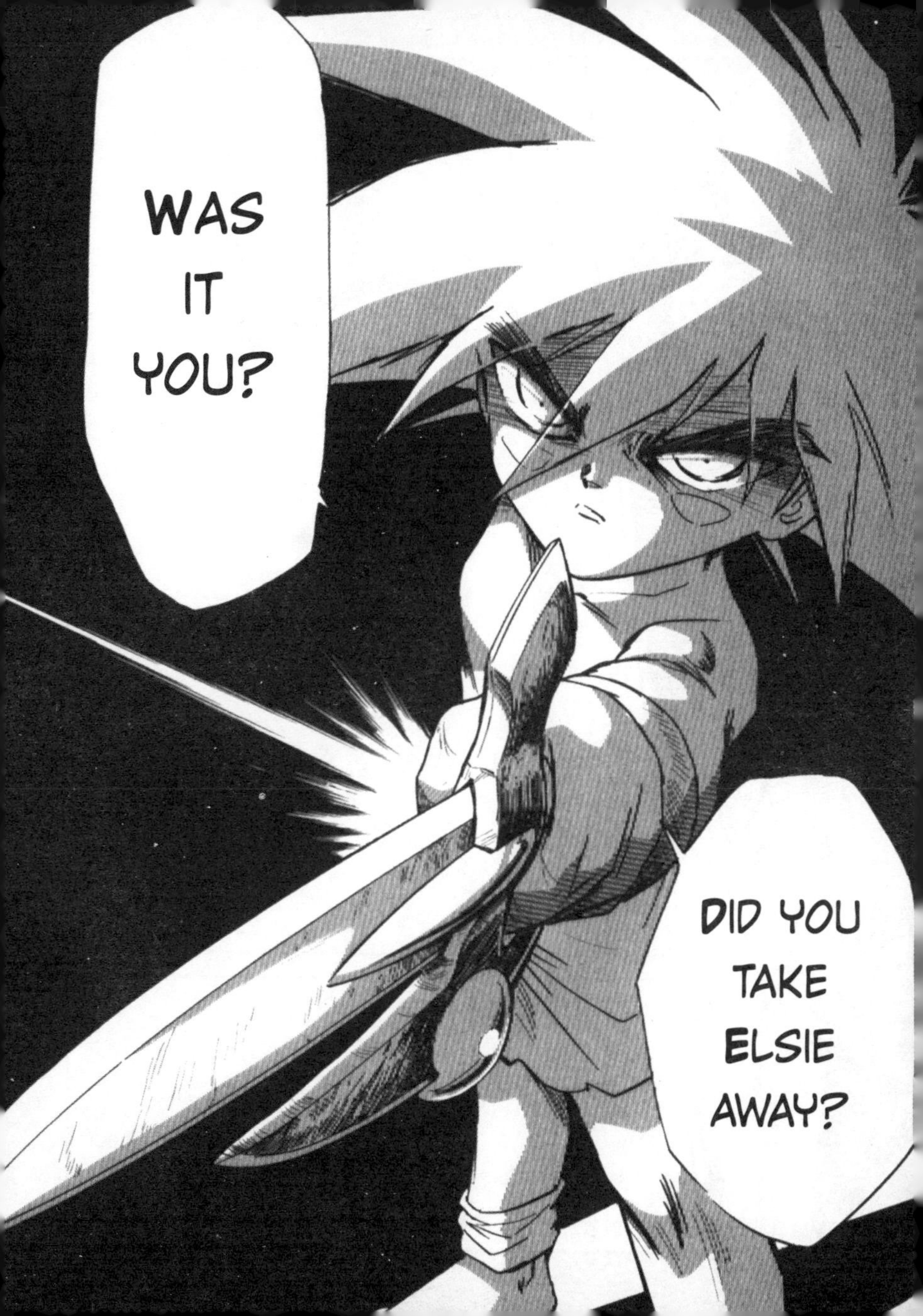
WAS IT YOU?
DID YOU TAKE ELSIE AWAY?

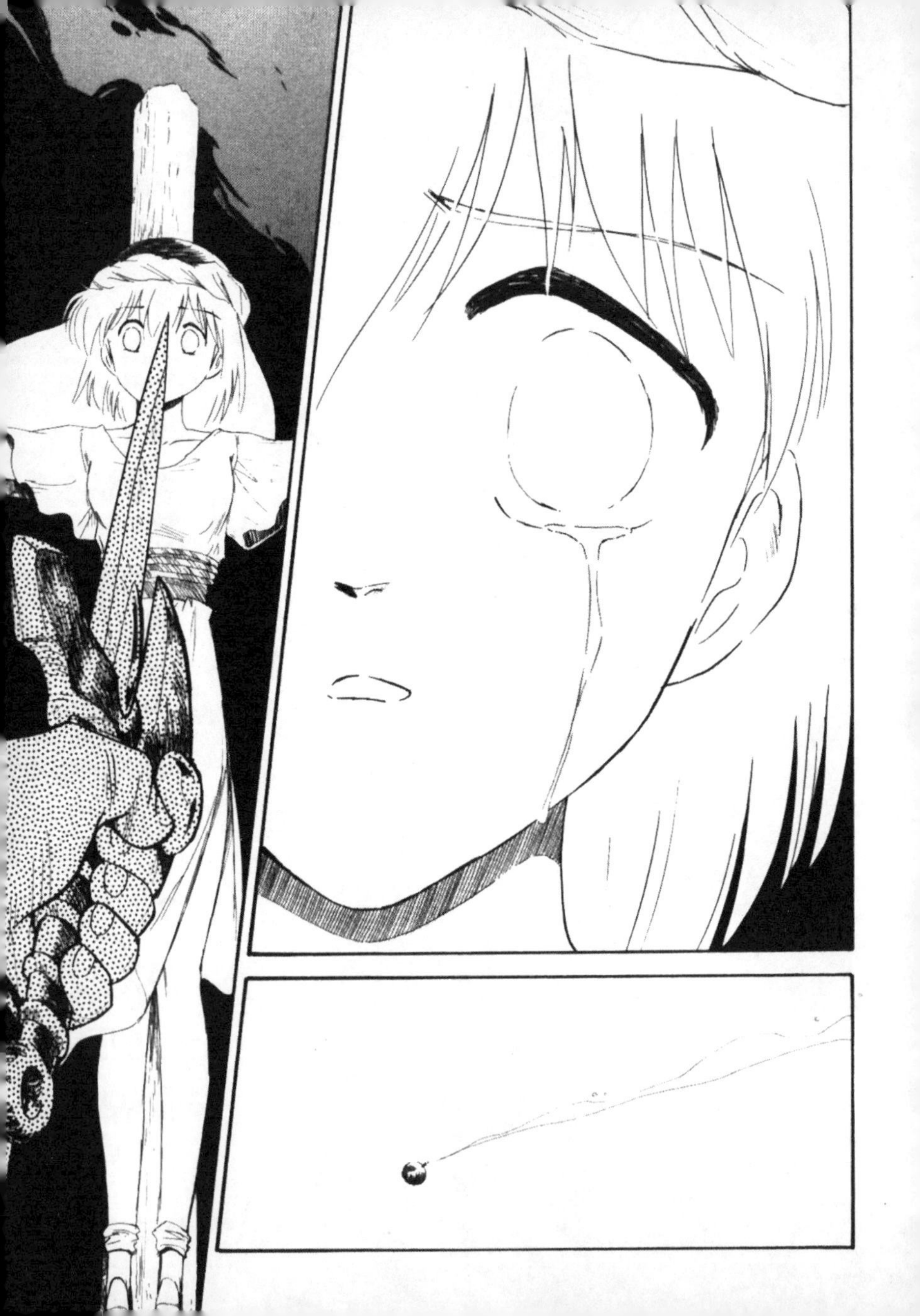

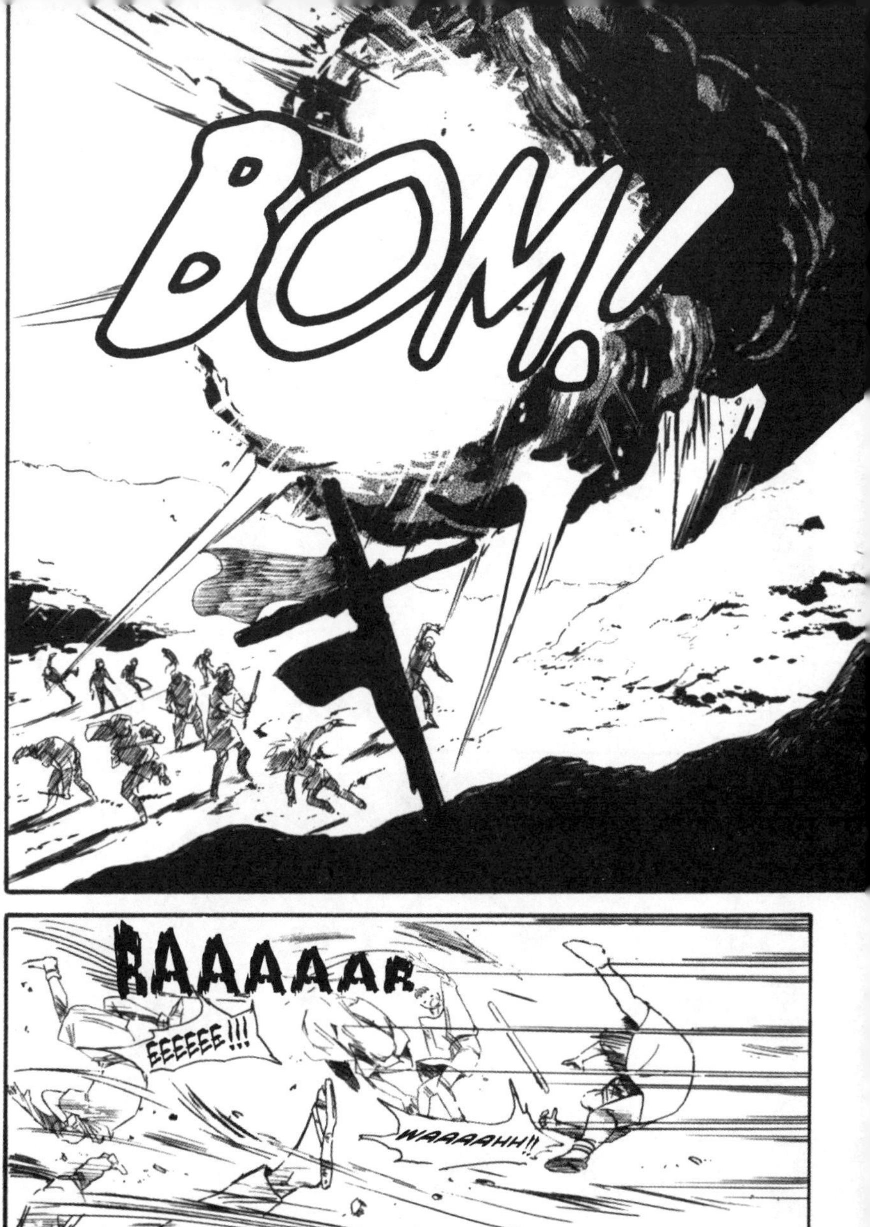
BOM!
RAAAAAR
EEEEEE!!!
WAAAAHH!!

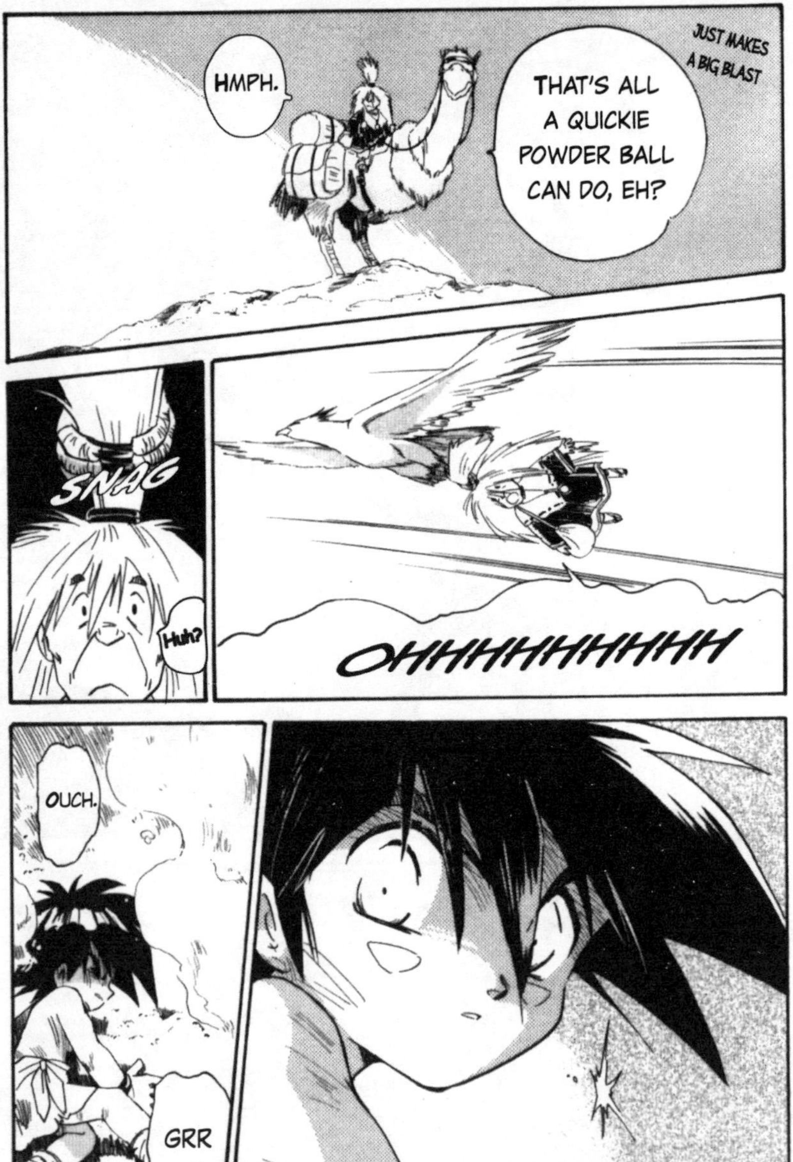
JUST MAKES A BIG BLAST
THAT'S ALL A QUICKIE POWDER BALL CAN DO, EH?
HMPH.
OHHHHHHHHHHH
SNAG
Huh?
OUCH.
GRR ...

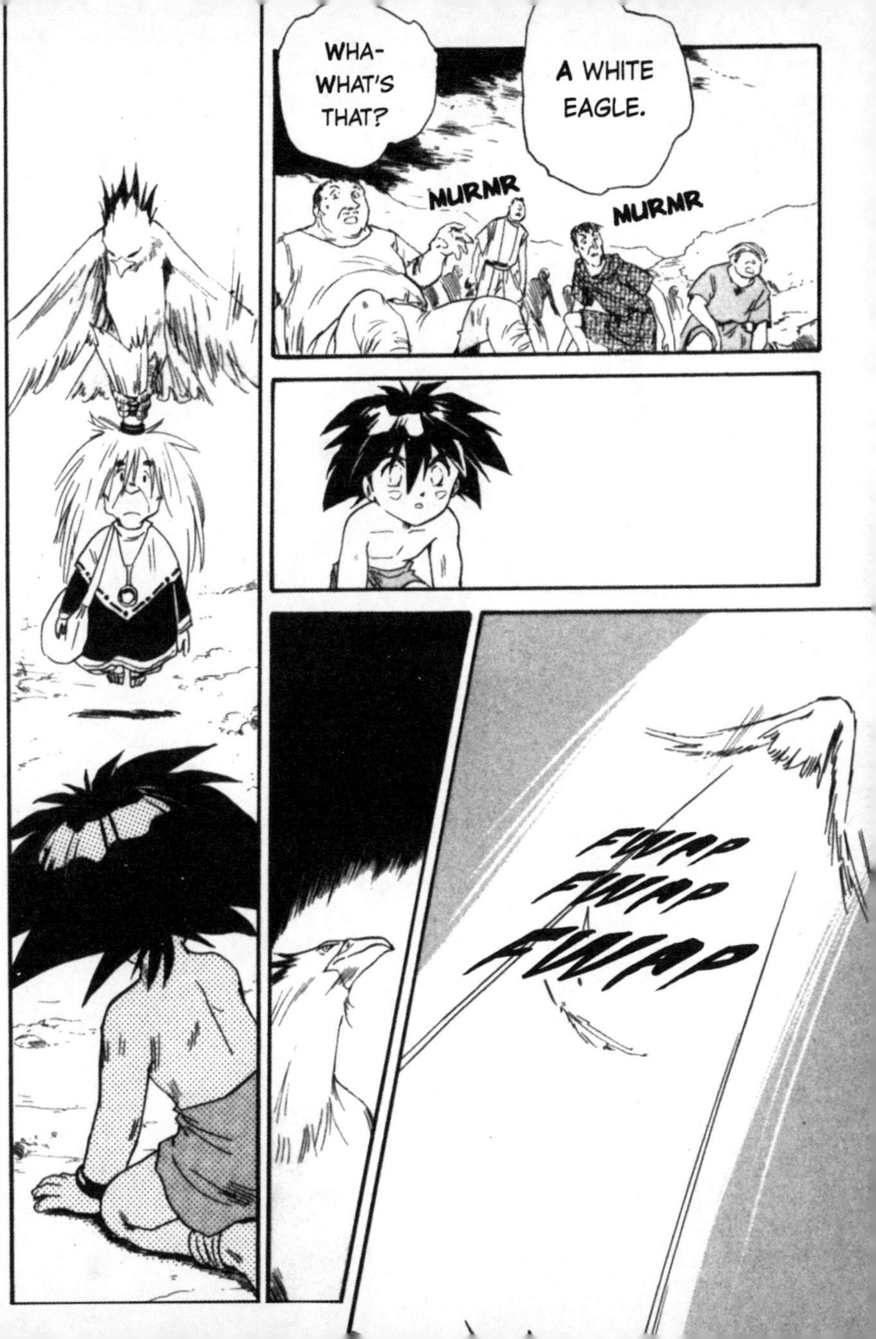
A WHITE EAGLE.
WHA- WHAT'S THAT?
MURMR
MURMR
FWAP FWAP FWAP

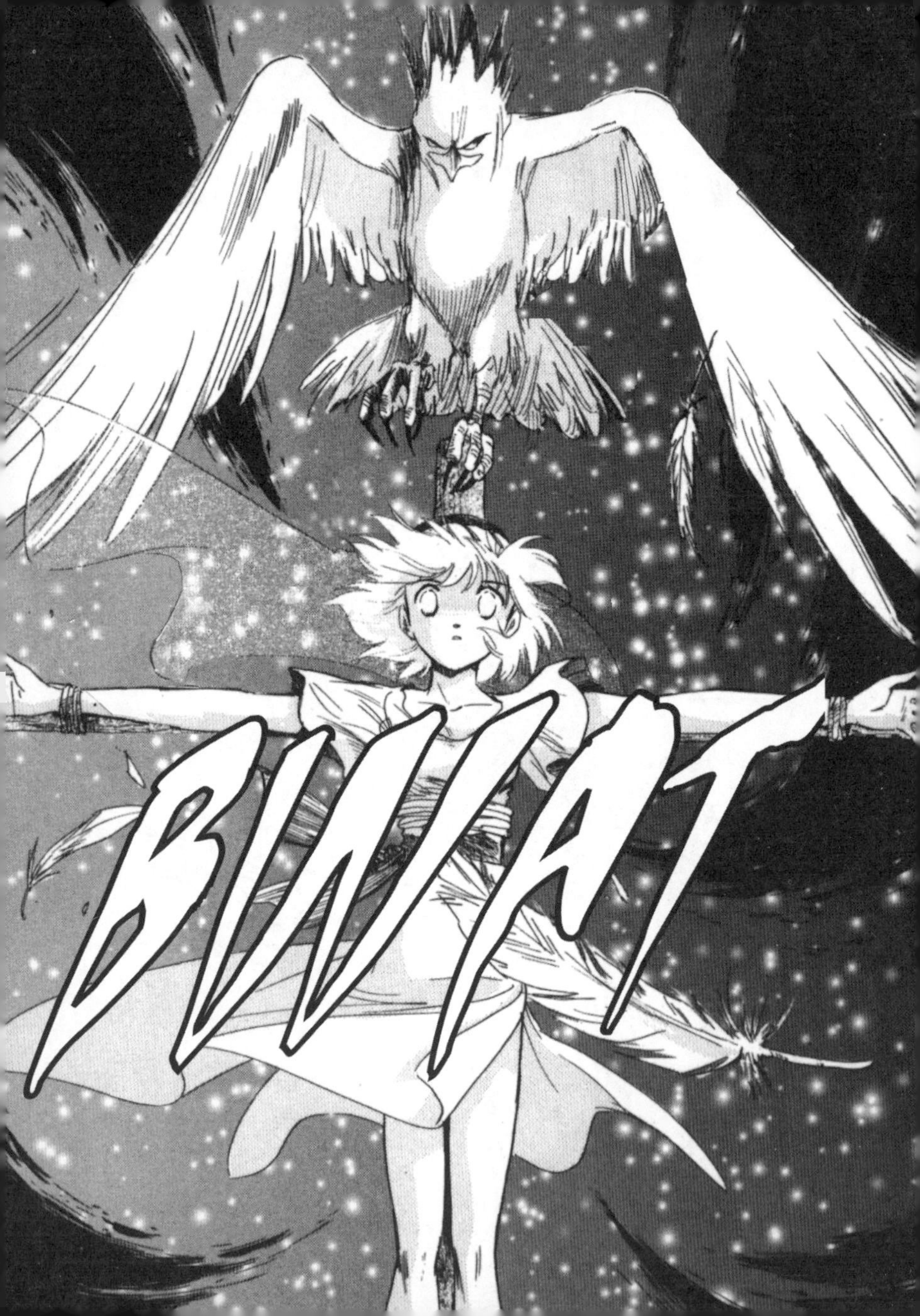
BWAT

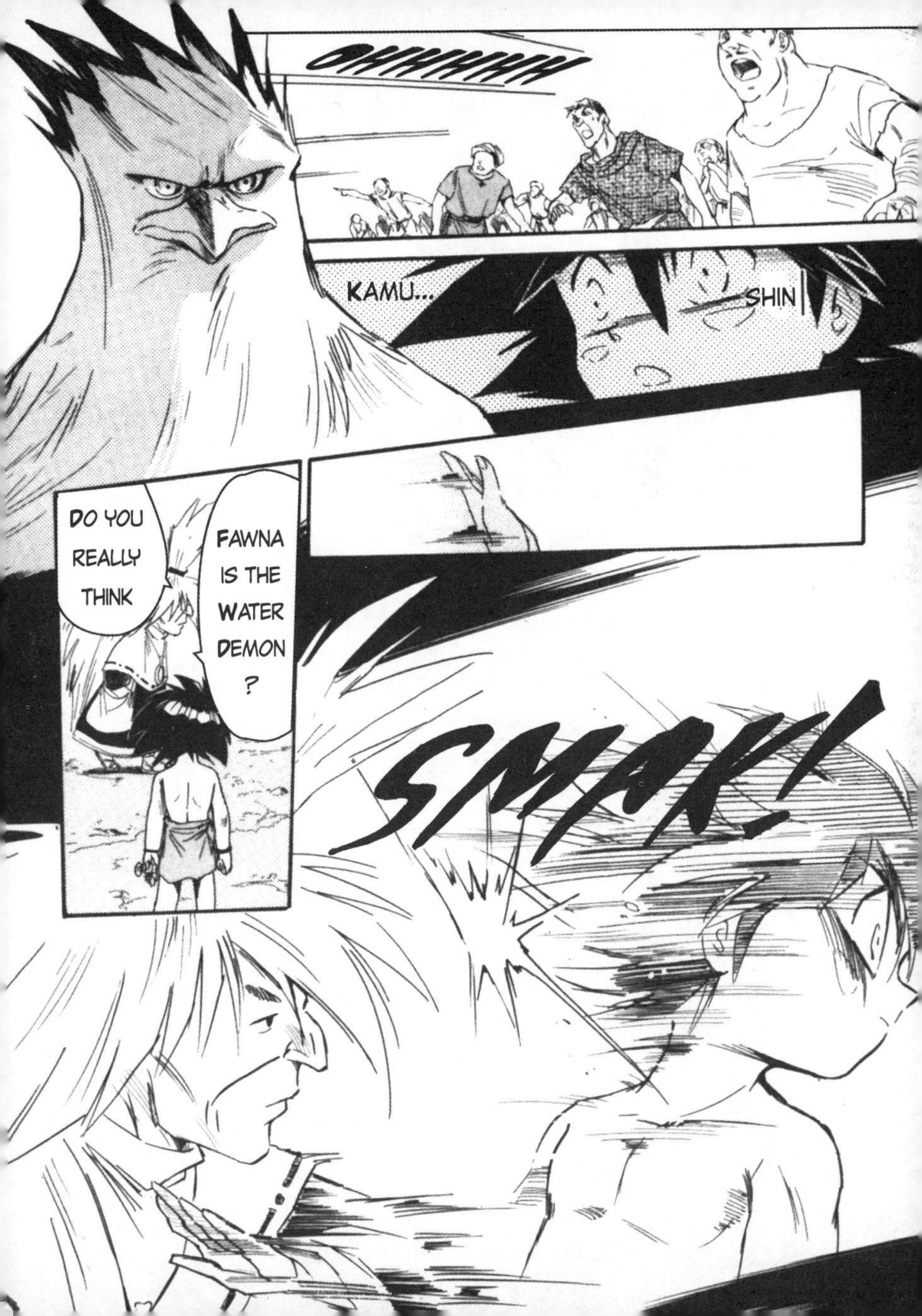
OHHHHHH
KAMU...
SHIN
DO YOU REALLY THINK
FAWNA IS THE WATER DEMON ?
SMAK!

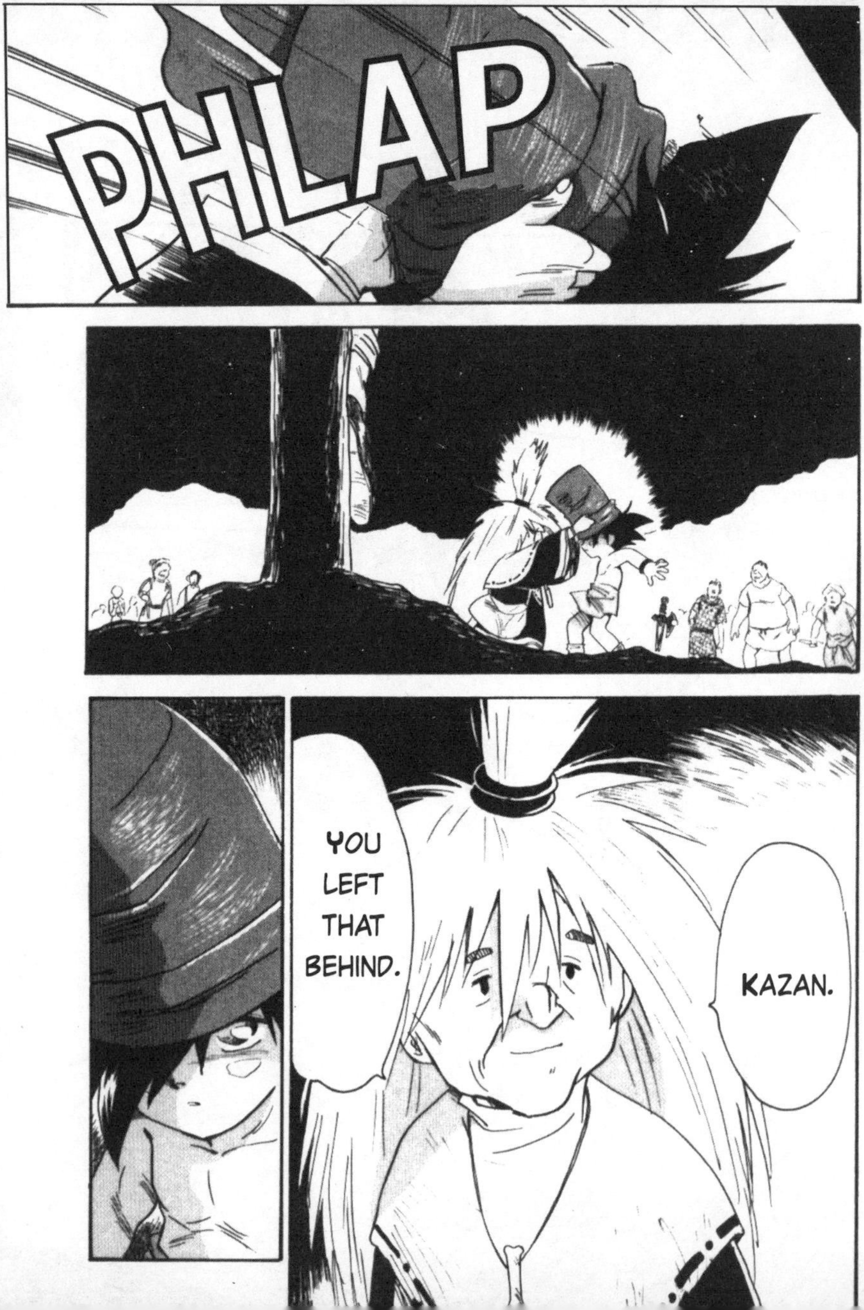
PHLAP
YOU LEFT THAT BEHIND.
KAZAN.

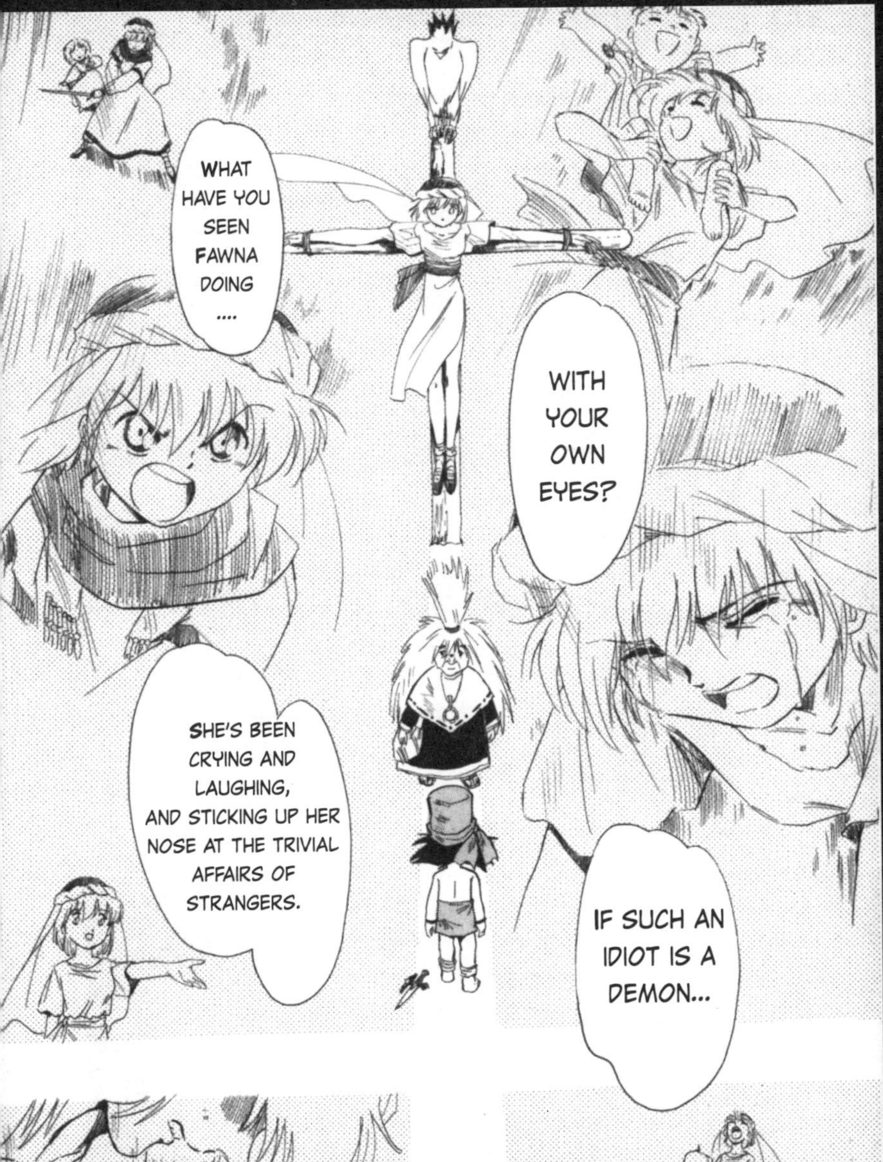
WHAT HAVE YOU SEEN FAWNA DOING ....
WITH YOUR OWN EYES?
SHE'S BEEN CRYING AND LAUGHING, AND STICKING UP HER NOSE AT THE TRIVIAL AFFAIRS OF STRANGERS.
IF SUCH AN IDIOT IS A DEMON...

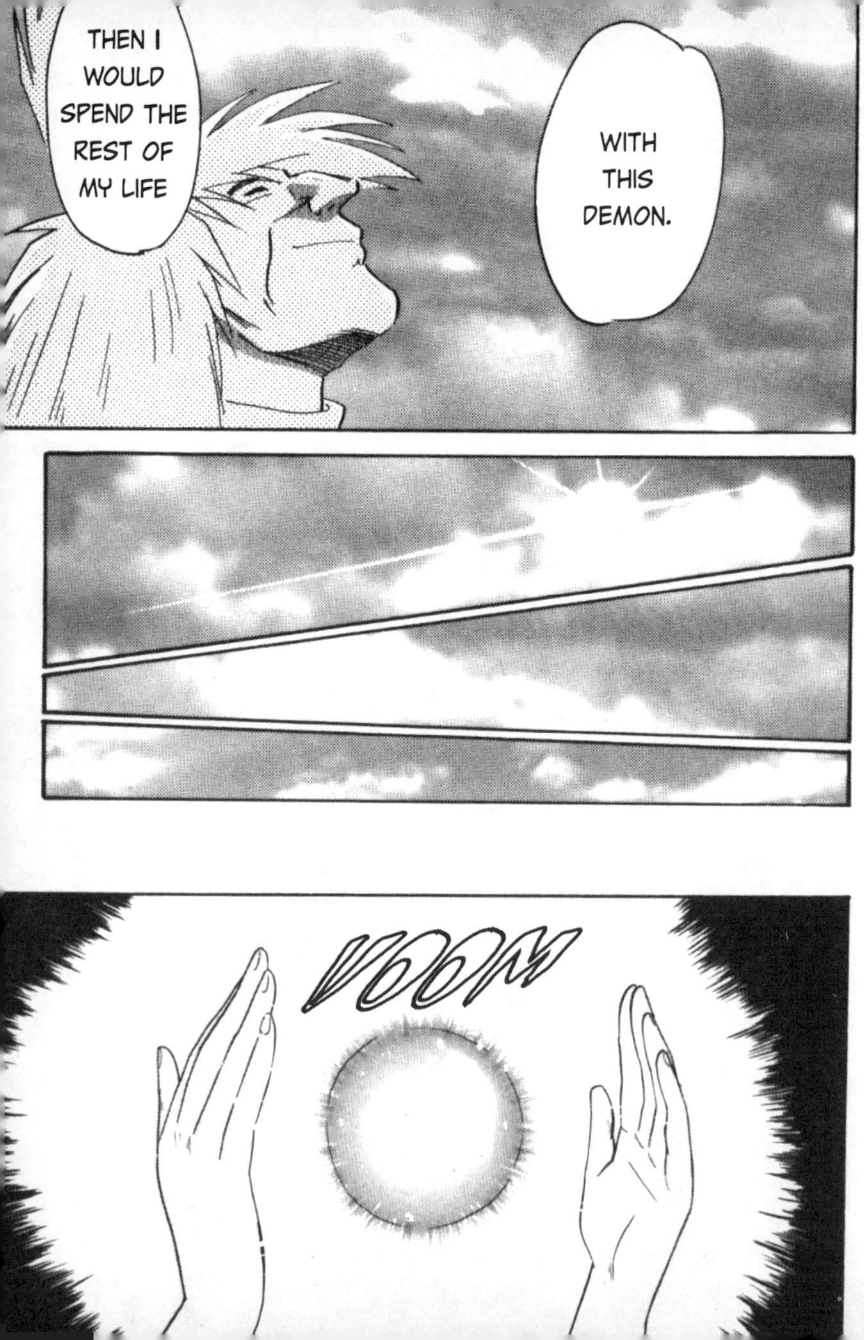
THEN I WOULD SPEND THE REST OF MY LIFE
WITH THIS DEMON.
VOOM

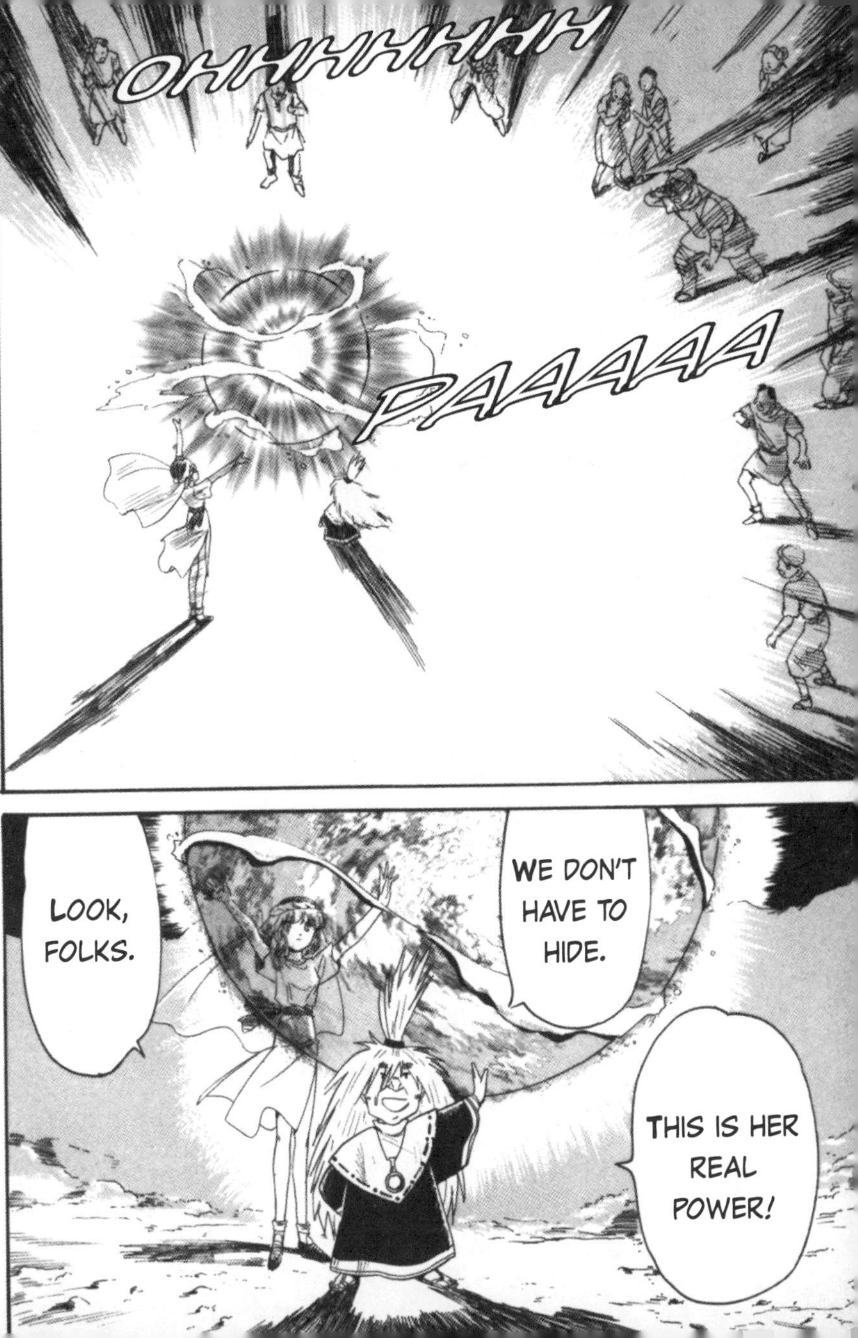
OHHHHHHHH
PAAAAAA
LOOK, FOLKS.
WE DON'T HAVE TO HIDE.
THIS IS HER REAL POWER!

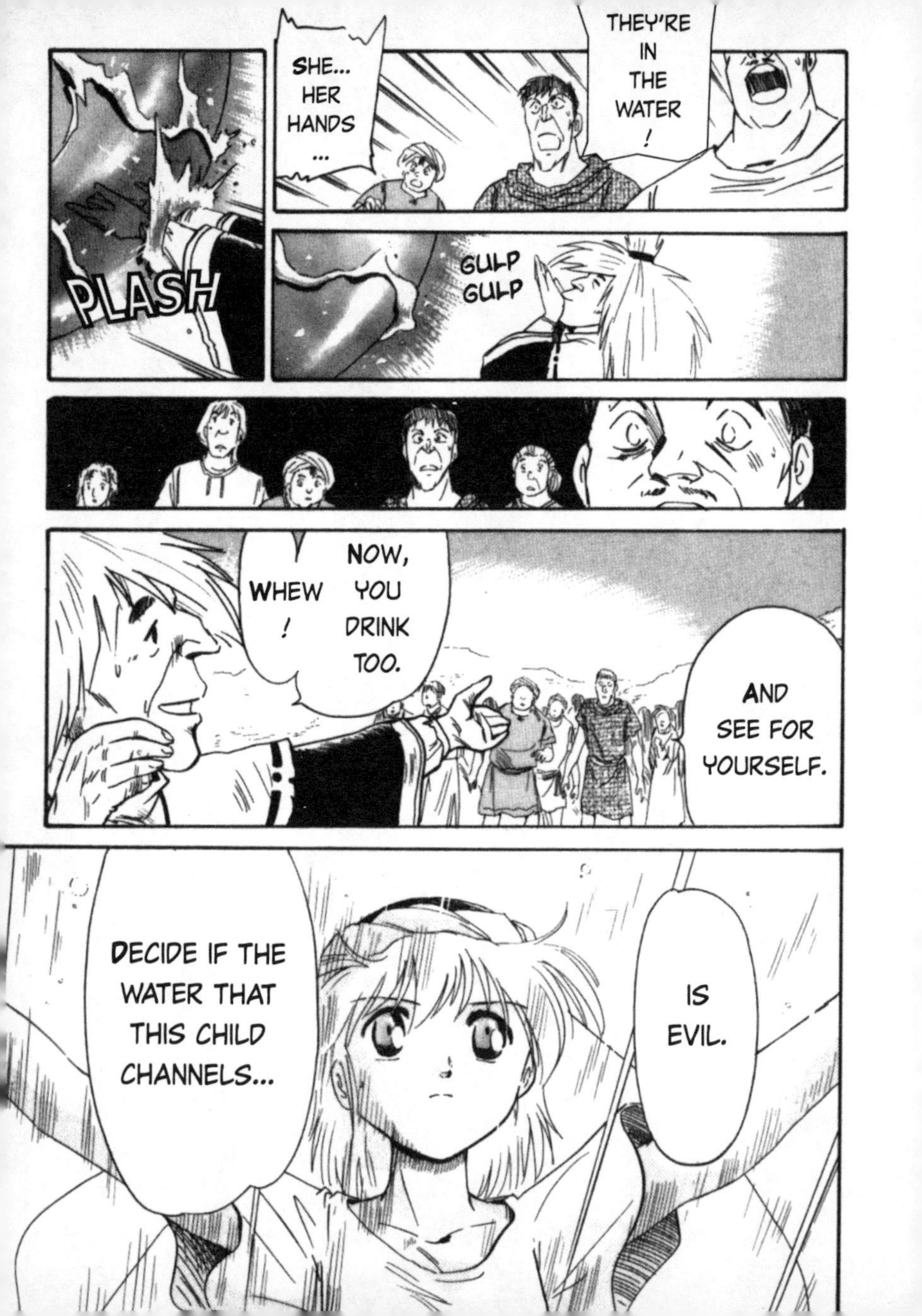
PLASH
SHE... HER HANDS ...
THEY'RE IN THE WATER !
GULP GULP
WHEW !
NOW, YOU DRINK TOO.
AND SEE FOR YOURSELF.
DECIDE IF THE WATER THAT THIS CHILD CHANNELS...
IS EVIL.

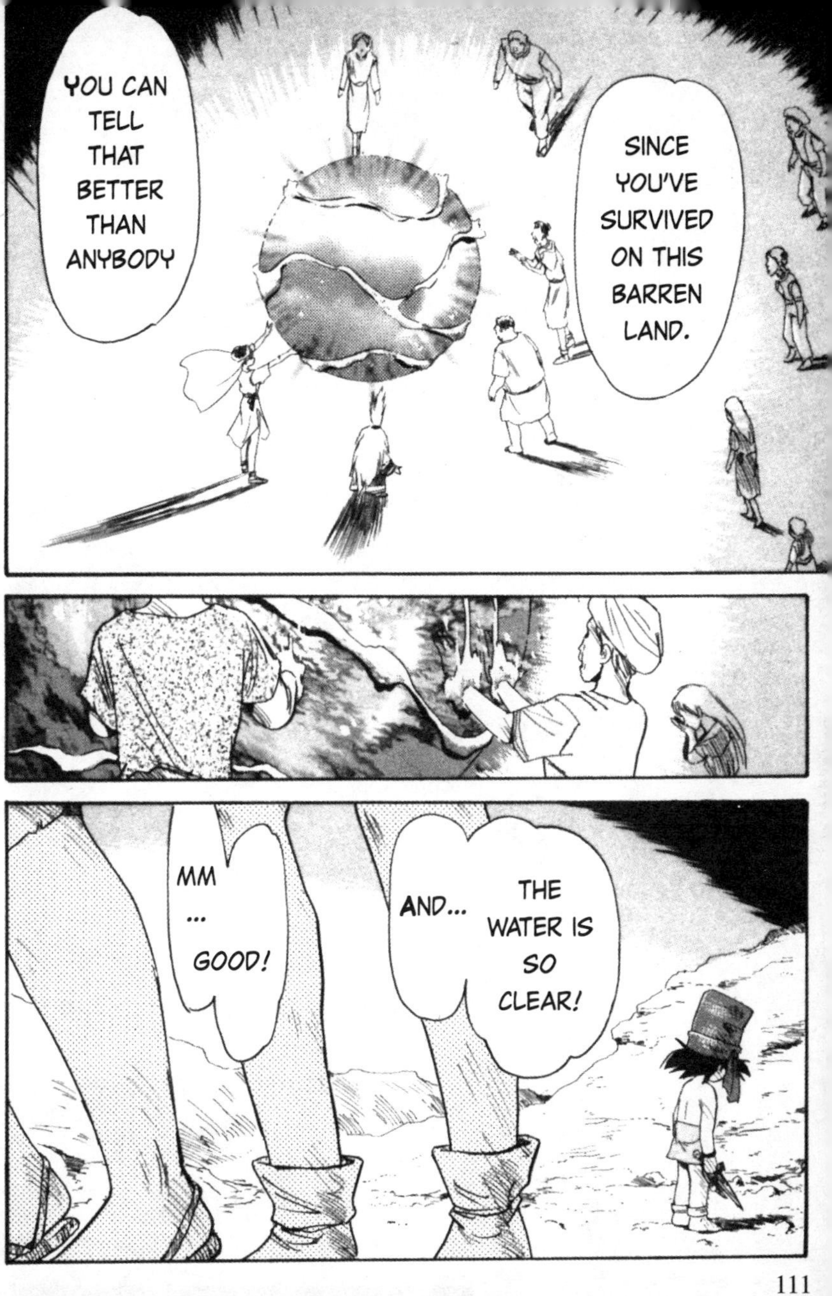
SINCE YOU'VE SURVIVED ON THIS BARREN LAND.
YOU CAN TELL THAT BETTER THAN ANYBODY
THE WATER IS SO CLEAR!
AND...
MM ... GOOD!

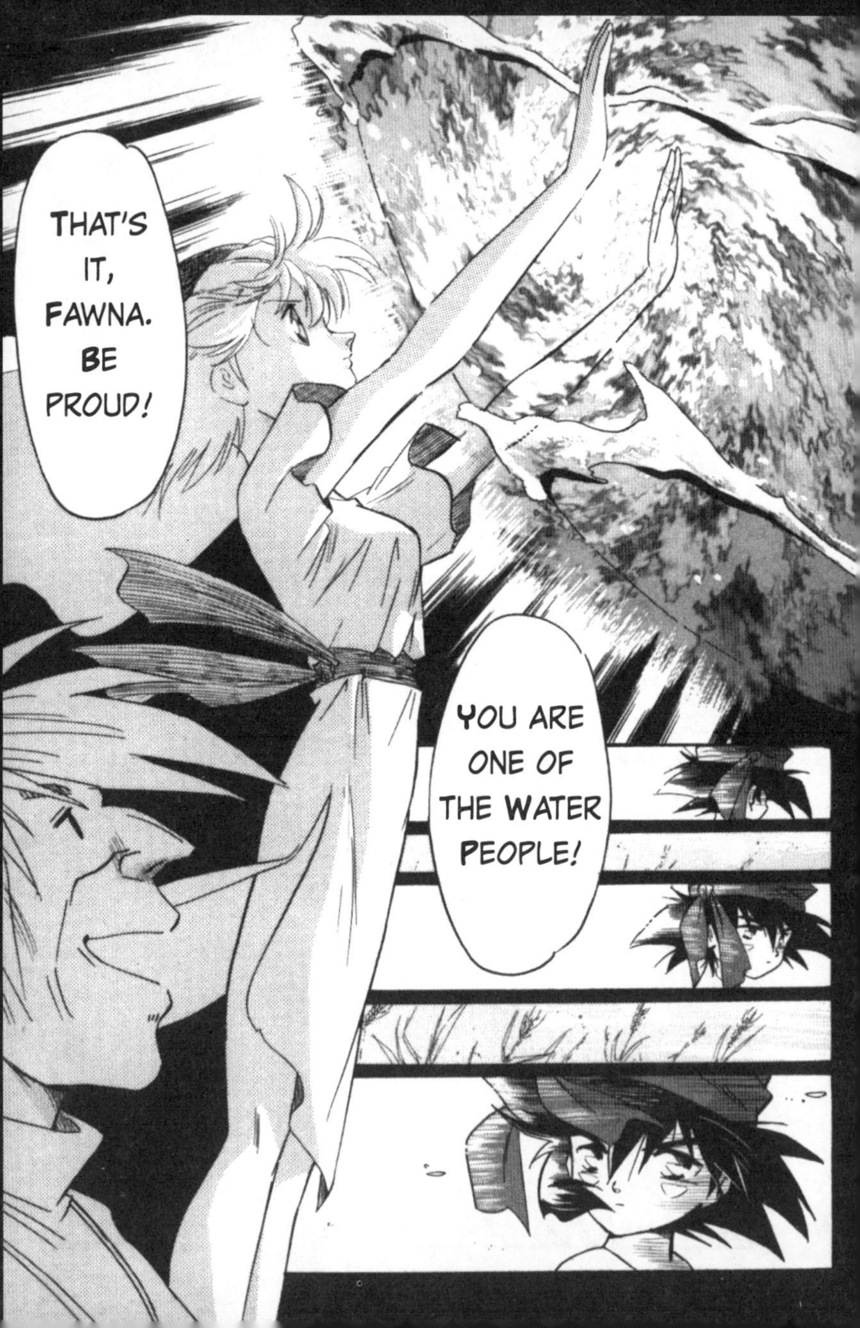
THAT'S IT, FAWNA. BE PROUD!
YOU ARE ONE OF THE WATER PEOPLE!

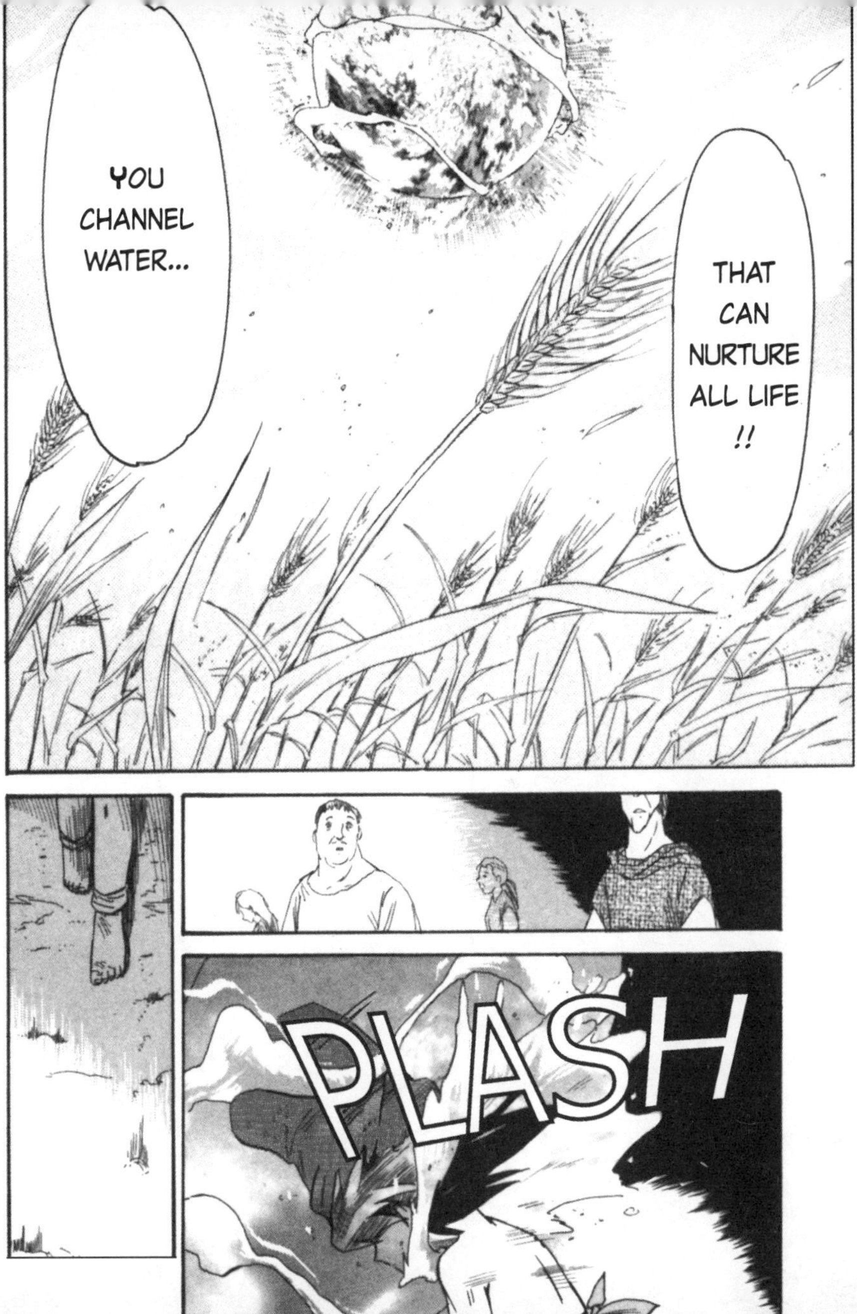
THAT CAN NURTURE ALL LIFE !!
YOU CHANNEL WATER...
PLASH

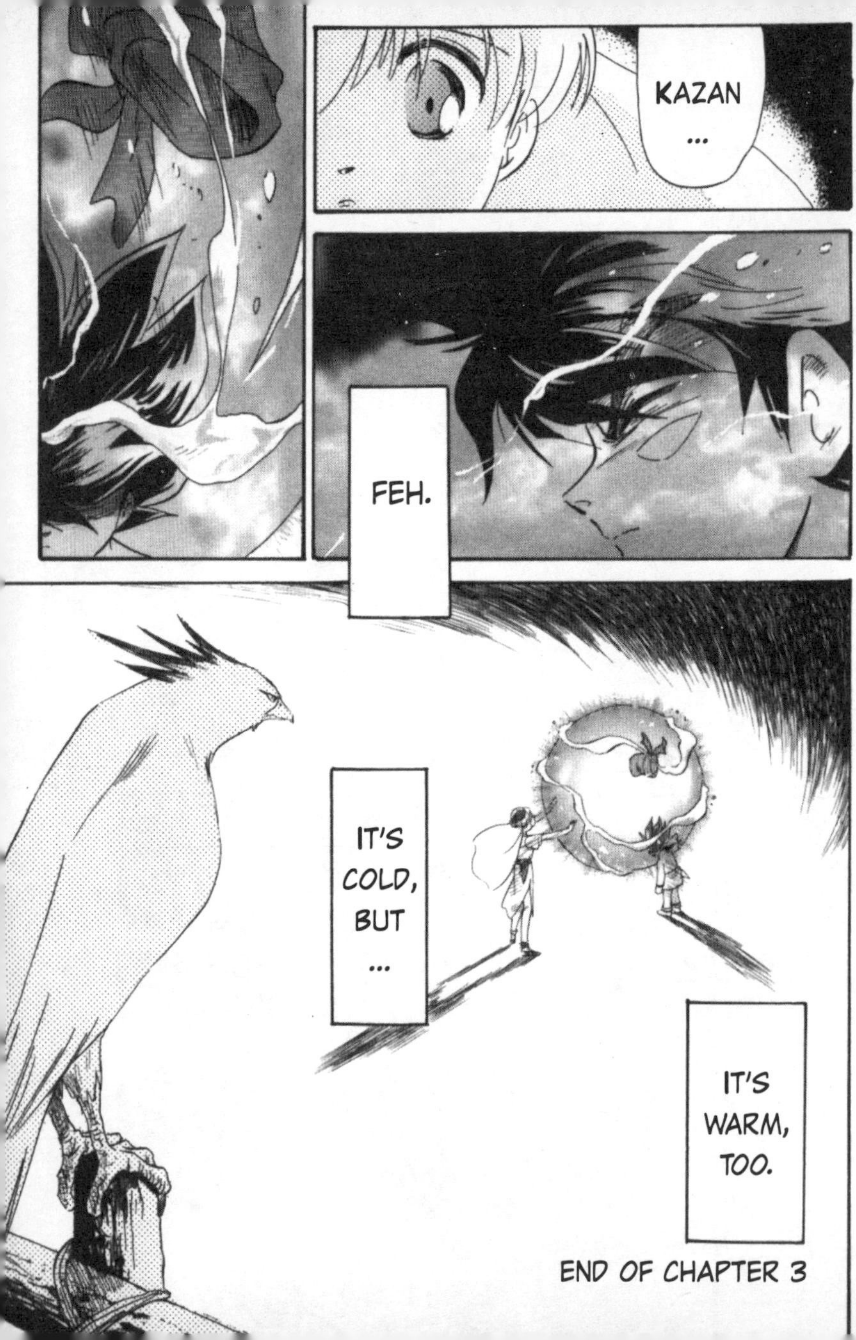
KAZAN
...
FEH.
IT'S COLD, BUT ...
IT'S WARM, TOO.
END OF CHAPTER 3

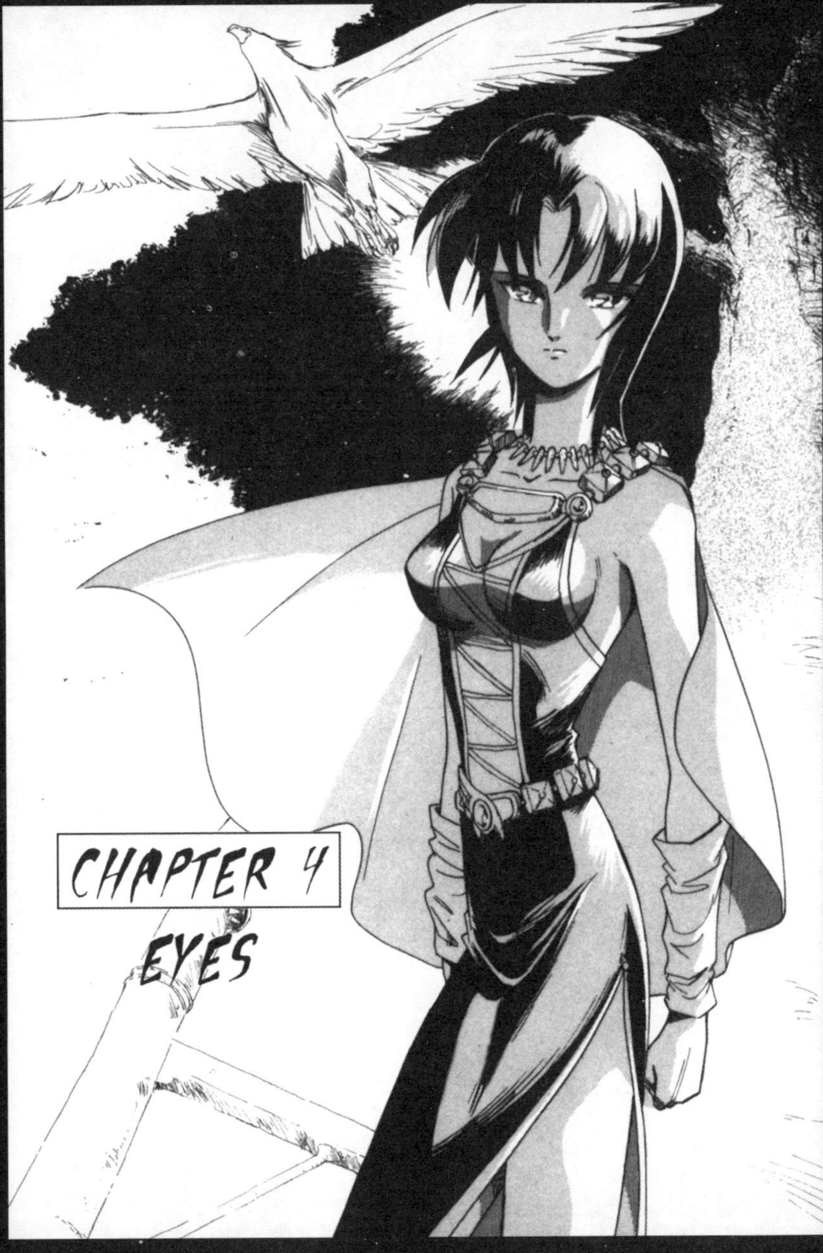
CHAPTER 4
EYES

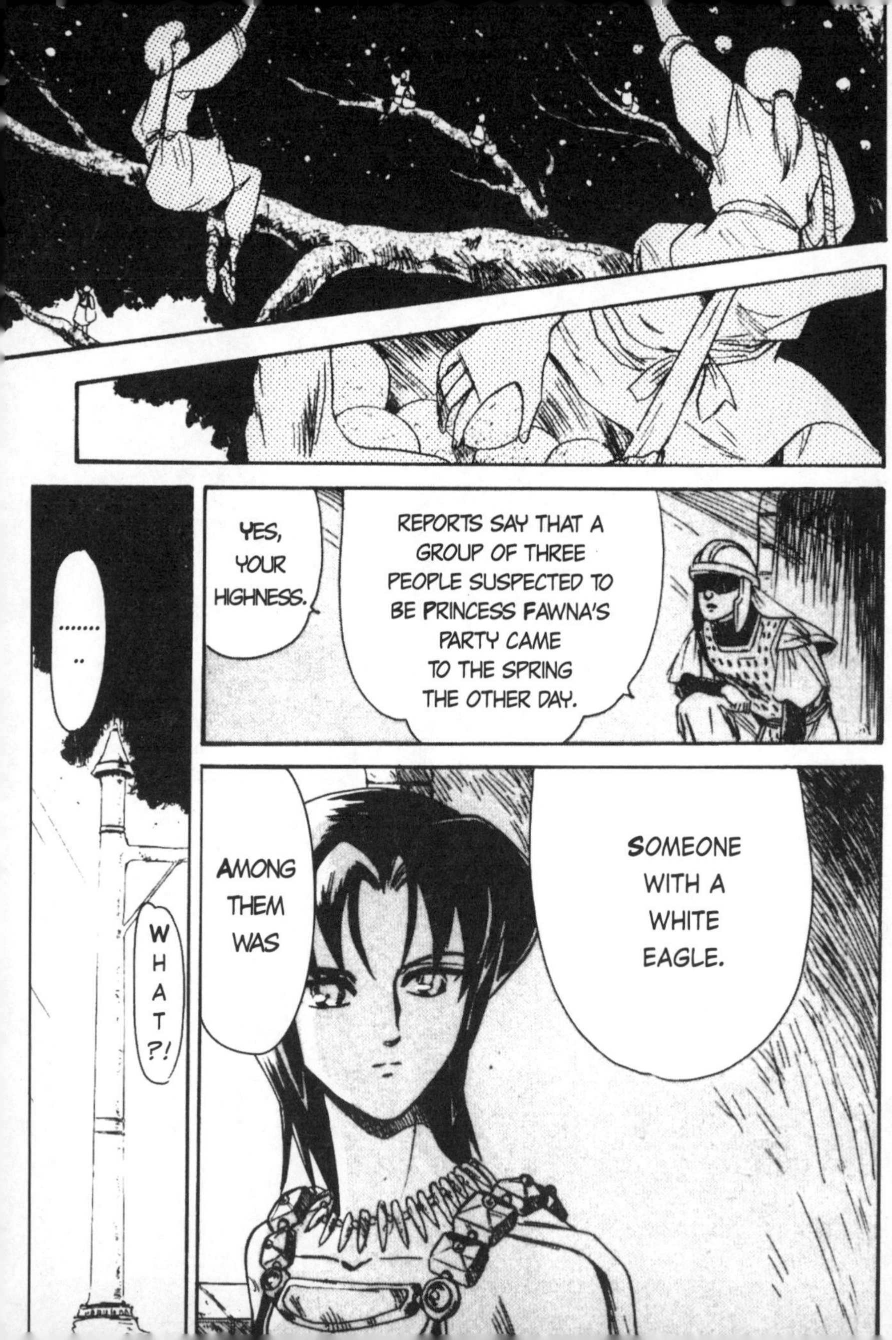
YES, YOUR HIGHNESS.
REPORTS SAY THAT A GROUP OF THREE PEOPLE SUSPECTED TO BE PRINCESS FAWNA'S PARTY CAME TO THE SPRING THE OTHER DAY.
....
AMONG THEM WAS
SOMEONE WITH A WHITE EAGLE.
WHAT?!

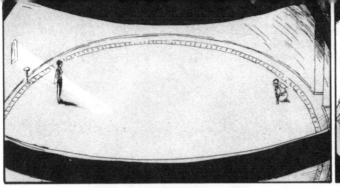

CAPTURE THAT WHITE EAGLE.

MAKE SURE...

TO TAKE IT ALIVE.

YES, MADAM.

WHAT SHALL I DO WITH ITS OWNER?

......

KILL HIM.

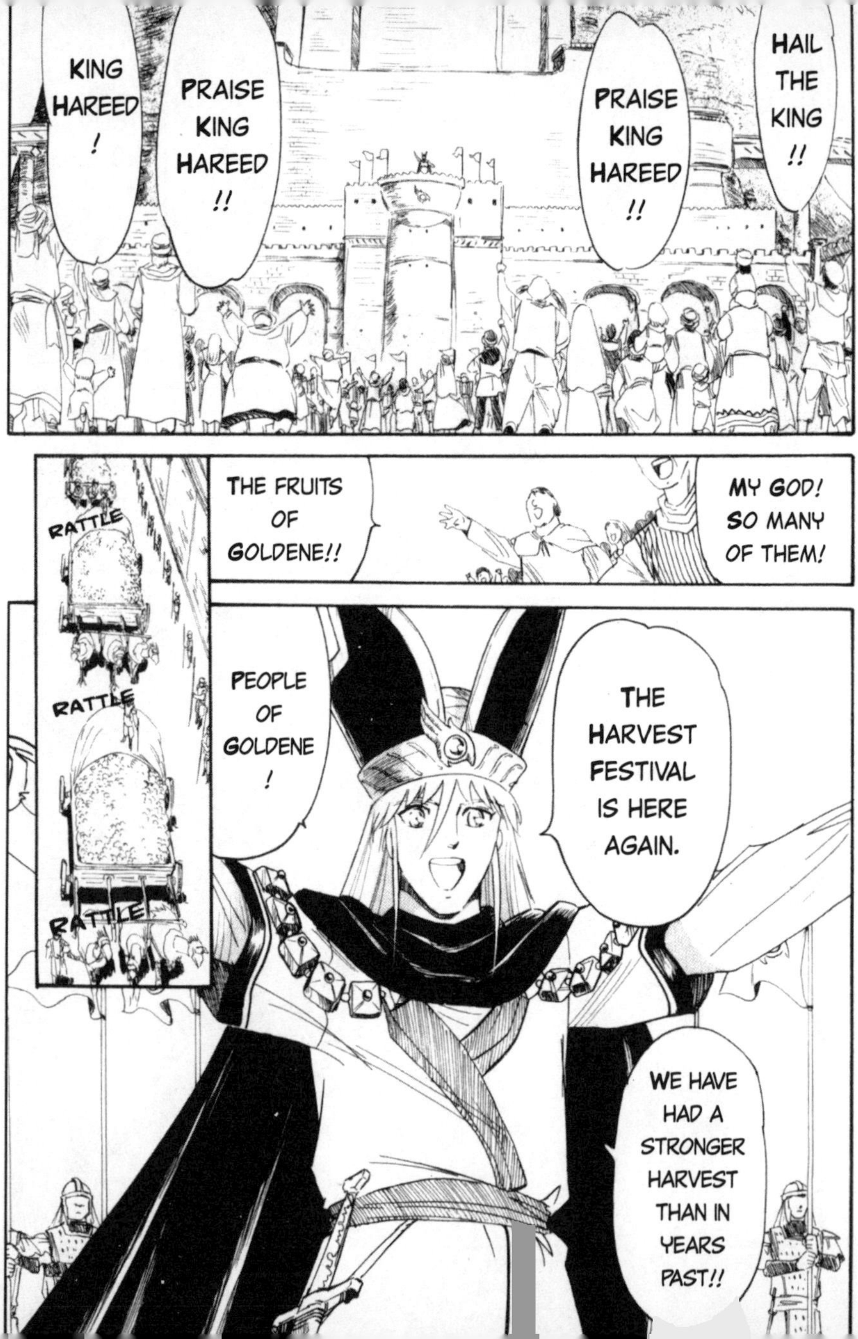
HAIL THE KING!!
PRAISE KING HAREED!!
PRAISE KING HAREED!!
KING HAREED!
MY GOD! SO MANY OF THEM!
THE FRUITS OF GOLDENE!!
RATTLE
RATTLE
RATTLE
THE HARVEST FESTIVAL IS HERE AGAIN.
PEOPLE OF GOLDENE!
WE HAVE HAD A STRONGER HARVEST THAN IN YEARS PAST!!

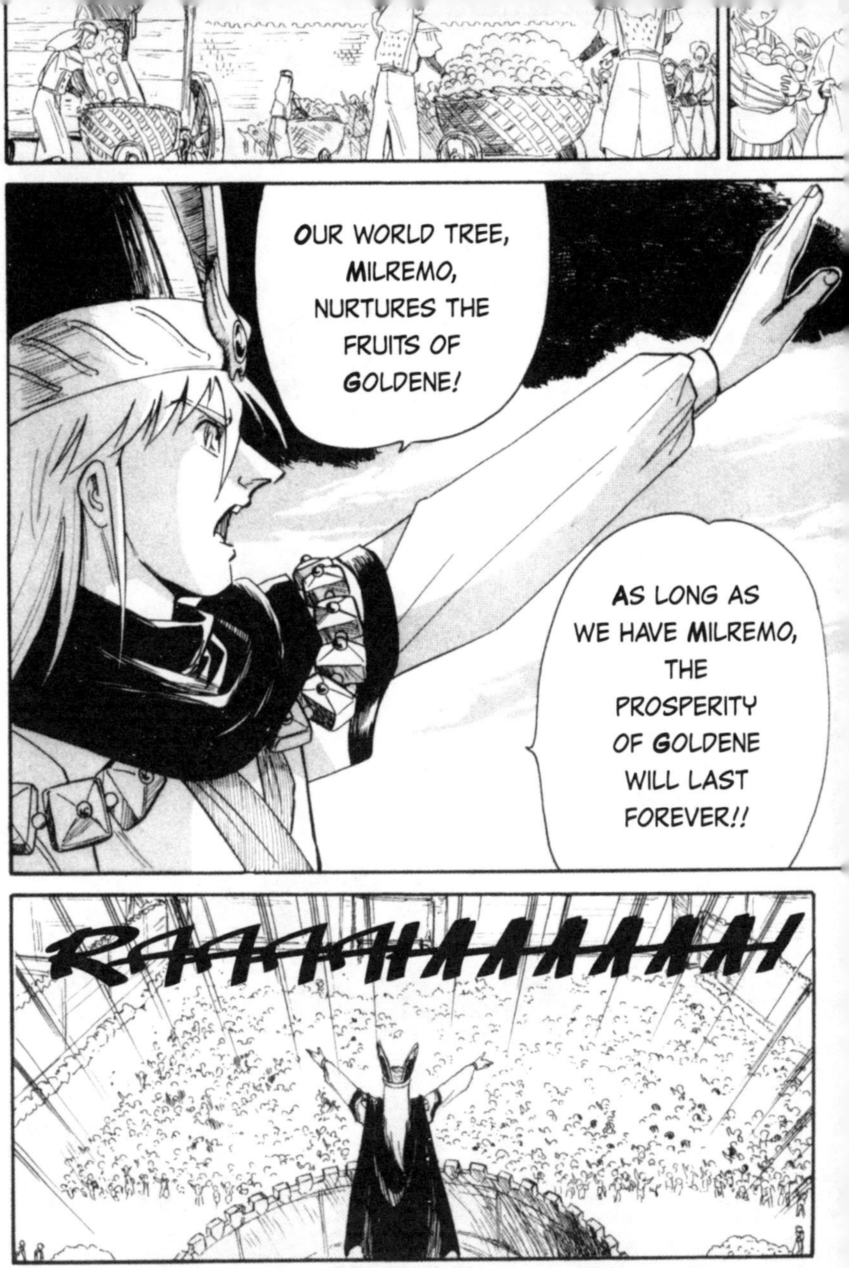
OUR WORLD TREE, MILREMO, NURTURES THE FRUITS OF GOLDENE!
AS LONG AS WE HAVE MILREMO, THE PROSPERITY OF GOLDENE WILL LAST FOREVER!!
RAAAAHHAAAAAAAH

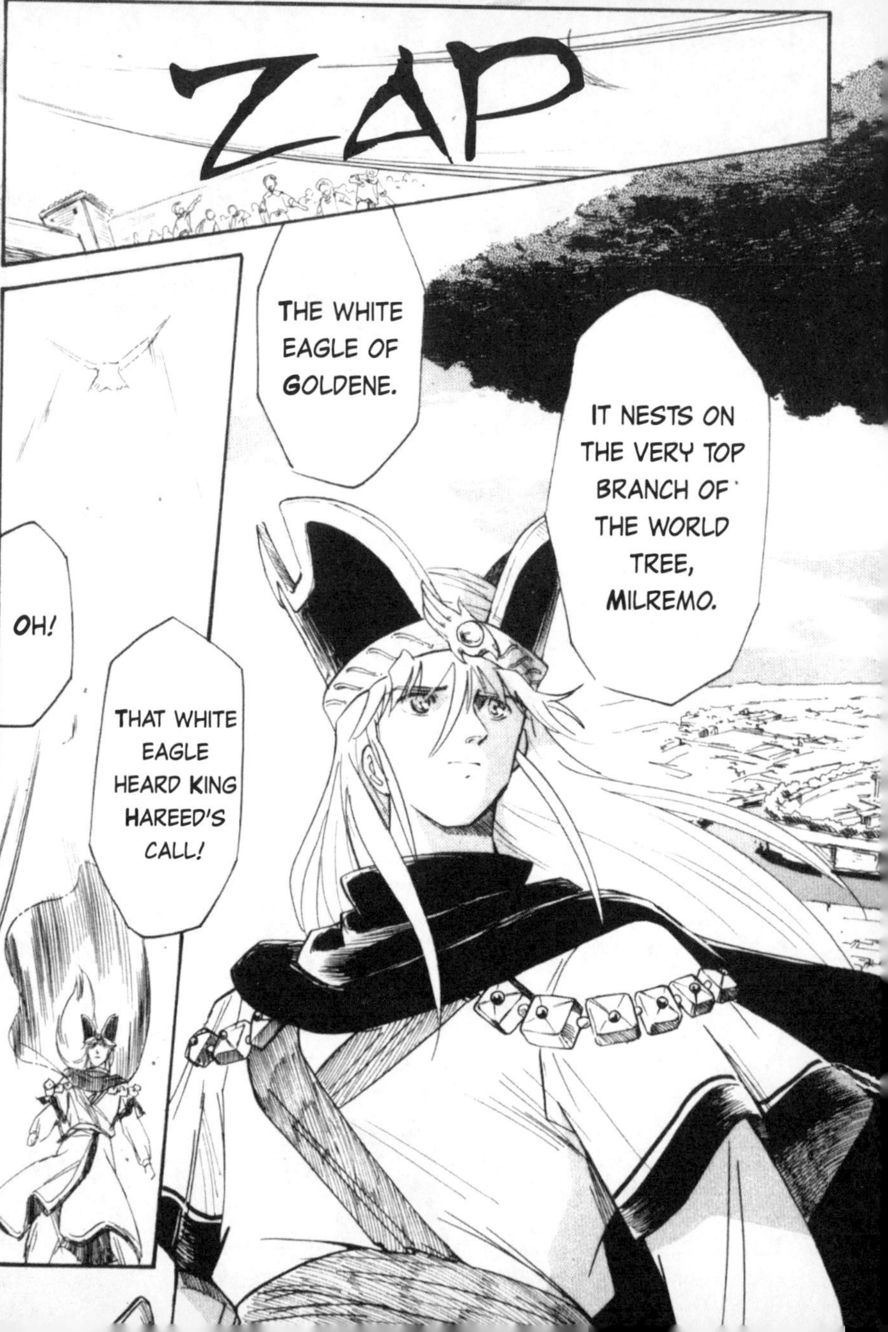
ZAP
THE WHITE EAGLE OF GOLDENE.
IT NESTS ON THE VERY TOP BRANCH OF THE WORLD TREE, MILREMO.
OH!
THAT WHITE EAGLE HEARD KING HAREED'S CALL!

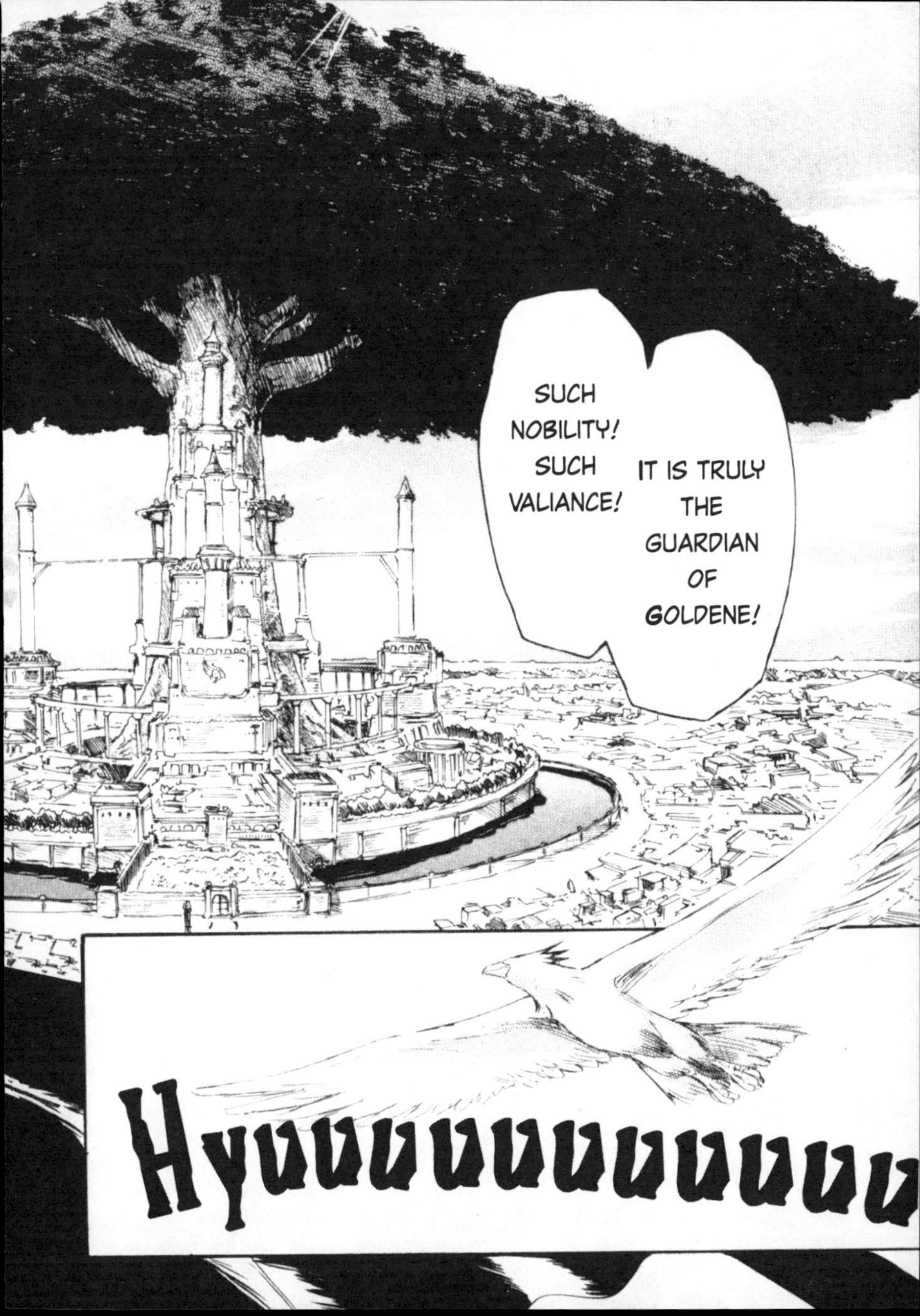
SUCH NOBILITY! SUCH VALIANCE!
IT IS TRULY THE GUARDIAN OF GOLDENE!
Hyuuuuuuuuuuuu

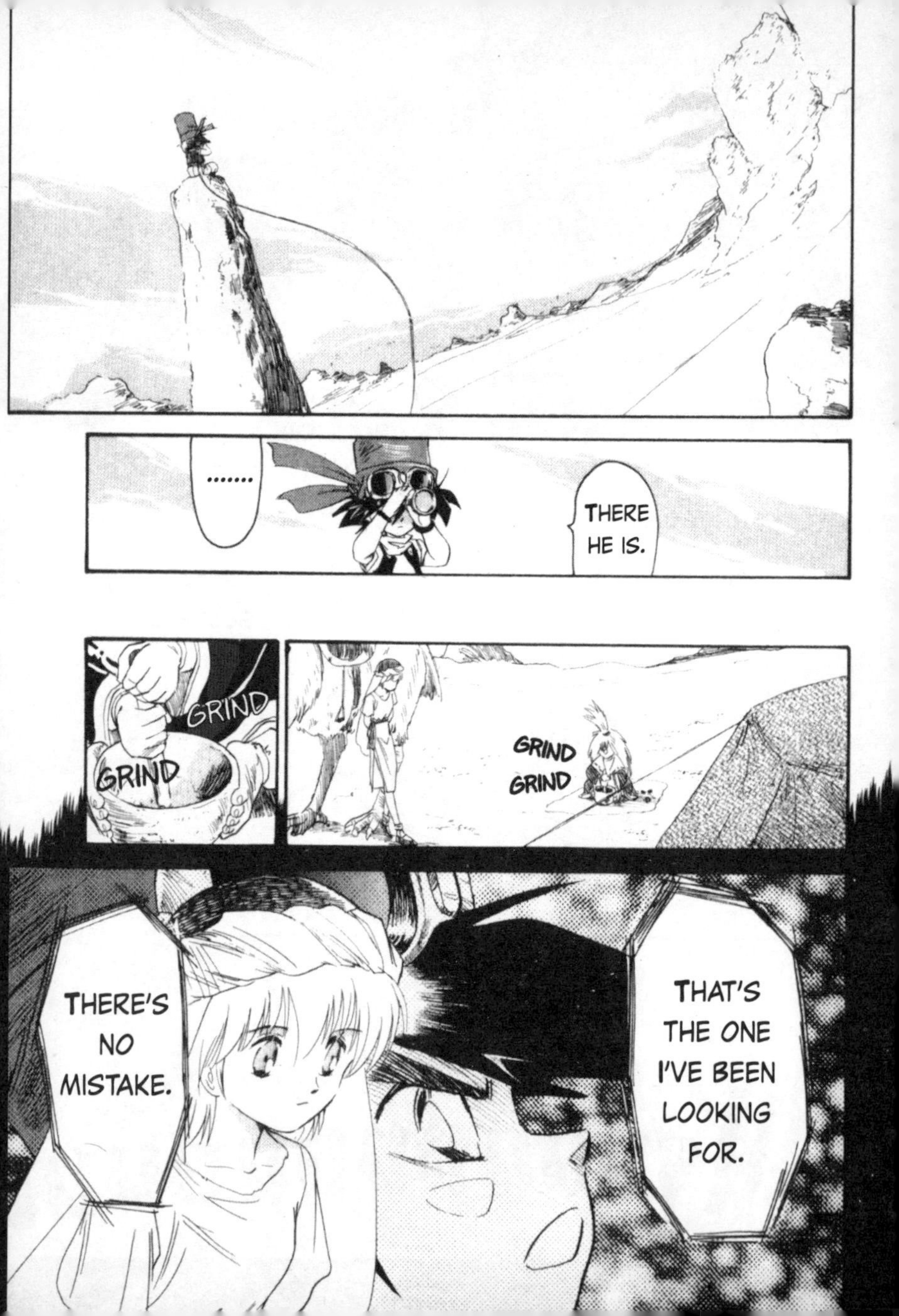

....
THERE HE IS.
GRIND
GRIND
GRIND GRIND
THAT'S THE ONE I'VE BEEN LOOKING FOR.
THERE'S NO MISTAKE.

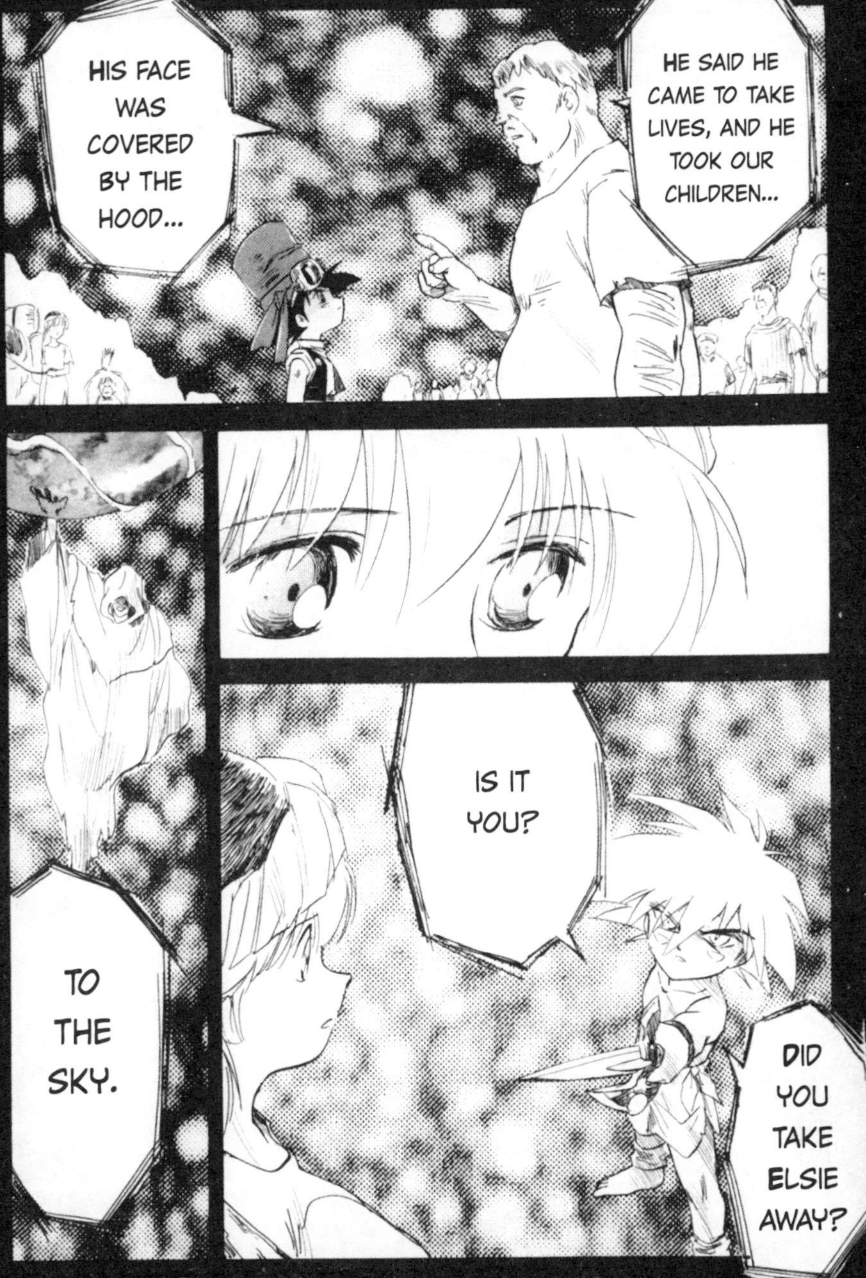
HE SAID HE CAME TO TAKE LIVES, AND HE TOOK OUR CHILDREN...
HIS FACE WAS COVERED BY THE HOOD...
DID YOU TAKE ELSIE AWAY?
IS IT YOU?
TO THE SKY.

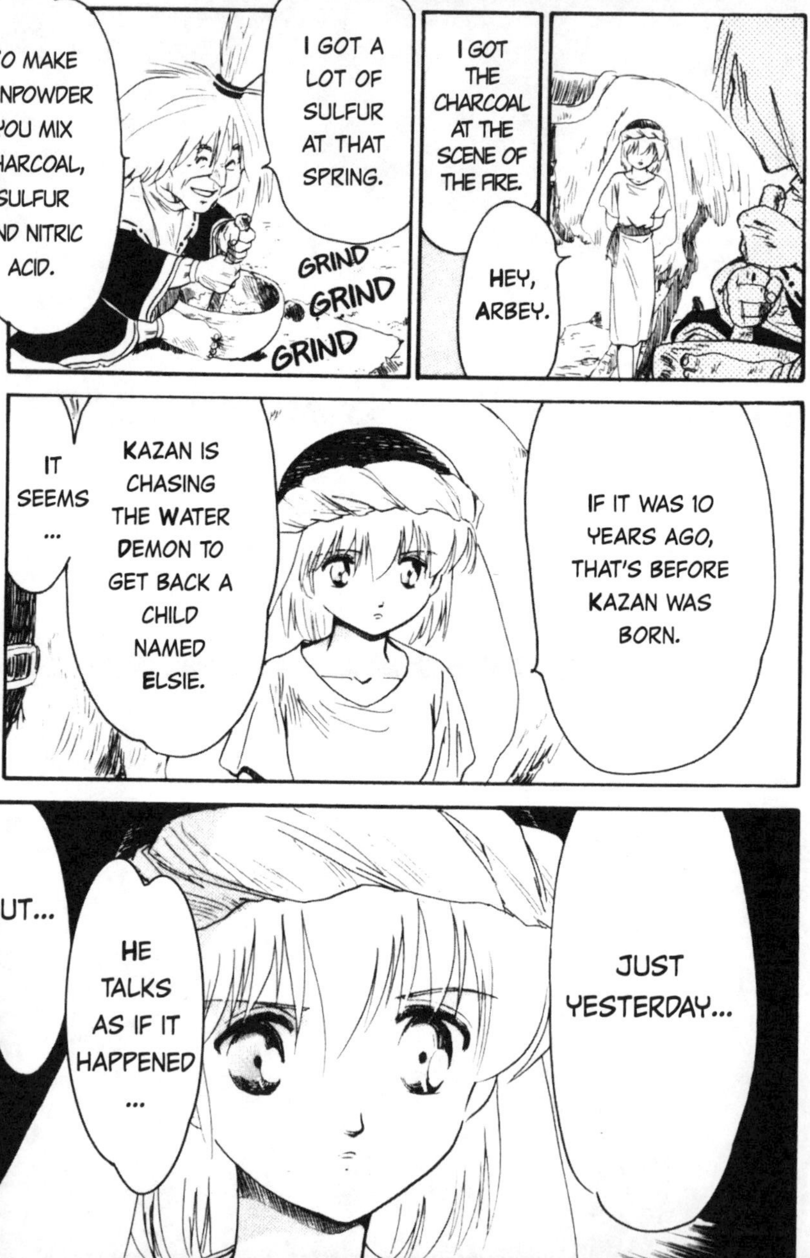
TO MAKE GUNPOWDER YOU MIX CHARCOAL, SULFUR AND NITRIC ACID.
I GOT A LOT OF SULFUR AT THAT SPRING.
GRIND GRIND GRIND
I GOT THE CHARCOAL AT THE SCENE OF THE FIRE.
HEY, ARBEY.
IT SEEMS ...
KAZAN IS CHASING THE WATER DEMON TO GET BACK A CHILD NAMED ELSIE.
IF IT WAS 10 YEARS AGO, THAT'S BEFORE KAZAN WAS BORN.
BUT...
HE TALKS AS IF IT HAPPENED ...
JUST YESTERDAY...

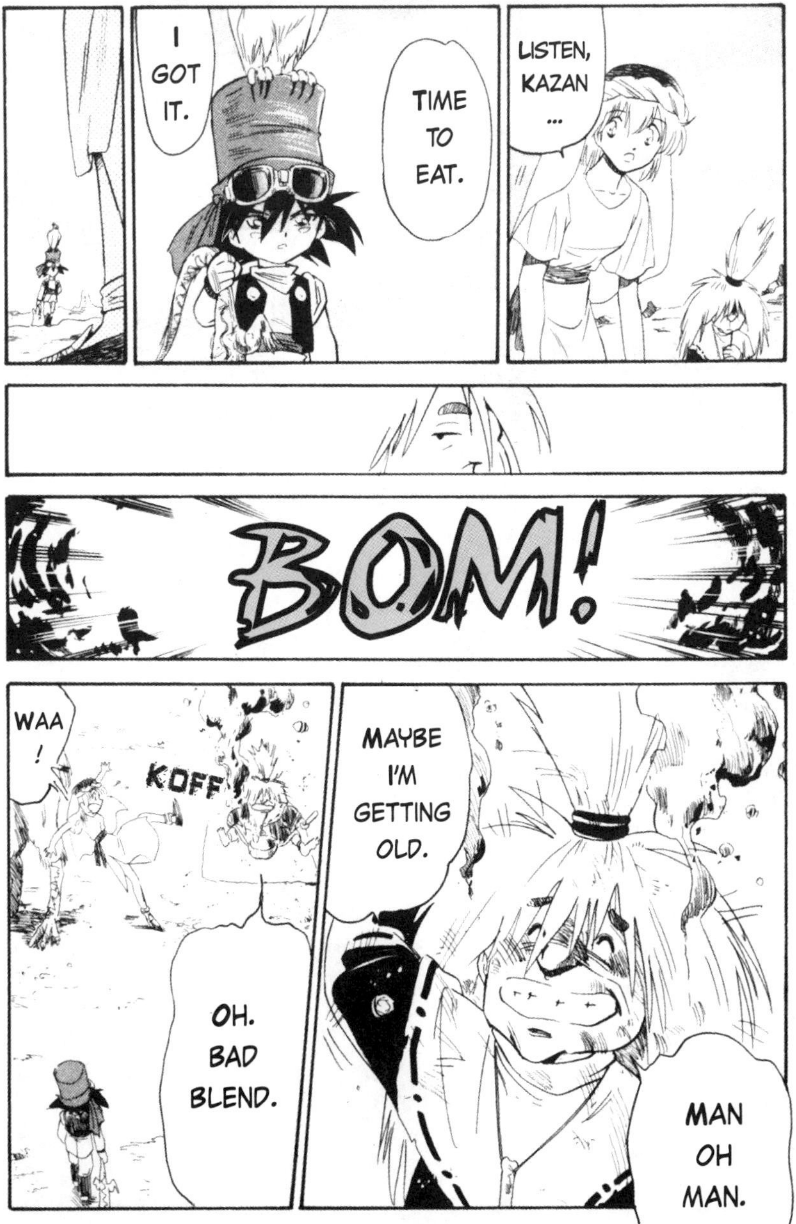
I GOT IT.
TIME TO EAT.
LISTEN, KAZAN ...
BOM!
WAA !
KOFF
MAYBE I'M GETTING OLD.
OH. BAD BLEND.
MAN OH MAN.

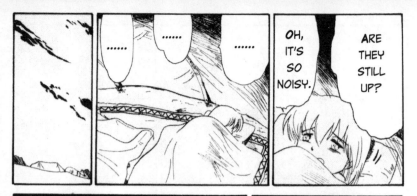

....

OH, IT'S SO NOISY.

ARE THEY STILL UP?

HOW ABOUT THIS?

MUCH SMALLER.

BUT DON'T REDUCE THE BLAST POWER.

AND ONE MORE ...

MAN ...

SUCH A DEMANDING KID.

MUTTER MUTTER

......

MY NAME IS KAZAN.

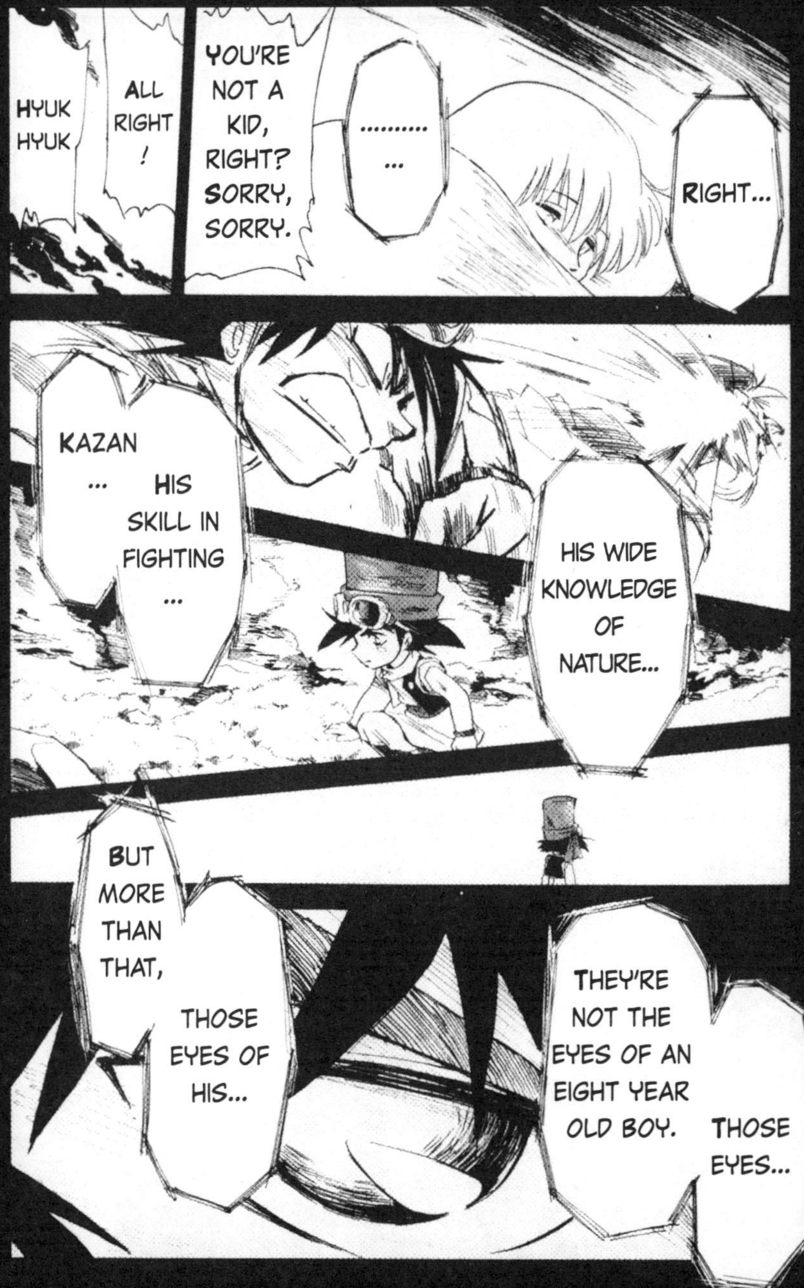
RIGHT...
....
YOU'RE NOT A KID, RIGHT? SORRY, SORRY.
ALL RIGHT!
HYUK HYUK
HIS WIDE KNOWLEDGE OF NATURE...
KAZAN... HIS SKILL IN FIGHTING...
THOSE EYES...
THEY'RE NOT THE EYES OF AN EIGHT YEAR OLD BOY.
THOSE EYES OF HIS...
BUT MORE THAN THAT,

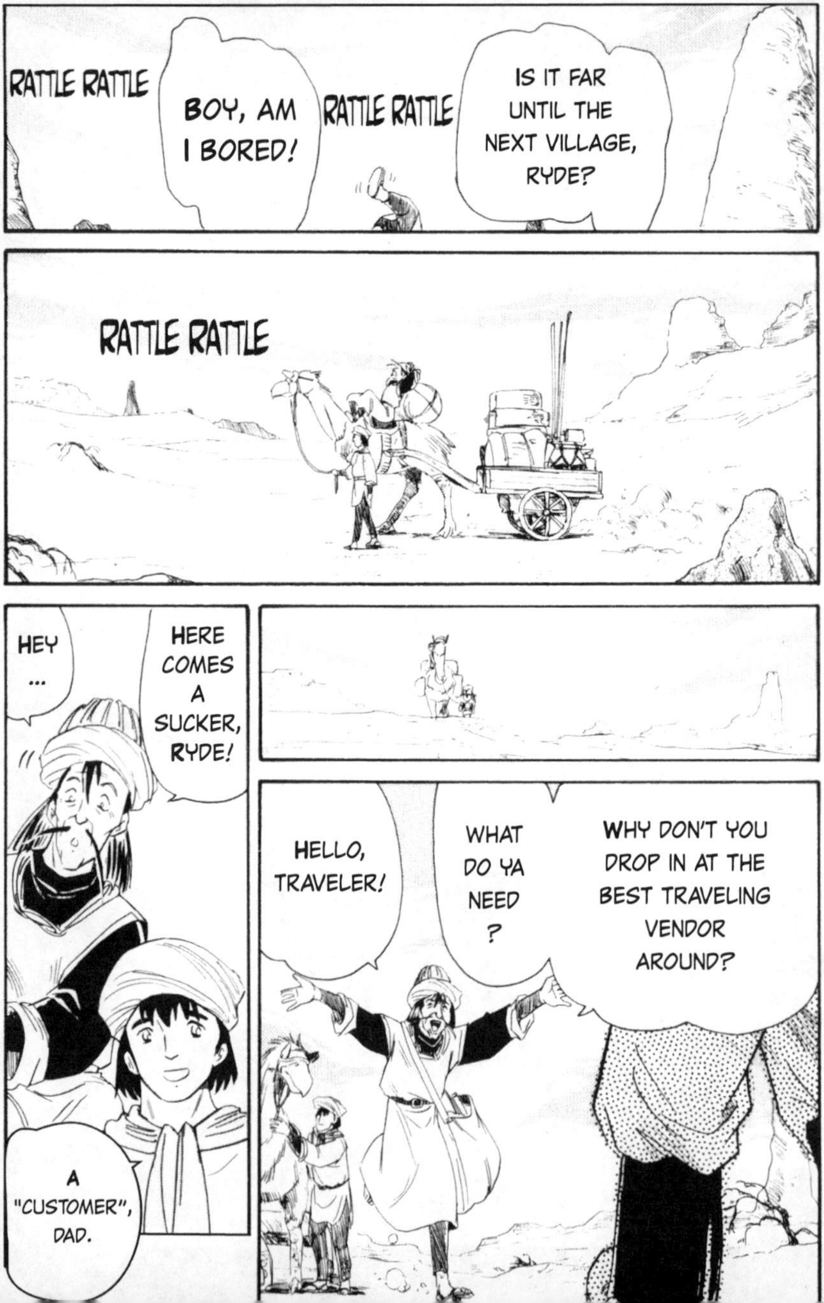
RATTLE RATTLE
BOY, AM I BORED!
RATTLE RATTLE
IS IT FAR UNTIL THE NEXT VILLAGE, RYDE?
RATTLE RATTLE
HEY ...
HERE COMES A SUCKER, RYDE!
A "CUSTOMER", DAD.
HELLO, TRAVELER!
WHAT DO YA NEED ?
WHY DON'T YOU DROP IN AT THE BEST TRAVELING VENDOR AROUND?

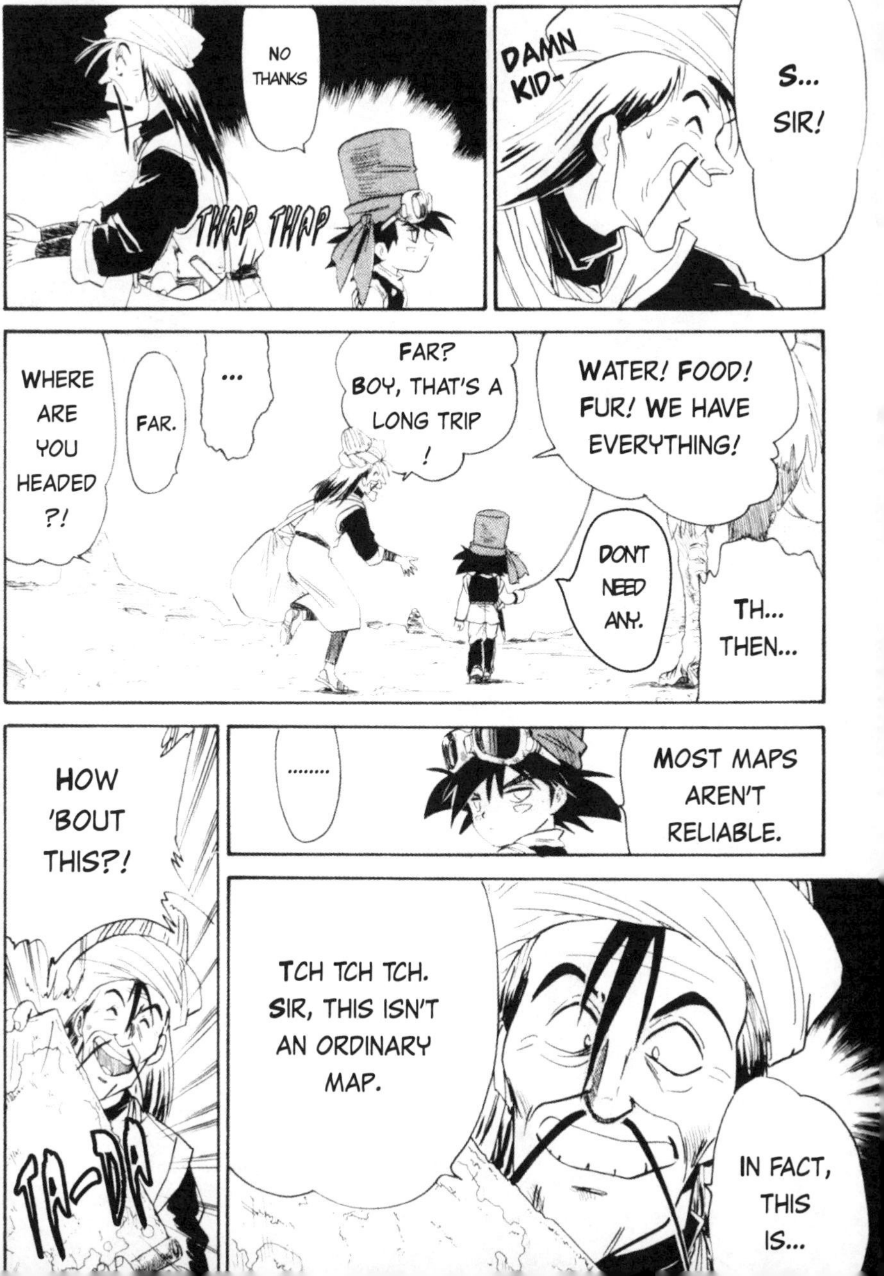
NO THANKS
THAP THAP
DAMN KID-
S... SIR!
WHERE ARE YOU HEADED?!
FAR.
...
FAR? BOY, THAT'S A LONG TRIP!
WATER! FOOD! FUR! WE HAVE EVERYTHING!
DON'T NEED ANY.
TH... THEN...
HOW 'BOUT THIS?!
TA-DA
MOST MAPS AREN'T RELIABLE.
....
TCH TCH TCH. SIR, THIS ISN'T AN ORDINARY MAP.
IN FACT, THIS IS...

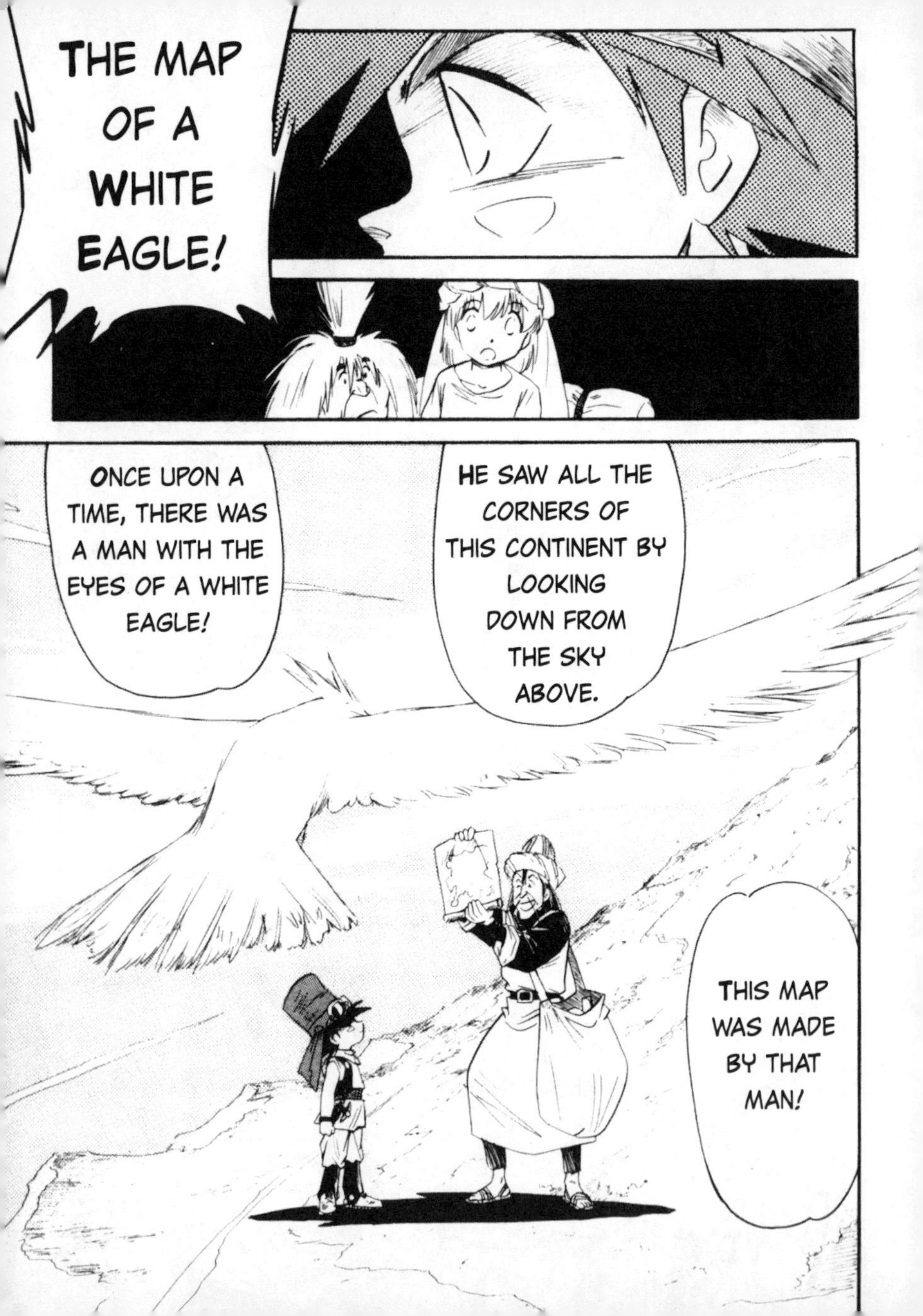
THE MAP OF A WHITE EAGLE!
ONCE UPON A TIME, THERE WAS A MAN WITH THE EYES OF A WHITE EAGLE!
HE SAW ALL THE CORNERS OF THIS CONTINENT BY LOOKING DOWN FROM THE SKY ABOVE.
THIS MAP WAS MADE BY THAT MAN!

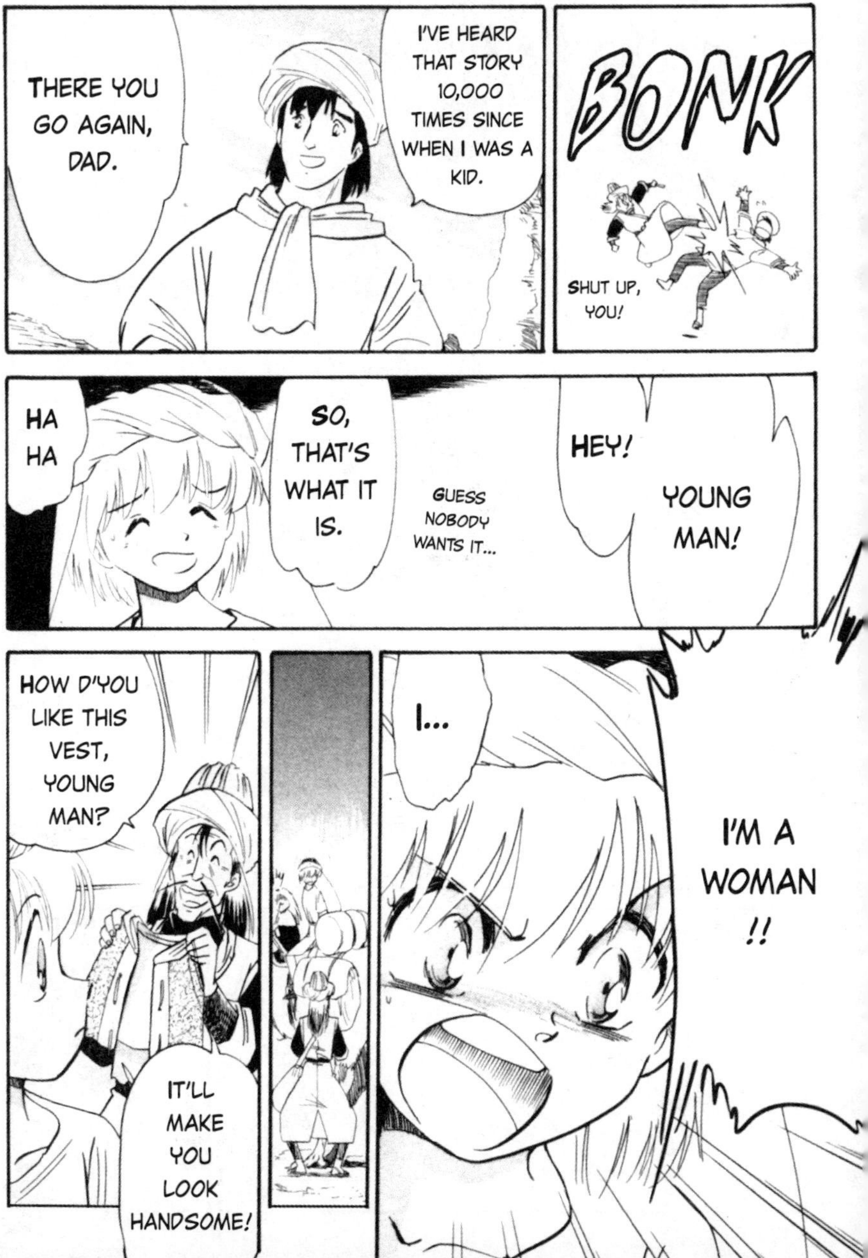
THERE YOU GO AGAIN, DAD.
I'VE HEARD THAT STORY 10,000 TIMES SINCE WHEN I WAS A KID.
BONK
SHUT UP, YOU!
HA HA
SO, THAT'S WHAT IT IS.
GUESS NOBODY WANTS IT...
HEY!
YOUNG MAN!
HOW D'YOU LIKE THIS VEST, YOUNG MAN?
IT'LL MAKE YOU LOOK HANDSOME!
I...
I'M A WOMAN !!

WAHAHWAHAHWAHAHAHA

HEE HEE HEE

D- DON'T LAUGH, ARBEY!

BAM! BAM! BAM!

LET'S GO, KAZAN!

HE MUST BE A CON MAN!

MI... MISS...

I HAVE WOMEN'S CLOTHES TOO.

SEE?

SLEHH!

HEY.

I'LL BUY THAT MAP.

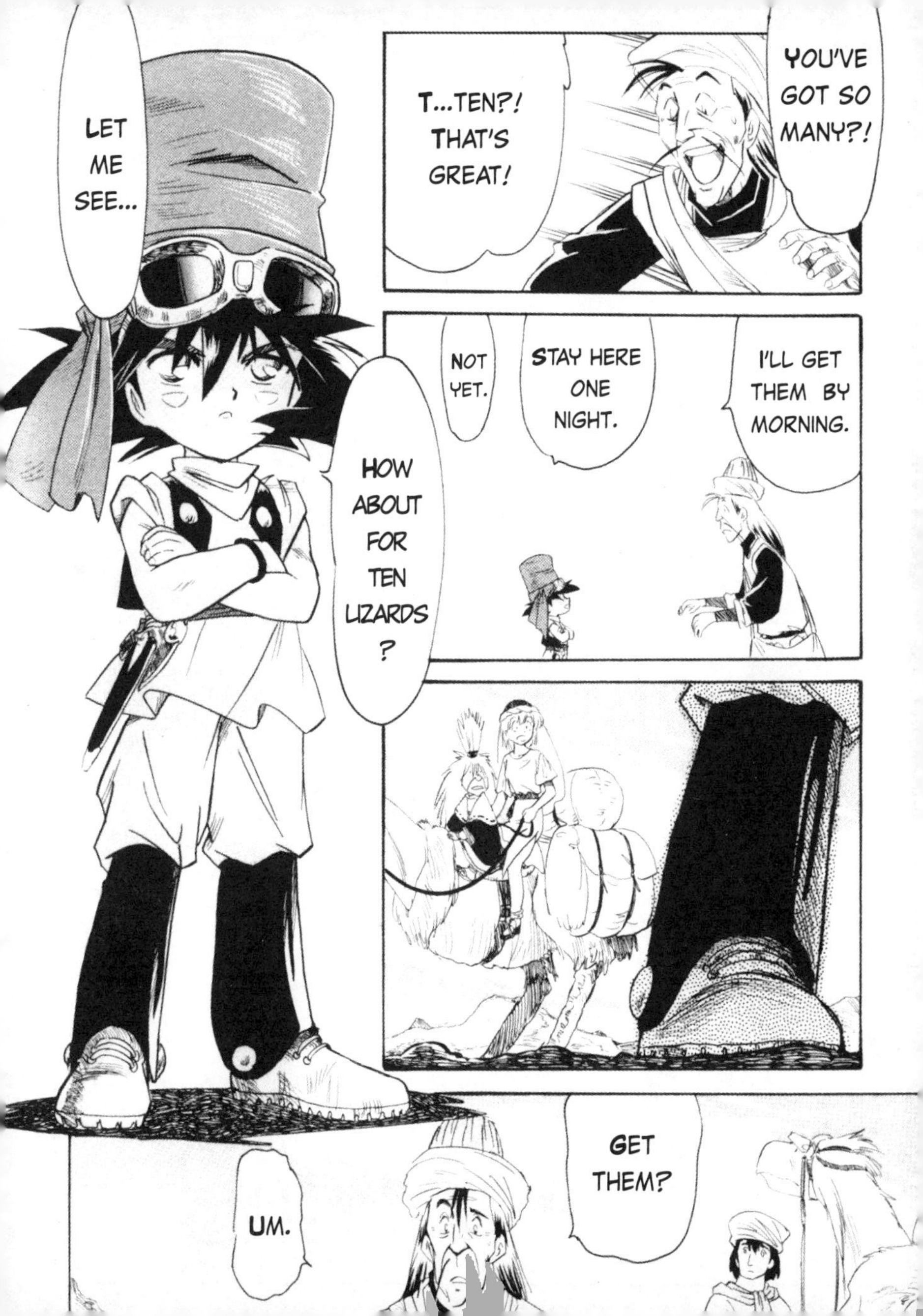
LET ME SEE...
HOW ABOUT FOR TEN LIZARDS?
YOU'VE GOT SO MANY?!
T...TEN?! THAT'S GREAT!
I'LL GET THEM BY MORNING.
STAY HERE ONE NIGHT.
NOT YET.
GET THEM?
UM.

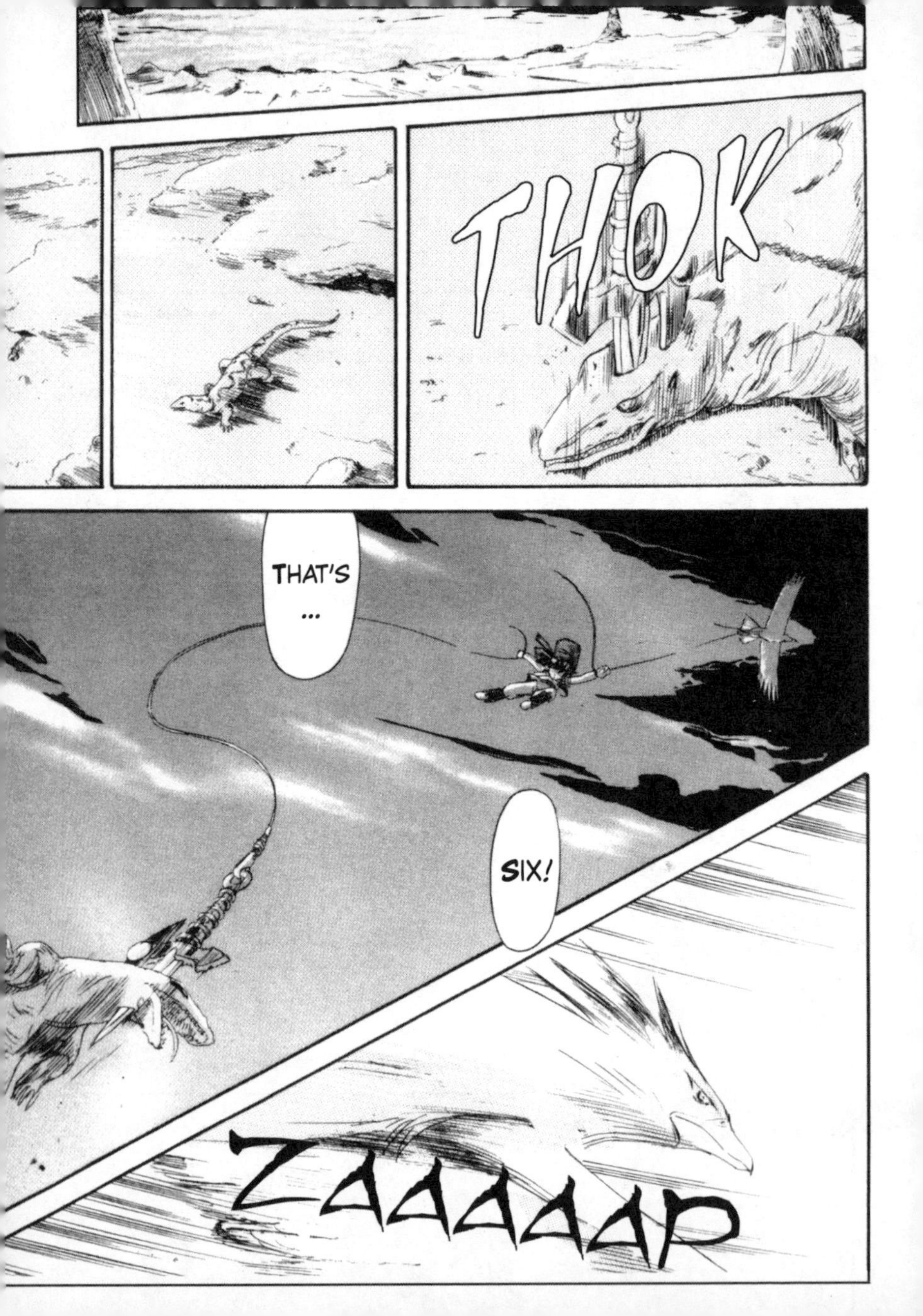
THOK
THAT'S ...
SIX!
ZAAAAAP

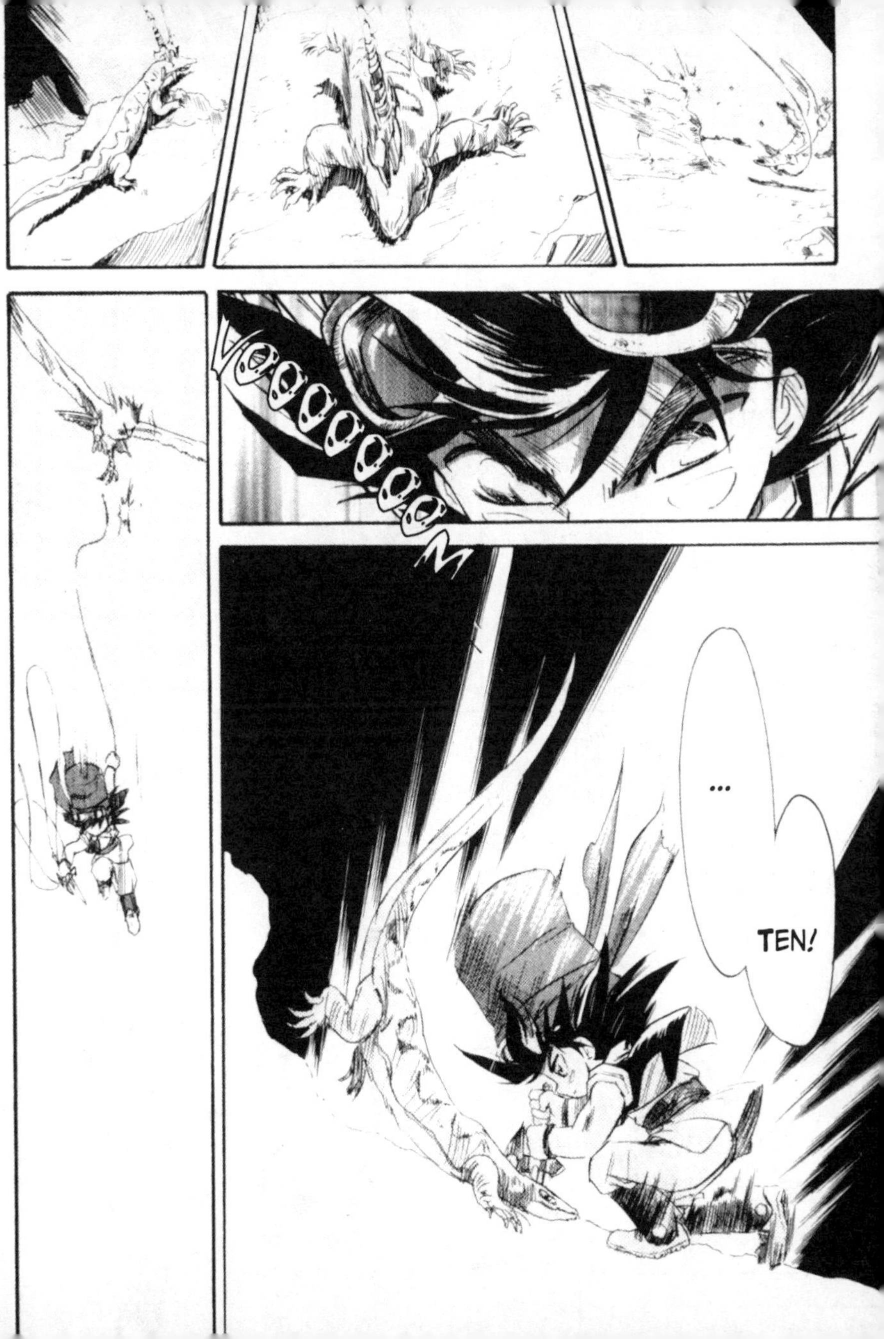
VOOOOOOOOOOM
...
TEN!

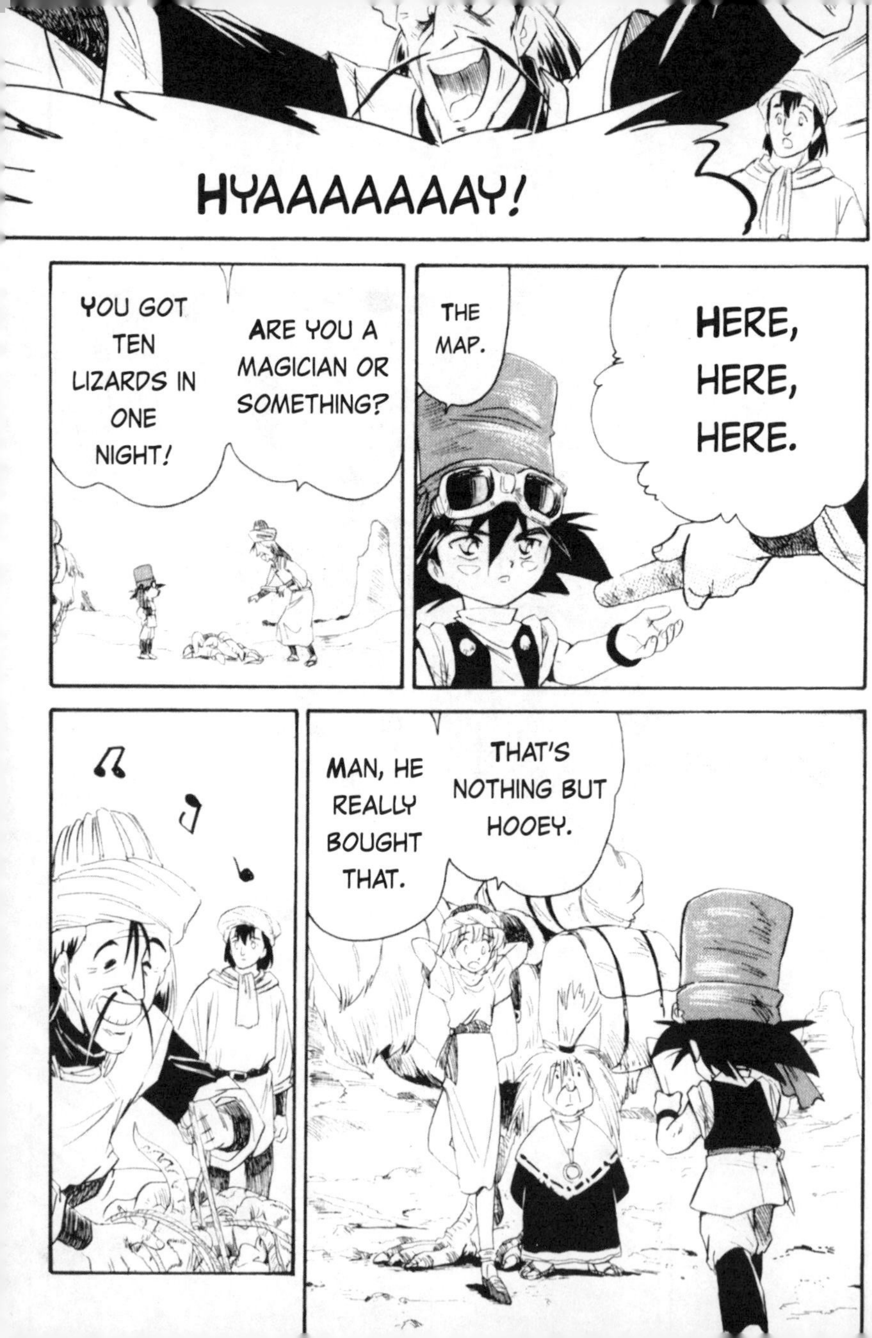
HYAAAAAAAY!
YOU GOT TEN LIZARDS IN ONE NIGHT!
ARE YOU A MAGICIAN OR SOMETHING?
THE MAP.
HERE, HERE, HERE.
MAN, HE REALLY BOUGHT THAT.
THAT'S NOTHING BUT HOOEY.

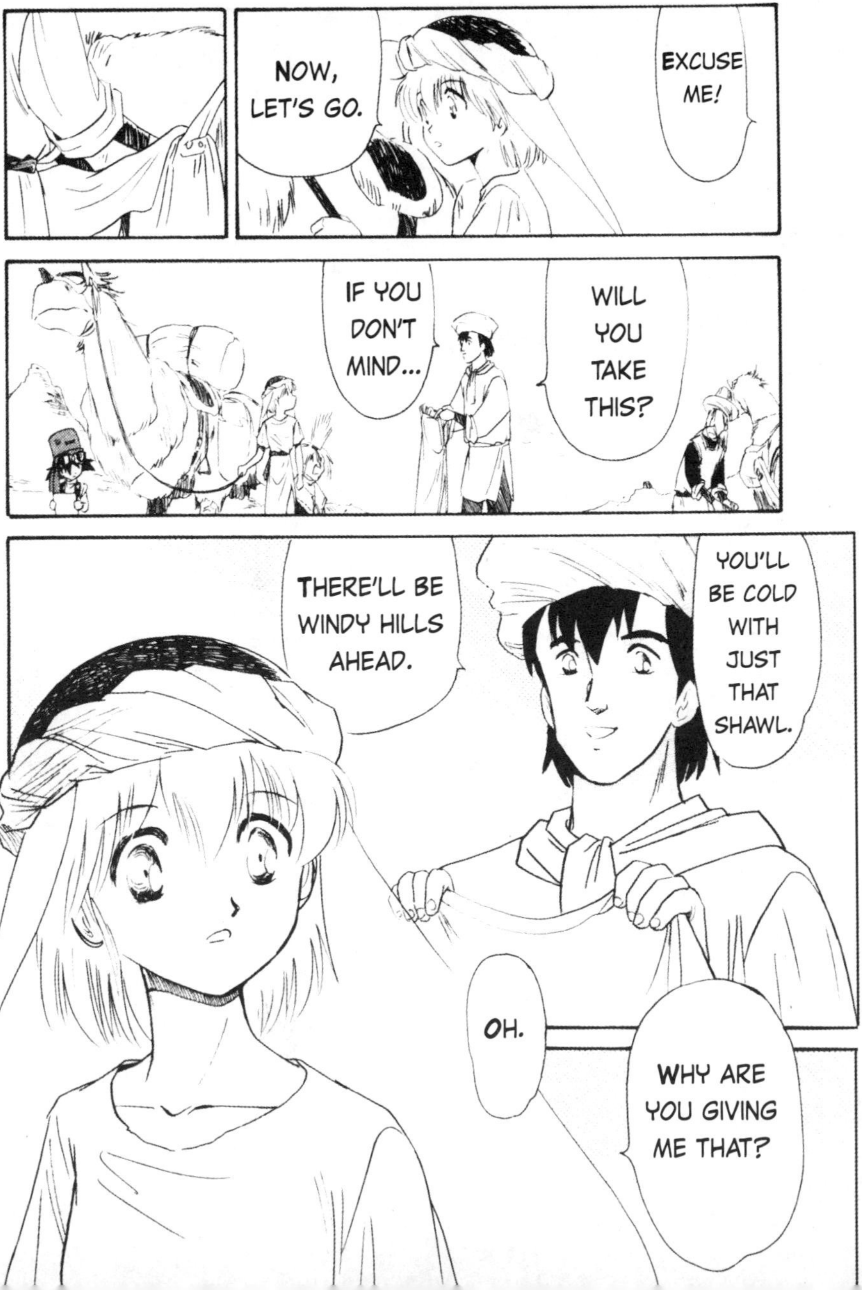
EXCUSE ME!
NOW, LET'S GO.
WILL YOU TAKE THIS?
IF YOU DON'T MIND...
YOU'LL BE COLD WITH JUST THAT SHAWL.
THERE'LL BE WINDY HILLS AHEAD.
WHY ARE YOU GIVING ME THAT?
OH.

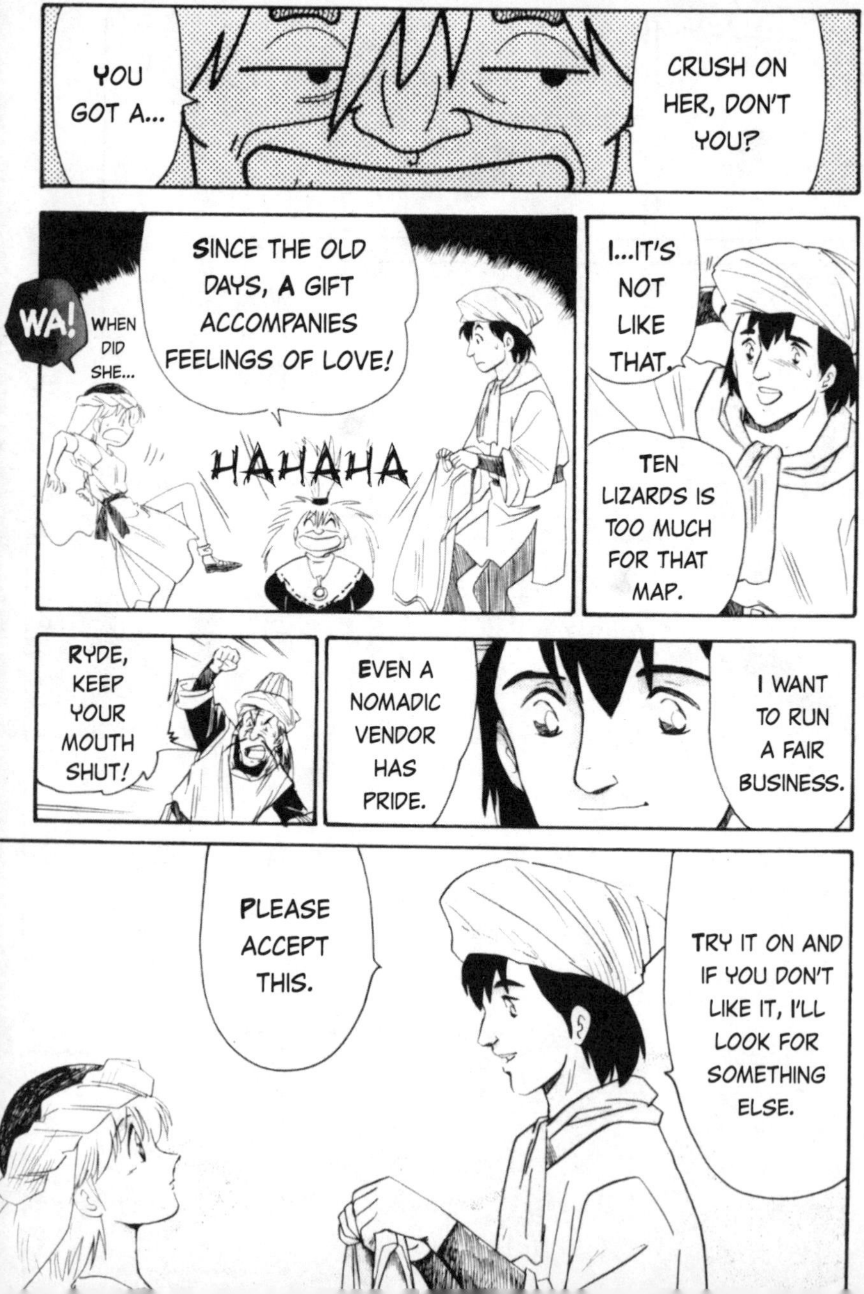
YOU GOT A...
CRUSH ON HER, DON'T YOU?
SINCE THE OLD DAYS, A GIFT ACCOMPANIES FEELINGS OF LOVE!
WA!
WHEN DID SHE...
HAHAHA
I...IT'S NOT LIKE THAT.
TEN LIZARDS IS TOO MUCH FOR THAT MAP.
RYDE, KEEP YOUR MOUTH SHUT!
EVEN A NOMADIC VENDOR HAS PRIDE.
I WANT TO RUN A FAIR BUSINESS.
PLEASE ACCEPT THIS.
TRY IT ON AND IF YOU DON'T LIKE IT, I'LL LOOK FOR SOMETHING ELSE.

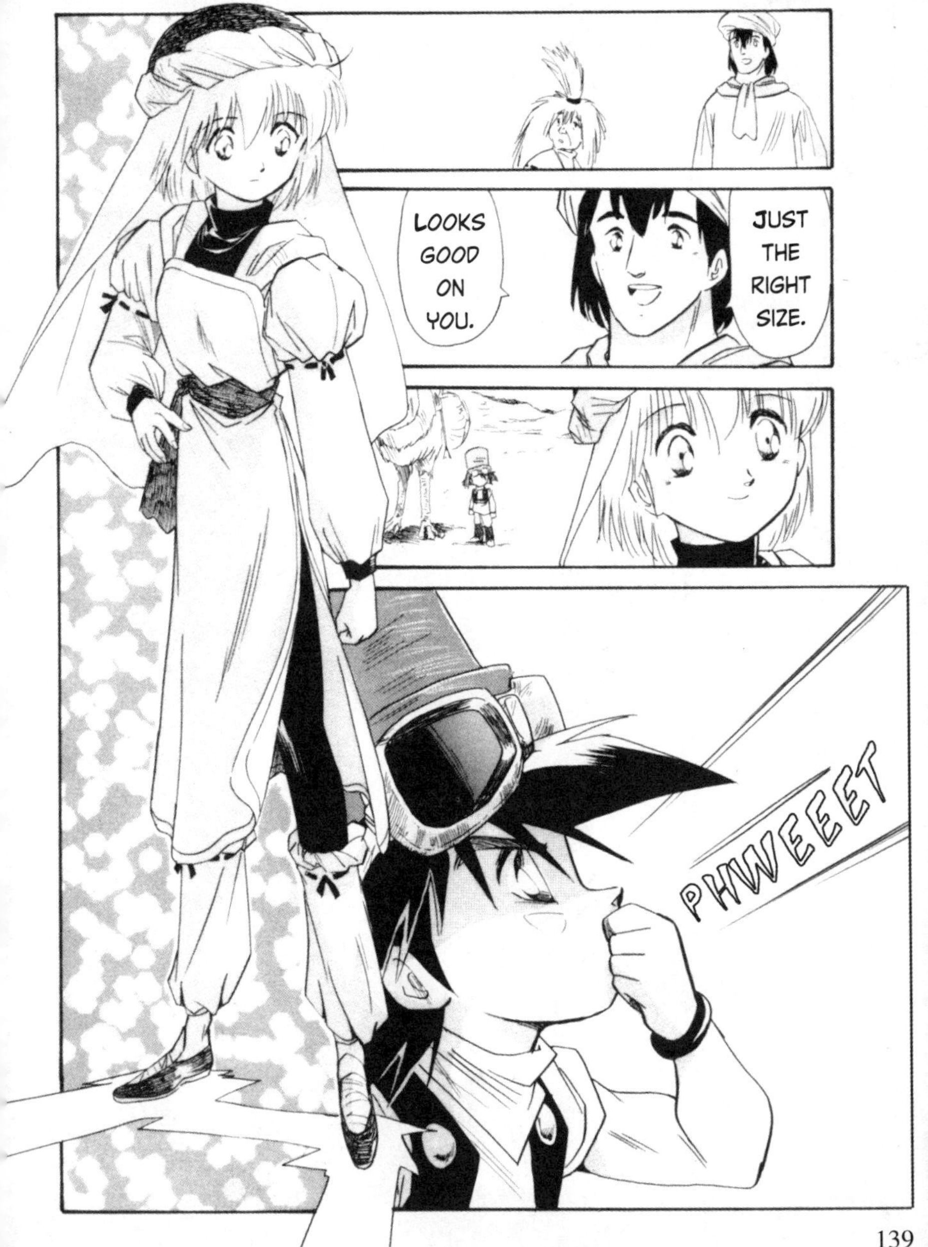
JUST THE RIGHT SIZE.
LOOKS GOOD ON YOU.
PHWEEET

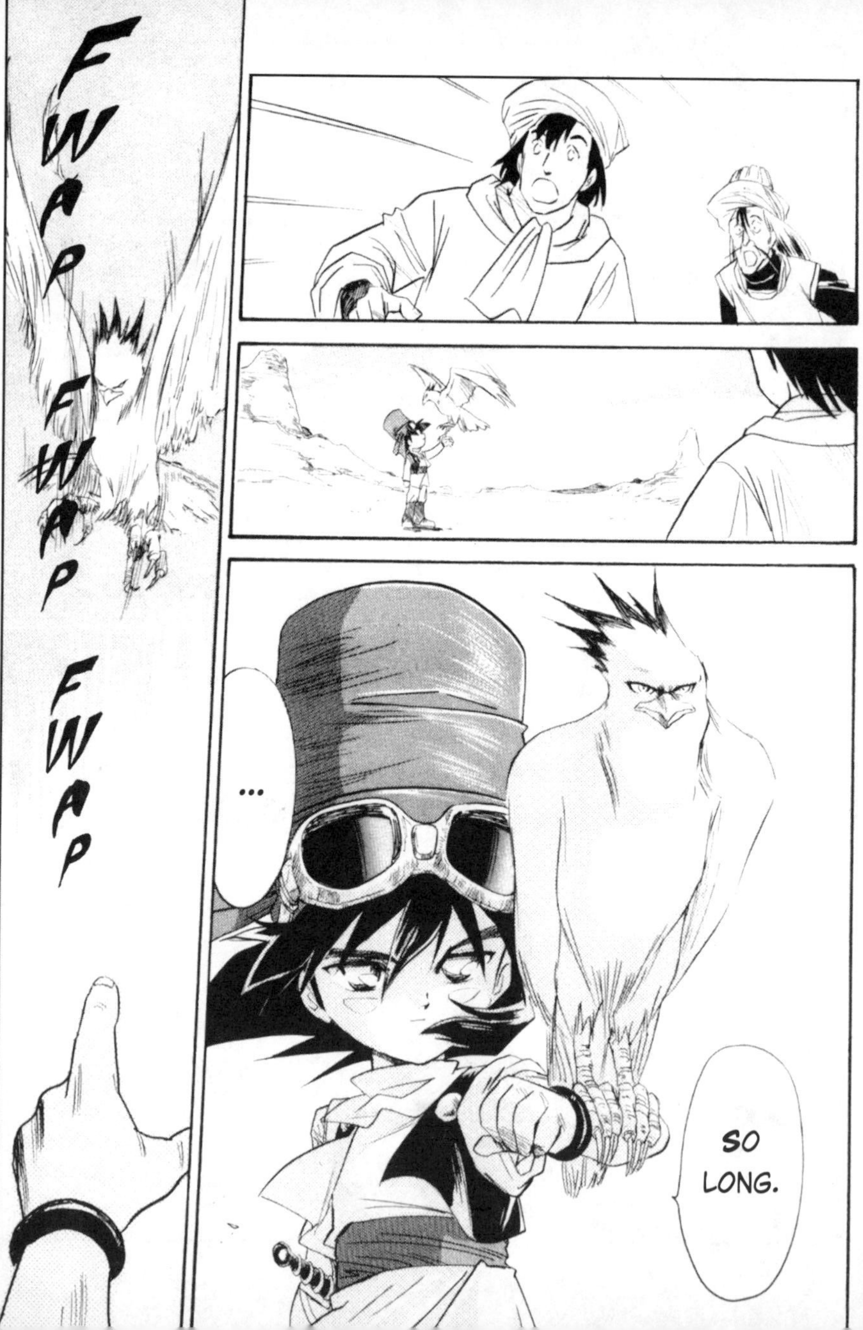
FWAP FWAP FWAP
...
SO LONG.

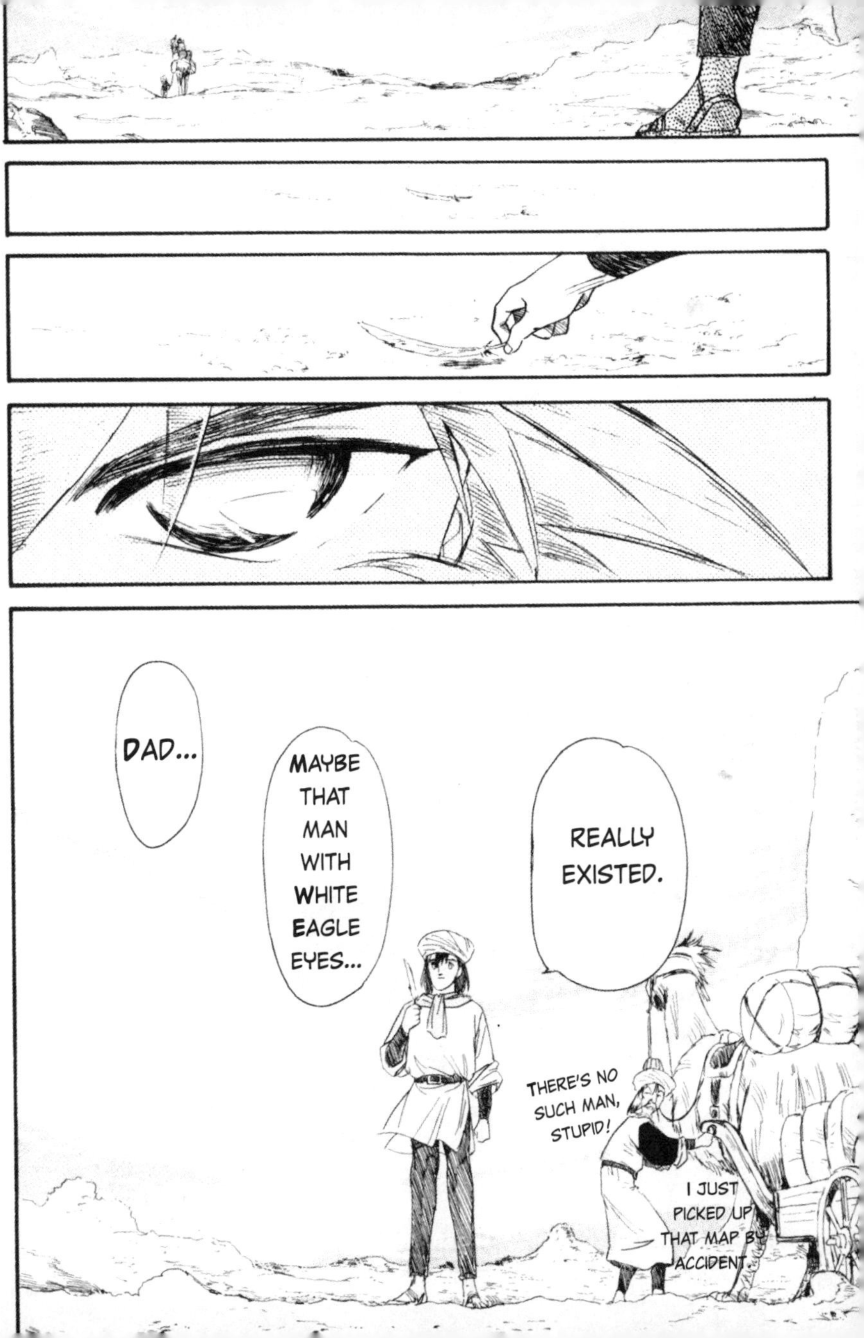
DAD...
MAYBE THAT MAN WITH WHITE EAGLE EYES...
REALLY EXISTED.
THERE'S NO SUCH MAN, STUPID!
I JUST PICKED UP THAT MAP BY ACCIDENT.

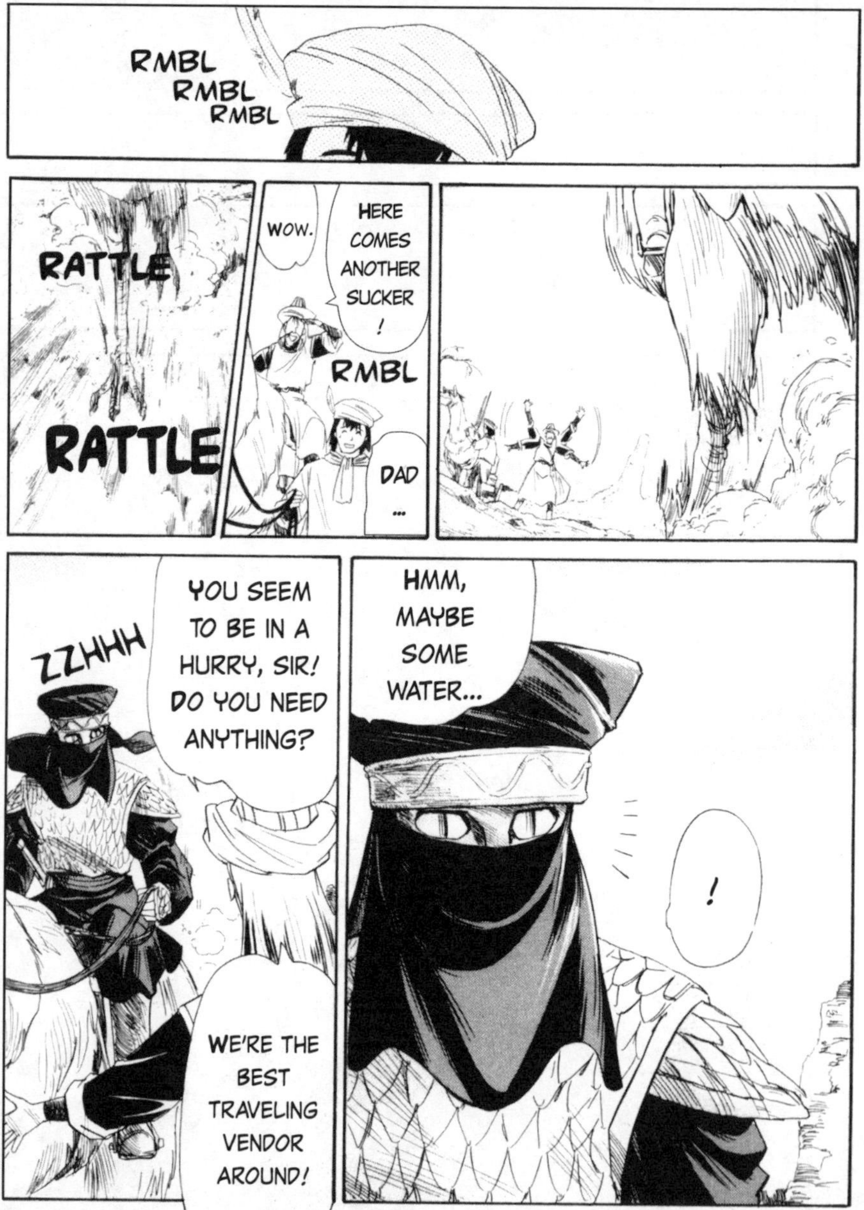
RMBL
RMBL
RMBL
RATTLE
RATTLE
WOW.
HERE COMES ANOTHER SUCKER!
RMBL
DAD...
ZZHHH
YOU SEEM TO BE IN A HURRY, SIR! DO YOU NEED ANYTHING?
WE'RE THE BEST TRAVELING VENDOR AROUND!
HMM, MAYBE SOME WATER...
!

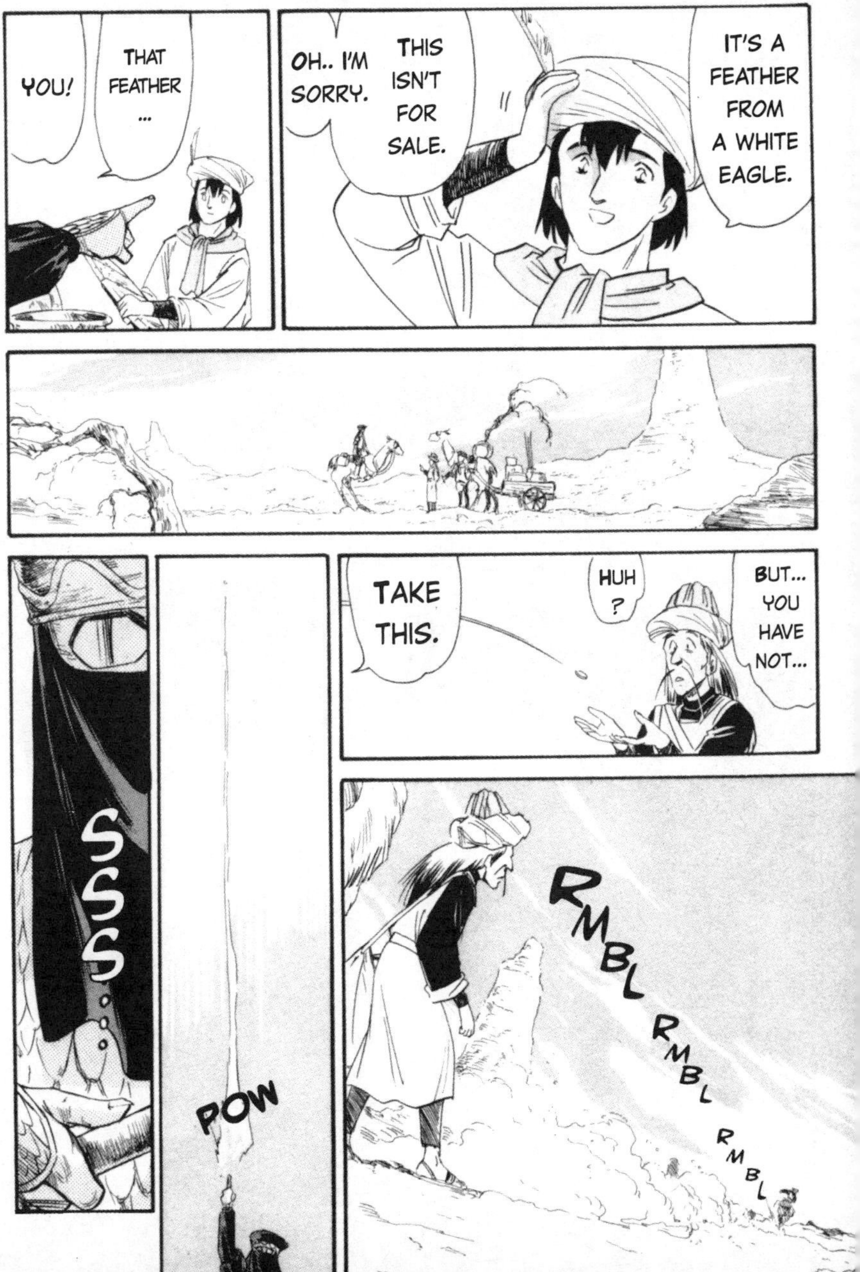
YOU!
THAT FEATHER ...
OH.. I'M SORRY.
THIS ISN'T FOR SALE.
IT'S A FEATHER FROM A WHITE EAGLE.
TAKE THIS.
HUH ?
BUT... YOU HAVE NOT...
SSSS
POW
RMBL RMBL RMBL

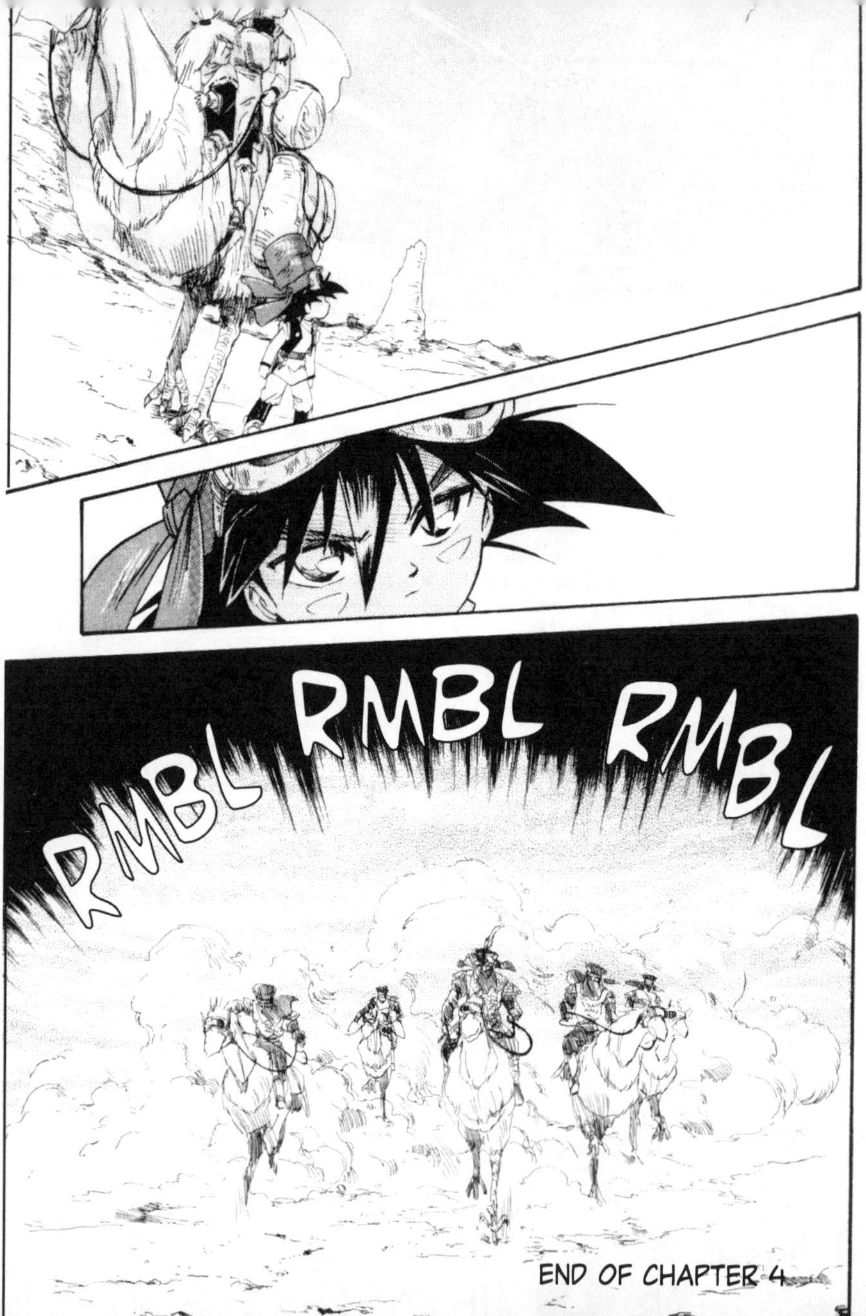
RMBL RMBL RMBL
END OF CHAPTER 4

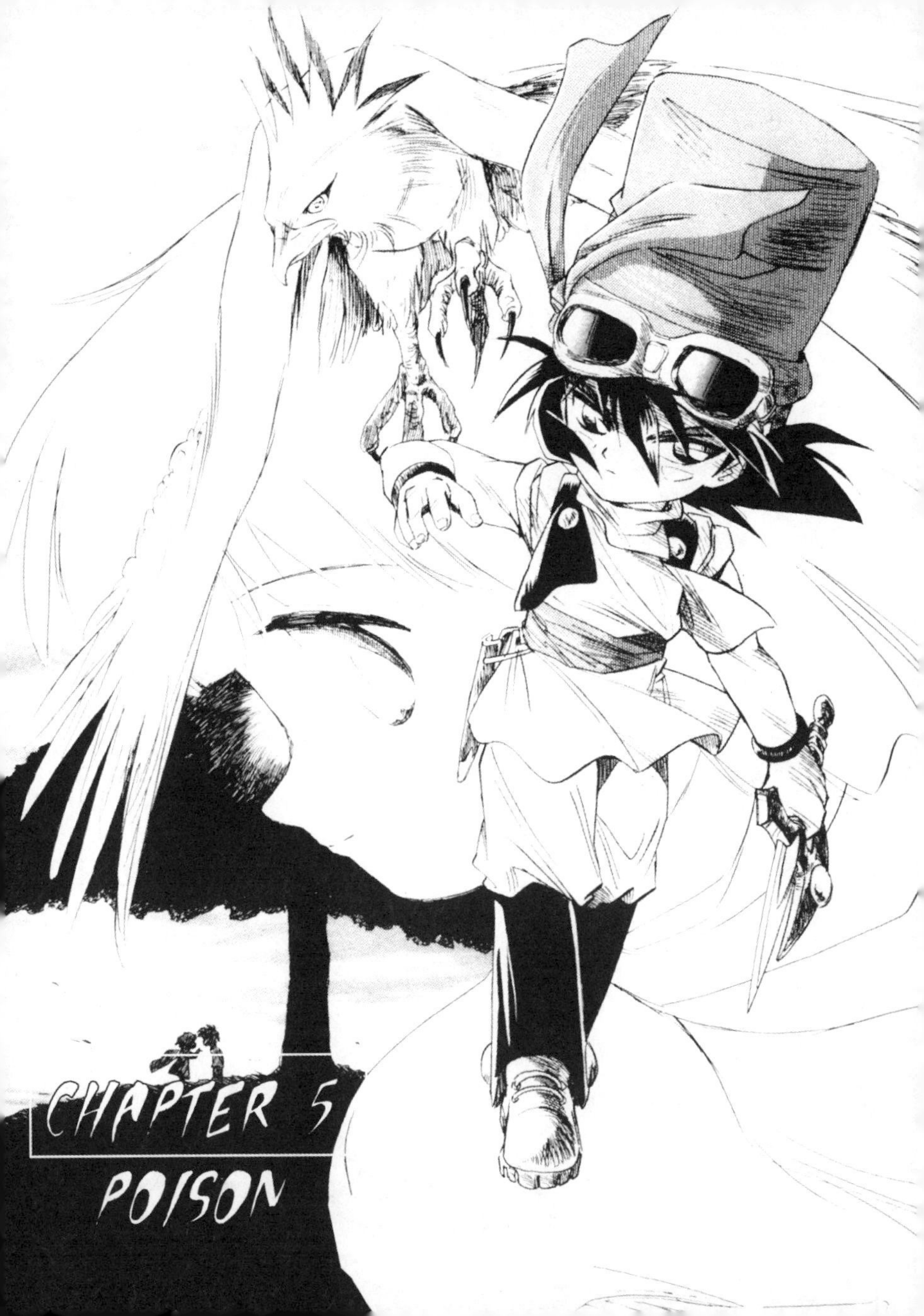
CHAPTER 5
POISON

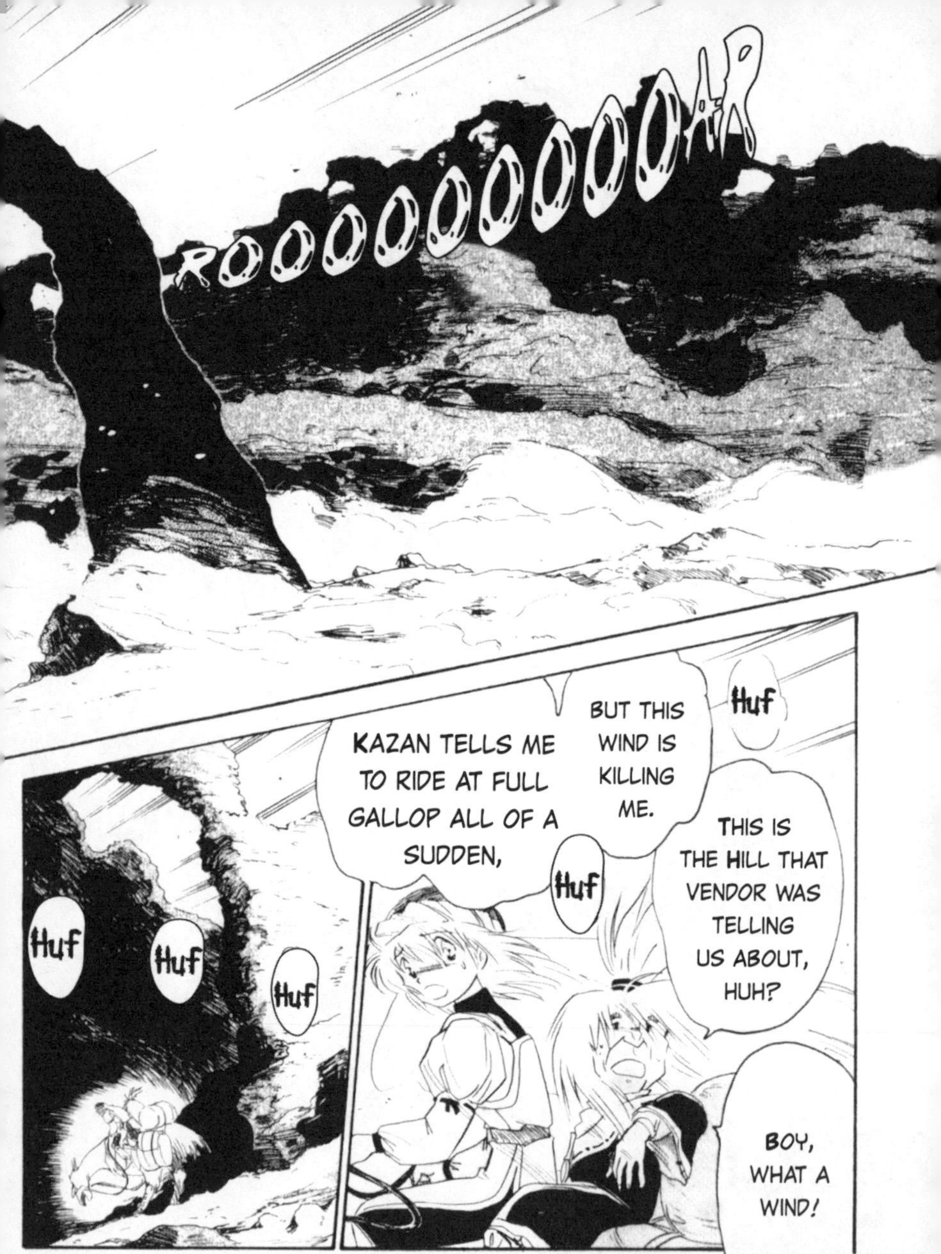
ROOOOOOOOOOOAR
Huf
Huf
Huf
KAZAN TELLS ME TO RIDE AT FULL GALLOP ALL OF A SUDDEN,
BUT THIS WIND IS KILLING ME.
Huf
Huf
THIS IS THE HILL THAT VENDOR WAS TELLING US ABOUT, HUH?
BOY, WHAT A WIND!

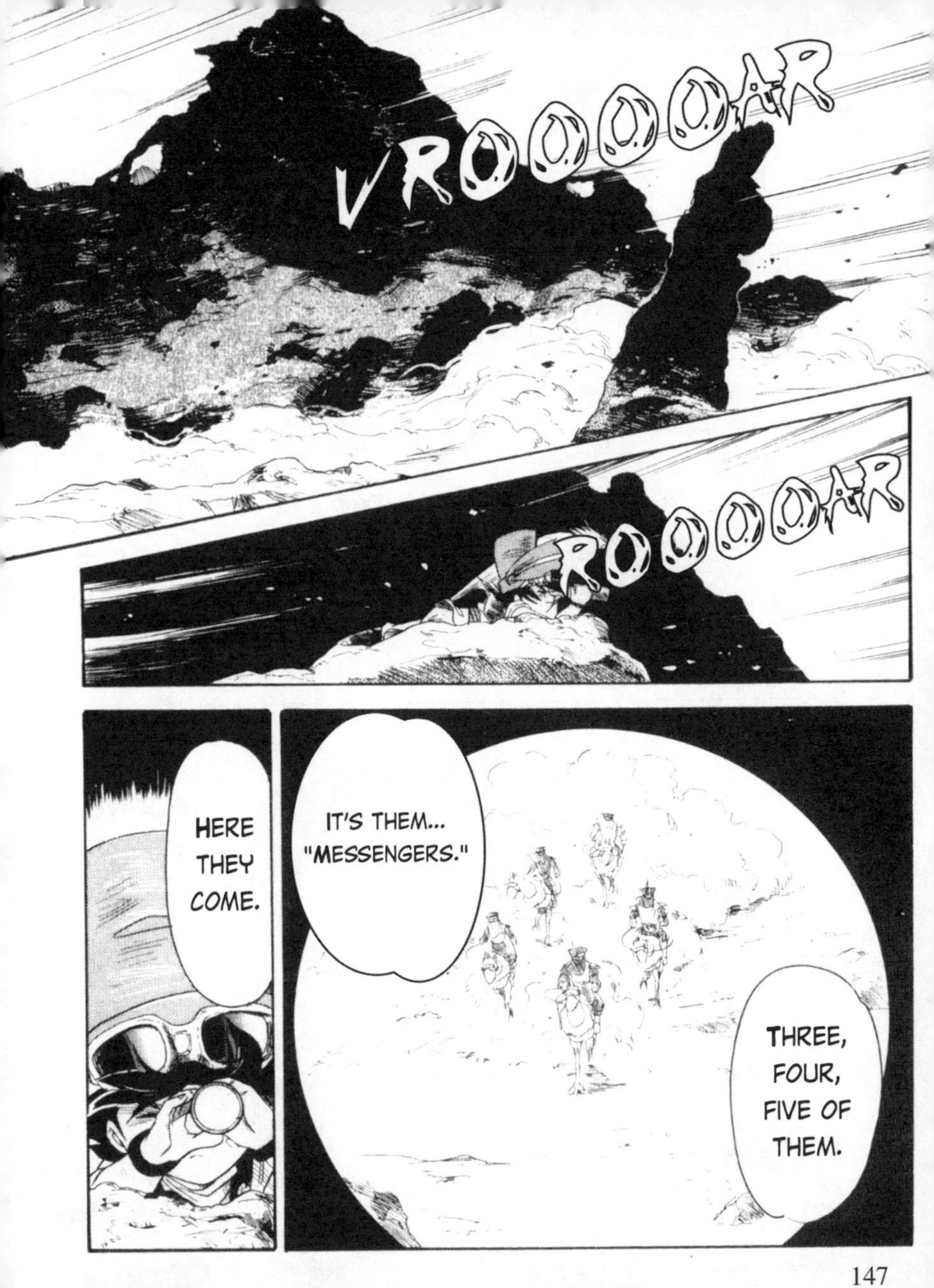
VROOOOAR
ROOOOAR
HERE THEY COME.
IT'S THEM... "MESSENGERS."
THREE, FOUR, FIVE OF THEM.

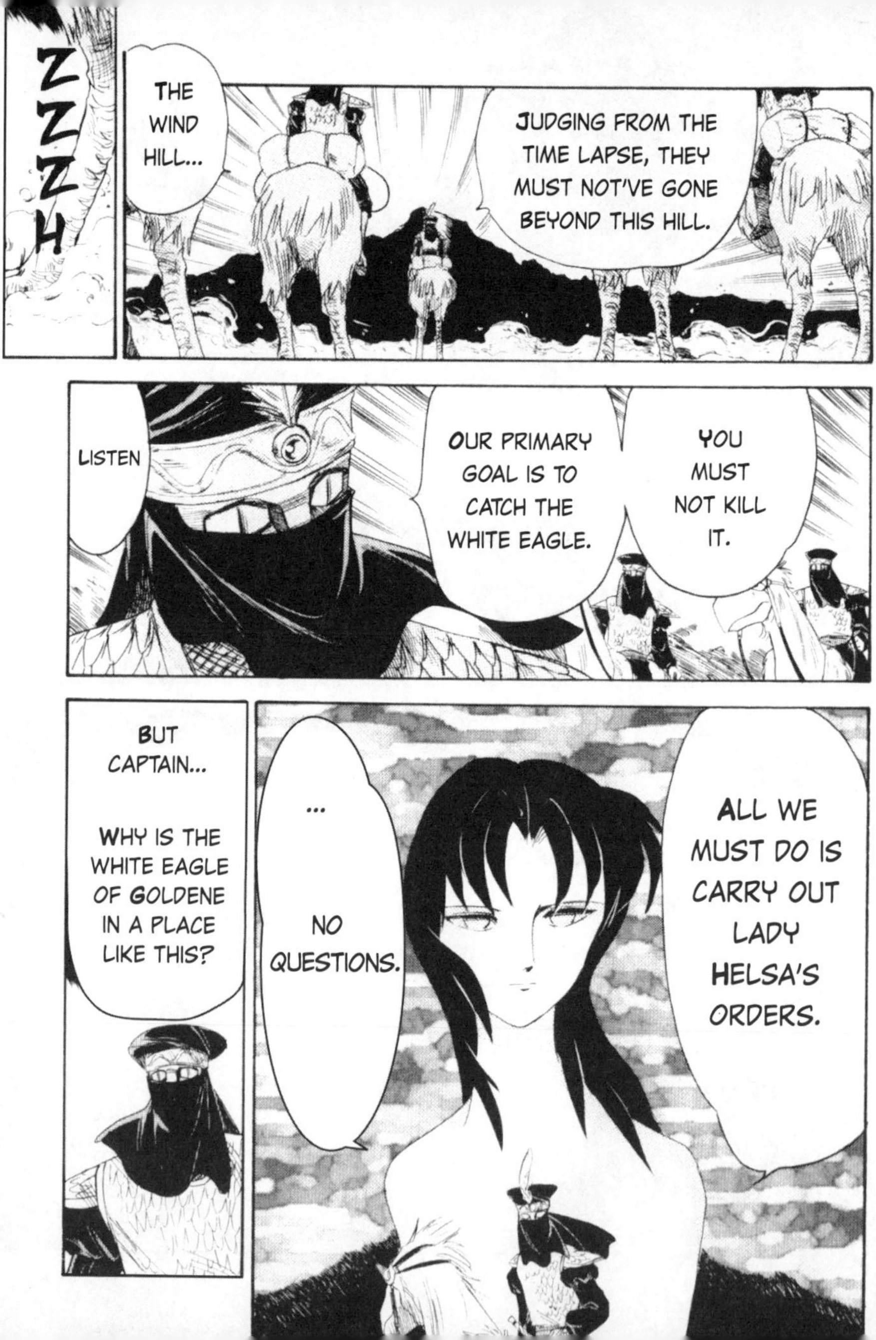
ZZZH
THE WIND HILL...
JUDGING FROM THE TIME LAPSE, THEY MUST NOT'VE GONE BEYOND THIS HILL.
LISTEN
OUR PRIMARY GOAL IS TO CATCH THE WHITE EAGLE.
YOU MUST NOT KILL IT.
BUT CAPTAIN...
WHY IS THE WHITE EAGLE OF GOLDENE IN A PLACE LIKE THIS?
...
NO QUESTIONS.
ALL WE MUST DO IS CARRY OUT LADY HELSA'S ORDERS.

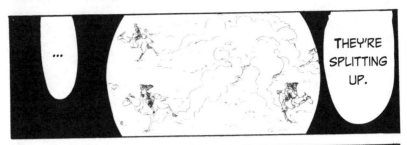

...

THEY'RE SPLITTING UP.

KAZAN!

IS THAT THEM?

YEAH. SAME AS THE ASSASSIN IN BLACK WHO ATTACKED FAWNA BEFORE.

THIS TIME THERE ARE FIVE OF THEM. IT'S NOT GONNA BE EASY.

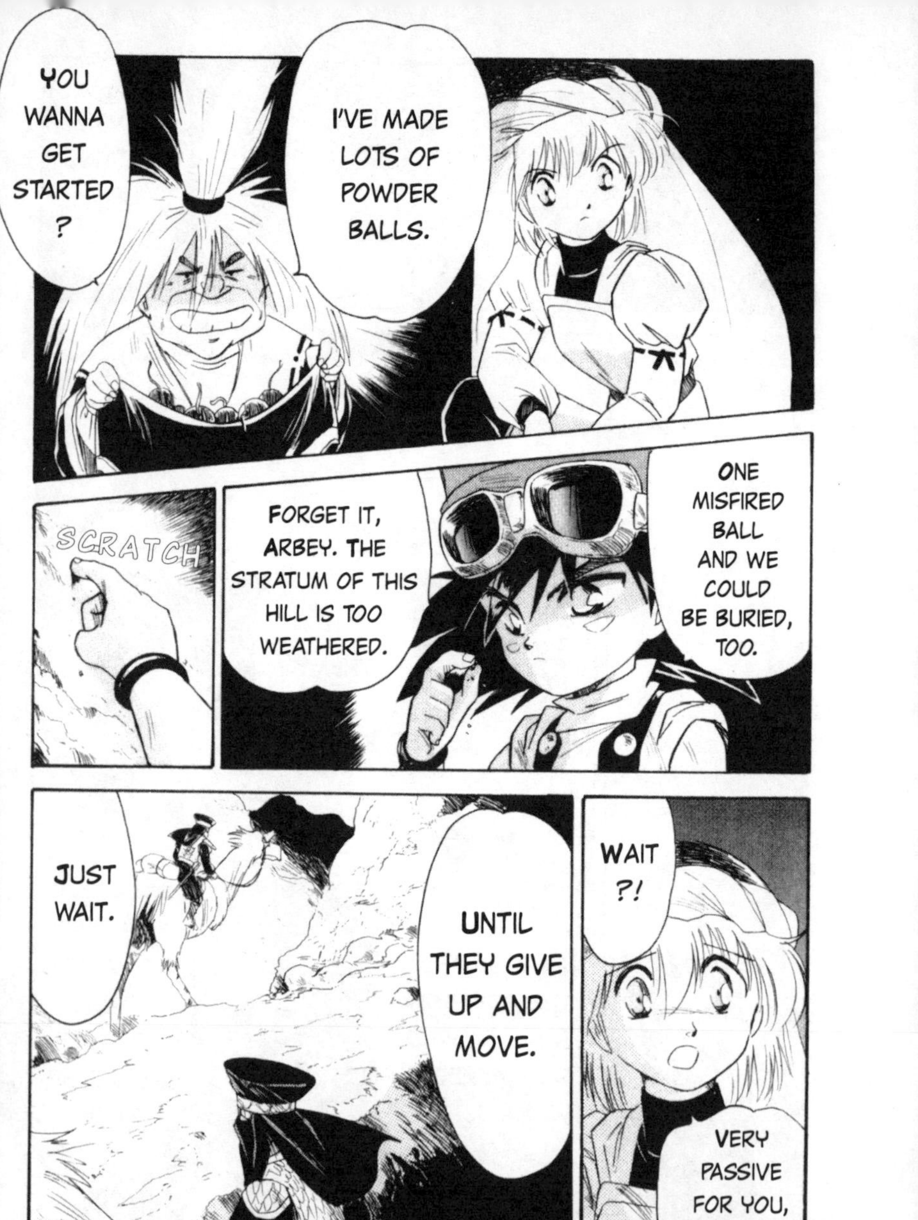
I'VE MADE LOTS OF POWDER BALLS.
YOU WANNA GET STARTED ?
ONE MISFIRED BALL AND WE COULD BE BURIED, TOO.
FORGET IT, ARBEY. THE STRATUM OF THIS HILL IS TOO WEATHERED.
SCRATCH
WAIT ?!
UNTIL THEY GIVE UP AND MOVE.
JUST WAIT.
VERY PASSIVE FOR YOU, ISN'T IT?

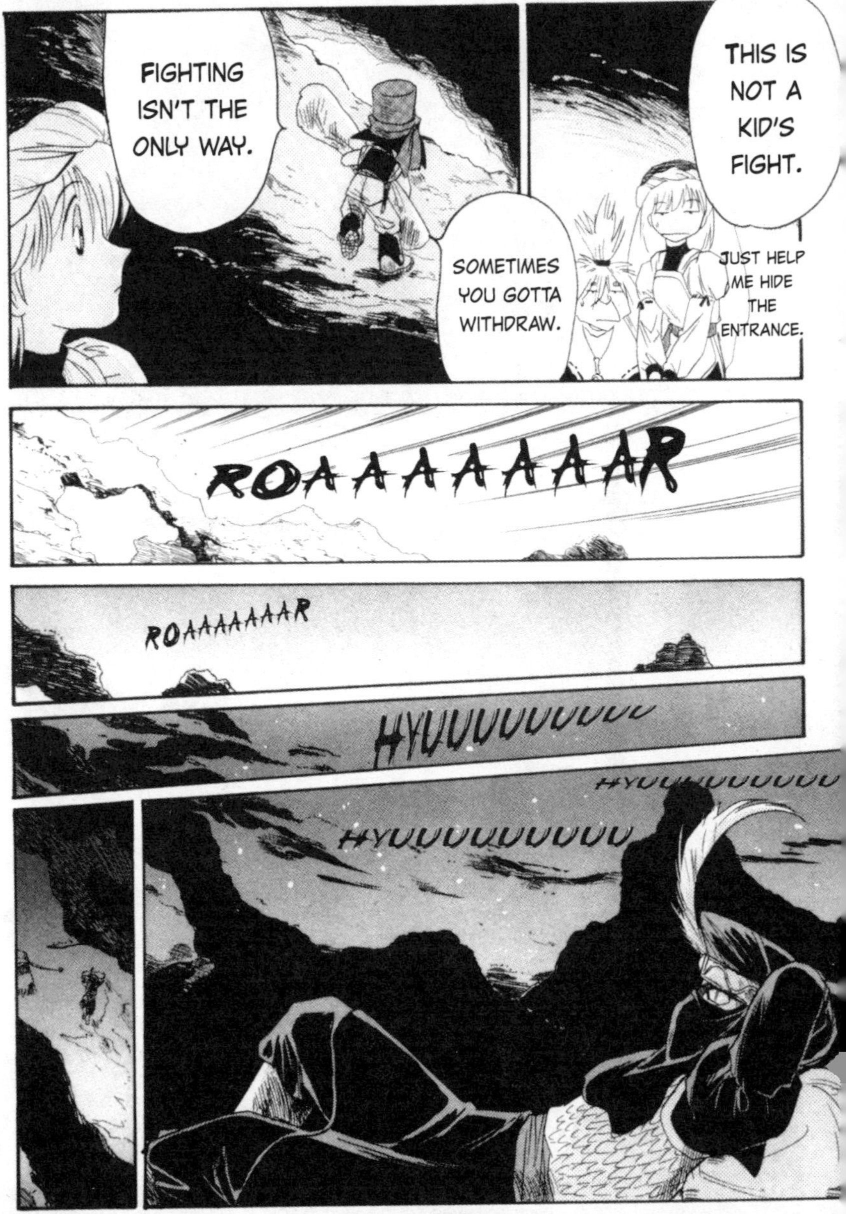
FIGHTING ISN'T THE ONLY WAY.
THIS IS NOT A KID'S FIGHT.
SOMETIMES YOU GOTTA WITHDRAW.
JUST HELP ME HIDE THE ENTRANCE.
ROAAAAAAAR
ROAAAAAAAR
HYUUUUUUUUU
HYUUUUUUUUU
HYUUUUUUUUU

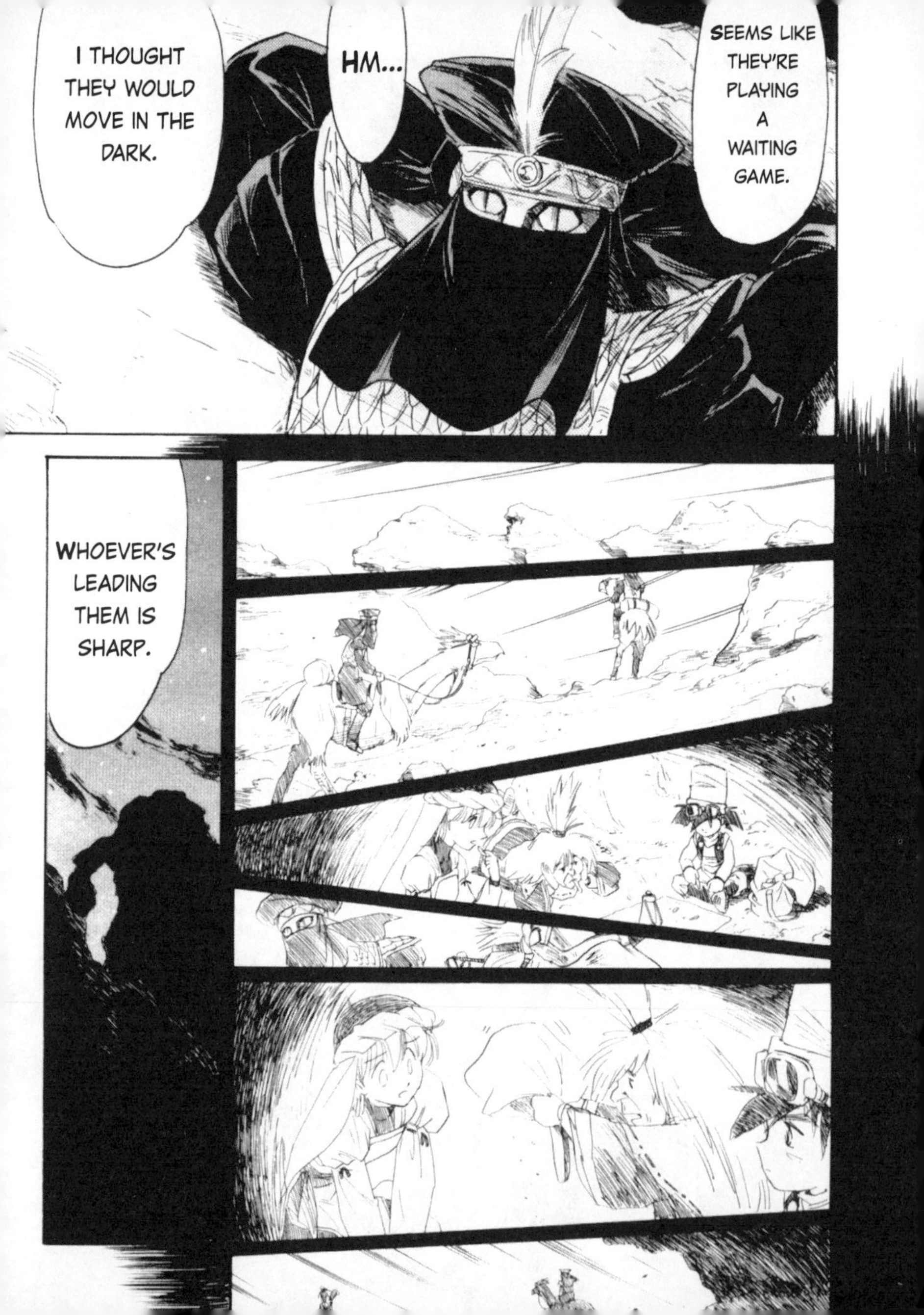
SEEMS LIKE THEY'RE PLAYING A WAITING GAME.
HM...
I THOUGHT THEY WOULD MOVE IN THE DARK.
WHOEVER'S LEADING THEM IS SHARP.

IT'S BEEN FIVE DAYS.

WE'VE RUN OUT OF FOOD. HOW LONG ARE WE GONNA STAY HERE, ARBEY?

QUIET. KAZAN IS CHECKING ON THEM NOW.

GURGLL

OH!

PHAP

NOPE.

STILL THERE.

.....

THEY'RE STARVING US OUT.

!

FWAP
FWAP
FWAP
FWAP

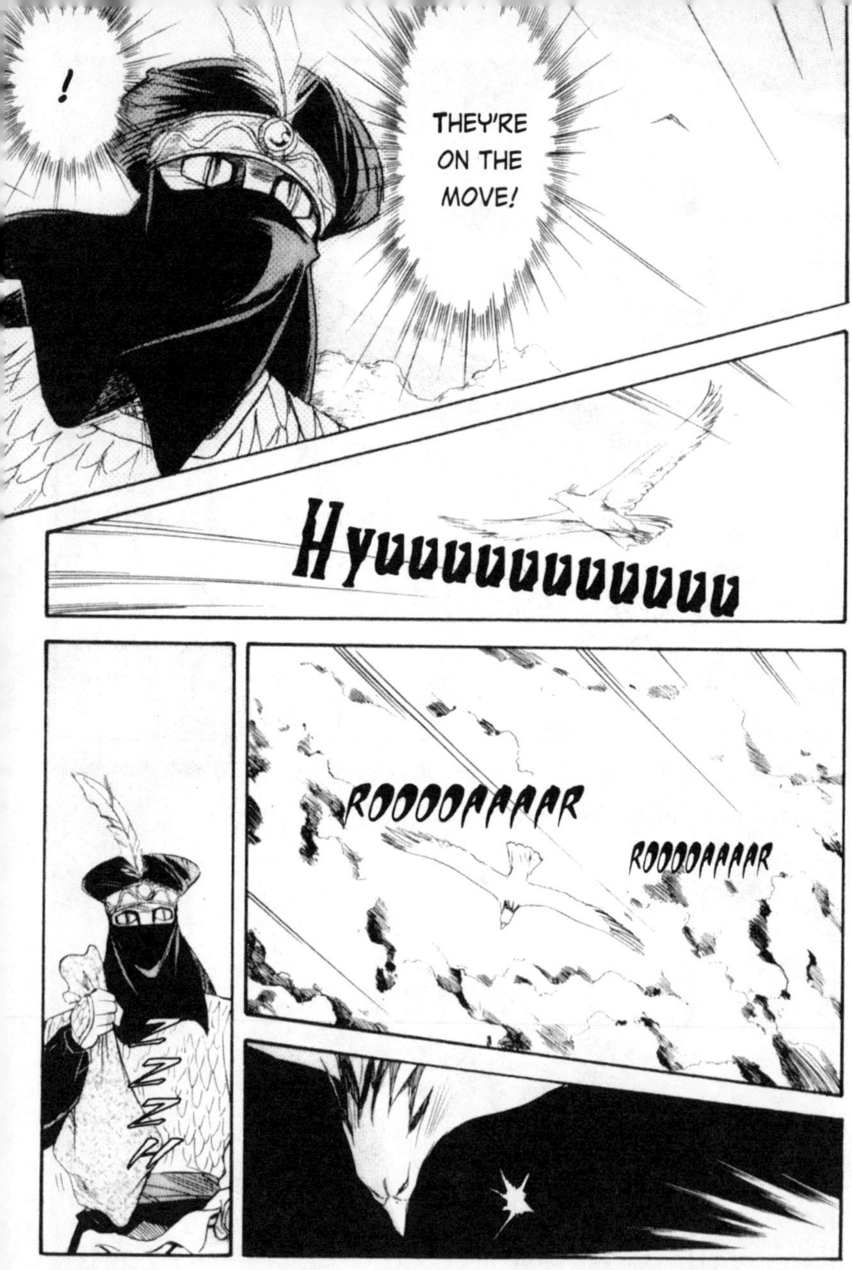
THEY'RE ON THE MOVE!
!
Hyuuuuuuuuuuu
ROOOOAAAAR
ROOOOAAAAR
ZZZH

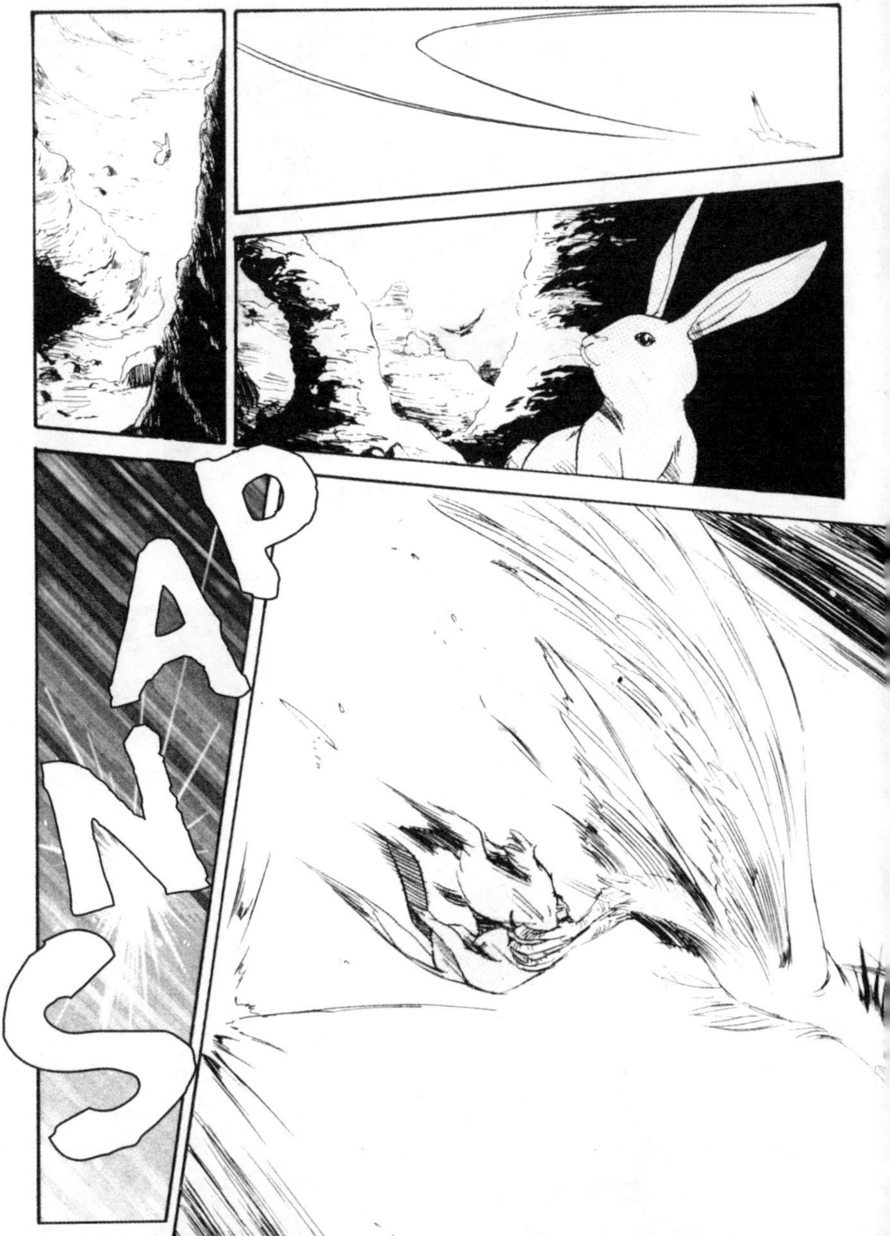
SNAP

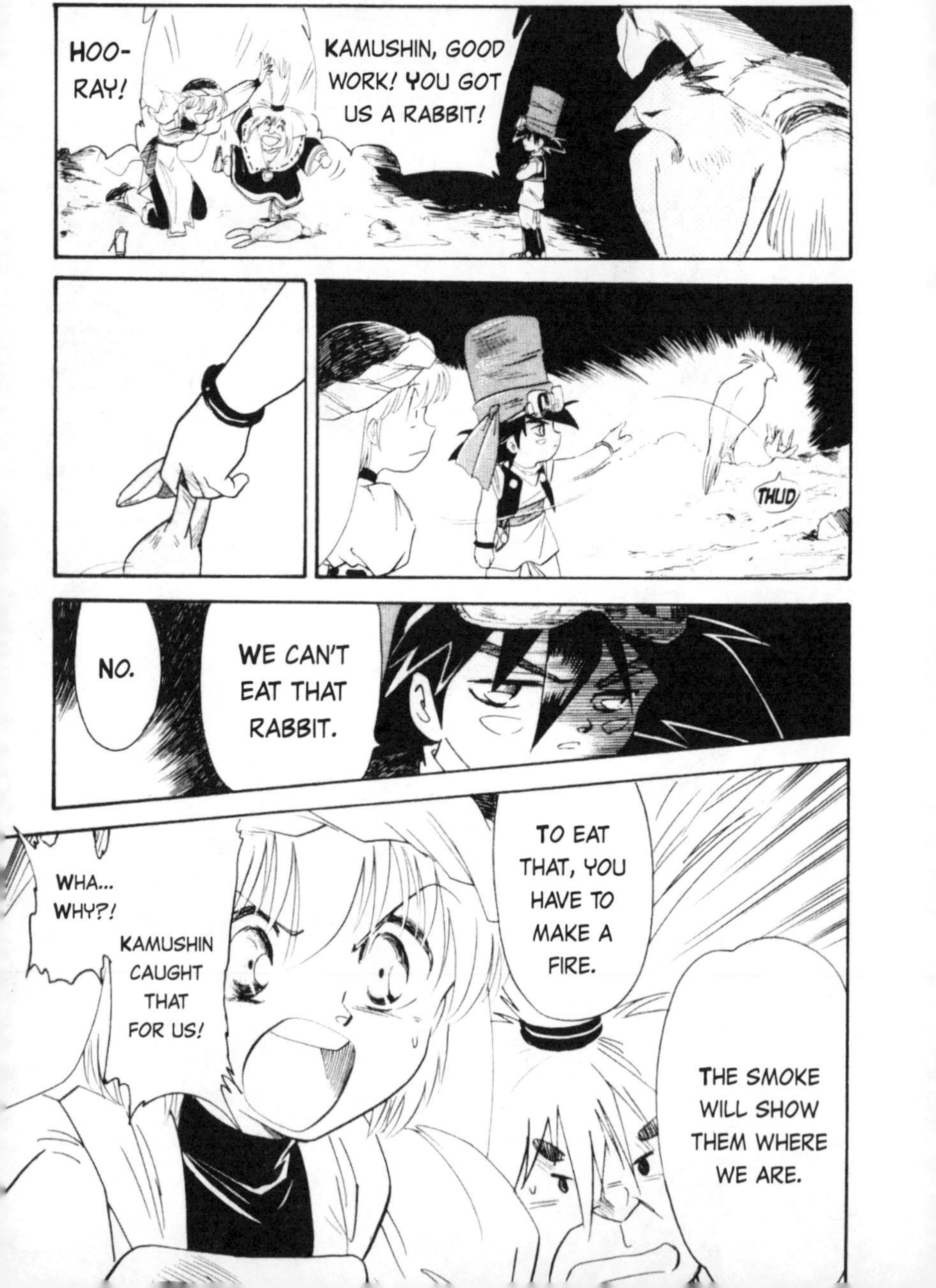
HOO-RAY!
KAMUSHIN, GOOD WORK! YOU GOT US A RABBIT!
THUD
NO.
WE CAN'T EAT THAT RABBIT.
WHA... WHY?!
KAMUSHIN CAUGHT THAT FOR US!
TO EAT THAT, YOU HAVE TO MAKE A FIRE.
THE SMOKE WILL SHOW THEM WHERE WE ARE.

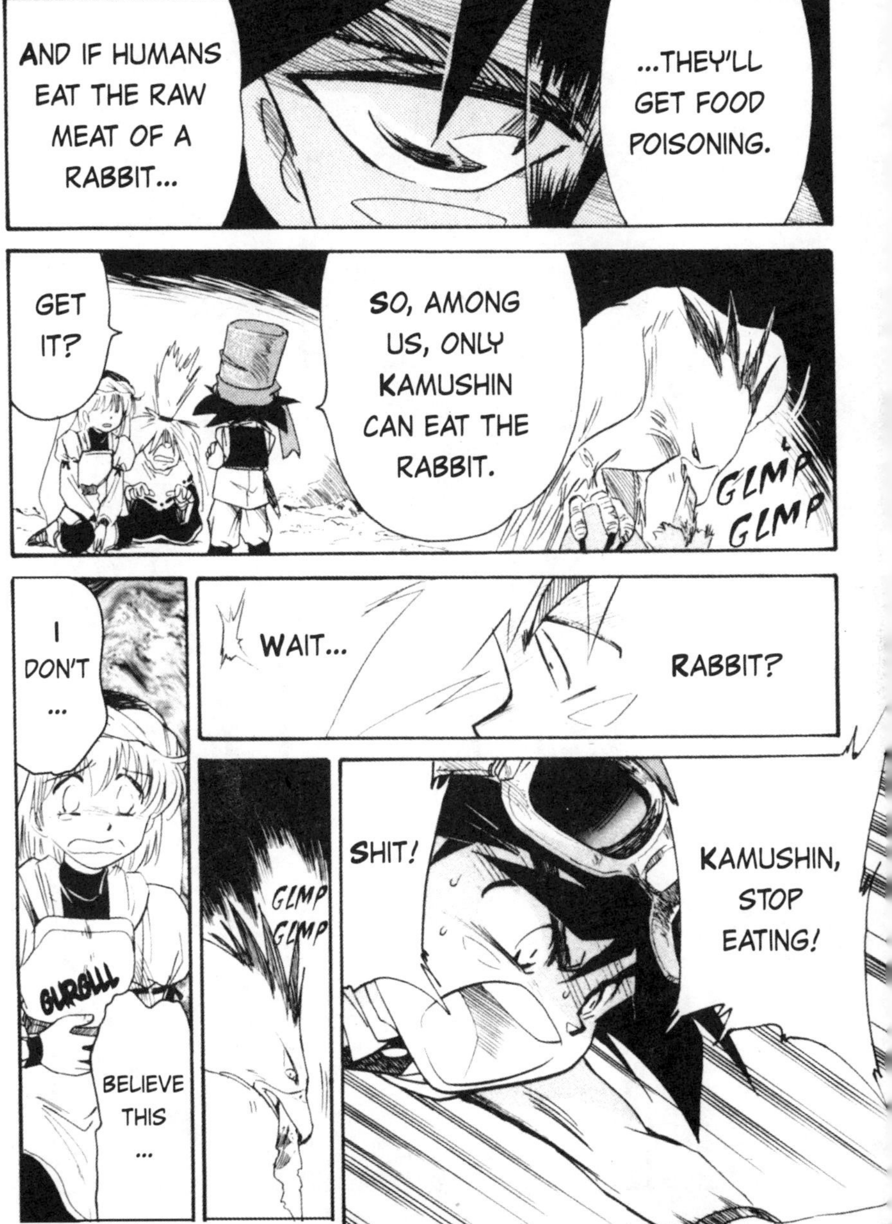
AND IF HUMANS EAT THE RAW MEAT OF A RABBIT...
...THEY'LL GET FOOD POISONING.
SO, AMONG US, ONLY KAMUSHIN CAN EAT THE RABBIT.
GET IT?
GLMP GLMP
WAIT...
RABBIT?
KAMUSHIN, STOP EATING!
SHIT!
GLMP GLMP
I DON'T ...
BELIEVE THIS ...
GURGLLL

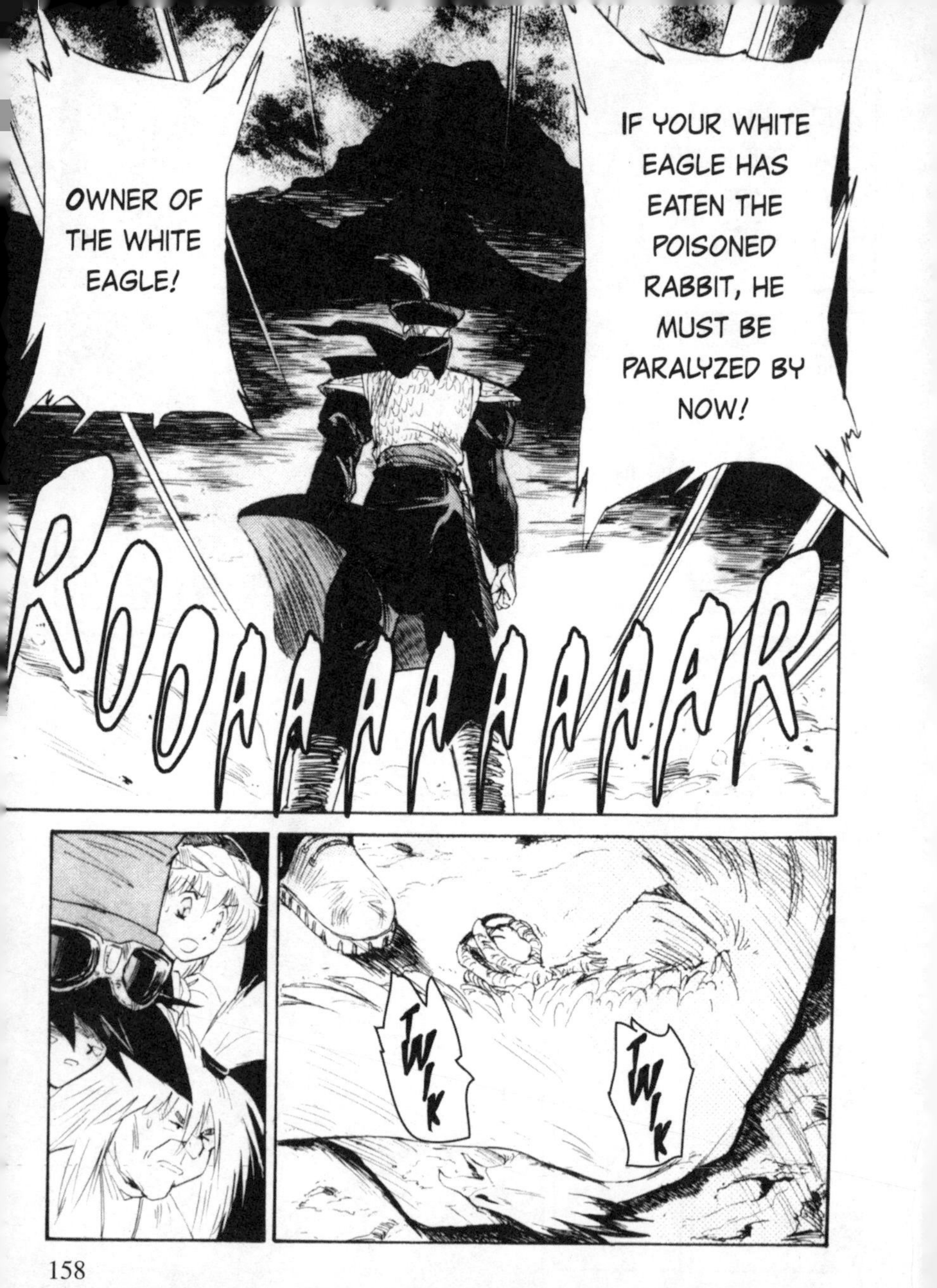
IF YOUR WHITE EAGLE HAS EATEN THE POISONED RABBIT, HE MUST BE PARALYZED BY NOW!
OWNER OF THE WHITE EAGLE!
ROOAAAAAAAAAR
TWIK
TWIK

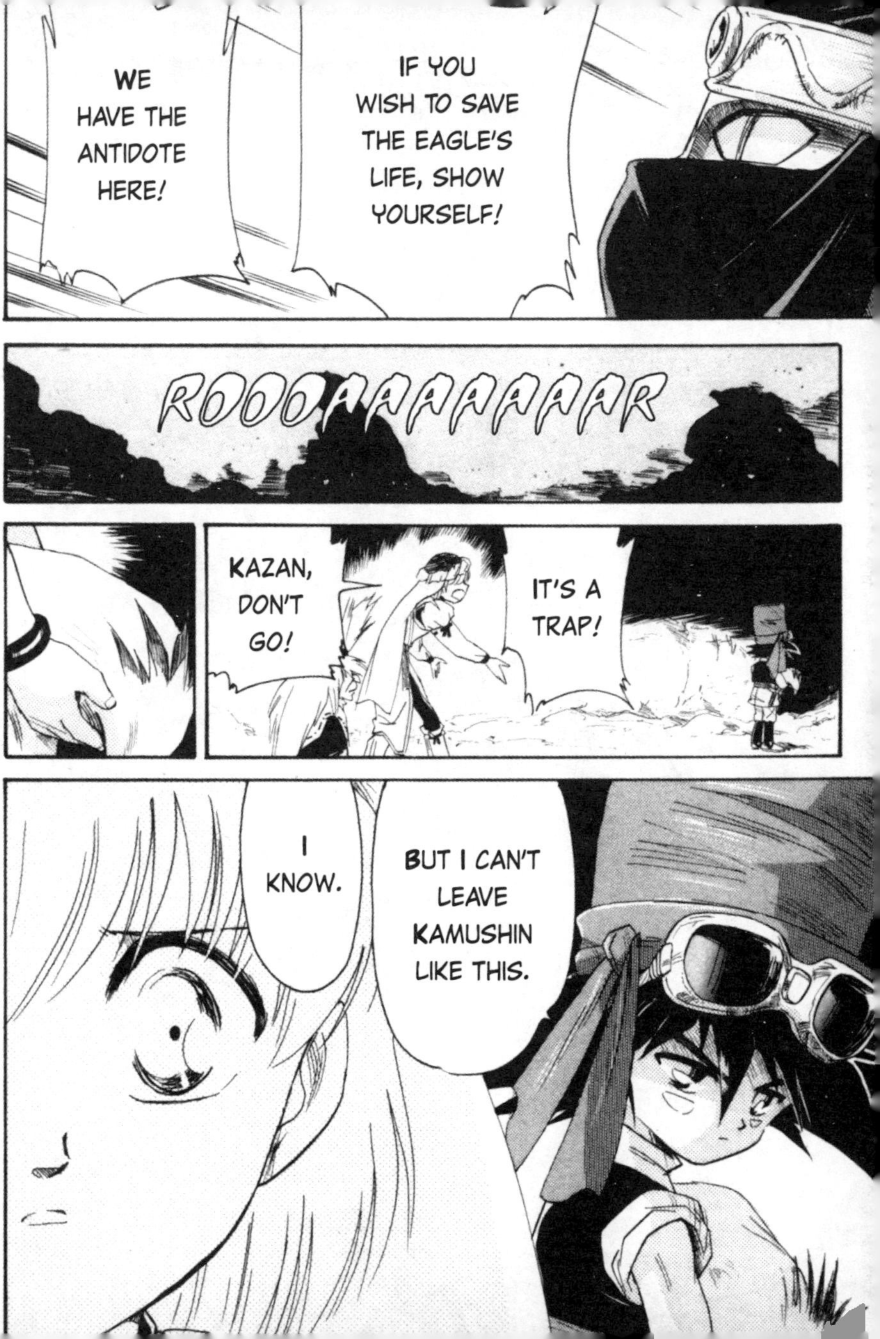
IF YOU WISH TO SAVE THE EAGLE'S LIFE, SHOW YOURSELF!
WE HAVE THE ANTIDOTE HERE!
ROOOAAAAAAAAR
IT'S A TRAP!
KAZAN, DON'T GO!
BUT I CAN'T LEAVE KAMUSHIN LIKE THIS.
I KNOW.

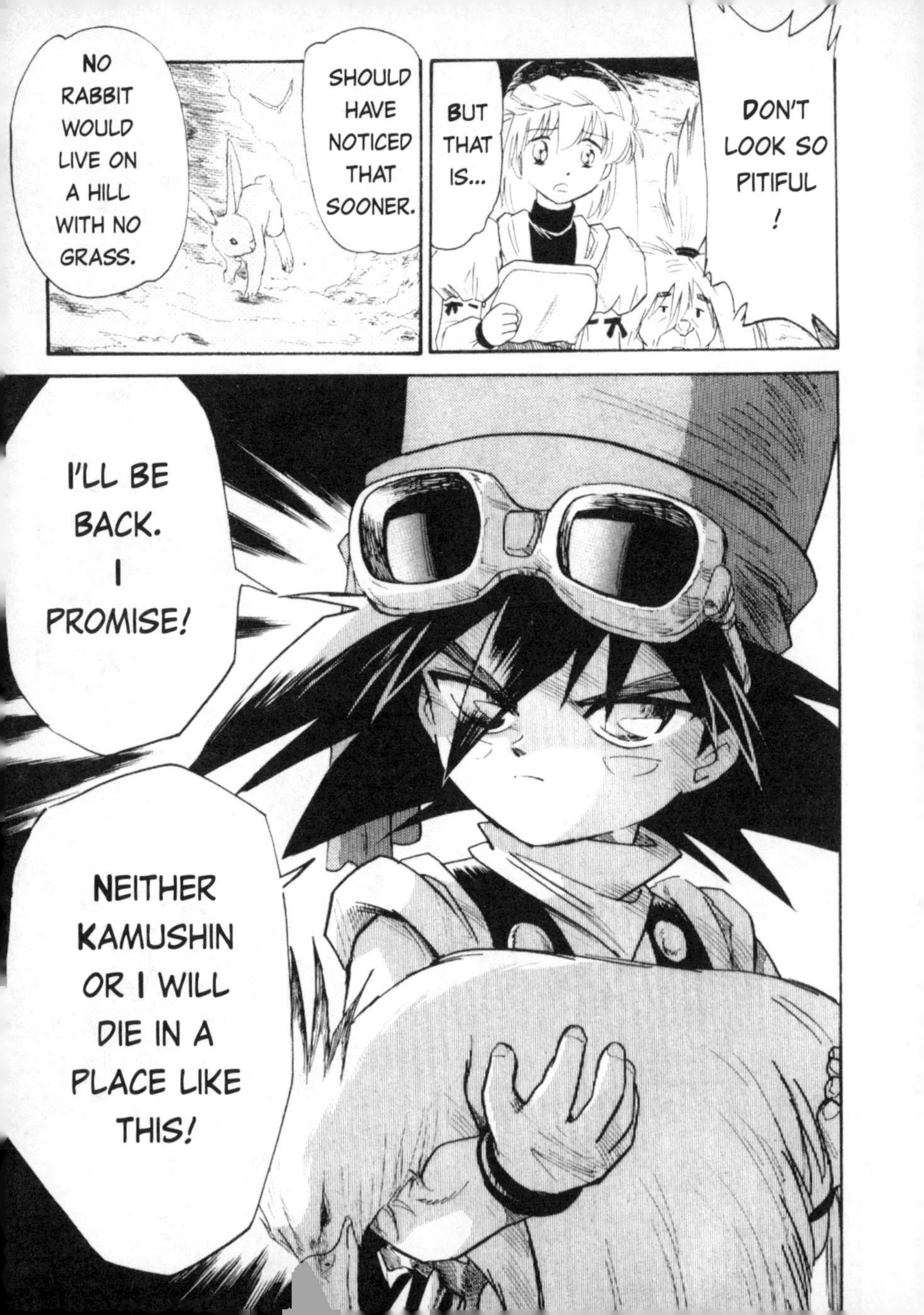
DON'T LOOK SO PITIFUL!
BUT THAT IS...
SHOULD HAVE NOTICED THAT SOONER.
NO RABBIT WOULD LIVE ON A HILL WITH NO GRASS.
I'LL BE BACK. I PROMISE!
NEITHER KAMUSHIN OR I WILL DIE IN A PLACE LIKE THIS!

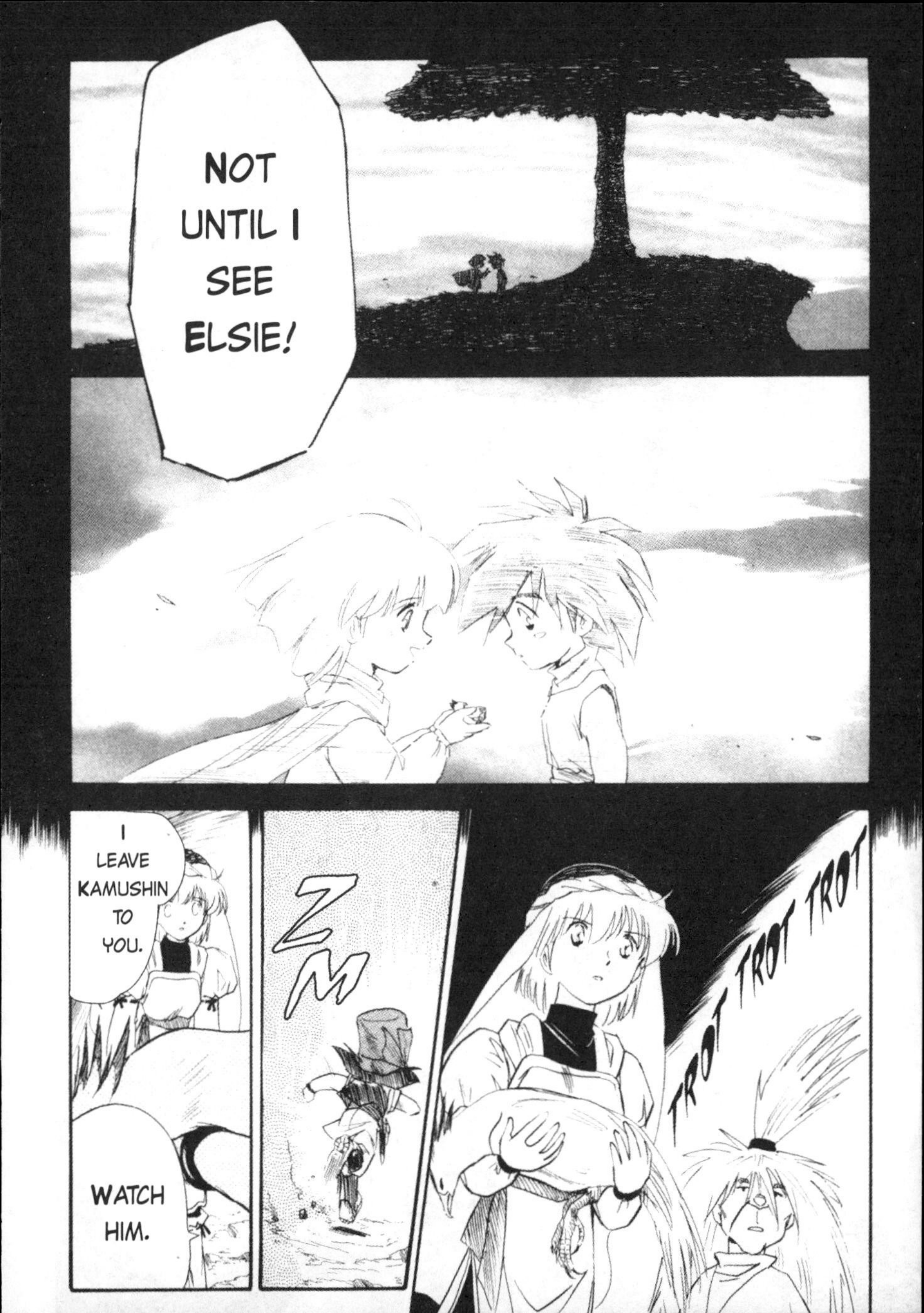
NOT UNTIL I SEE ELSIE!
I LEAVE KAMUSHIN TO YOU.
WATCH HIM.
ZM
TROT TROT TROT

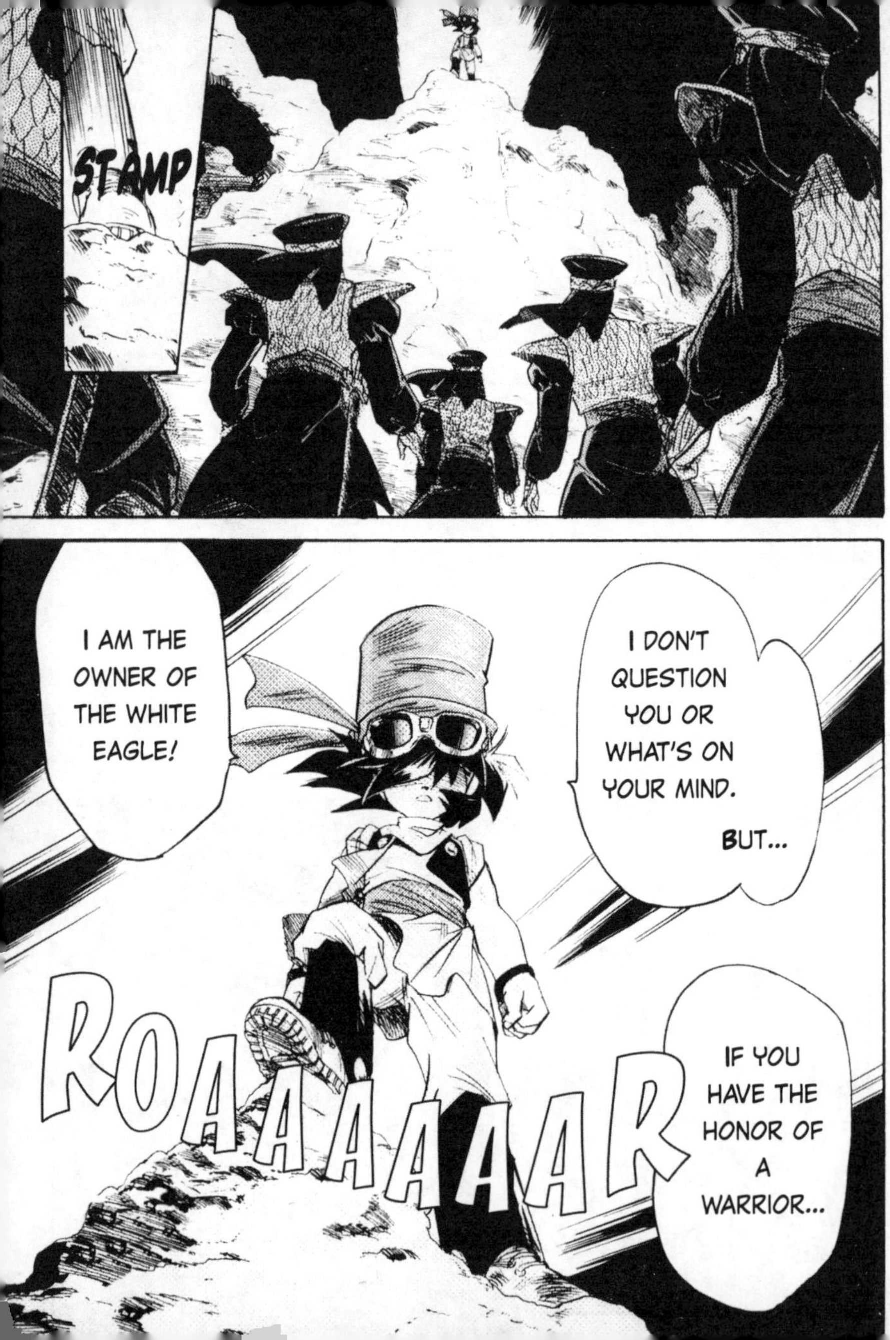
STAMP
I DON'T QUESTION YOU OR WHAT'S ON YOUR MIND.
BUT...
I AM THE OWNER OF THE WHITE EAGLE!
IF YOU HAVE THE HONOR OF A WARRIOR...
ROAAAAAAAR

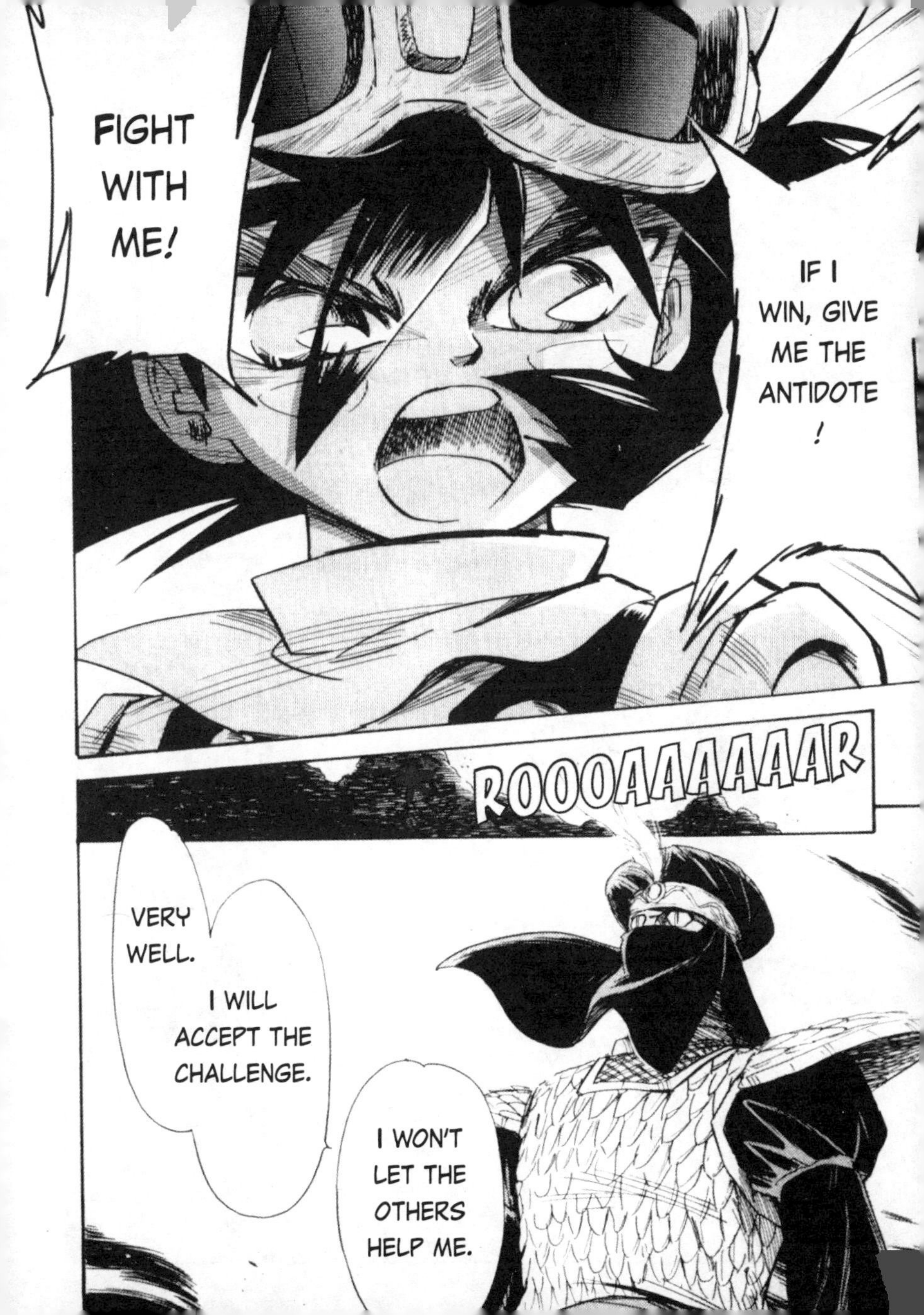
IF I WIN, GIVE ME THE ANTIDOTE!
FIGHT WITH ME!
ROOOAAAAAAR
VERY WELL.
I WILL ACCEPT THE CHALLENGE.
I WON'T LET THE OTHERS HELP ME.

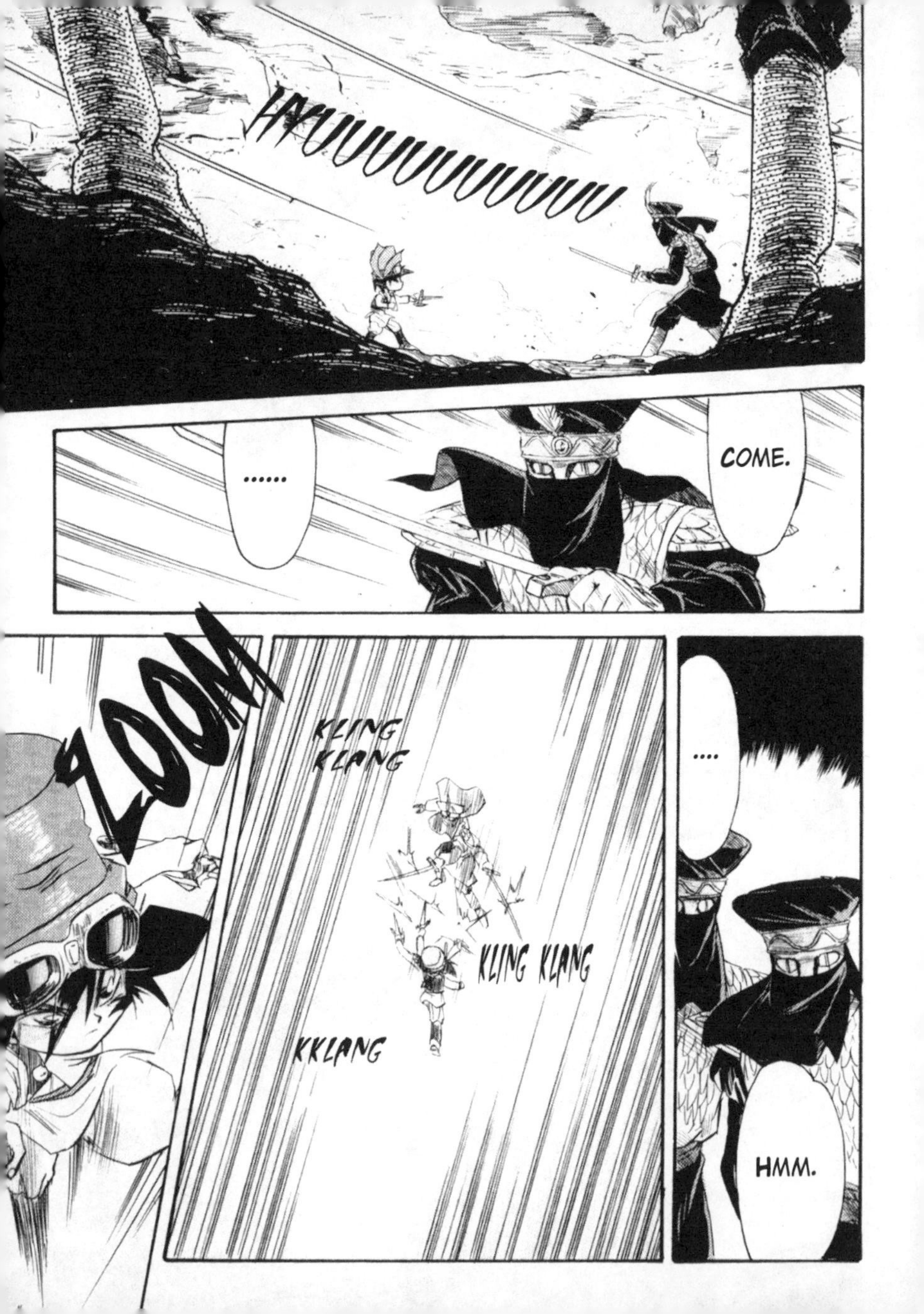
HYUUUUUUUUUUUU
COME.
......
ZOOM
KLING KLANG
KLING KLANG
KKLANG
....
HMM.

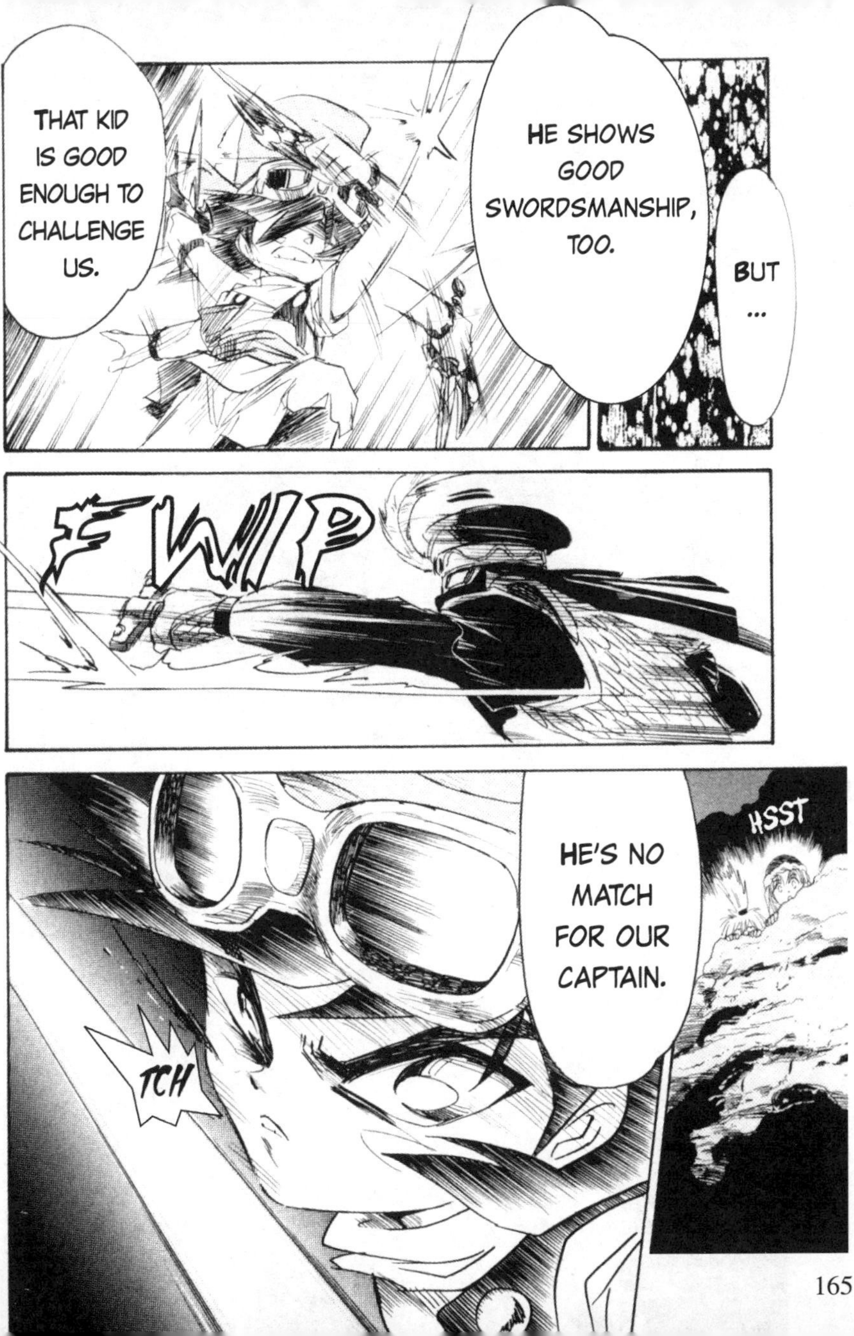
HE SHOWS GOOD SWORDSMANSHIP, TOO.
THAT KID IS GOOD ENOUGH TO CHALLENGE US.
BUT ...
FWIP
HSST
HE'S NO MATCH FOR OUR CAPTAIN.
TCH

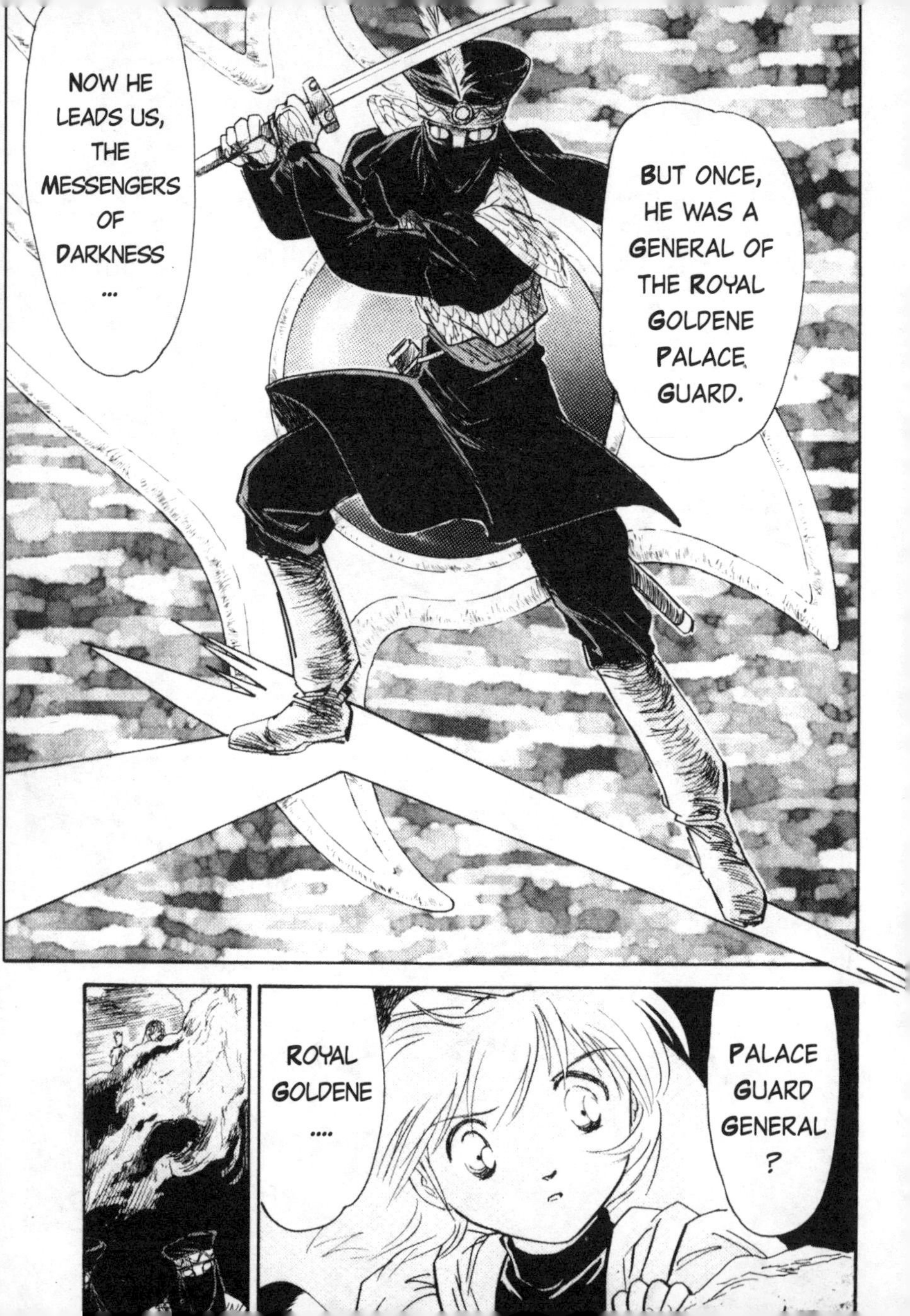
BUT ONCE, HE WAS A GENERAL OF THE ROYAL GOLDENE PALACE GUARD.
NOW HE LEADS US, THE MESSENGERS OF DARKNESS ...
PALACE GUARD GENERAL ?
ROYAL GOLDENE ....

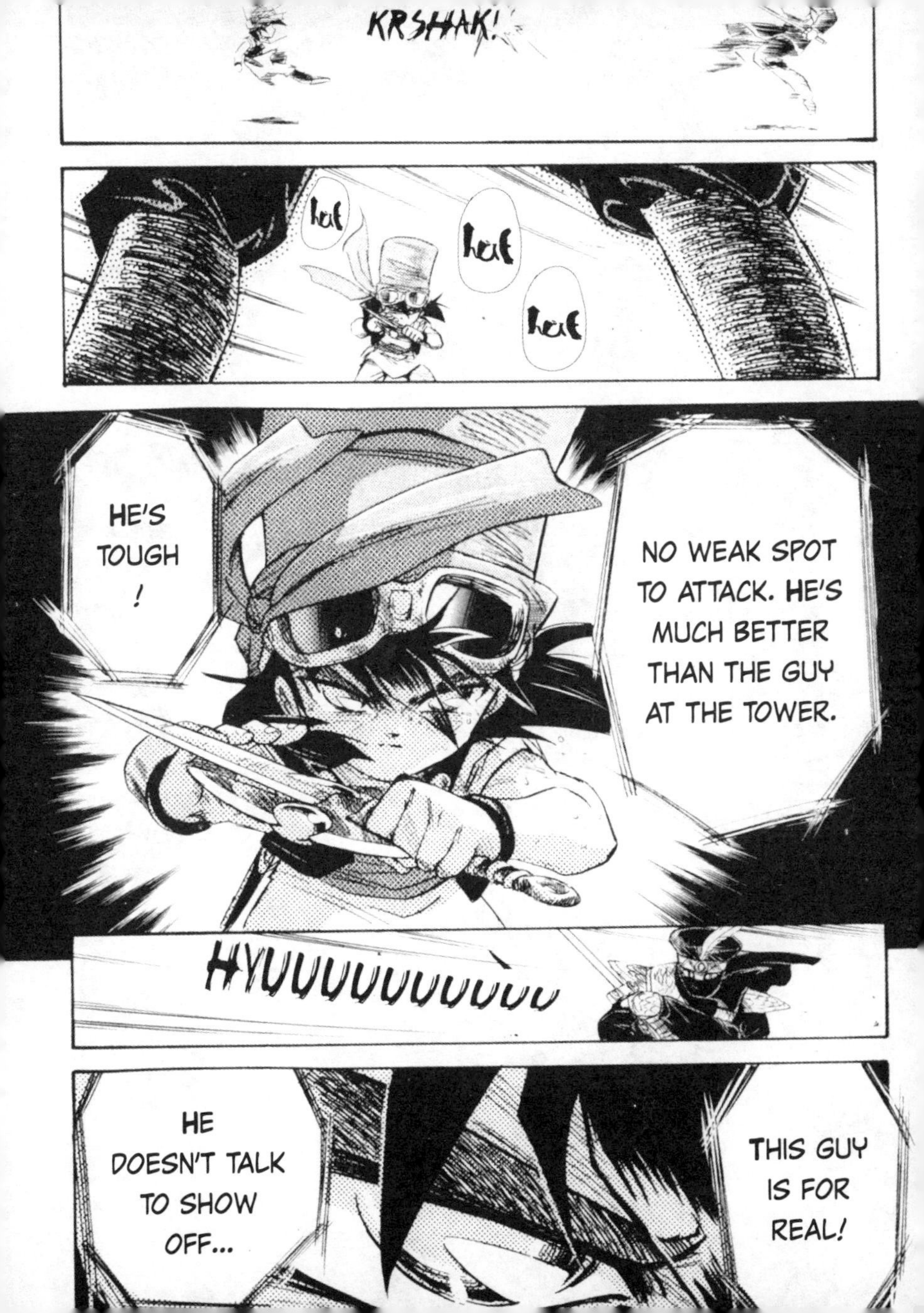
KRSHAK!
haf
haf
haf
HE'S TOUGH!
NO WEAK SPOT TO ATTACK. HE'S MUCH BETTER THAN THE GUY AT THE TOWER.
HYUUUUUUUUUUU
THIS GUY IS FOR REAL!
HE DOESN'T TALK TO SHOW OFF...

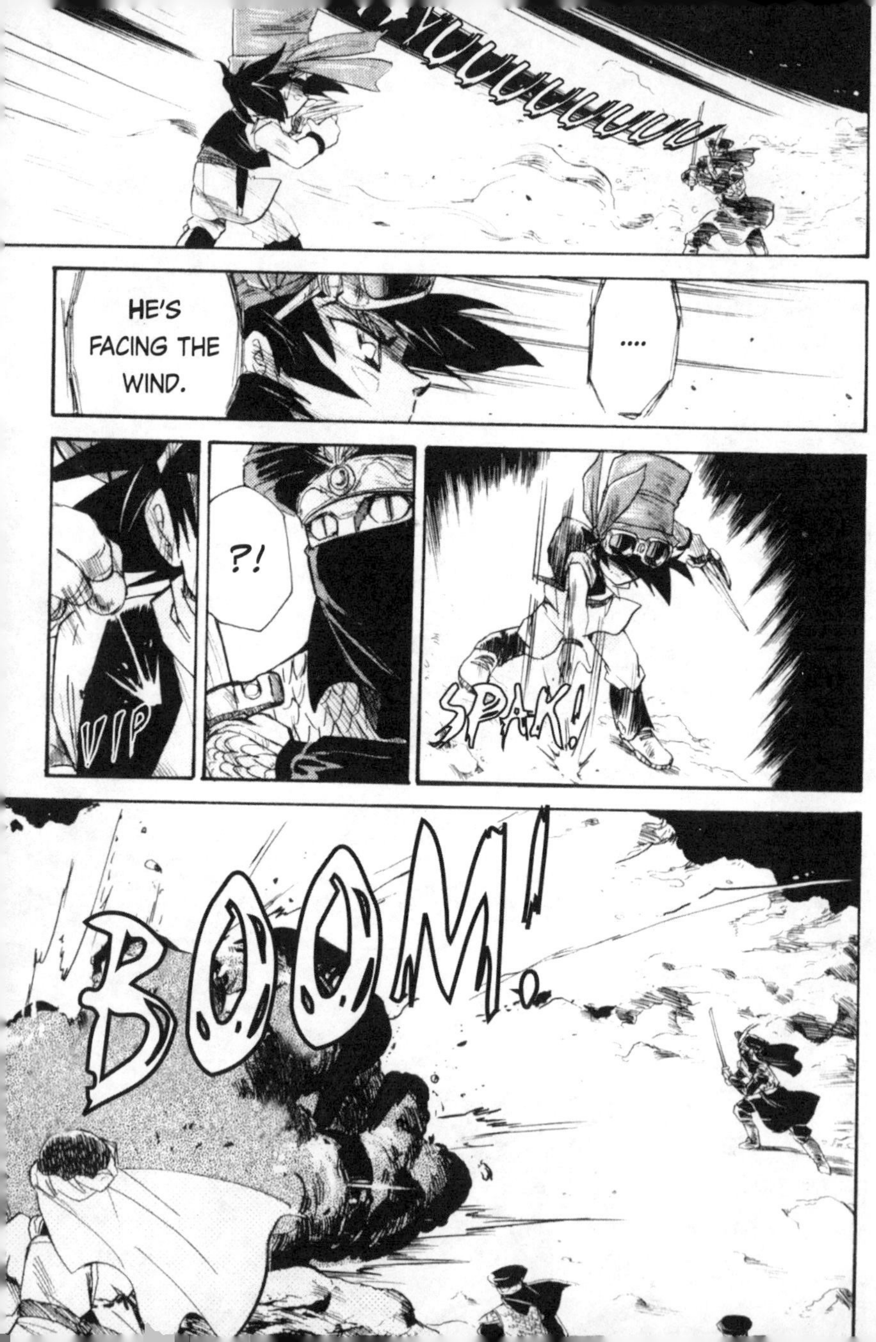
YUUUUUUUUU
HE'S FACING THE WIND.
....
VIP
?!
SPAK!
BOOM!

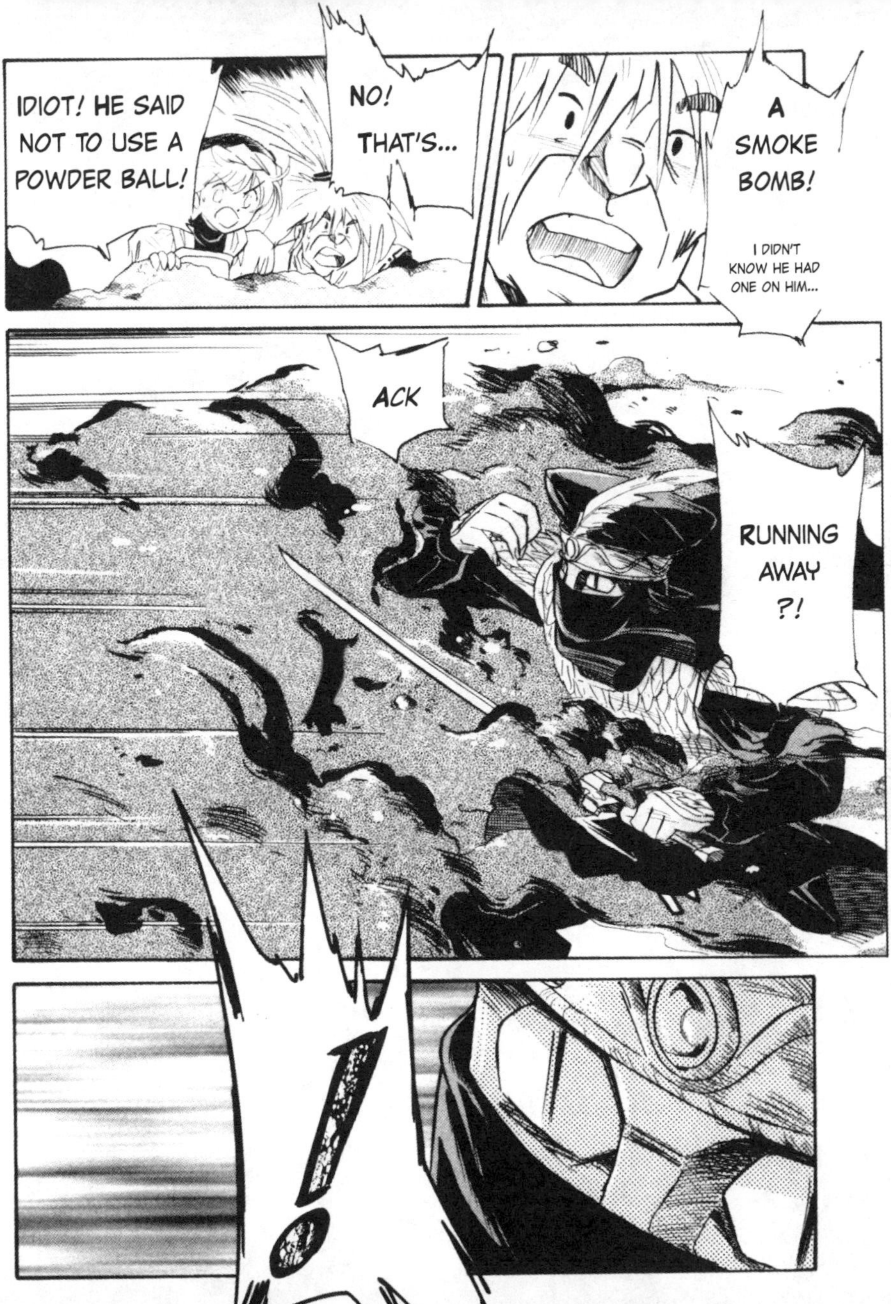
IDIOT! HE SAID NOT TO USE A POWDER BALL!
NO! THAT'S...
A SMOKE BOMB!
I DIDN'T KNOW HE HAD ONE ON HIM...
ACK
RUNNING AWAY ?!

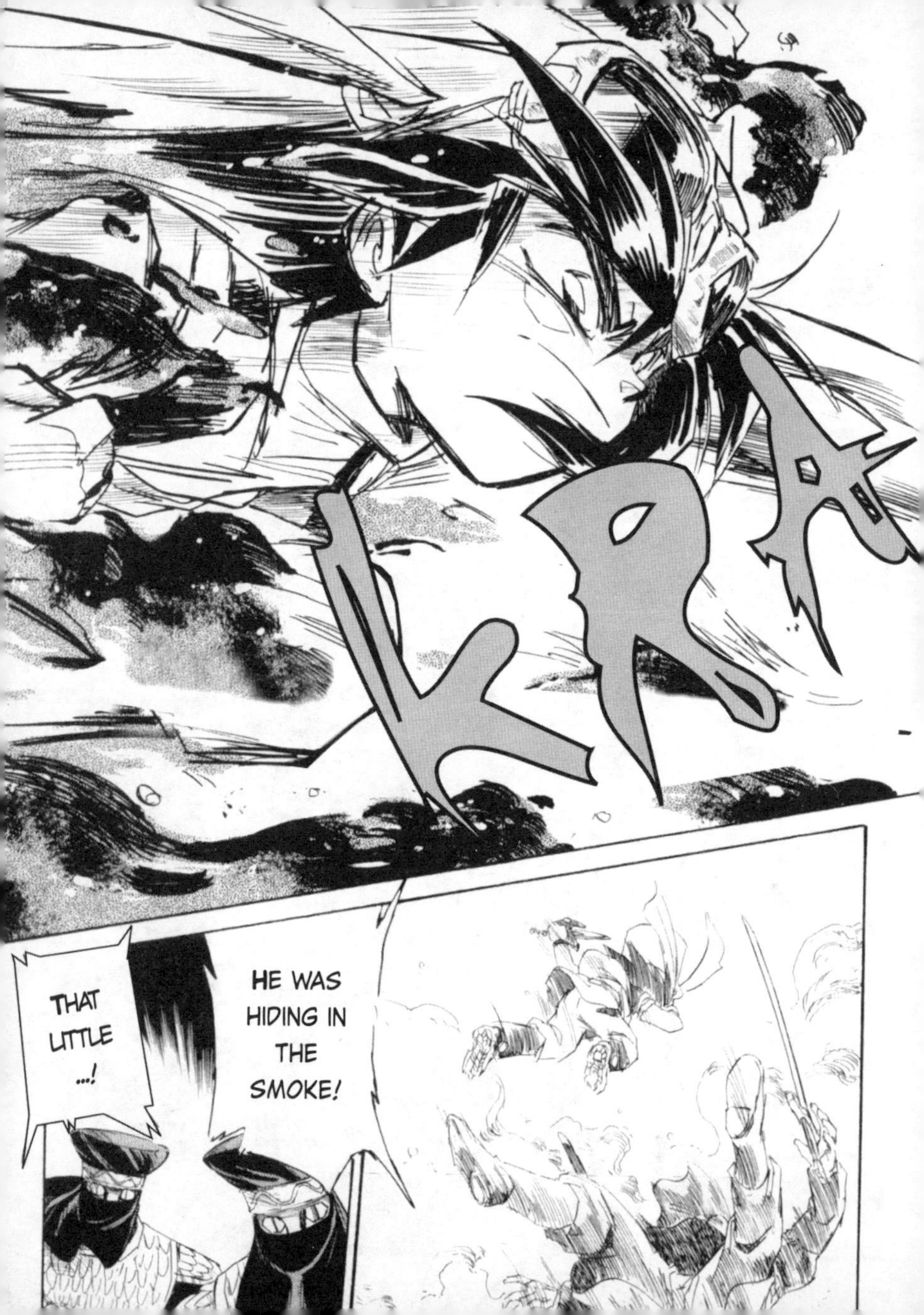
KRA
HE WAS HIDING IN THE SMOKE!
THAT LITTLE ...!

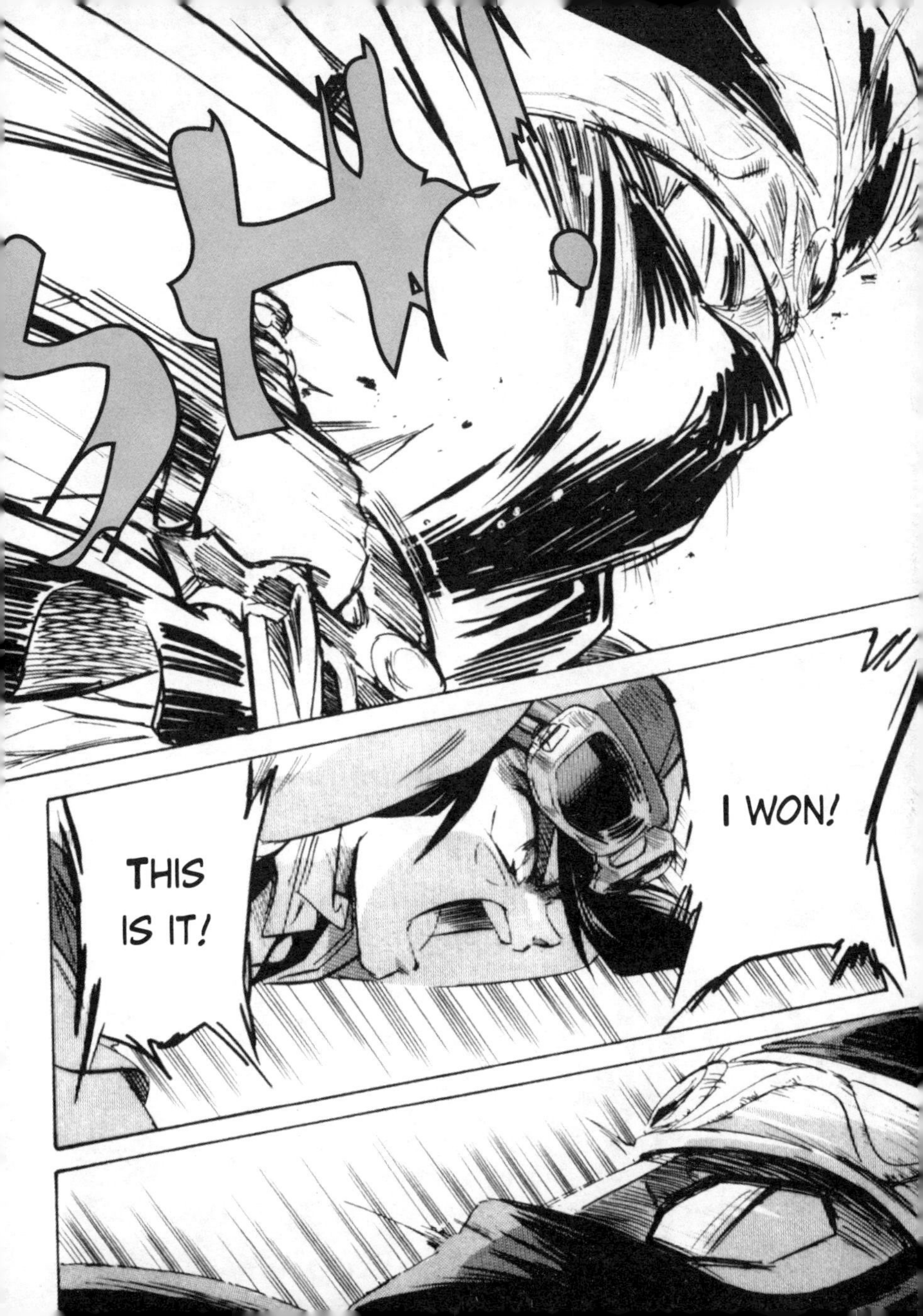
I WON!
THIS IS IT!

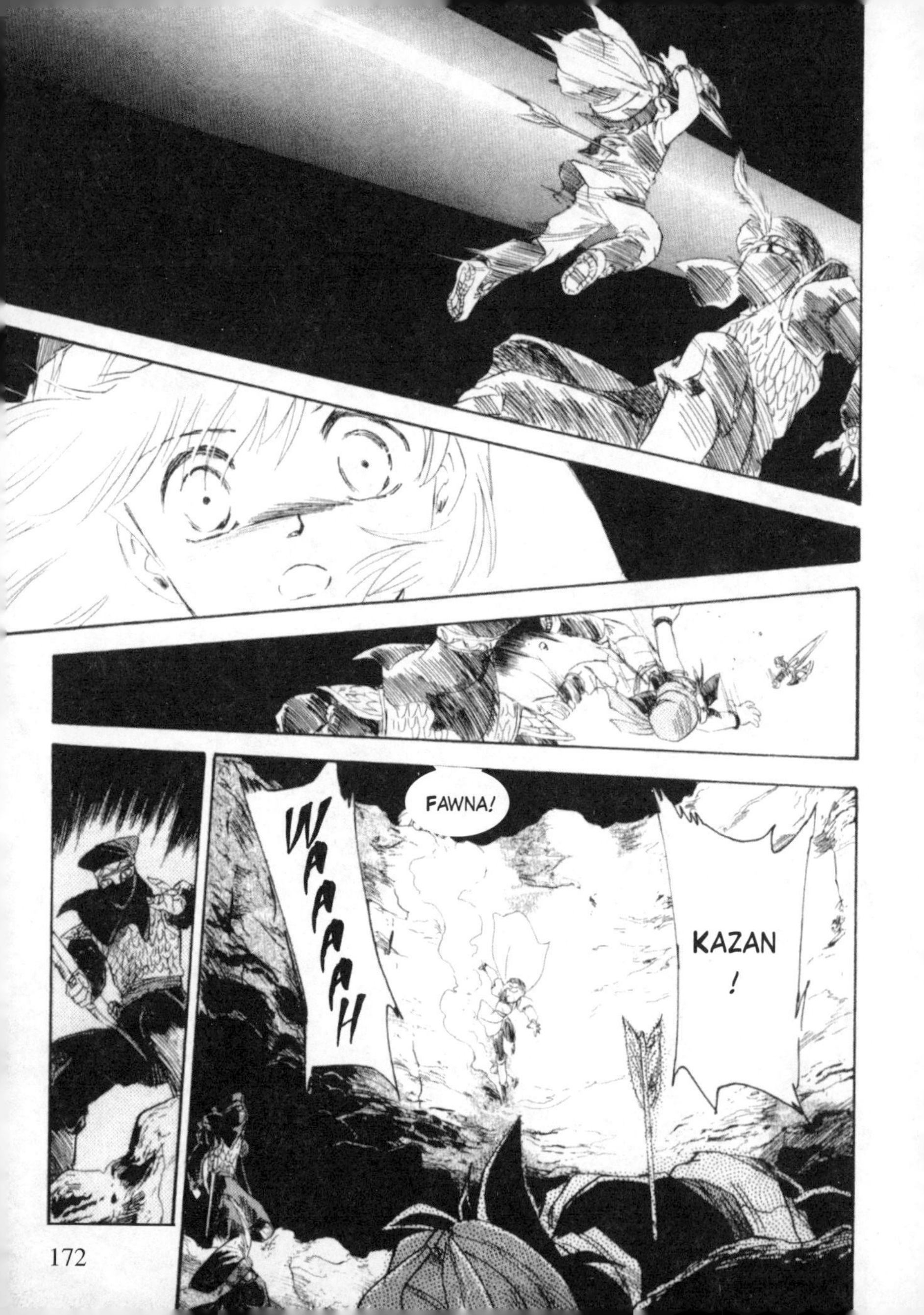
FAWNA!
WAAAAAH
KAZAN
!

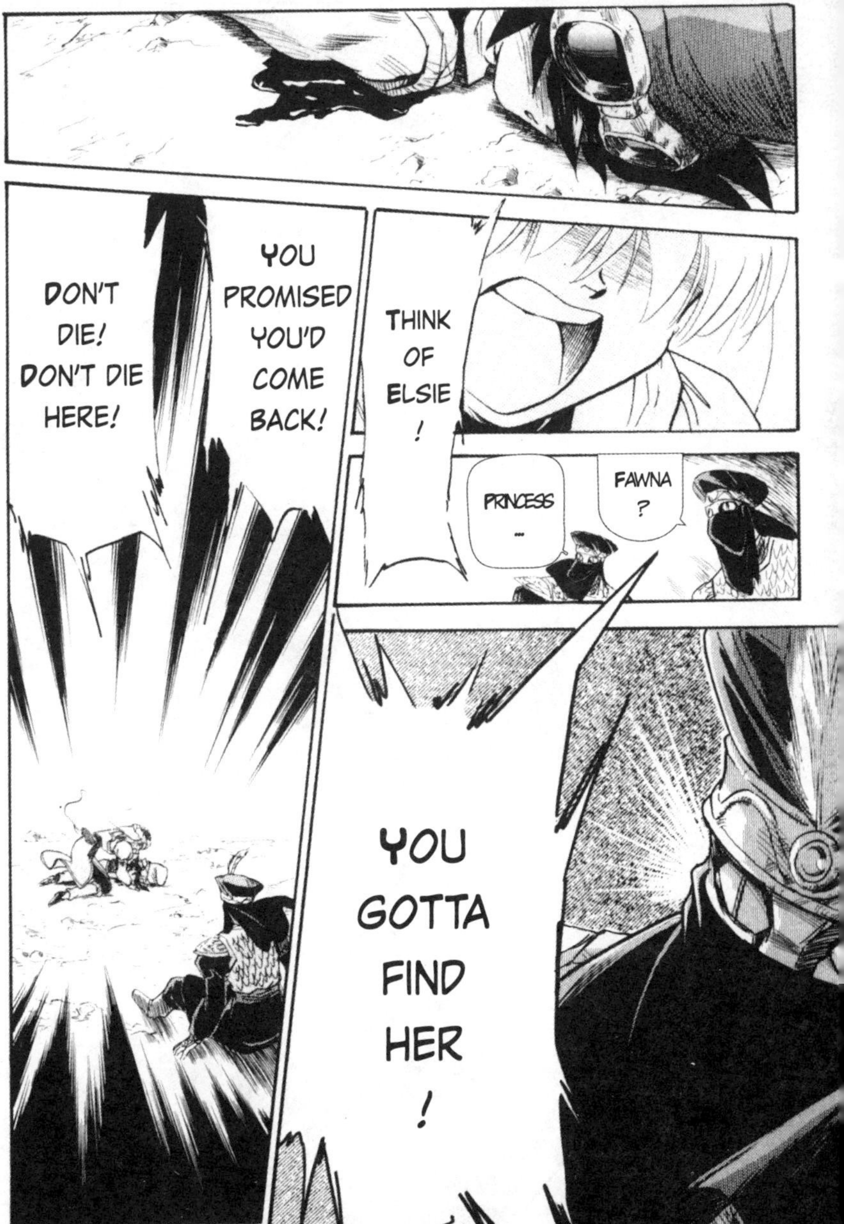
THINK OF ELSIE!
YOU PROMISED YOU'D COME BACK!
DON'T DIE! DON'T DIE HERE!
FAWNA?
PRINCESS...
YOU GOTTA FIND HER!

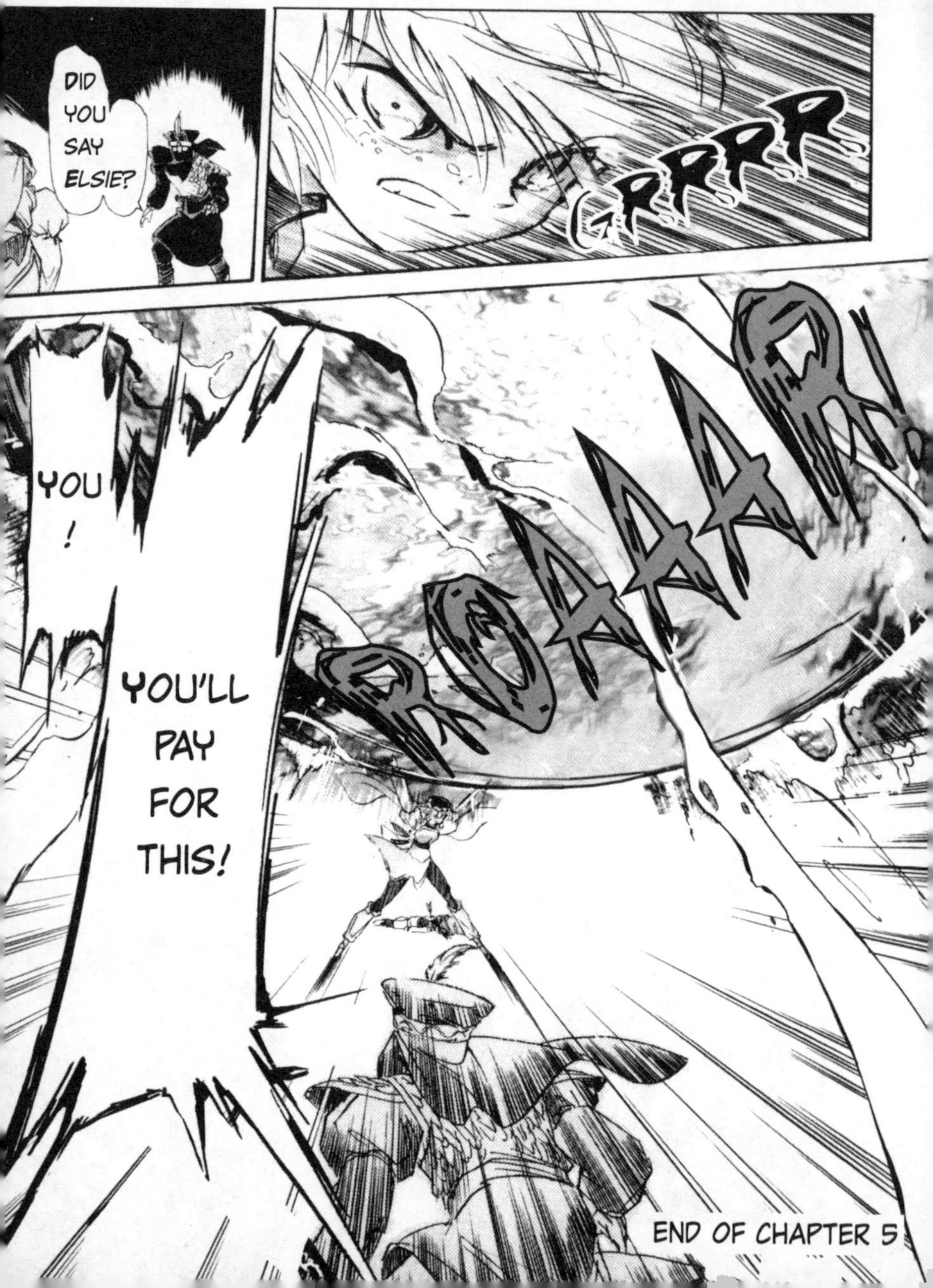
DID YOU SAY ELSIE?
GRRRRR
YOU!
YOU'LL PAY FOR THIS!
ROAAAR!
END OF CHAPTER 5

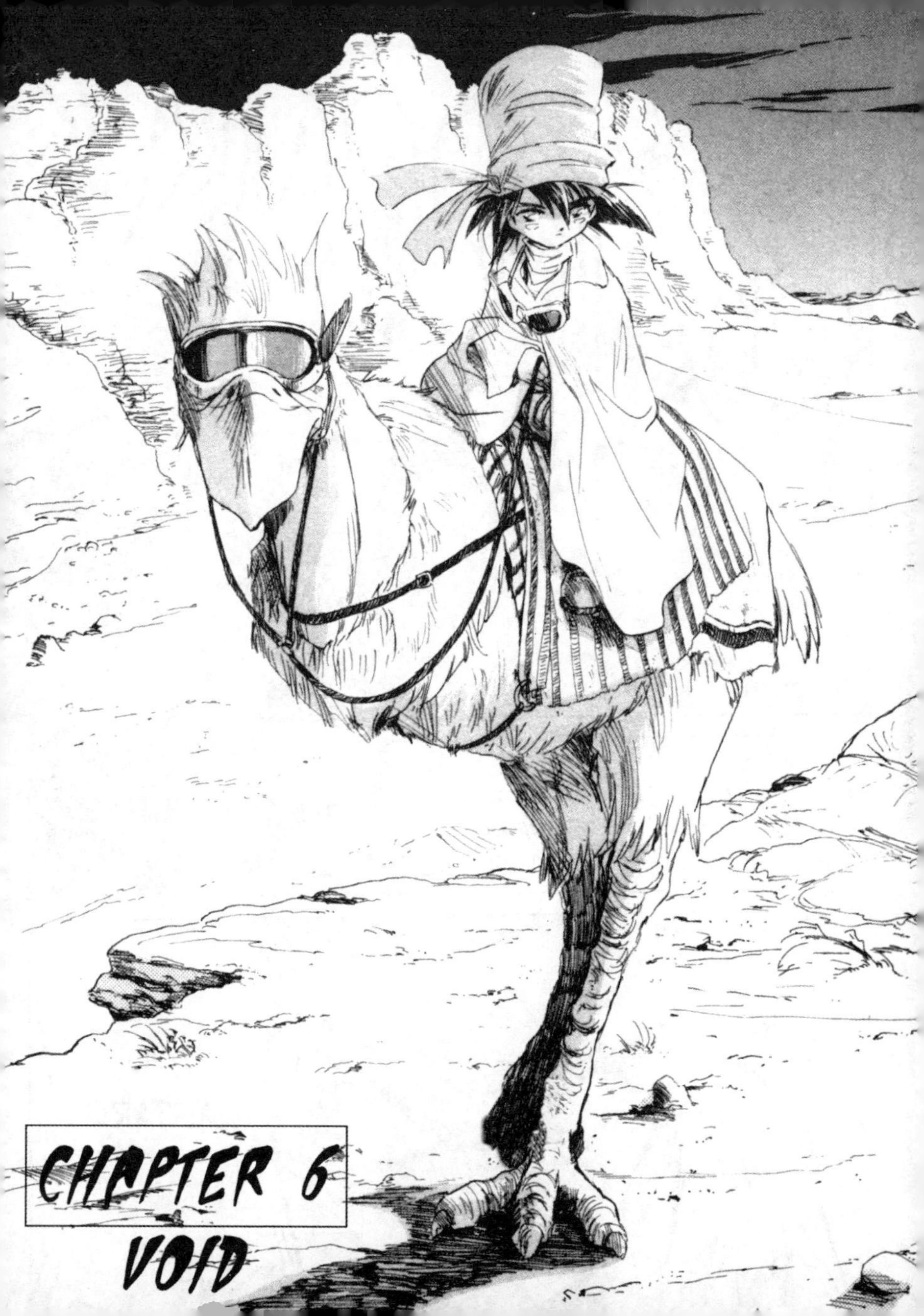
CHAPTER 6
VOID

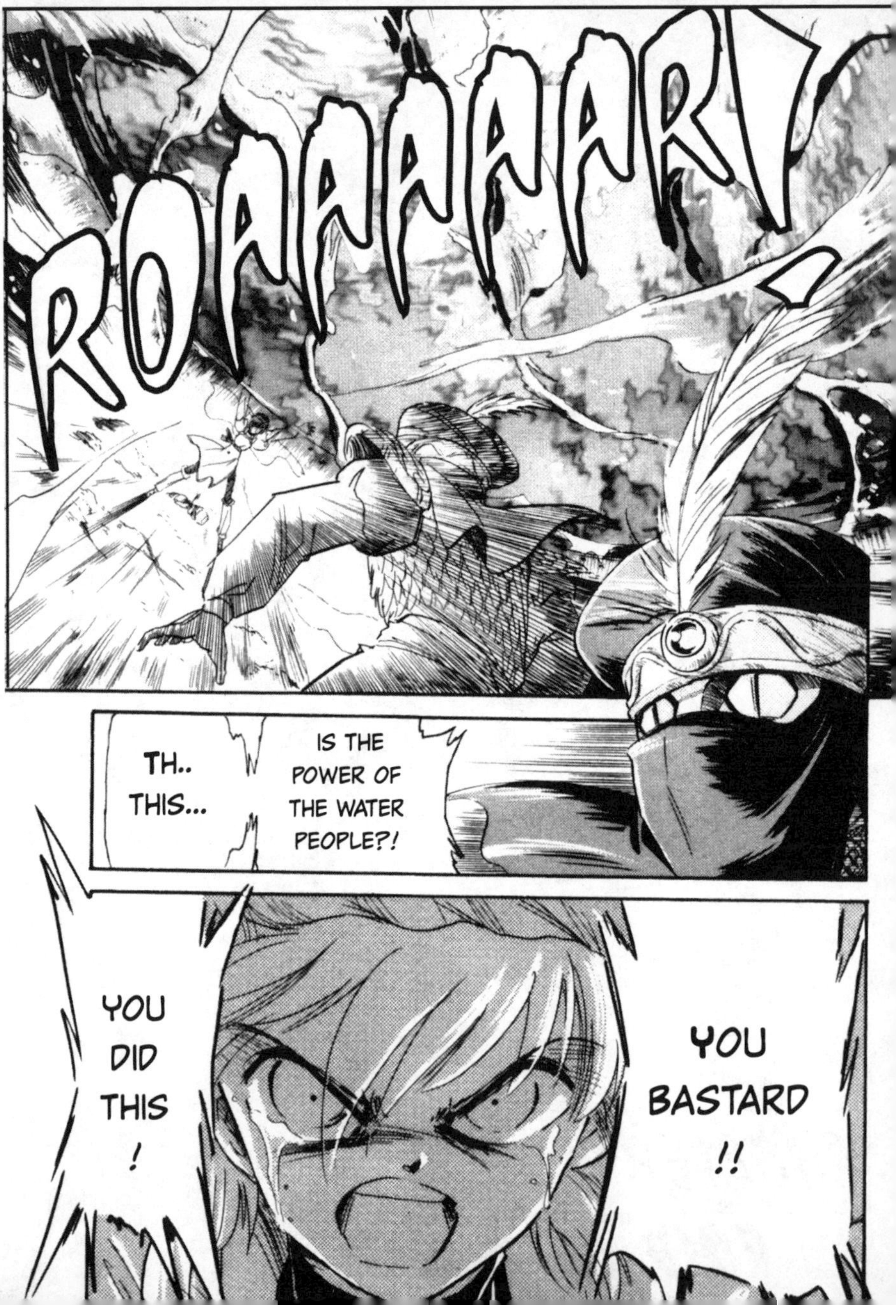
ROAAAAAR!
TH.. THIS...
IS THE POWER OF THE WATER PEOPLE?!
YOU BASTARD!!
YOU DID THIS!

YOU SAID YOU WOULDN'T LET THE OTHERS HELP!

LOOK AT WHAT YOU DID TO HIM!

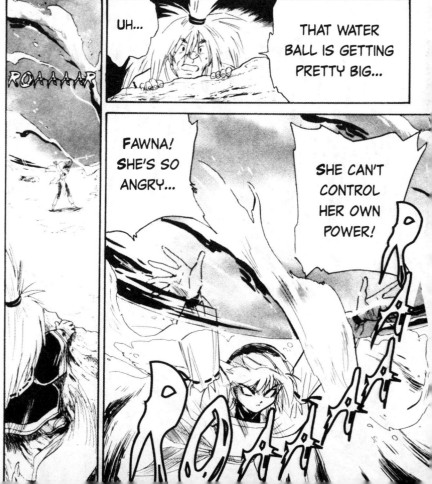

ROAAAAR

UH...

THAT WATER BALL IS GETTING PRETTY BIG...

FAWNA! SHE'S SO ANGRY...

SHE CAN'T CONTROL HER OWN POWER!

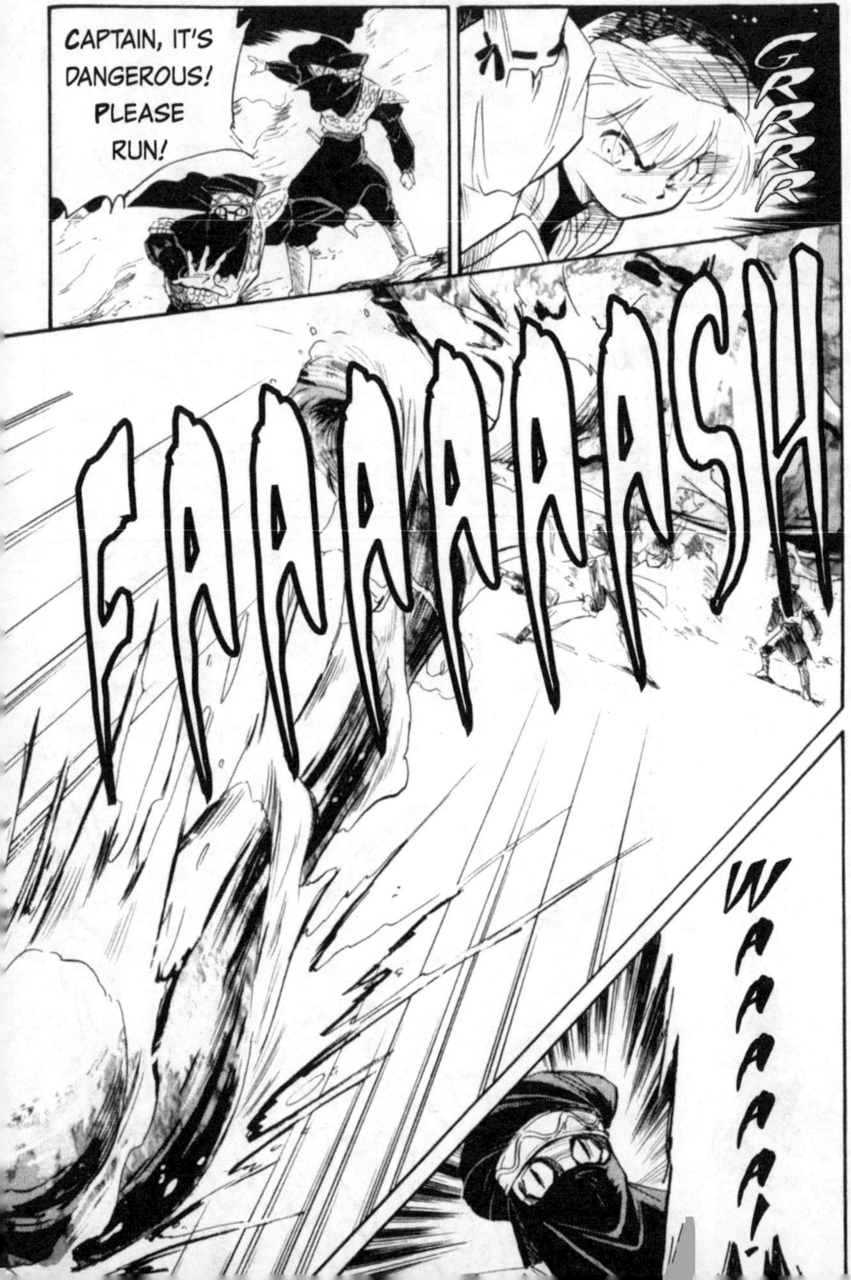

CAPTAIN, IT'S DANGEROUS! PLEASE RUN!
GRRRR
FAAAAASH
WAAAAAAAI-

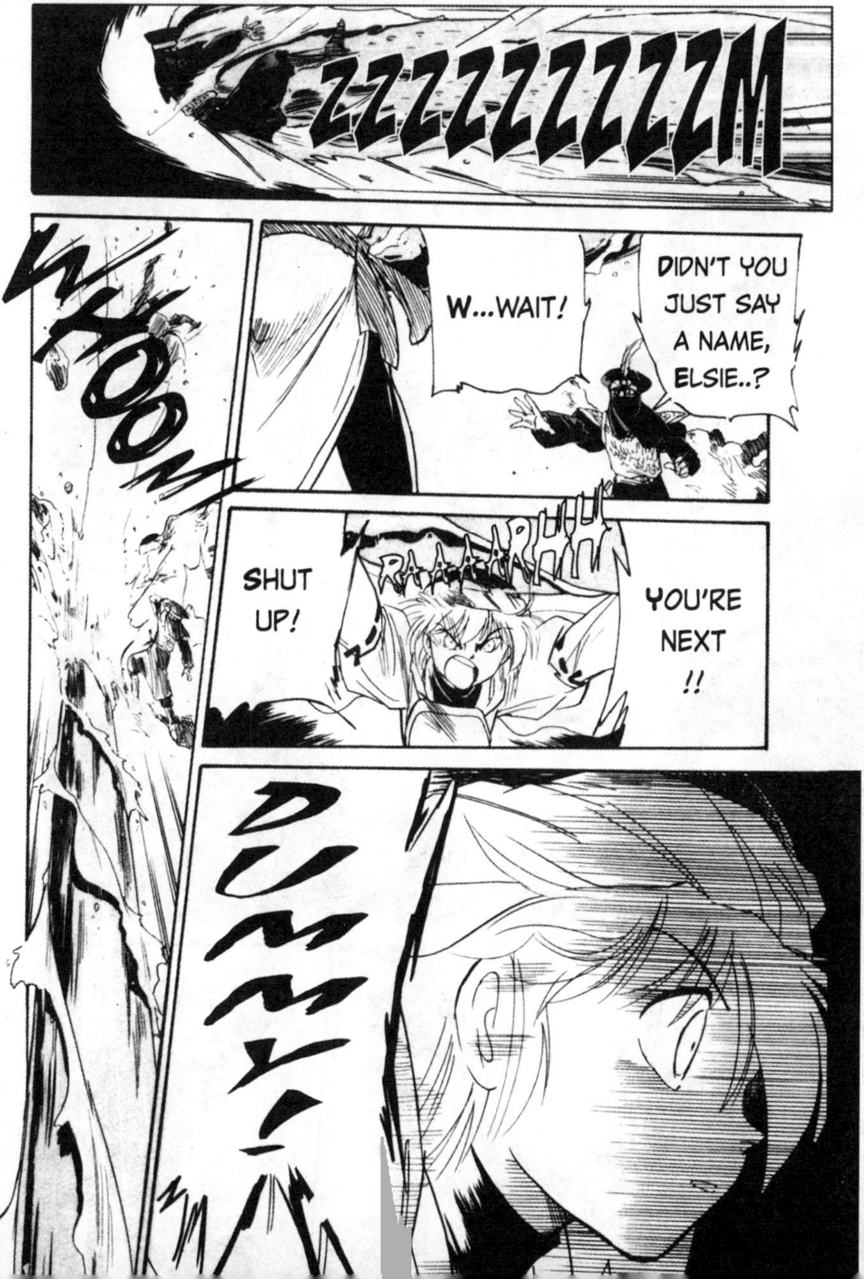
ZZZZZZZZZZZM
WHOOM!
W...WAIT!
DIDN'T YOU JUST SAY A NAME, ELSIE..?
RAAAARHH
SHUT UP!
YOU'RE NEXT !!
DUMMY!

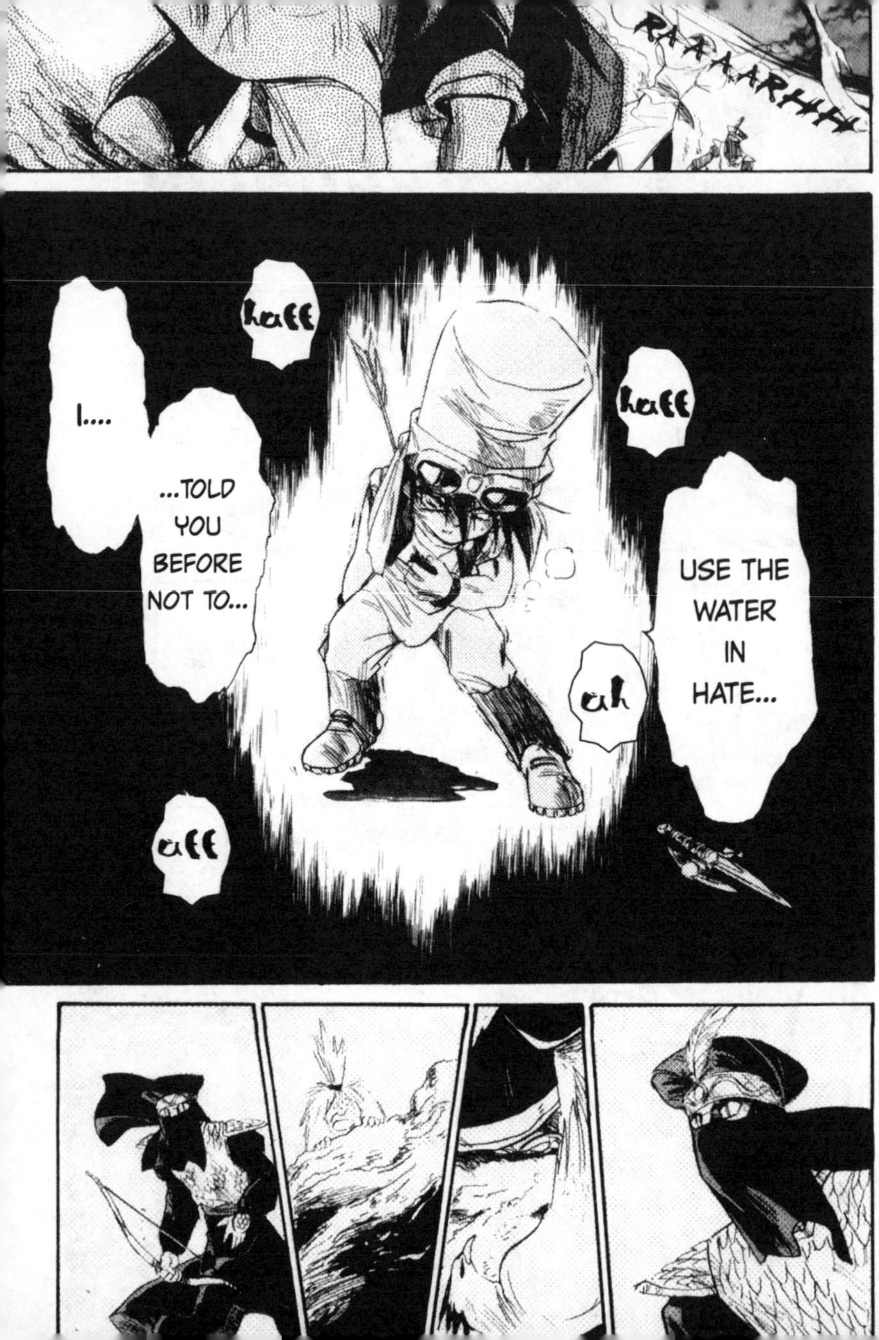
RAAAARHHH
haff
haff
I....
...TOLD YOU BEFORE NOT TO...
USE THE WATER IN HATE...
ah
aff

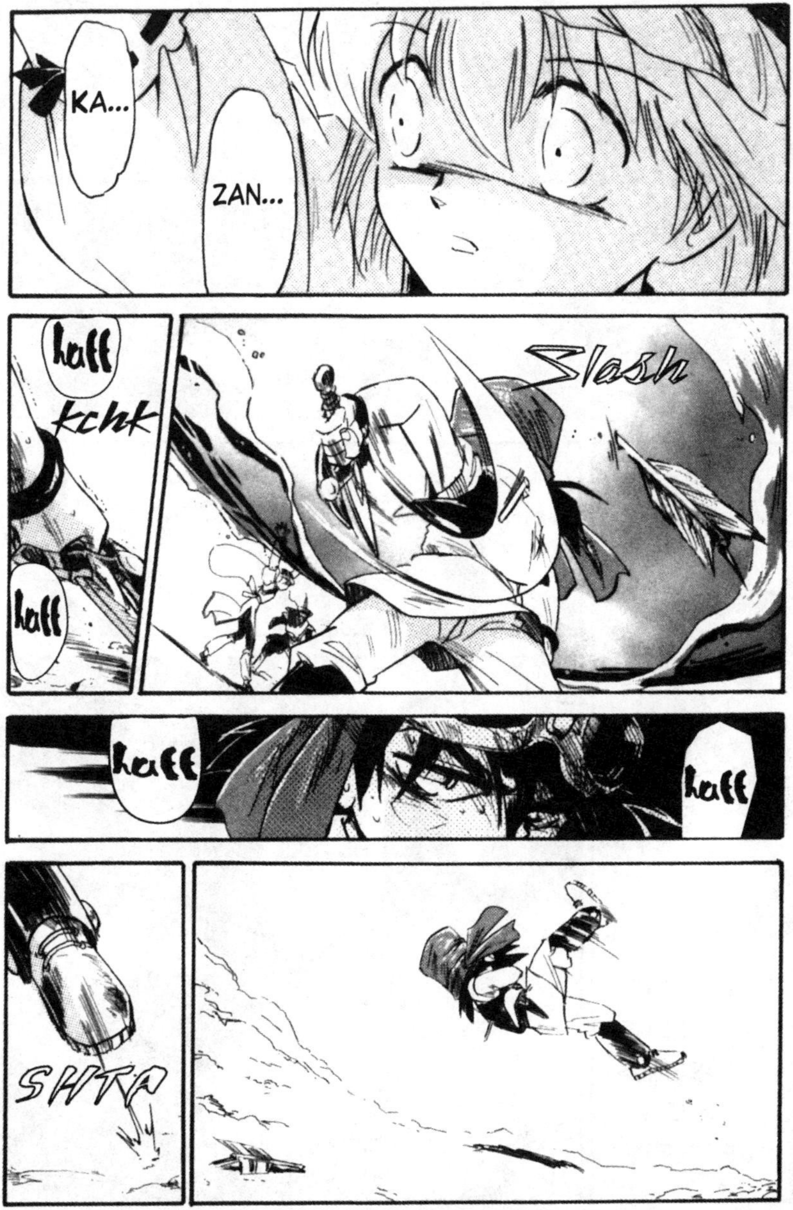

KA...
ZAN...
Slash
haff
kchk
haff
haff
haff
SHTA

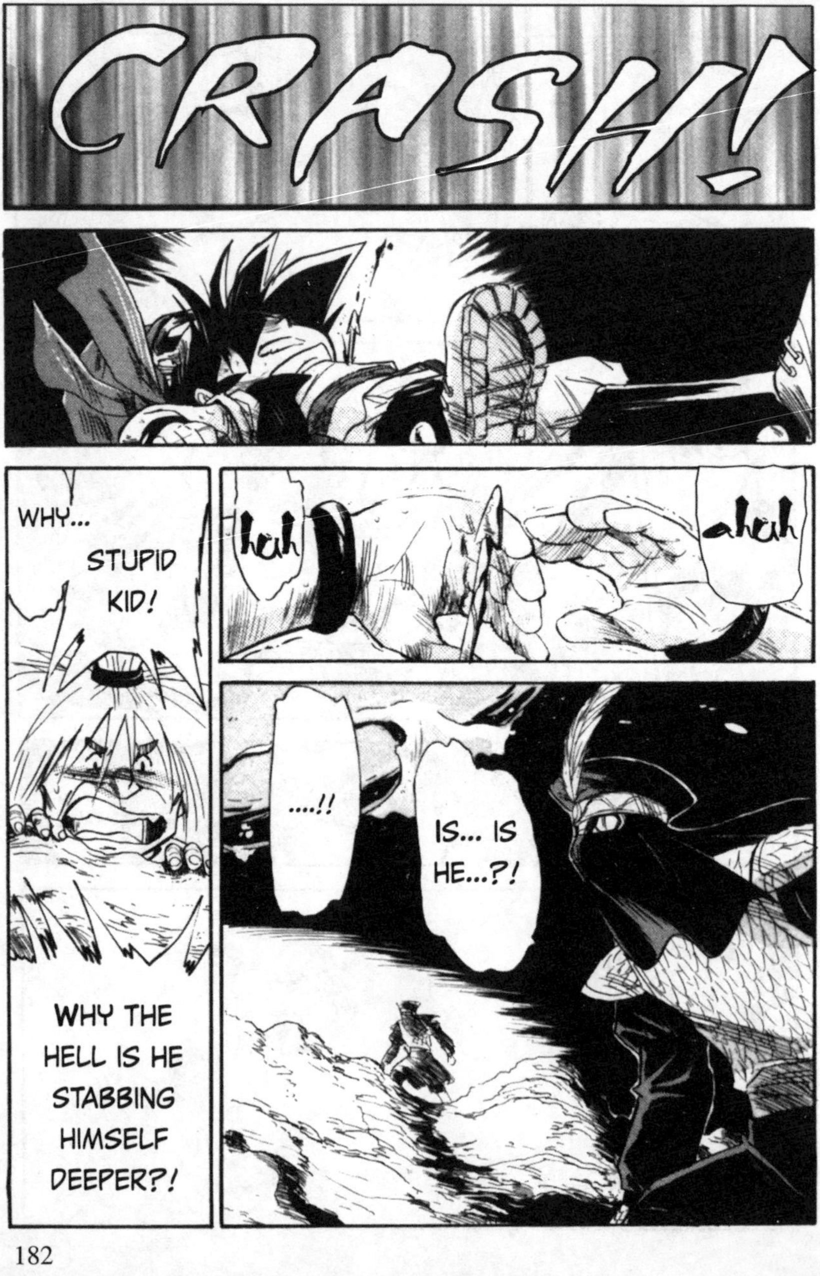
CRASH!
hah
ahah
WHY...
STUPID KID!
WHY THE HELL IS HE STABBING HIMSELF DEEPER?!
...!!
IS... IS HE...?!

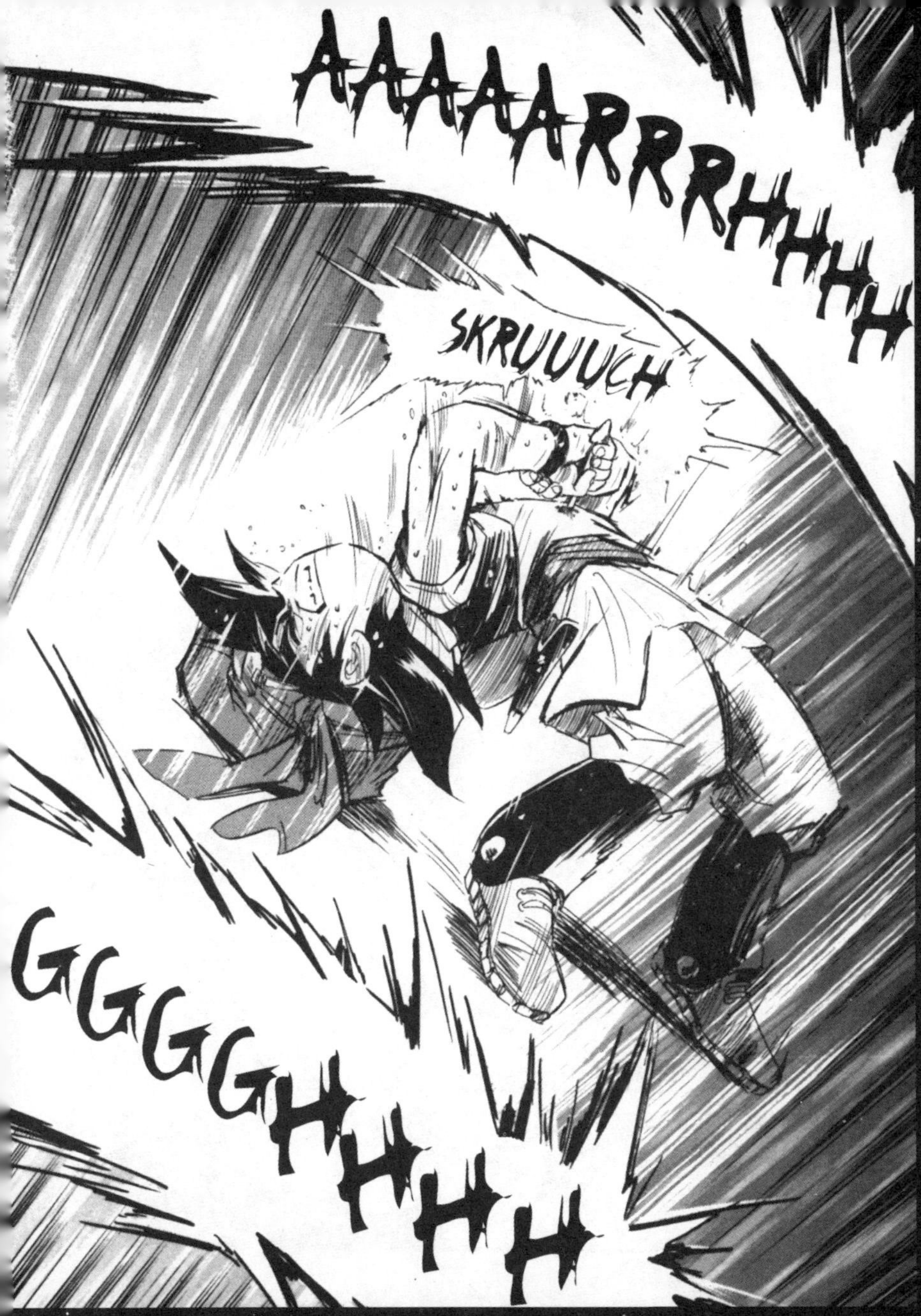
AAAAARRRRHHHHH
SKRUUUCH
GGGGGHHHHHH

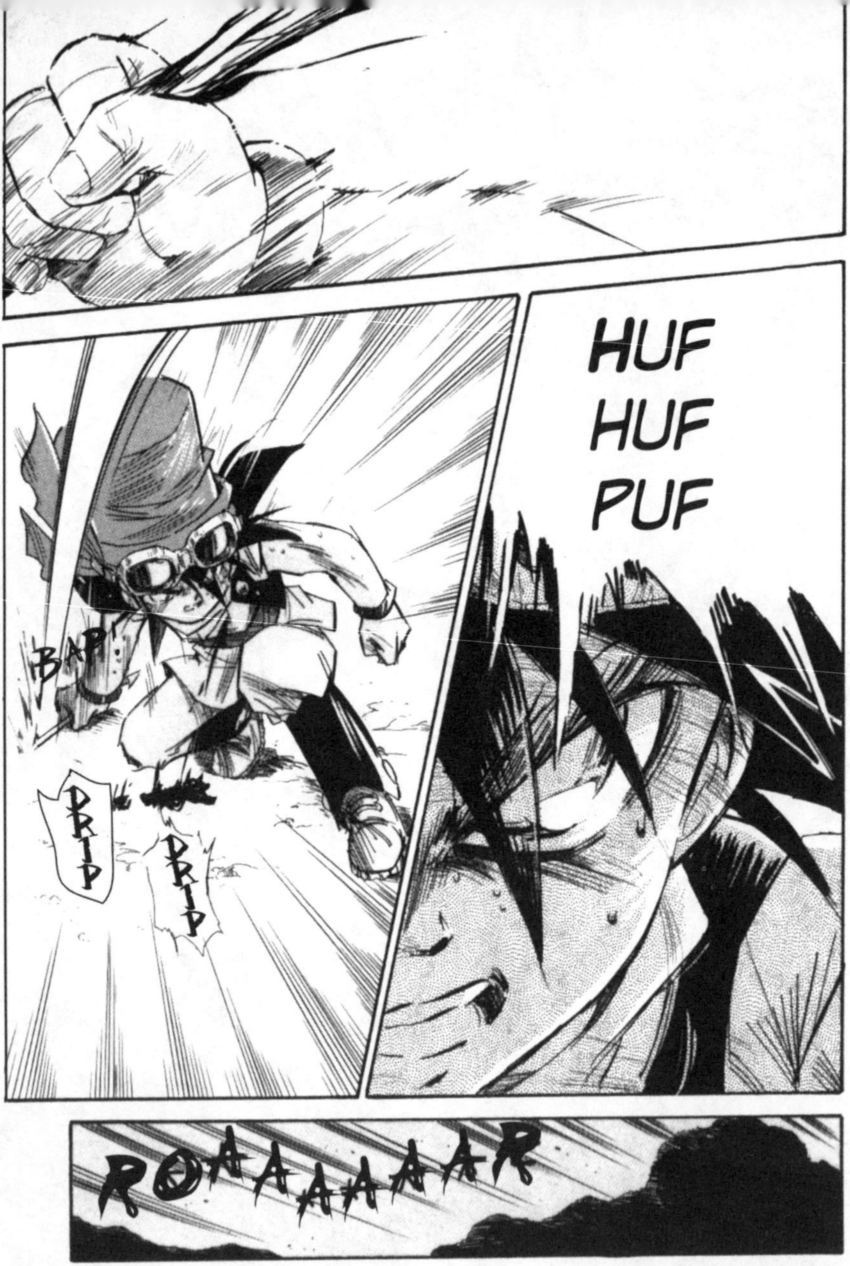
HUF
HUF
PUF
BAP!
DRIP
DRIP
ROAAAAAAR

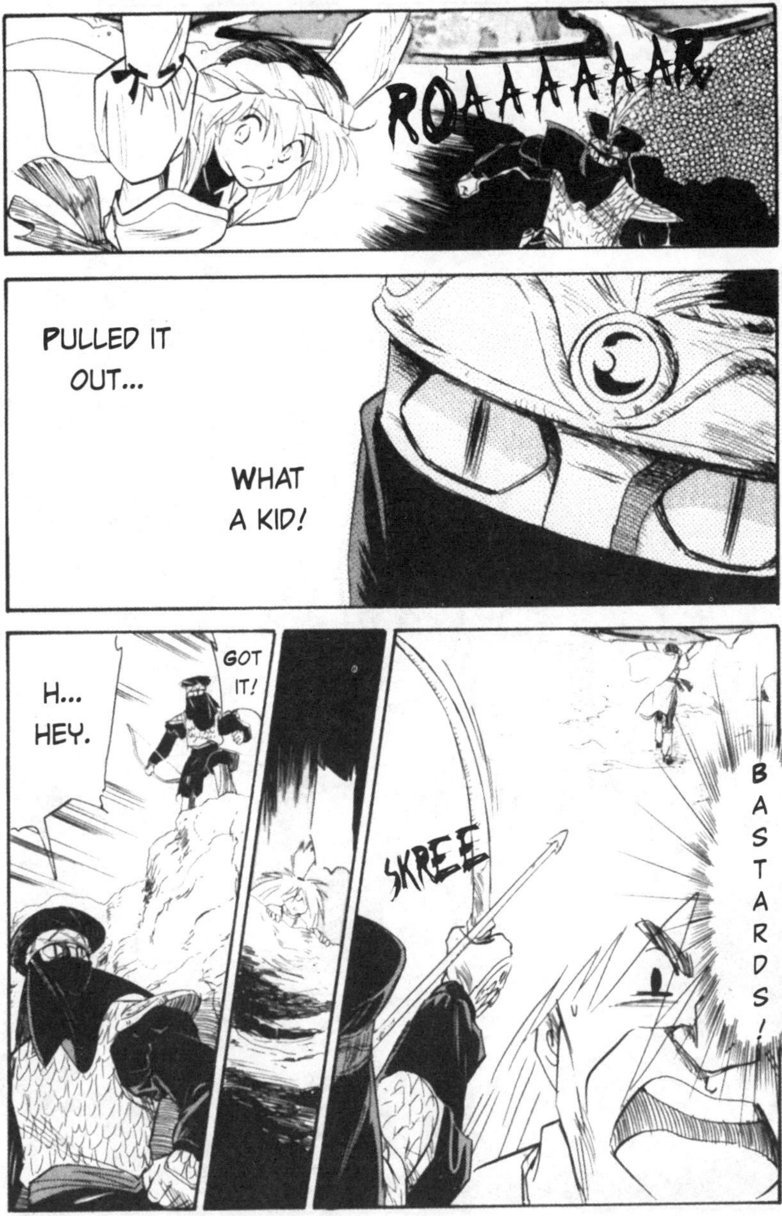
ROAAAAAAAR
PULLED IT OUT...
WHAT A KID!
BASTARDS!
SKREE
GOT IT!
H... HEY.

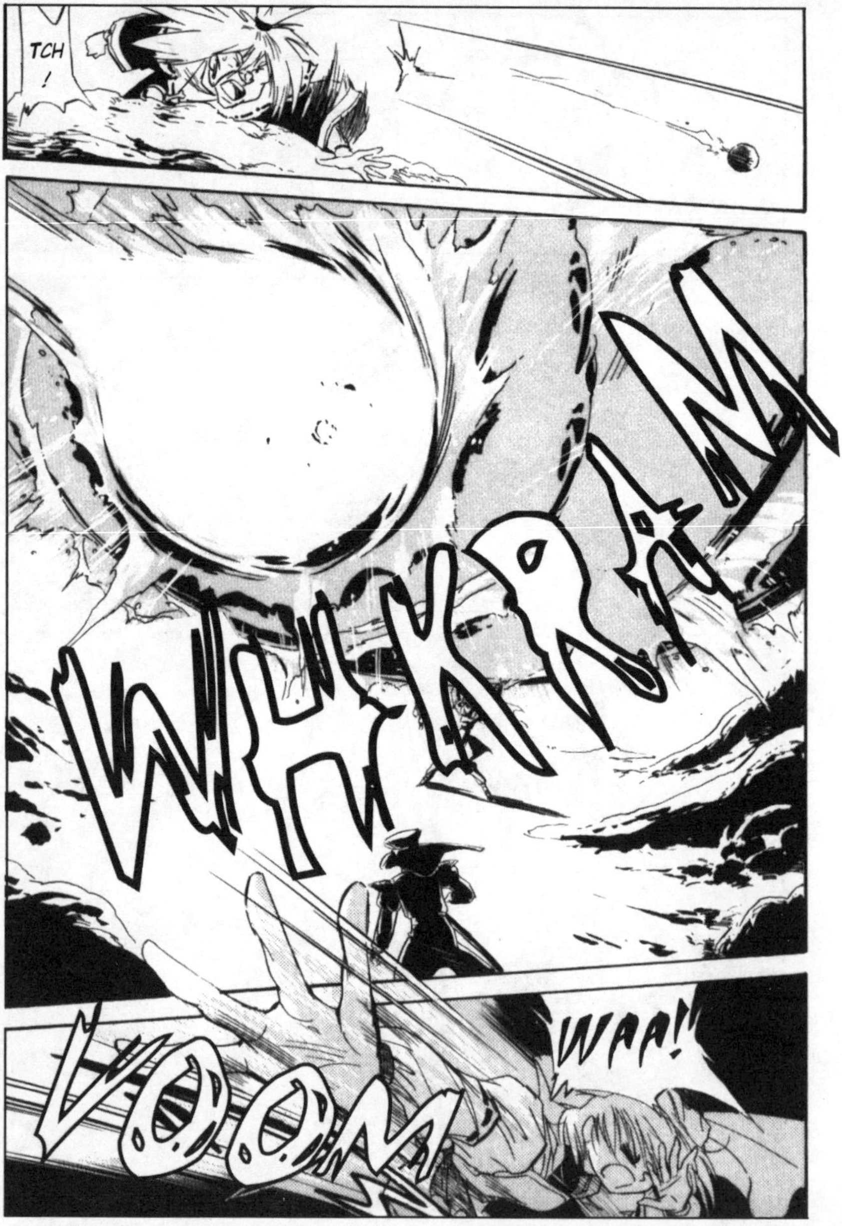
TCH
!
WHKRAM
WAA!
VOOM

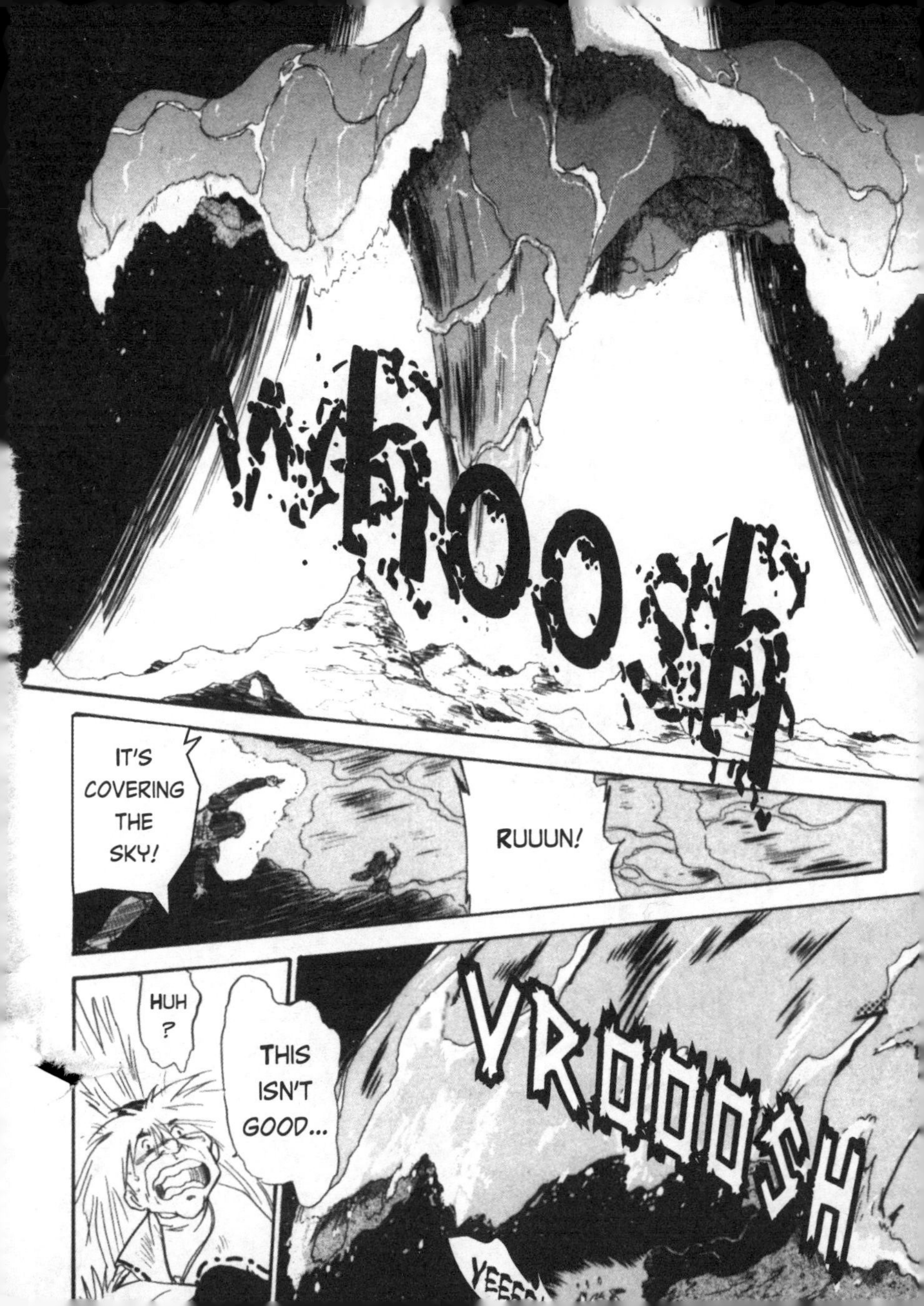

IT'S COVERING THE SKY!
RUUUN!
HUH?
THIS ISN'T GOOD...
VROOOOSH

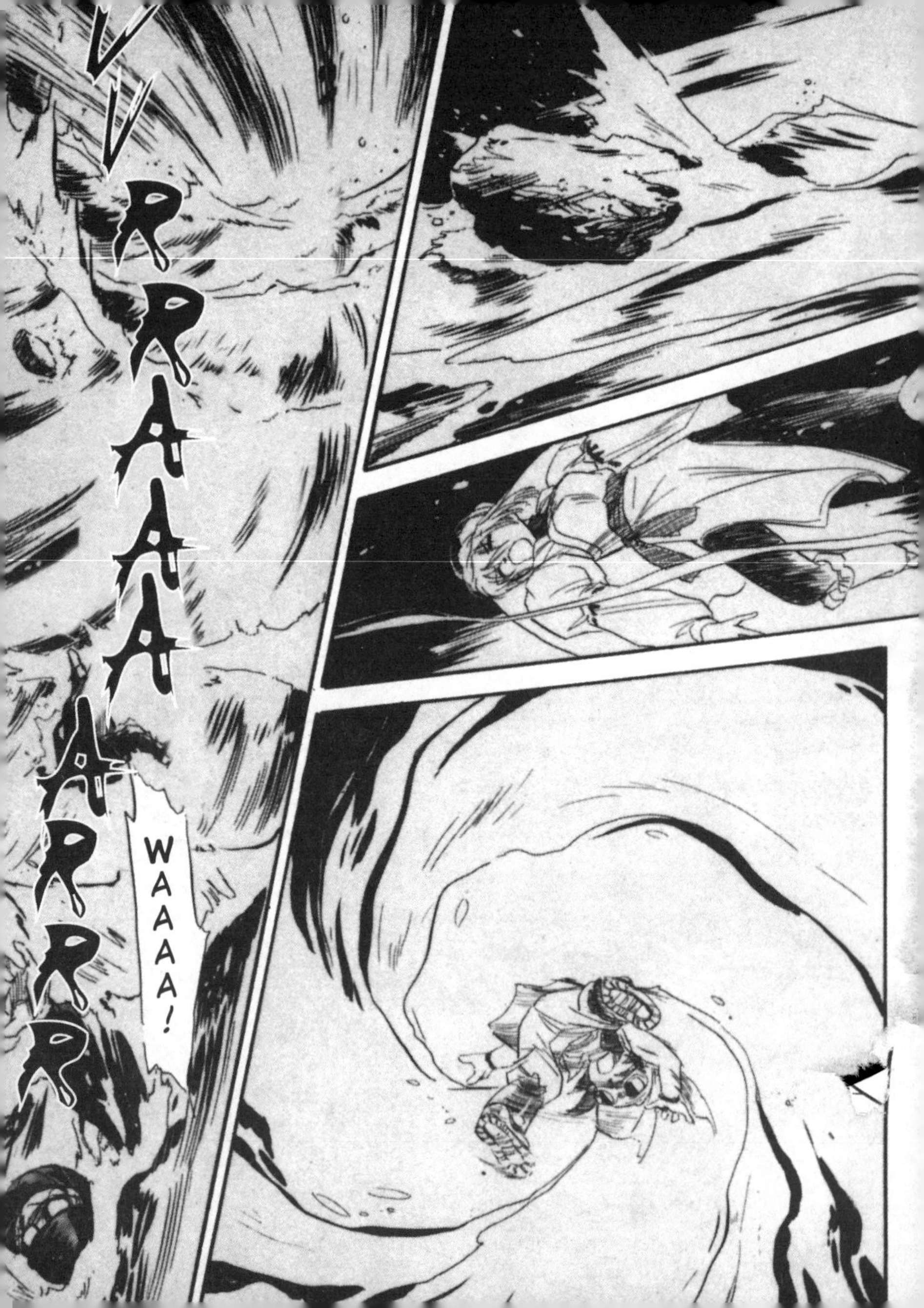

VVRRAAAAARRRR
WAAAAA!

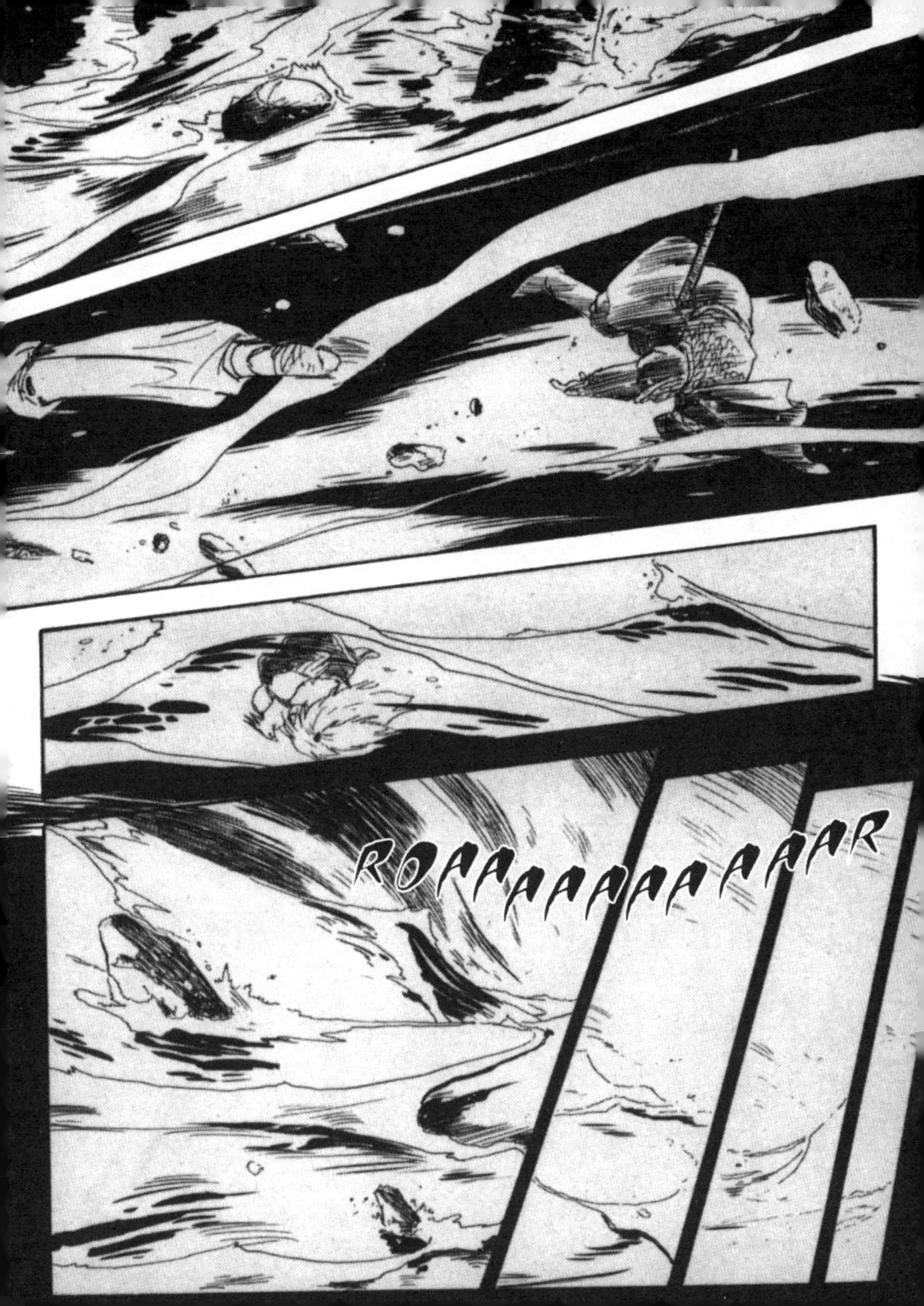
ROAAAAAAAAAAR

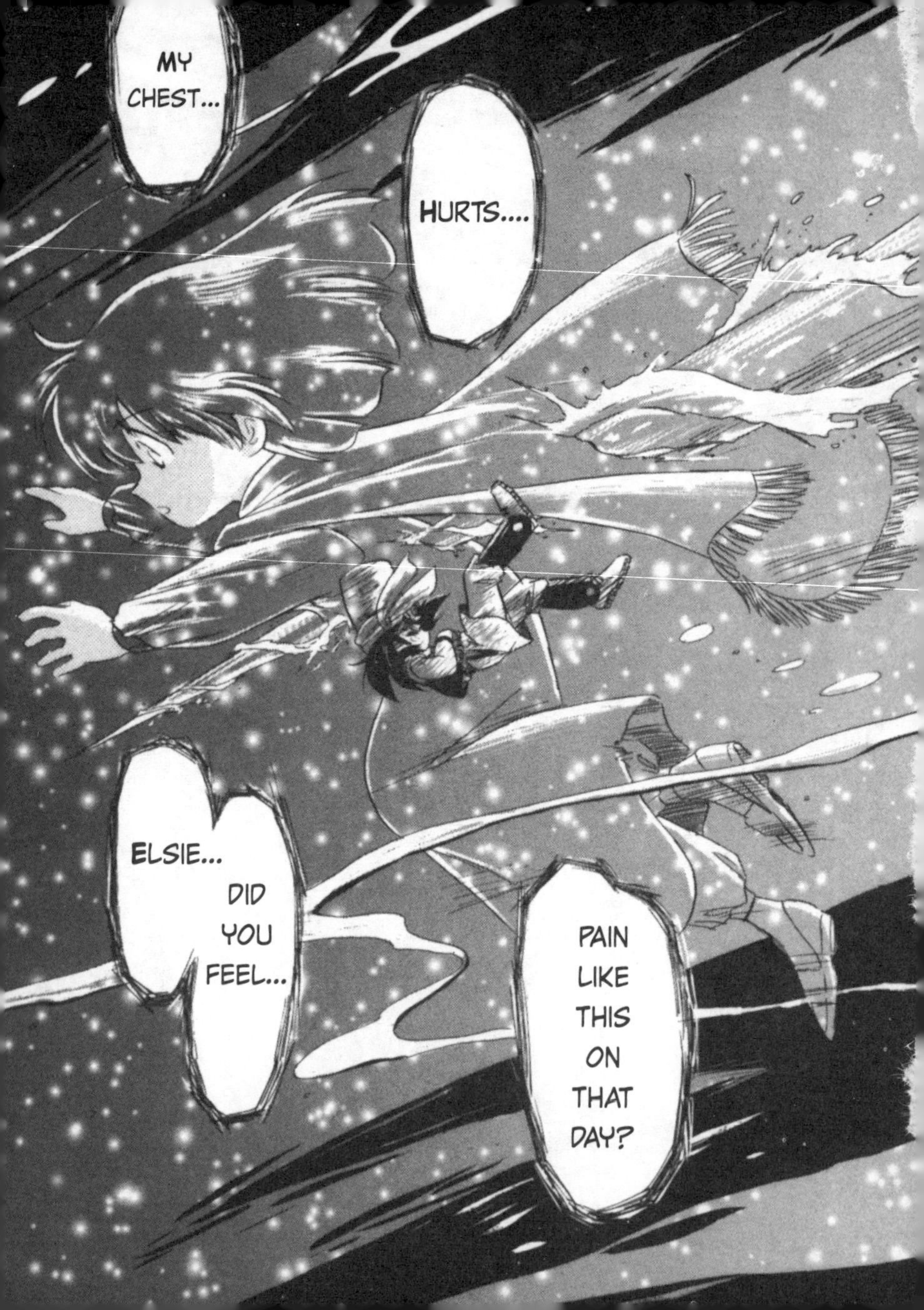
MY CHEST...
HURTS....
ELSIE... DID YOU FEEL...
PAIN LIKE THIS ON THAT DAY?

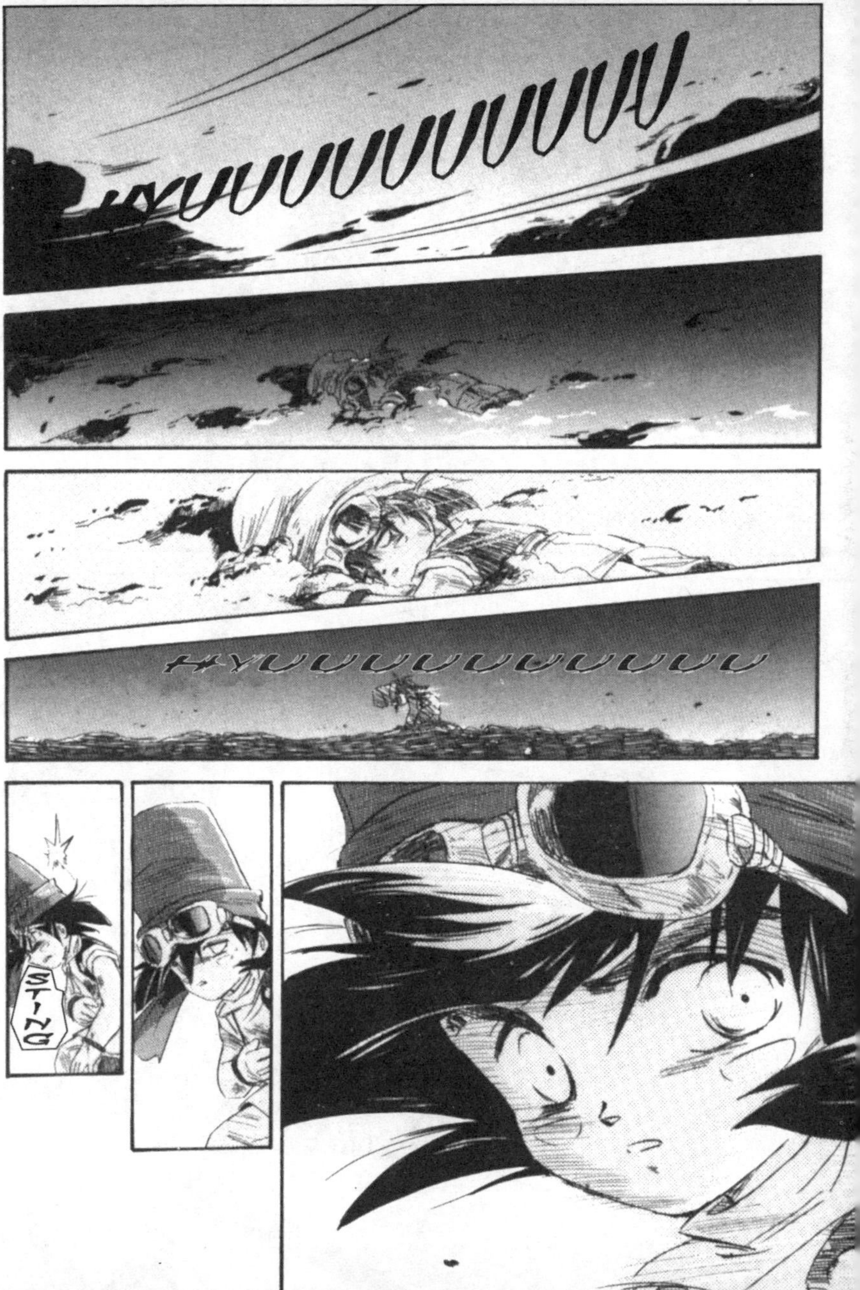
HYUUUUUUUUUUUU
HYUUUUUUUUUUUU
STING

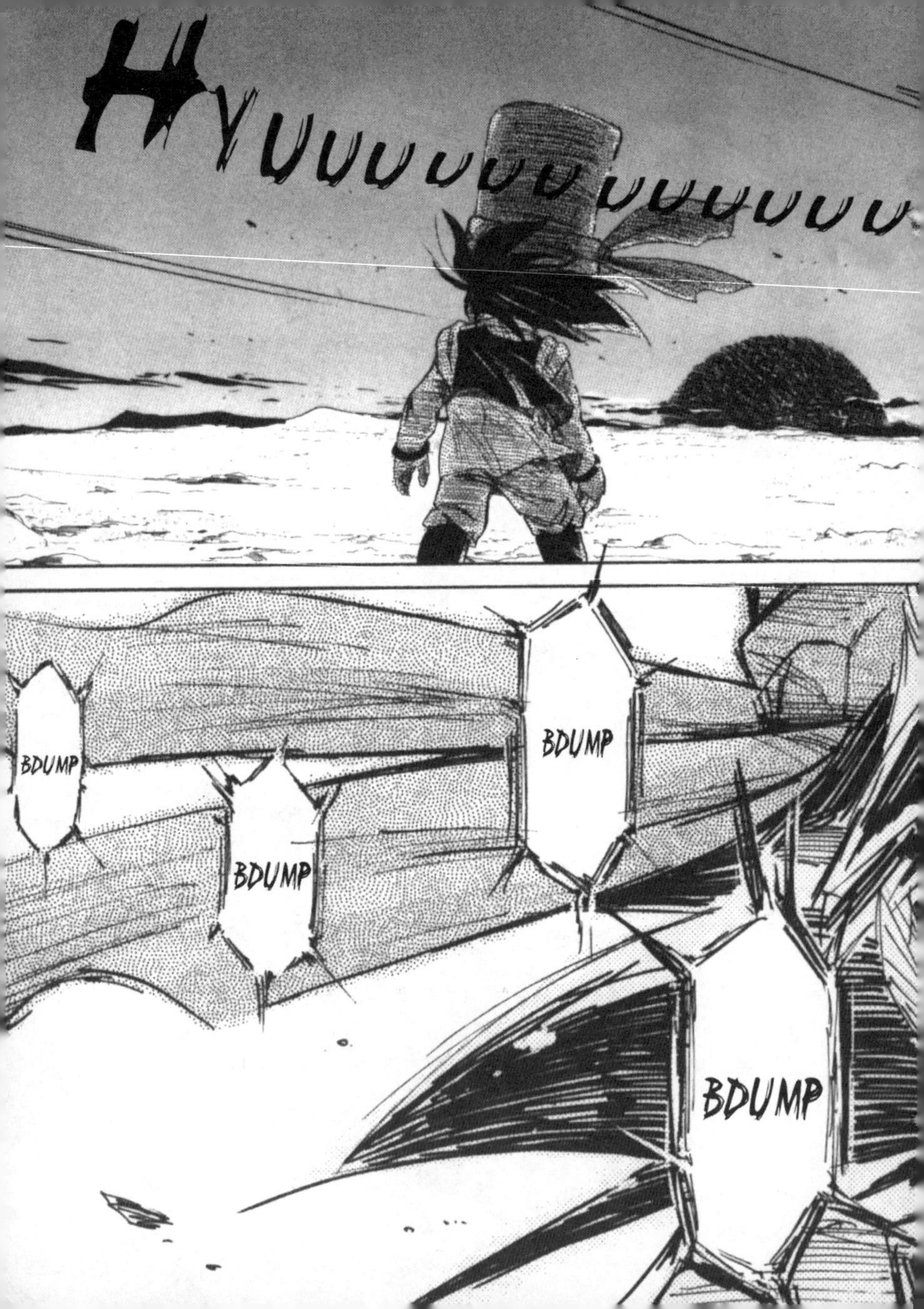
HYUUUUUUUUUUUUUU
BDUMP
BDUMP
BDUMP
BDUMP

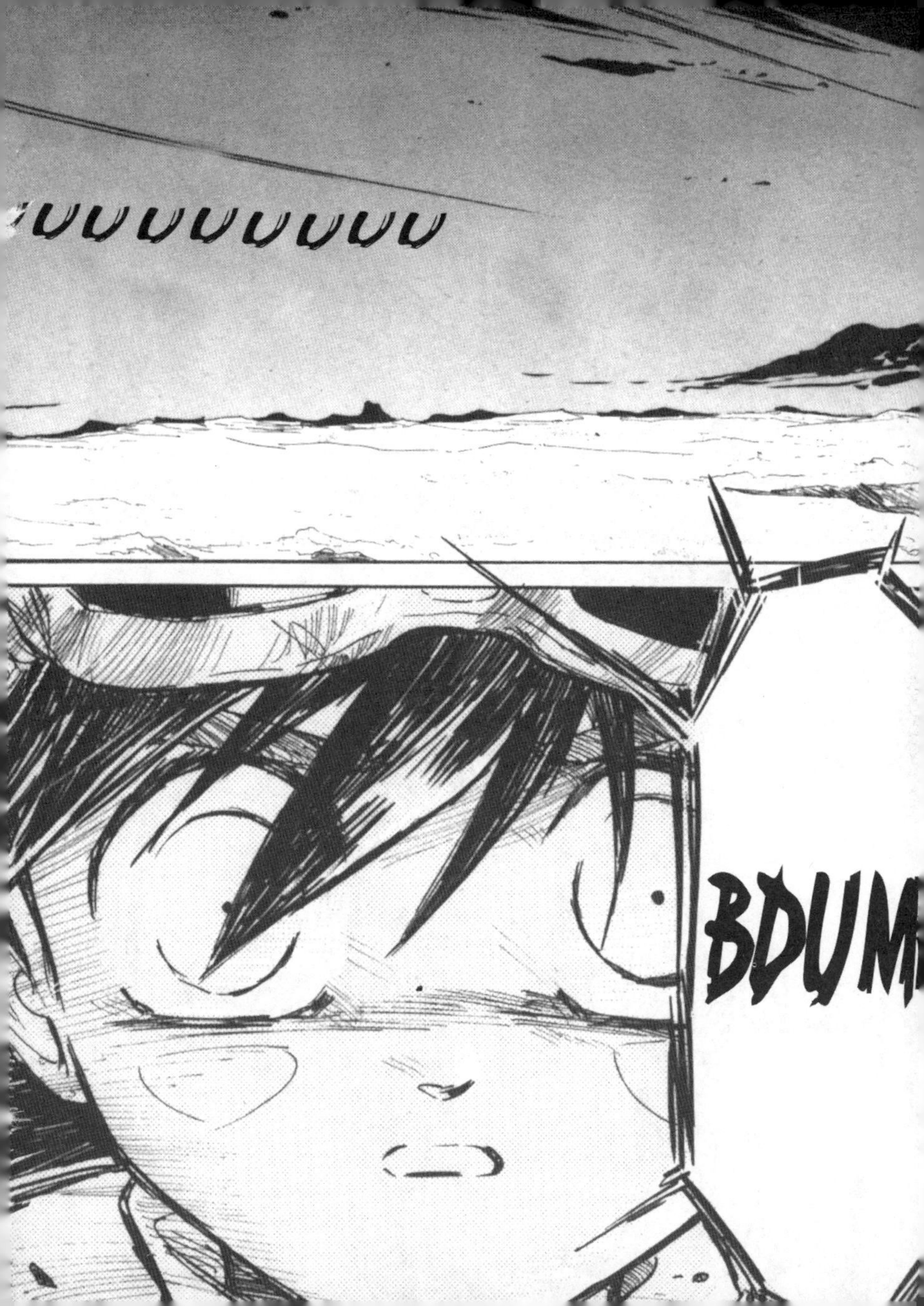

OOOOOOOOOOO
BDUM

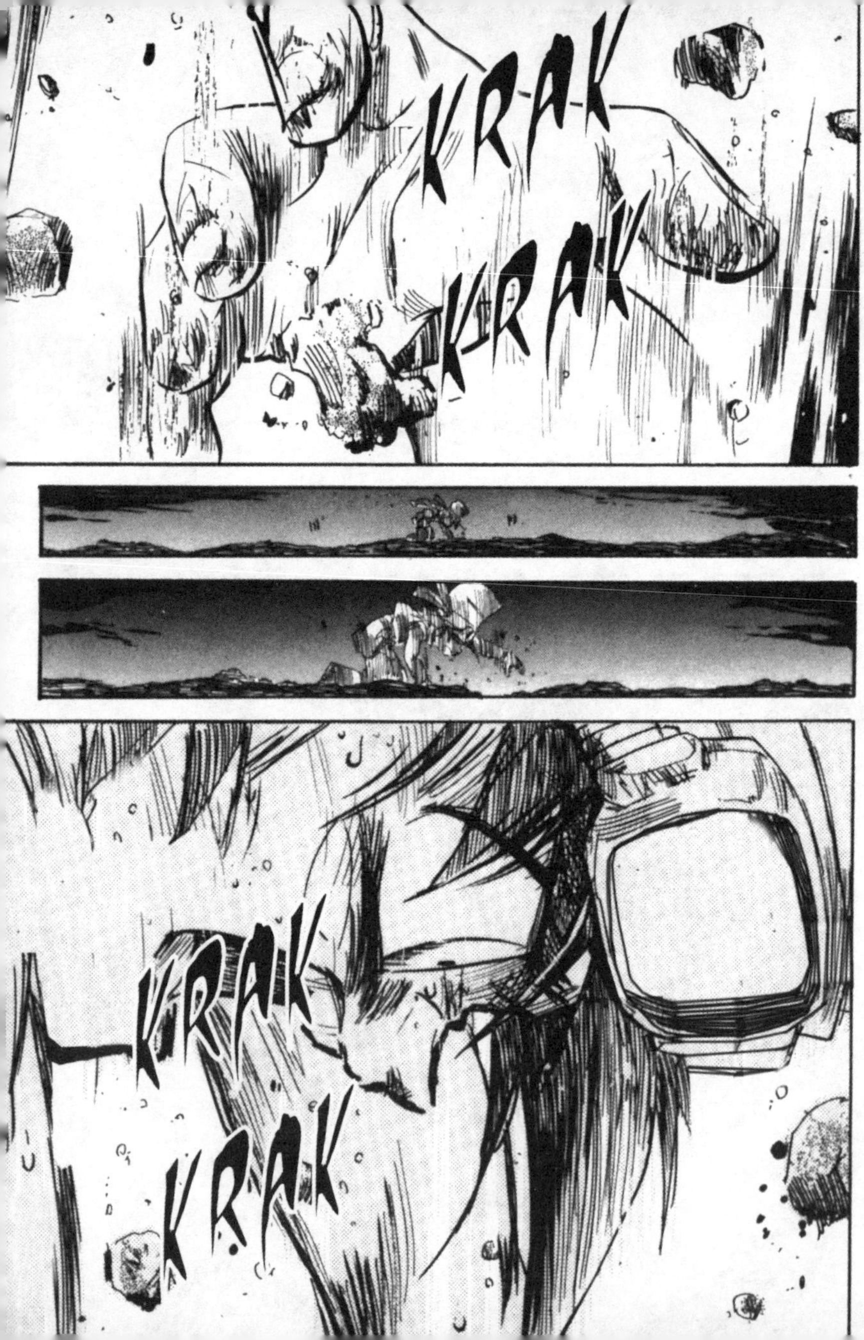
KRAK
KRAK
KRAK
KRAK

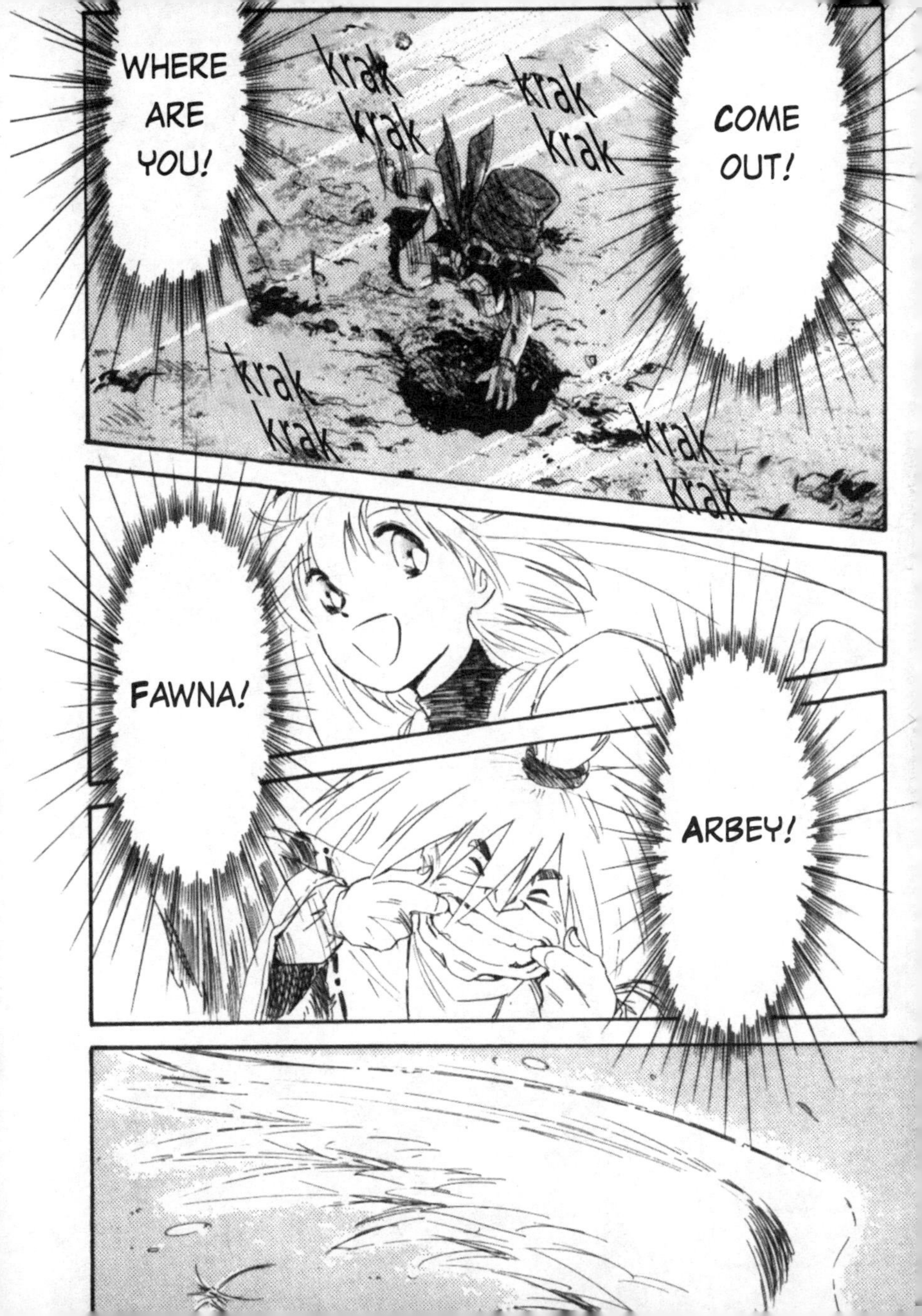
COME OUT!
WHERE ARE YOU!
krak krak
krak krak
krak krak
krak krak
ARBEY!
FAWNA!

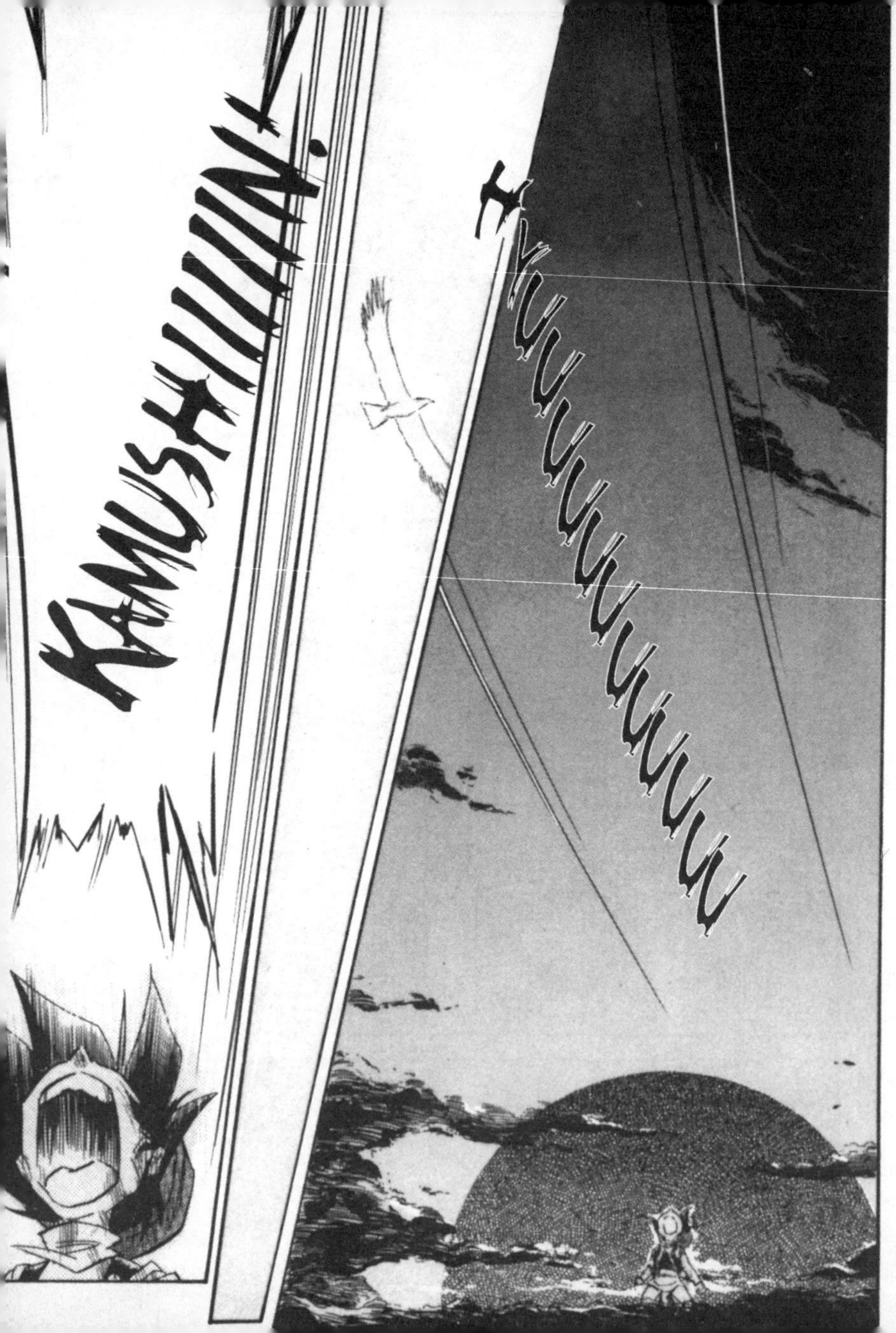
KAMUSHIIIIIN!
FYUUUUUUUUUUUUU

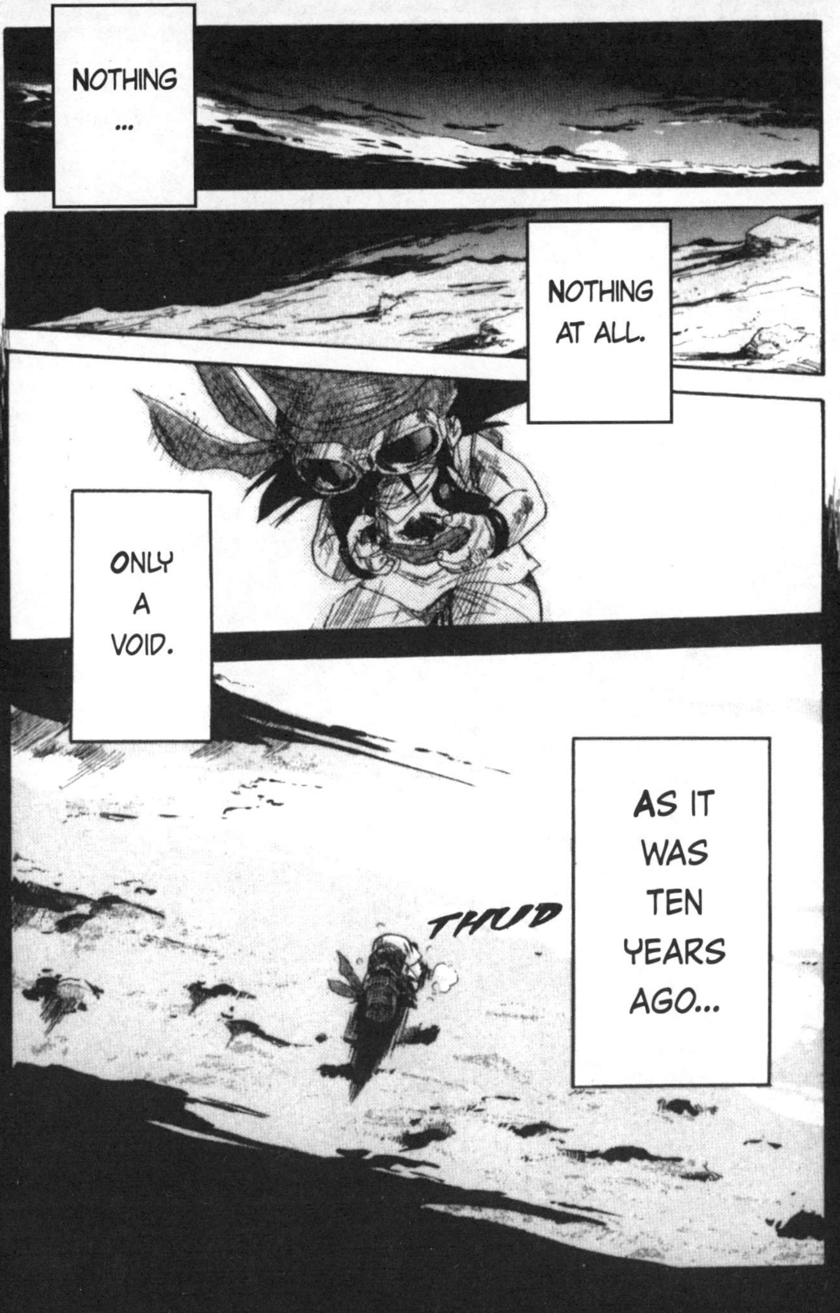
NOTHING ...
NOTHING AT ALL.
ONLY A VOID.
AS IT WAS TEN YEARS AGO...
THUD

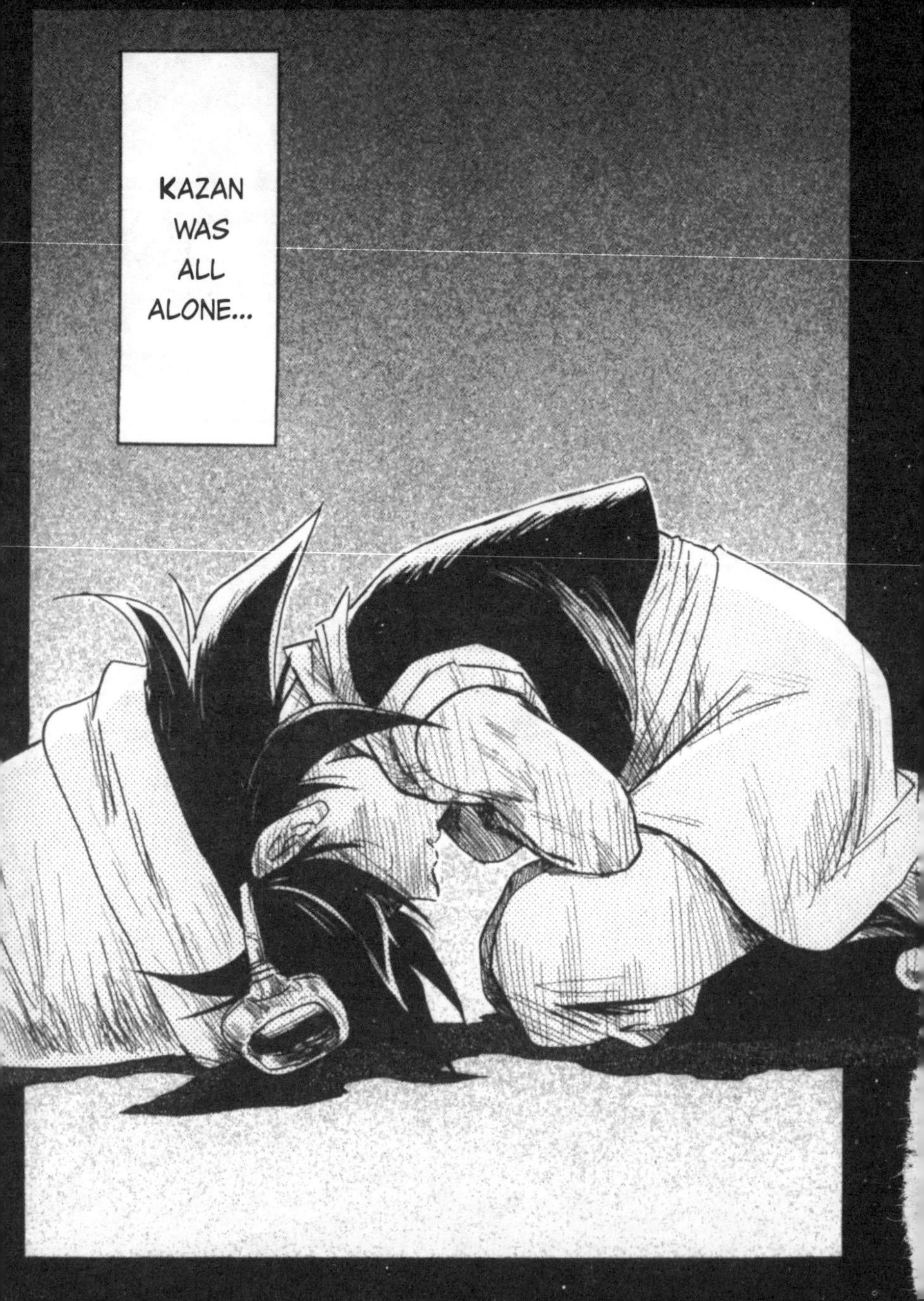
KAZAN WAS ALL ALONE...

KAZAN
END OF VOLUME 3

CONTINUED IN VOLUME 4